"Serhii Plokhy has alighted upon a fascinating episode in the history of Soviet intelligence. Not long after Stalin's death, Communist Party leader Nikita Khrushchev ordered a campaign of assassinations directed against defectors and those campaigning for the dissolution of the Soviet Union, most notably the Ukrainian nationalists led by Stepan Bandera. One of the most accomplished assassins, Bogdan Stashinsky, defected, however, and uncovered the entire ghastly affair in 1961. Plokhy, a leading Harvard professor, details the story in startling clarity and pinpoint accuracy from an impressive array of sources, German, Russian, Ukrainian, and American. Yet he carries his learning lightly, which makes for a very readable story that could as well have emerged from the pen of a spy thriller writer."

—**Jonathan Haslam, George F. Kennan Professor,
School of Historical Studies, Institute for Advanced Study, Princeton,
and author of *Near and Distant Neighbors: A New History of Soviet Intelligence***

"This book often reads like an Ian Fleming spy novel, but it is actually about real events that occurred during the tensest phase of the Cold War in the late 1950s and early 1960s. Serhii Plokhy provides a riveting account of the exploits of a Soviet assassin who used poison gas to kill exiled opponents of the Soviet regime amid East–West preparations for all-out war. Plokhy's meticulously researched book sheds valuable light on the Soviet regime's continued use of political assassinations in foreign countries long after the death of Joseph Stalin. A wonderful read for scholars and spy novel fans alike."

—**Mark Kramer, director, Cold War Studies, Harvard University**

THE MAN WITH THE POISON GUN

THE MAN

WITH THE

POISON GUN

A COLD WAR SPY STORY

SERHII PLOKHY

BASIC
BOOKS
New York

An imprint of Perseus Books, a division of PBG Publishing, LLC,
a subsidiary of Hachette Book Group, Inc.

Books published by Basic Books are available at special discounts for
bulk purchases in the United States by corporations, institutions, and other
organizations. For more information, please contact the
Special Markets Department at the Perseus Books Group,
2300 Chestnut Street, Suite 200, Philadelphia, PA 19103,
or call (800) 810-4145, ext. 5000,
or e-mail special.markets@perseusbooks.com.

Designed by Cynthia Young

Library of Congress Cataloging-in-Publication Data
Names: Plokhy, Serhii, 1957– author.
Title: The man with the poison gun : a Cold War spy story / Serhii Plokhy.
Description: New York : Basic Books, [2016] |
Includes bibliographical references and index.
Identifiers: LCCN 2016019612 | ISBN 9780465035908 (hardcover)
Subjects: LCSH: Stashinsky, Bogdan, 1931– | Spies—Soviet
Union–Biography. | Bandera, Stepan, 1909–1959—Assassination. | Rebet,
Lev, 1912–1957—Assassination. | Espionage, Soviet—Germany—History. |
Political refugees—Germany (West)—Biography. |
Ukrainians—Germany—Biography. | Poisoning—Germany—History—20th
century. | Political crimes and offenses—Germany—History—20th century.
| Ukraine—Politics and government—1945–1991.
Classification: LCC DK266.3 .P463 2016 | DDC 327.1247043092 [B]—dc23
LC record available at https://lccn.loc.gov/2016019612

10 9 8 7 6 5 4 3 2 1

CONTENTS

PART III
MOSCOW NIGHTS

PART IV
ESCAPE FROM PARADISE

PART V
PUBLICITY BOMB

THE COLD WAR EUROPE

FINLAND

NORWAY

ESTONIA

Baltic Sea

SWEDEN

LATVIA

North Sea

LITHUANIA

DENMARK

EAST
PRUSSIA

USSR

NETHERLANDS

Berlin

Warsaw

Bonn

EAST
GERMANY

POLAND

BELGIUM

LUX. Frankfurt

Prague

WEST
GERMANY

CZECHOSLOVAKIA

UKRAINE

Lviv

FRANCE

Munich

Vienna

Budapest

SWITZER-
LAND

AUSTRIA

HUNGARY

ROMANIA

Trieste

Bucharest

Belgrade

YUGOSLAVIA

Black
Sea

ITALY

BULGARIA

Sofia

Tirana

ALBANIA

GREECE

TURKEY

Mediterranean Sea

⊛ City divided into Soviet and Western Occupation Zones

•••••••• pre-World War II borders

●●●●●●● Iron Curtain

Occupied by the USSR in the course of World War II

Areas under Communist Control

0   100 mi

0   100 km

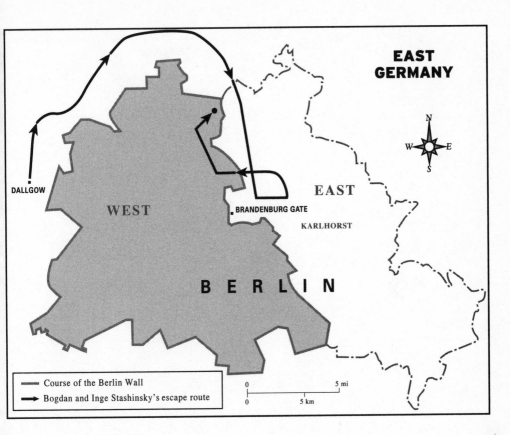

EAST
GERMANY

DALLGOW

WEST

EAST

BRANDENBURG GATE

KARLHORST

B E R L I N

N
W · E
S

Course of the Berlin Wall

Bogdan and Inge Stashinsky's escape route

0   5 mi

0   5 km

PREFACE

In the fall of 1961, as American and Soviet tanks faced one another at Checkpoint Charlie in the newly divided city of Berlin, and David Cornwell, a British spy more commonly known as John le Carré, was contemplating the writing of his first bestselling novel, *The Spy Who Came in from the Cold*, the West German police were interrogating a Soviet spy.

The slim thirty-year-old man had papers in the name of an East German, Josef Lehmann, but claimed that his real name was Bogdan Stashinsky and that he was a citizen of the Soviet Union. Stashinsky admitted during questioning that he was singlehandedly responsible for tracking down and killing two Ukrainian émigrés hiding in Munich, where they had been conspiring to liberate their country and destroy the Soviet Union. He had used a new, specially designed secret weapon—a spray pistol delivering liquid poison that, if fired into the victim's face, killed without leaving a trace. The Soviet leader Nikita Khrushchev, who had spent a good part of his career in Ukraine, had regarded the émigré leaders as personal enemies. They had been the primary targets of multiple KGB assassination attempts, and ultimately victims of Stashinsky's poison gun.

Stashinsky's testimony, implicating the Kremlin rulers in political assassinations carried out abroad, was a bombshell, shaking the worlds of espionage and international politics. The Stashinsky case changed how the Soviets fought the Cold War, forcing the KGB to abandon its practice of foreign assassination. It also ended the career of the KGB chief Aleksandr Shelepin, who had aspired to replace Nikita Khrushchev and then Leonid Brezhnev at the top of the Soviet power pyramid. In West Germany, the

Stashinsky trial changed how Nazi criminals were prosecuted. Using the Stashinsky case as a precedent, many defendants in such cases claimed, as had the Soviet spy, that they were simply accessories to murder, while their superiors, who ordered the killings, were the main perpetrators. West German legislators eventually changed the law to make it impossible for Nazi perpetrators to claim the "Stashinsky defense."

In the United States, Stashinsky's case was investigated by a subcommittee of the US Senate, and the evidence he provided was considered in the conclusions of the Warren Commission on the assassination of John F. Kennedy. Many conspiracy theorists still believe that Lee Harvey Oswald was trained by the KGB in the same facility as Bogdan Stashinsky.

Stashinsky's story captured the imagination of the Western world. It was featured in a long article in *Life* magazine, and made it into successive editions of *Great True Spy Stories*, compiled by former CIA chief Allen Dulles. In Ian Fleming's last James Bond novel, *The Man with the Golden Gun*, Bond, brainwashed by the Soviets, tries to assassinate his boss by shooting him with a cyanide-loaded poison gun. The Stashinsky story served as the basis of a number of radio and television features around the world. It inspired numerous books and documentary films, at least two novels, two theater plays, and one movie.

For decades, the KGB denied any involvement in the Stashinsky assassinations, and for decades, CIA officers could never be entirely sure whether Stashinsky's story was true or false. Even today, some authors claim that Stashinsky was in fact a loyal KGB agent who had been sent to the West in order to bear false witness, and thereby shield the prized KGB agent who actually did the job. By tapping into new, previously unavailable sources, this book finally puts to rest many earlier theories and speculations about Stashinsky's assassinations. It also places the Stashinsky story into the broad context of the Cold War—the relentless battle of ideologies and cultures between East and West—and demonstrates the crushing impact that the Soviet police state had on the population living east of the Iron Curtain.

Most of what we know today about Bogdan Stashinsky, his crime, and his punishment comes from the testimony that he gave at his trial in Karlsruhe, Germany, in October 1962. We can now supplement that data with information from recently declassified files of the Central Intelligence Agency; KGB and Polish security archives; and memoirs and interviews of former KGB officers. The study of graveyard records in a Berlin suburb made it possible to corroborate parts of the story originally told by Stashinsky, and my interview with a former head of the South African police allowed me to trace the former Soviet assassin to that country. He is probably still living there, always looking over his shoulder, aware that the old habits of the KGB die hard, if at all.

PROLOGUE

On the sunny morning of October 15, 1959, a tram coming from downtown Munich made its regular stop on the Ludwig Bridge across the Isar River. "Deutsches Museum," announced the conductor. The German Museum of Masterpieces of Science and Technology, which had housed the world's largest collection of scientific exhibits before the war, was a few hundred yards away, its main building located on an island in the middle of the river. While the museum still showed signs of damage suffered during the Allied bombing of the city, the passengers could also see signs of postwar revival. The museum building was being restored, and new houses had been built on the bombed-out Zeppelinstrasse on the right bank of the river. The doors of the tram car opened, allowing passengers to enter and exit.

A slim, flat-chested man with sloping shoulders in his late twenties waited on the Ludwig Bridge, but showed no interest in hopping onto the tram. He also missed a tram going in the opposite direction, toward Karlsplatz and the Hauptbahnhof—the main railway station. Nor was he on his way to the museum. He stood on the bridge, looking toward the river and Zeppelinstrasse. After a moment, he left the bridge, walking along Zeppelinstrasse toward building no. 67, near which a dark blue Opel Kapitan was parked. The man came close enough to read the sedan's license plate. He then returned to his post on the bridge, where he kept an eye on the car and the building nearby. Finally, around noon, activity caught his attention: a man in his early fifties left the building with a younger woman and got into the car. The Opel Kapitan pulled away from the curb and proceeded along Zeppelinstrasse away from the Ludwig Bridge. The young man watched the car until it disappeared from sight. Then he boarded the downtown train.

At a quarter past noon, the young man from the Ludwig Bridge was on the other side of the city, getting off the tram on the Massmannplatz. From there he walked toward the Kreittmayrstrasse and then in the direction of St. Benno's Catholic Church at the end of the street. He paused at the recently constructed apartment building at no. 7 and looked into its archway, which led to the courtyard and garages, but the dark blue Opel Kapitan was nowhere in sight. He walked along the street once again, repeatedly checking his watch. Finally he spotted the Opel Kapitan approaching in his direction. He could see the license plate. It was the same car, but the driver was alone.

When the Opel Kapitan turned into the archway at no. 7, the young man headed for the main entrance and opened the door with a key. He locked the door from the inside and took the stairs to the ground floor, deciding to wait there until the owner of the Opel Kapitan entered the hallway. Suddenly he heard voices upstairs. "*Wiedersehen*—until we meet again," said a female voice, and someone began to descend the stairs. The young man panicked; he was caught on the stairs between this unknown resident and the owner of the Opel Kapitan, who could appear any moment. Finally he decided to return to the ground floor, turned his face toward the elevator door, and pressed the elevator button. A few seconds later he heard steps behind him: it was a woman, as he could tell from the click of her high heels. She opened the door and left the building.

Relieved, the young man returned to his previous position behind the first turn of the stairs, out of sight of anyone entering. A few moments later he looked out and saw the man he was waiting for—the owner of the Opel Kapitan from Zeppelinstrasse. The man was short, stocky, and balding. He was struggling to remove his key from the main door. He carried some bags under his arm. One of them was open, and the young man could see that it contained tomatoes. The young man bent down and pantomimed tying his shoelace—he knew that the gesture looked unnatural, but he wanted to avoid approaching the man with the tomatoes while the entrance door was still open. The young man straightened up and resumed his movement toward the door. "*Funktioniert es nicht*—Isn't it working?" he heard himself say. "*Doch es funktioniert*—Now it's working," responded the owner of the Opel Kapitan.

The young man grasped the outside doorknob with his left hand. His right hand, in which he held a rolled-up newspaper, came up, with one end pointed toward the man's face. There was a soft pop. He saw the older man's body moving backward and to the side. He did not see it fall. He stepped outside and closed the entrance door behind him. On the street, he un-rolled the newspaper and removed the eight-inch cylinder which had been concealed within. The gun went into his pocket. The mission was over. Stashinsky had finally done it.[1]

PART I

KGB MAN

1

STALIN'S CALL

Nikita Khrushchev, the balding, overweight, but surprisingly energetic future leader of the Soviet Union, was in the middle of a speech when a note was delivered to the podium asking him to call Moscow as soon as possible.

It was December 1, 1949, and Khrushchev, then a party boss of Ukraine, was addressing professors and students in the Western Ukrainian city of Lviv. The city and its environs had belonged to Poland before World War II but were annexed to the Soviet Union in 1939 as a result of the Molotov-Ribbentrop Pact. After the short-lived Soviet-German alliance was dissolved, the Soviets lost the region to invading Germans in June 1941, but reclaimed it in July 1944. Ever since, they had unsuccessfully tried to convince the local Ukrainian population to accept life under Soviet rule. It was a difficult proposition: the Ukrainians wanted their own state. A few weeks before Khrushchev's speech, Ukrainian nationalist guerrillas had scored a major victory by assassinating Yaroslav Halan, a communist author and one of the main propagandists of the new regime. Khrushchev came to Lviv to personally oversee the investigation and lead the hunt for Halan's killers. One of them had turned out to be a student, and Khrushchev was now addressing local college administrators and party activists among the students to alert them to the dangers of nationalism.

The request to call Moscow caught Khrushchev by surprise. He finished his speech, calling on the students to fight nationalism in their ranks and stand on guard against the guerrillas, left the meeting, and placed a call to the Kremlin. On the other end of the line was Stalin's right-hand man, Georgii Malenkov, the party boss responsible for the appointment and dismissal of Soviet officials. Khrushchev had been called back to the Kremlin. "How urgent is it?" asked Khrushchev. "Very. Get a plane first thing tomorrow morning," came the answer. "I left ready for anything, trying to anticipate all sorts of unpleasant surprises," recalled Khrushchev later.[1]

Three years earlier, in 1946, Stalin had removed Khrushchev as first secretary of the Communist Party of Ukraine, assigning him to the less important office of head of the Ukrainian Cabinet. The appointment was punishment for Khrushchev's demands that Moscow help relieve the Ukrainian famine of 1946–1947. Stalin, whose insistence on high grain-procurement quotas had caused the famine, refused to listen or to help. Annoyed with Khrushchev's demands, he replaced him with Lazar Kaganovich, one of the organizers of the Great Famine of 1932–1933, which had claimed the lives of as many as 4 million Ukrainians. Chastised, Khrushchev fell into line and showed no mercy in extracting grain from the exhausted Ukrainian peasantry. Close to 1 million people died as a result. In the fall of 1947, Stalin reinstalled Khrushchev in his former post of party boss of Ukraine.[2]

But what did Stalin want now? Was the summons to Moscow related to the assassination of Yaroslav Halan and Khrushchev's perceived inability to end the Ukrainian resistance? The guerrilla fighters were universally known as Banderites—a name derived from that of the leader of the "revolutionary" (most militant) branch of the Organization of Ukrainian Nationalists (OUN), Stepan Bandera. Judging by Khrushchev's memoirs, he had first heard of Bandera in 1939. That year, as head of the Communist Party of Ukraine, Khrushchev oversaw the incorporation of Western Ukraine into the Ukrainian Soviet Socialist Republic. Bandera, who was serving a life sentence for his role in the 1934 assassination of the Polish minister of the interior, had walked out of the prison in 1939 following the

German invasion of Poland, slipping through Soviet hands. "We were impressed by Bandera's record as an opponent of the Polish government, but we should have taken into account the fact that men like him were also enemies of the Soviet Union," remembered Khrushchev later.

As Stalin shared the spoils of the Molotov-Ribbentrop Pact with Hitler, taking control of first Western Ukraine and Belarus and then the Baltic states and the Romanian provinces of Moldavia and Bukovyna, Bandera led a revolt against the old leadership of the Organization of Ukrainian Nationalists and offered the services of his faction of the OUN to Germany. The German-Soviet alliance turned out to be short-lived. On June 22, 1941, the German armies crossed the Soviet border and began their movement eastward, pushing the retreating Red Army out of Western Ukraine. On June 30, 1941, a week after Germany's attack on its former ally, Bandera and his people declared the creation of an independent Ukrainian state.

But an independent Ukraine had no place in German plans: they wanted *Lebensraum* (living space)—a territory cleansed of the local population and made ready for German settlement. The Gestapo arrested Bandera and his associates, demanding that they rescind their declaration. Bandera refused and spent most of the war in the German concentration camp of Sachsenhausen. Two of his brothers died in Auschwitz. "It's true that when Bandera realized that the Hitlerites did not intend to keep their promise to sponsor an independent Ukraine he turned his units against them," recalled Khrushchev. "But even then he did not stop hating the Soviet Union. During the second half of the war he fought both against us and the Germans."[3]

By 1944, the Ukrainian nationalists had organized a guerrilla force numbering as many as 100,000 men. Formally, they constituted the Ukrainian Insurgent Army; informally, they were known as Banderites. "As we pushed the Germans west, we encountered an old enemy—Ukrainian nationalists," recalled Khrushchev. "The Banderites were setting up partisan detachments of their own." After his release from Sachsenhausen, Bandera fled to Austria. The insurgency was run by others, who had little, if any, contact with their faraway leader, but Bandera's name remained closely linked with the underground. All aspects of guerrilla warfare, good and bad, became associated with Bandera—the self-sacrifice of young men and women who gave their lives for the cause of Ukrainian independence as well as the ethnic cleansing of Poles in Western Ukraine, the participation of the individual members of the nationalist underground in the Holocaust, and the gruesome assassinations of Soviet "collaborators" such as Yaroslav Halan.[4]

The Soviets employed tens of thousands of regular troops, thousands of members of special detachments, and locally formed militias to fight the nationalist underground. They reported killing more than 100,000 "bandits" and arresting another quarter of a million in 1944–1946. Hundreds of thousands of civilians were deported from Western Ukraine to Siberia and Kazakhstan. The commanders of the Ukrainian Insurgent Army, which now numbered fewer than 5,000 soldiers, switched to small-scale attacks on Soviet government institutions and military installations. Individual terror against representatives of Soviet rule and local "collaborators" became the new modus operandi. The insurgents understood that they could not win in a pitched battle. Their only remaining hope for personal survival and the creation of an independent Ukrainian state was a new global war, this time between the United States and the Soviet Union.

Slowly but relentlessly, Soviet counterinsurgency operations and terror against the local population delivered results. By 1948, Ukrainian nationalist resistance had weakened sufficiently to allow the Soviets to begin the mass collectivization of agriculture—the centerpiece of their program of socialist transformation. Soviet agents penetrated many of the remaining insurgent units and tried to gain control over communications between local insurgents and Bandera's émigré followers, who were headquartered in Munich, the center of the American occupation zone in Germany. Still, the Soviet secret police could not reach the leadership of the Insurgent Army or prevent assassinations of regime supporters like Yaroslav Halan.[5]

Nikita Khrushchev had known Halan personally. In 1946, Halan had represented the Soviet Ukrainian media at the Nuremberg Trials of major war criminals, where he had demanded the extradition of Stepan Bandera from the American occupation zone of Germany. Back home, he attacked the Ukrainian nationalists with his fiery pamphlets. Halan also targeted the Ukrainian Catholic Church. Its hierarchs were arrested and its priests forced to accept the jurisdiction of the Russian Orthodox Church as part of the Soviet struggle against the Vatican and its political, religious, and cultural influences in the Soviet-controlled part of Europe. The church's faithful were driven underground. Halan's vitriolic attacks on the church did not go unnoticed in Rome, and in July 1949 Pope Pius XII excommunicated him. Halan responded with a new pamphlet, in which he wrote: "I spit on the pope." Many believed that the phrase sealed Halan's fate in the eyes of the insurgents, who allied themselves with the persecuted Ukrainian Catholic Church.[6]

Khrushchev was immediately informed of Halan's death and called Moscow to let Stalin know what had happened in Lviv. The aging and ever more paranoid Soviet dictator was not pleased. The assassination left no doubt that more than five years after the Red Army had recaptured Western Ukraine from the retreating Germans, and more than four years after the red banner had been flown atop the Reichstag building in central Berlin, the Ukrainian underground was still fighting the victorious Soviet superpower. And not somewhere on the periphery of the communist world, but in its very heart, within the borders of the USSR. Stalin dispatched his best secret police forces to Ukraine. They were told that "Comrade Stalin has rated the work of the security organs combating banditry in Western Ukraine as highly unsatisfactory." They were ordered to find the assassins and crush the remaining Ukrainian resistance.[7]

Khrushchev knew that his job was on the line. That is why he not only came to Lviv in person to oversee the investigation, but also brought along a full team to help increase police and party control over locals: the minister of the interior, the secretaries of the Central Committee of the Ukrainian Communist Party, and even the first secretary of the Ukrainian branch of the Komsomol—the Young Communist League. Khrushchev wanted his underlings to turn Lviv and Western Ukraine into a fortress. According to one account, he was prepared to introduce drastic measures to remove the recruitment base for the underground: he would round up young men and send them to the Donbas Mines or to trade schools in Eastern Ukraine, or even, perhaps, place the population under strict control through a system of internal passports, a step that would have turned the whole region into a huge prison camp outside of Soviet laws. Khrushchev dropped that idea only after Stalin's security experts protested his plans. One of them believed that Khrushchev's proposed measures would drive Ukrainian youth into the forests, directly into the hands of the insurgents.[8]

Upon receiving a call from the Kremlin, Khrushchev put his plans on hold and flew to Moscow, as ordered. "I did not know what my status would be when I returned to Ukraine—or even if I would return at all," he remembered later. The trip turned out to be the most fateful of his career. Instead of being reprimanded or arrested, Khrushchev was promoted. The aging dictator wanted Khrushchev by his side in Moscow, and he gave him control of the city's party organization to fight internal enemies. Stalin was purging party cadres of real and alleged supporters of the "Leningrad group" of Soviet officials, who were accused of attempting to form a separate Russian Communist Party—a potential threat to the unity of the All-Union Communist Party led by Stalin. Khrushchev, the longtime leader of Ukraine, seemed a natural ally in the struggle against Russian particularism, which threatened to topple the empire.

Khrushchev was more than relieved. He thanked Stalin for his trust in him. "I've been treated well, and I am thankful to everyone who has helped with the supervision of Ukraine," he told the dictator. "But I will nonetheless be glad to get back to Moscow." Stalin wanted him to go back to Ukraine, wrap up unfinished business there, and return to the Soviet capital in time for the lavish celebration of his seventieth birthday, scheduled for December 21, 1949. On that day, Stalin seated Khrushchev next to himself. On Stalin's other side was the leader of Communist China, Mao Zedong.

Khrushchev had begun his assent to the summit of Soviet power. But he would never forget the scare caused by Stalin's unexpected summons and the person he believed responsible for Ukrainian resistance to the Soviets, Stepan Bandera.[9]

2

MASTER KILLER

As Khrushchev took part in the celebrations for Stalin's birthday in Moscow, his former subordinates in Ukraine continued their hunt for the leaders of the Ukrainian underground. Many of them celebrated New Year's Day 1950 in Lviv instead of returning to Kyiv or Moscow and spent months after that in Western Ukraine. Among them was General Pavel Sudoplatov, the most senior security official to be sent from Moscow to Lviv with the task of destroying the leadership of the armed resistance. Sudoplatov followed his orders. Killing leaders of the Ukrainian movement was in fact his specialty.

Sudoplatov had been given his first assignment in that line of work in November 1937, when he was a thirty-year-old foreign intelligence officer. He was first summoned to the office of Stalin's people's commissar (minister) of the interior, Nikolai Yezhov, and then taken to meet Stalin himself. At the time, Sudoplatov, a native of Ukraine and a fluent Ukrainian speaker, had infiltrated Ukrainian émigré circles in Europe by posing as a representative of the Ukrainian underground based in the Soviet Union. Stalin, eager for a status report on relations among the leaders of the various Ukrainian organizations, had summoned Sudoplatov to his office. Sudoplatov revealed that they were all competing with one another for positions in the future government of independent Ukraine, but the most dangerous of all was Yevhen Konovalets, the head of the Organization of Ukrainian Nationalists. Konovalets was then the superior of Stepan Bandera, and the OUN had the backing of German military intelligence, the Abwehr.

"What are your suggestions?" asked Stalin. Sudoplatov had none. Stalin gave him a week to prepare a plan for combating Konovalets and his organization. A week later, Sudoplatov came back to Stalin's office with a plan for penetrating the Abwehr by means of Soviet agents in Konovalets's organization.

This plan was clearly not what Stalin had in mind. Stalin gave the floor to Hryhorii Petrovsky, an old Bolshevik and one of the leaders of Soviet Ukraine, who had been invited to sit in on the meeting. As Sudoplatov later recalled, Petrovsky "solemnly announced that the Ukrainian socialist state had, in absentia, condemned Konovalets to death for grave crimes against the Ukrainian proletariat"—that is, assassination, albeit couched in political justification. He referred specifically to Konovalets's role in the suppression of the Bolshevik uprising in Kyiv in 1918, during which Konovalets had served as a military commander for a short-lived government of independent Ukraine. Stalin spoke up in support of Petrovsky's suggestion: "This is not just an act of revenge, although Konovalets is an agent of German fascism. Our goal is to behead the movement of Ukrainian fascism on the eve of the war and force the gangsters to annihilate one another in a struggle for power."

Stalin obviously had assassination in mind when he first summoned Sudoplatov: he simply did not want to be the first to suggest it to the potential assassin. When Sudoplatov failed to guess the leader's wish, Stalin had Petrovsky step in to suggest assassination and provide legal justification for the killing. The idea was wholly Stalin's, not Petrovsky's—only a few days before their meeting, Sudoplatov had met with Petrovsky individually, and he had suggested nothing of the sort. Now, with the idea of assassination on the table, Stalin pressed his intelligence agent. "What are the personal tastes of Konovalets? Try to exploit them," said Stalin. Sudoplatov, who had met with Konovalets more than once in the course of his work abroad, told Stalin that wherever they went, the Ukrainian leader would always buy a box of chocolates. "Konovalets is overly fond of chocolate candies," he told his Kremlin host. Stalin suggested that Sudoplatov think about that.

Before parting ways, Stalin asked the future assassin whether he understood the political importance of the mission entrusted to him. Sudoplatov assured Stalin that he did and that he was prepared to give his life to fulfill the task. Stalin wished him success and shook his hand. Konovalets's activities during the revolution provided legal justification for the proposed act of individual terror, his ties with the Abwehr the political rationale, and the characterization of his nationalist movement as fascist the ideological excuse. The latter would become a major weapon in the Soviet effort to discredit the Ukrainian nationalist movement, which was radical and rightist in ideological orientation, but branded fascist only by its Soviet opponents. Stalin was getting ready for the coming war with Germany and wanted confusion in the ranks of his enemies. Konovalets had to die.

The Soviet secret police followed Stalin's suggestion to exploit Konovalets's weakness. Technical experts constructed a bomb disguised as a box of chocolates. Turning the box from a vertical position to a horizontal one would start the clock mechanism, with a thirty-minute countdown to detonation. On May 23,1938, Sudoplatov met with Konovalets in downtown Rotterdam in the restaurant of the Hotel Atlanta and gave him the box. The assassin then left the restaurant and went into a shop on a nearby street, where he bought a hat and a raincoat to disguise his appearance. Shortly after noon, he heard the explosion and saw people running in the direction from which he had just come. Sudoplatov went to the railway station and boarded a train for Paris. "The gift was presented. The parcel is now in Paris, and the tire of the car in which I traveled had a blowout while I was shopping," read the encoded telegram sent that day from Paris to Moscow.[1]

Konovalets was killed on the spot, as Sudoplatov would learn from a newspaper. Immediately after the assassination, Sudoplatov developed an excruciating headache, but he never regretted what he had done. "The prospect of war was regarded as inevitable by the spring of 1938, and we knew that he would fight for the Germans," wrote Sudoplatov later about his victim. The assassination he carried out was considered a classic by generations of KGB officers: elegant, efficient, and politically expedient. As Stalin had planned, the death of Konovalets produced a power struggle in the nationalist underground. Two years after the assassination, the young and ambitious Stepan Bandera led his radical allies in revolt against Konovalets's longtime aide and successor, Colonel Andrii Melnyk. Bandera managed to wrest control of most of the organization from Melnyk, but the split between the two factions, which resulted in open conflict between them, would last for decades, weakening the nationalist camp.[2]

The assassination made Pavel Sudoplatov a celebrity in the ranks of the Soviet secret police and gave his career a significant boost. His status was further enhanced during the war, when he found himself in charge of all diversionary and assassination activity behind the German lines. His skills remained in high demand after the war. In September 1946, he entered the compartment of a train car heading from Saratov to Moscow. His victim was Oleksandr Shumsky, the people's commissar of education of Ukraine in the 1920s, who had been accused of Ukrainian nationalism and, after years of imprisonment and internal exile, had insisted on his right to return to Ukraine. Along with Sudoplatov was one of his subordinates, Colonel Grigorii Mairanovsky, the head of the special secret-police poison lab. "At night the members of the group led by Sudoplatov entered the compartment and covered Shumsky's mouth, after which Mairanovsky injected the poison," read a later report about the assassination. The autopsy conducted afterward found no trace of the poison used by Mairanovsky—curare, a plant extract. The cause of death was given as a stroke.

Sudoplatov and Mairanovsky's next victim was an archbishop of the Ukrainian Catholic Church, Teodor Romzha. He was the head of the church in Transcarpathia, which had belonged to Czechoslovakia before World War II. According to Sudoplatov, in 1947 Soviet intelligence received reports that the Vatican was lobbying the United States and Britain to support Ukrainian Catholics and their allies in the nationalist underground. Romzha was the last unimprisoned Ukrainian Catholic bishop, and thus exceedingly dangerous. In February 1947, a plan to kill Romzha was submitted to Moscow by the Ukrainian minister of security. The first attempt took place in late October 1947, when the carriage in which the archbishop was riding was hit by a truck. Romzha survived the attack and was taken to a local hospital. Sudoplatov and Mairanovsky finished the job when a nurse recruited by the secret police injected the bishop with poison supplied by Mairanovsky.

Sudoplatov's memoirs and Soviet secret-police archives indicate that all the killings committed by Sudoplatov and Mairanovsky, his "Dr. Death," were done with Stalin's personal approval. No one else had the authority to decide the fate of the secret victims of Sudoplatov's death squad. But the initiative to put people on the list could come from other members of the Soviet leadership as well. Sudoplatov claimed that the killings of Shumsky and Romzha were carried out at the insistence of Nikita Khrushchev, who allegedly met with Mairanovsky on his way to Uzhhorod. Sudoplatov claims to have been present during a telephone conversation between General Sergei Savchenko, the Ukrainian security minister, and Khrushchev in which the latter gave the final go-ahead for the operation to kill Romzha. Whether that is true or not, there is no doubt that the original plan to assassinate Romzha was drafted in Kyiv, not Moscow, and could not have been submitted there without Khrushchev's personal approval.[3]

In December 1949, Sudoplatov was given his most significant assignment yet: to locate and kill the commander in chief of the Ukrainian Insurgent Army, Roman Shukhevych. The seasoned forty-two-year-old nationalist leader had learned his military skills as the commander of Nachtigall, the Abwehr Special Forces Battalion in 1941, and he had taken control of the Bandera faction of the Organization of Ukrainian Nationalists while Bandera was imprisoned in Sachsenhausen. Sudoplatov and the deputy security minister of Ukraine, General Viktor Drozdov, mobilized a whole army of secret-police officers and agents to hunt down Shukhevych. The breakthrough came in early March 1950, when a former member of the underground betrayed Shukhevych's courier, twenty-five-year-old Daria Husiak. Upon her arrest, Sudoplatov interrogated Husiak personally, but she did not betray her superior. The secret police then put her in a cell with a female informer, who got a note from Husiak to be passed to

Shukhevych in a village near Lviv. More than six hundred officers quickly descended on the village of Bilohorshcha in search of the resistance leader.

When Soviet forces broke into the house that Shukhevych occupied, he tried to fight his way out and was killed in action. "Our group, which entered the house, began the operation, in the course of which Shukhevych was asked to surrender," read Sudoplatov's report. "In answer to that, Shukhevych put up armed resistance and began firing a machine gun with which he killed Major Revenko, a department head of the Ministry of State Security of the Ukrainian SSR, and, despite measures taken to capture him alive, he was killed by a sergeant of the MDB in the course of the gunfight." One of Shukhevych's wounds suggested that at some point in the shootout he killed himself to keep from falling into the hands of the secret police. But Sudoplatov could report to Moscow that his mission had been fulfilled. Another leader of the Ukrainian movement was down.[4]

With Shukhevych gone, Stepan Bandera's symbolic importance as leader of the underground and emblem of its continuing resistance grew disproportionately to his actual involvement in Ukrainian developments. The assassination of the Soviet propagandist Yaroslav Halan by the members of the nationalist underground had only solidified Bandera's position at the top of the list of the enemies of the Soviet regime. Nikita Khrushchev demanded his head. According to some accounts, it was in the fall of 1949 that the Soviet Supreme Court had passed a death sentence on Stepan Bandera. Sudoplatov recalled later that once Khrushchev was in Moscow, he asked him to prepare a plan "for liquidating the Bandera leadership of the Ukrainian fascist movement in Western Europe, which is arrogantly insulting the leadership of the Soviet Union."[5]

3

SECRET AGENT

On a summer evening in 1950, a plainclothes policeman showed up on the doorstep of a modest peasant house in the village of Borshchovychi near Lviv. The house belonged to the well-respected Stashinsky family. The father worked as a carpenter and was known for his love of books; the mother ran the household. They had three children—two daughters and a son—all in their late teens or early twenties.[1]

The family had less than two acres of land, but they had never welcomed the communist regime. They were committed Ukrainian patriots, and it was in their home that many of their neighbors had first heard the Ukrainian national anthem, or seen a trident—the coat of arms of the short-lived Ukrainian state that was crushed by a Bolshevik invasion in 1920. The region was under Polish rule until 1939, so the singing of the Ukrainian anthem and the display of the Ukrainian coat of arms were by no means innocent manifestations of local patriotism. After the Soviet takeover of the region, the Stashinskys found themselves among the victims of Bolshevik terror. In October 1940, the Soviet agents arrested a close relative, the thirty-six-year-old Petro Stashinsky, an activist of the Ukrainian cultural movement and a member of the Organization of Ukrainian Nationalists. In June 1941, Petro Stashinsky was shot in a Lviv prison, just days, if not hours, before the Soviets withdrew from the city.

He shared the fate of thousands of Ukrainian patriots. The family took Petro's arrest and killing very hard.

When the Soviets returned in 1944, the members of the Stashinsky family were strong supporters of the OUN. They helped the men from the forest in any way they could, and their home became a safe haven. Sometimes twenty to thirty men would arrive, and Mrs. Stashinsky would go around the neighborhood and collect food for them. The two daughters, Iryna and Maria, became couriers for the underground. Both sisters were arrested and held for a time by the secret police. "When they were reported, they were taken to the prison in Yarychiv," recalled one of the family's neighbors years later, referring to a prison in a neighboring town. "And they beat and assaulted them so badly that . . . Maria had given up any hope of ever being married. She used to say: 'What good am I to anyone when I'm so destroyed?'" Iryna was fired from her position as a teacher in the local school. The Stashinskys were put on the secret police list of suspects, and the father of the girls kept a supply of dry bread on hand in case he was arrested and forced to undertake the long journey to Siberia.[2]

Now, the policeman wanted to talk to nineteen-year-old Bogdan Stashinsky. He was the pride of the family—the first to go to college. He was also popular with the local girls. A slim youngster with an open, rather long face, a pronounced nose, and a noticeable cleft in the middle of his chin, he wore his hair high and fluffy, held his lanky body erect, and cultivated a carefully groomed appearance. Born on November 4, 1931, Stashinsky had been educated under the Poles, the Soviets, the Germans, and then the Soviets again. Under the Poles, the main language of education was Polish; under the Germans and Soviets, it was Ukrainian. Depending on the occupiers, either German or Russian was considered by the curriculum as a foreign language. In 1945, when the war ended, he moved to Lviv, seventeen kilometers from his native village, to continue his education. He dreamed of becoming a medical doctor but did not get into medical school. Instead he studied mathematics at the local teachers' college. He went home every few days for a supply of food, taking a train, which he could not afford. He usually snuck in without paying the fare.

The plainclothes policeman told Bogdan he would have to come to the railway police station immediately to talk about a ticket incident that had taken place a few days earlier. Bogdan had been caught taking the train without paying, and officers had already taken his name and address and then let him go. Now they wanted Bogdan back. Given the family's background and ties to the underground, this seemed to be a minor problem. He could have been charged with a serious crime; maybe now he would be. Bogdan followed the policeman to the station. To his surprise, there was a senior officer awaiting him. "Captain Konstantin Sitnikovsky," the officer introduced himself. He was welcoming, and seemed more interested in the young student's life and attitudes than in the incident on the train. He asked questions about Bogdan's studies, his family, and his parents. That was it. After the friendly talk, he was allowed to go home. He did not know whether there would be a follow-up invitation for another talk. For the moment, the police were leaving him alone. This was good news; when one of Maria Stashinsky's colleagues in the underground had been arrested for her role in the resistance, Captain Sitnikovsky had beaten her up and put a gun to her head, imitating execution.[3]

From his friends in Lviv, Bogdan knew that the secret police had been paying special attention to students since the assassination of Yaroslav Halan. One of the identified killers, the eighteen-year-old Ilarii Lukashevych, was a student at the local agricultural college. Almost immediately, the authorities either arrested or expelled any students who were close to Lukashevych. They also intensified the ideological harassment of students from the region. The campaign was led personally by the first secretary of the Ukrainian Komsomol (Young Communist League) and future head of the Soviet KGB, Vladimir Semichastny. In October and November 1949, the secret police arrested more than one hundred university students and employees. Soon after Khrushchev delivered his speech, interrupted by the note demanding that he call the Kremlin, fifty students were expelled from Lviv colleges. Over the course of the year, the Lviv Polytechnical Institute lost 344 students, amounting to 8 percent of its student body. Overall, up to 2 percent of Lviv students, almost all of them from recently annexed Western Ukraine, were affected by the purge.[4]

The secret police simultaneously stepped up its efforts to recruit informers among Lviv students whose families lived in the countryside—an area infested with guerrillas. Some transferred to other colleges in order to avoid the attention of the secret police; others switched to correspondence programs and left Lviv to go back to their families. One of those who had to leave Lviv in the summer of 1950 was a future leading Ukrainian historian, Mykola Kovalsky. In the fall of 1949, he was removed as head of a student trade-union cell; in March 1950, he was forced to join the Komsomol; and in the summer, at the end of the academic year, he packed up his belongings and signed a request to transfer to a correspondence program. He attributed his decision to leave the city to the atmosphere of "ideological and political terror inflicted on Western Ukrainian youth in the higher educational institutions of Lviv during the era of rampaging Stalinism, when [secret police] informers, denunciations to the police, and betrayal were imposed from above." Kovalsky's closest friend, also a future historian, Zenon Matysiakevych, was not so lucky. He was expelled from the university altogether. Neither Kovalsky nor Matysiakevych belonged to the underground.[5]

Bogdan Stashinsky would also be unlucky. In a few days, the same policeman showed up on his doorstep once again and invited him to another meeting with Captain Sitnikovsky. This time, the captain wanted to talk about the underground and the involvement of members of his family in its activities. It sounded as if he knew almost everything already. "Sitnikovsky knew of my sister's collaboration with the underground and was familiar with the situation in our village," recalled Stashinsky later. There was no doubt that Sitnikovsky was trying to recruit Stashinsky as an informer. "He presented me with a choice: either I could extricate myself from this situation and help my parents or I would be arrested and sentenced to twenty-five years' imprisonment, and my parents would be sent to Siberia," he recalled, describing his second meeting with Sitnikovsky. He knew that what the officer said was no empty threat. On a regular basis, the secret police were arresting people for "crimes" much less serious than those his family had committed.[6]

Bogdan Stashinsky's village of Borshchovychi was surrounded by forests where a detachment of the Ukrainian Insurgent Army was active. It was led by a native of a neighboring village named Ivan Laba, who took nom de guerre "Karmeliuk" after a famous nineteenth-century Ukrainian peasant rebel. Laba had joined the nationalist movement in 1941, soon after the Germans had driven Bandera's followers underground. Like many other Ukrainian nationalists, Laba had been captured by the Gestapo and sent to Auschwitz, where he had managed to survive the war. At the end of the war he rejoined the guerrillas and became one of their local leaders. Laba dated Bogdan Stashinsky's younger sister, Maria, and knew Bogdan personally. Bogdan knew many other members of the underground as well—they came to his house on a fairly regular basis.[7]

Captain Sitnikovsky explained that resistance was senseless. Stashinsky did not disagree with the officer. He knew that going to the forest was equivalent to a death sentence: the chances were nine out of ten that anyone who did so would be caught or killed by the police. Should he save himself and his family by cooperating? If he refused, he would lose his dream of getting an education. Furthermore, he would go to prison, and so would the members of his family. Sitnikovsky did not request a formal agreement right away. "Although he was recruiting me, he did not ask me directly," recalled Stashinsky later, "and he took a careful approach so that I would not see myself as a traitor." To save his family members, he would now have to spy on them. "I knew that if I accepted the proposal, I would quarrel with my parents, but I found myself in such circumstances that it was clear to me that it would be better to accept his proposal," remembered Stashinsky. "I believed that in that way I would succeed in protecting my parents from Siberia and my sisters from prison."

Stashinsky left the meeting without saying either yes or no. But his yes was implicit in his silence. He did not confide in his family or try to figure out a solution with their help. He convinced himself that he was saving his family, even if it was against what they would wish. Stashinsky was also saving himself. He was nineteen years old, not active in politics, and dreaming about the bright future ahead of him. With that future now under threat, he decided to cooperate. Some of his village acquaintances believed that he simply got scared. His next meeting with Sitnikovsky took place at the captain's private apartment.

The new secret agent received the Ukrainian code name "Oleh," a name with origins that went back to one of the first princes of medieval Kyiv. From now on, Stashinsky would sign all his reports with that name. Most of them dealt initially with information about the underground that he learned from his sister Iryna. But this was not enough. To rehabilitate himself completely in the eyes of the authorities and protect his family, said Sitnikovsky, the young man would have to carry out one more mission— that of penetrating the resistance group led by Ivan Laba. His task was of enormous political importance. Captain Sitnikovsky had learned that one of Halan's assassins had recently joined the group. Stashinsky was to locate him in the forest, gain his trust, and discover who had ordered the killing. Stashinsky was promised that this would be his last mission. After that, he would be allowed to continue his studies. Once again, he felt that he had no choice but to agree. Once again he chose not to turn to his family.

Stashinsky knew about the assassination of Halan from the papers. He also knew that one of the assassins, the forestry college student Ilarii Lukashevych, had been apprehended and sentenced to death. What he did not know was that he had already met the second killer, Mykhailo Stakhur, whom he knew only by his nom de guerre, "Stefan." Stakhur was in the vicinity of his village as part of Laba's group. In March and April 1951, the secret police spread the rumor that they were going to arrest Stashinsky for his ties with the underground. They pretended to look for him. Stashinsky returned from Lviv to his native village and told his relatives that the secret police were hot on his heels. Everyone agreed that under the circumstances he had no choice but to flee to the forest and join the guerrillas.

Bogdan's sister Iryna sent a message to her friends in the forest, and Ivan Laba came in person to pick him up. Some members of the underground were suspicious of Bogdan's intentions, but Iryna insisted, and Laba took him in. Laba admitted to Bogdan that he did indeed have under his command an insurgent who had assassinated Halan. In May 1951, Stashinsky met Mykhailo Stakhur, who confirmed that he had worked with Lukashevych in the murder. The two had gone to Halan's apartment and, in the middle of a conversation with him, had asked the writer to close the window. When he turned his back to his visitors, Stakhur killed him with a small axe that he had brought along and hidden under his coat. Once he had this information, Stashinsky had all he needed to complete his mission. He had found the killer, had learned the circumstances of the assassination, and could now tell Captain Sitnikovsky where the culprit was hiding.

In mid-June 1951, Stashinsky unexpectedly left the underground group. He went to report the results of his mission to Sitnikovsky. Less than a month later, on July 8, a special secret-police unit arrested Stakhur. The secret police forced an elderly local family that had supplied food to the insurgents to put sleeping powder into a fruit compote offered to the rebels. When the powder took effect, the officers arrested Stakhur together with three of his comrades. One of them was Yaroslav Kachor, who had advised Laba a few months earlier against taking in Stashinsky. Stakhur was put on trial and hanged in October 1951.[8]

Stashinsky's disappearance and the subsequent arrest of Stakhur had blown his cover, leaving no doubt that he was acting on behalf of the secret police. The news came as a shock to the other members of the Stashinsky family, who were now shunned by their fellow villagers, many of them supporters of the underground. The very people whom Bogdan had tried to save now turned against him, refusing to recognize him as their son and brother. Stashinsky's world had crumbled around him. He had earned the right to continue his education, but he could not do so without the continuing support of his family. Educational loans were nonexistent, and scholarships were small. Students who had little or no support from home often lived up to six in a dormitory room, surviving on cheap fish and considering potatoes a major feast.[9]

The secret police kept its word, however. While others were arrested, the Stashinsky family was left alone. They also gave Bogdan Stashinsky a choice: he could continue his education, or he could join a secret police unit with a monthly salary of between 800 and 900 rubles—three times the wages of a village librarian, and a fortune by student standards. "It was [only] a proposal," remembered Stashinsky later, "but I had no alternative to accepting it and continuing to work for the NKVD. By now, there was no way back for me." Indeed, Stashinsky had nowhere to go. He had saved his family by betraying it. They did not want to have him around anymore. The secret police would become his new home and family.[10]

4

PARACHUTIST

Bogdan Stashinsky was assigned to a special unit of the MGB—the Ministry of State Security, a predecessor of the KGB—that consisted of former insurgents who had agreed to work for the other side, either voluntarily or under duress.

Such units were first created in 1944, as the Red Army began to take over the Western Ukrainian territories formerly under German control. Disguised as units of the Ukrainian Insurgent Army, they engaged in terror, deception, and sabotage, including atrocious crimes against the civil population designed to turn public sentiment against the insurgents. Altogether, the undercover secret-police killed more than a thousand people and arrested twice as many. Some of the members of undercover units had second thoughts and returned to the forest, revealing the methods of MGB counterintelligence operations to the real insurgents. But most felt trapped and stayed where they were: with the blood of their own people on their hands, they, like Stashinsky, had nowhere else to go.

By the time Stashinsky joined the MGB, there were close to 150 special agents divided into small units of up to ten men. The Lviv department of state security had three such groups, named "Thunderstorm," "Typhoon," and "Meteor." The agents had at their disposal the products of the secret police special laboratories: concealed bombs that exploded upon delivery, for example, and toothpaste containers filled with poison gas and special sleeping powder called Neptune 47, which incapacitated within minutes anyone who drank water containing the substance.[1]

Stashinsky's group excelled in conducting an operation that became standard for all similar units. An insurgent in police captivity who had proved resilient to torture would be turned over to the members of a group dressed in Soviet uniforms, allegedly to be transported to another location. The truck carrying the group would unexpectedly break down near a farm occupied by the rest of the MGB team, dressed as resistance fighters. The second group would attack the first one, apparently killing its members and "liberating" the captive. The fight was well staged: both sides would fire blanks at each other, and members of the secret-police detachment, apparently dead, would be seen lying in pools of blood—packages of chicken blood were prepared ahead of time.

Then the deception would take an even more unexpected twist. Those pretending to be insurgents would claim that they had found the newly liberated prisoner's interrogation records, which showed that he had betrayed the secrets of the underground. They would threaten to execute the confused victim for treason if he did not establish his bona fides by telling them everything he knew about the resistance. Unless the terrified captive was alerted to the deception by sympathetic "actors"—themselves once members of the underground—he almost always gave up any information he had. No sooner was the interrogation over than a new secret-police group, dressed in Soviet uniforms, would appear and attack the "insurgents," recapturing the now thoroughly confused prisoner. He was back in custody, his genuine confession recorded by the secret police, and Stashinsky and his group could go to Lviv for rest and entertainment.[2]

One of the commanders overseeing the activities of the MGB special groups, Ihor Kupriienko, later wrote that his agents "prepared and acted entire plays with staging. This was the work of true actors." Kupriienko himself played a major role in an MGB episode that would change Stashinsky's life. It began in June 1951, the same month that Stashinsky left the insurgent group in the forest and joined the secret police. That month, a

special MGB unit consisting of former members of the underground established contact with a man dubbed by the secret police as "Maisky," or "the
one who came in May." His real name was Myron Matviyeyko, he was the
chief of Stepan Bandera's security service, and a Brithish agent.

The British had high hopes for Myron Matviyeyko and his group. With
the Soviets producing an atomic bomb of their own in the summer of 1949,
and China going communist a few months later, both the British and the
Americans were gearing up for a possible military confrontation in Europe.
It was believed that only America's nuclear monopoly prevented the USSR
from using its numerically superior armed forces in Europe. If war was
about to break out, the West needed as much intelligence about the Soviet
Union as it could get. MI6, the British military intelligence service, wanted
information on the Soviet Army and its technical capabilities and infra-
structure. In exchange for technical support and supplies, they wanted the
entire guerrilla network in Ukraine to be placed at their disposal. To this
end, the British parachuted Matviyeyko into Ukraine on May 15, 1951, in
the first of many such planned missions.[3]

Matviyeyko was thirty-seven years old and an experienced security operative when he began preparing for the airdrop. He was known in the
Bandera organization under the code name "Smiley" (Usmikh), but now
he received a new code name, "Moody," from his British instructors. The
original plan was to parachute Matviyeyko into Ukraine along with Bandera, who was supposed to lead the group, but the plan changed a few
weeks before the start of the operation. The British refused to include Bandera, arguing that if the operation failed, they would be accused not simply
of spying on the USSR but also of conspiring to overthrow the existing
government by helping to bring in the leader of the largest anti-Soviet
organization in the West. Nor did they want to take responsibility for Bandera's safety: the risk was too great. Matviyeyko would have to go to
Ukraine without his boss.

In May 1951, Stepan Bandera traveled to London to bid farewell to
Matviyeyko and give him his parting instructions. For Bandera, gaining
the trust of the resistance leaders was Matviyeyko's top priority. He wanted

Matviyeyko to convince Vasyl Kuk, the new commander in chief of the Ukrainian Insurgent Army and head of the Organization of Ukrainian Nationalists, to support Bandera in his struggle for control of the Ukrainian emigration. Matviyeyko was also to launch an investigation into the circumstances of the death at Soviet hands of the previous insurgent commander, Roman Shukhevych. There were rumors that Kuk had been responsible for a breach in Shukhevych's security. Should Kuk refuse to take Bandera's side, Matviyeyko had orders to take over the leadership of the guerrilla forces himself and, if necessary, liquidate the "traitor."[4]

On May 7, 1951, Matviyeyko and five members of his team were supplied with British military uniforms, handed documents issued in the name of Polish nationals, and flown on a British military airplane to Malta. Their subsequent flight to Ukraine was delayed because of bad weather, and they spent a long, anxious week on Malta waiting to be cleared for the airdrop. Finally, on the evening of May 14, Matviyeyko and his people took off from a British airbase on a flight of some six hours that took them across Greece, Bulgaria, and Romania. At a quarter past midnight on May 15, the plane flew low over the Dniester valley, whose high forested banks hid it from Soviet radar, and dropped the parachutists onto Western Ukrainian soil. The plane then turned west and dropped another group of Ukrainian parachutists over Poland.

The Soviets knew about Matviyeyko's group long before it left Malta. One of their sources was Kim Philby, the MI6 liaison officer with the CIA and a double agent recruited by Soviet military intelligence in the 1930s. Matviyeyko's was one of many groups betrayed by Philby, for whom it was a routine operation. "I do not know what happened to the parties concerned," wrote Philby in his memoirs. "But I can make an informed guess." Most of people he betrayed were captured, interrogated, and shot. The lucky ones received long sentences in the Gulag.

Soviet radar detected the British airplane violating Soviet air space but did nothing to stop it. The MGB commanders were lying in wait, with 14 aircraft and almost 1,100 officers and soldiers mobilized to locate the landing area and arrest the parachutists. But Myron Matviyeyko appeared to be extremely lucky on that score. Not only was the plane not intercepted by the Soviets, but the airdrop went exactly as planned, and the group did not lose any of its members. They all managed to find one another and avoid capture by the Soviet search teams. Besides Spanish Llama pistols, British Sten submachine guns, and large amounts of Soviet and foreign cash, the parachutists had substantial supplies of canned food and could survive in the woods for a long time without making contact with the locals. During the last week of May, they managed to establish contact with the only individual they really cared about, the leader of the Ukrainian resistance, Vasyl Kuk.

The commander in chief of the Ukrainian Insurgent Army sent his people to bring Matviyeyko to the headquarters of one of his local commanders. Matviyeyko was eager to come. After years in exile, he wanted to meet those waging war behind enemy lines. They, in turn, were glad to see an emissary from the West. They shared food and drink and were about to smoke a cigarette or two when the alleged Kuk people, upon hearing the words, "Let's have a smoke," suddenly attacked and incapacitated Matviyeyko. He felt too weak to resist—the water he had just drunk was laced with the sleeping powder Neptune 47. The "insurgents" were in fact agents of the Soviet police, members of a group similar to the one Stashinsky would join only a few months later.

For Matviyeyko, the game seemed to be over, but his captors thought otherwise. They told him that the real game was only about to begin. Matviyeyko, the head of a fearsome security service responsible for the interrogation, torture, and execution of those who fell out with Bandera and his organization, had no doubt that the MGB had means to make him talk at its disposal. He said as much to General Pavel Sudoplatov, Stalin's master killer, who personally interrogated Matviyeyko when he was brought to Moscow. Sudoplatov recalled that Matviyeyko decided to cooperate after he realized how much the Soviets already knew about his organization; they seemed to be lacking only the names of the second-tier operators. There were probably other reasons for Matviyeyko's cooperation as well. Given his leadership of a group that the Soviets considered "British spies," and his position at the head of Bandera's security service, he doubtless made what Kim Philby would have called an "informed guess" that unless he cooperated, he would not just be sent to the Gulag, but shot.

Matviyeyko was prepared to listen to what his captors had to say. They wanted Bandera's emissary to become a key figure in a radio game that they were eager to play with the British and Bandera's nationalists. Matviyeyko would work under MGB control, sending radio telegrams composed by his handlers to London and Munich. His messages would contain some genuine information for the British and Bandera and a lot of disinformation for both. Matviyeyko would report on the alleged successes and real difficulties of the Ukrainian insurgency, which was already on its last legs as an organized movement, having been thoroughly penetrated by MGB agents and crushed by Soviet interior forces. The British and Bandera would inform Matviyeyko about each and every airdrop they were planning to execute—information that would go straight to the MGB. Matviyeyko accepted the conditions offered him.

The radio game began in earnest in late June 1951, a little more than a month after Matviyeyko's airdrop and about three weeks after his capture. Ihor Kupriienko was one of its supervisors. Under his and his colleagues' supervision, the MGB created a sham guerrilla group in the woods. Its members established a base in the countryside and began to spread rumors that they had Bandera's personal emissary with them. From their base, Matviyeyko would send his radio messages abroad. In the course of a year, the MGB sent thirty-two radio telegrams to the British center in Cologne and received twenty-nine telegrams with instructions from London.

The British and the Bandera people could not have been happier. In their minds, their previous sporadic contacts with the resistance, conducted through couriers, had finally become regular. They were getting intelligence that perhaps was not first-rate but, to all appearances, genuine. The Soviets, however, were triumphant. The MGB handlers got a unique opportunity to learn about their enemies' plans, feed them false information, and frustrate their activities in their very center. The MGB never managed to persuade Bandera to visit Matviyeyko in Ukraine, but it succeeded brilliantly in deepening existing divisions among nationalist factions by providing disinformation that pitted one leader against another.[5]

The arrival of Matviyeyko in Ukraine, his confession, and the information gathered from the radio game highlighted the increasing importance of Stepan Bandera's headquarters in the resistance struggle being conducted by the remnants of the Ukrainian Insurgent Army in Ukraine. While interrogating Matviyeyko, Pavel Sudoplatov paid special attention to information about Bandera's whereabouts and his living conditions, habits, and contacts in the Ukrainian emigration. The MGB officers abroad were charged with the task of locating and killing Bandera and other leaders of the Ukrainian emigration. Bogdan Stashinsky, a novice member of the MGB special tasks unit, would play an important role in the realization of those plans.

In the summer of 1952, after serving with his unit for close to a year, Stashinsky was summoned to Kyiv, the capital of Ukraine, and offered two years of training for clandestine work abroad. Stashinsky must have been a good agent. His level of education was also significantly higher than that of his comrades. Many of the former resistance fighters were young boys who knew nothing but their mountains and had never seen a city or traveled by train. Few of them were high school graduates. Even among the officers and agents of the secret police, only 13 percent had a university education, and less than half had finished high school. Stashinsky, with several years of university courses behind him, was clearly an exception. The proposal must have come as a relief, as he would no longer have to betray his own family or face the danger of being killed in a shootout with actual insurgents. He agreed, and then he began the training that would put his life and Bandera's on a collision course.[6]

5

STREETS OF MUNICH

As the Cold War heated up, Joseph Stalin set out to reform and re-structure his intelligence services. In November 1952, he issued recommendations on how the new service should be organized. "Our main enemy is America," declared the elderly leader. "But the main pressure should not be directed against America itself. Illegal residencies should be established first and foremost in neighboring states. The first base where we need to have our people is West Germany." He wanted agents who would be prepared to carry out any order coming from Moscow. "Communists who look askance at espionage, at the work of the Cheka [the earlier name for the communist secret police], who are afraid to get their hands dirty should be thrown headfirst into the well," continued the dictator.[1]

Bogdan Stashinsky, who had joined the foreign intelligence school in the summer of 1952, was indeed trained to perform any task the Soviet leaders could think of. His future country of deployment was West Germany—the centerpiece of Stalin's intelligence plan. During his two years in Kyiv, Stashinsky studied espionage craft, from photography to driving and shooting. He also took German classes with a private tutor. In the summer of 1954, Stashinsky was finally ready to start his journey westward. By now he was an employee of the KGB—the name the Soviet secret police had assumed that March. The name change came with the cleansing of the old cadres from the Soviet security services. After Stalin's death in March 1953, Nikita Khrushchev, the former boss of Ukraine and now the head of the Communist Party apparatus, staged a coup against Stalin's most powerful aide, the former head of the security services, Lavrentiy Beria. Khrushchev and his allies arrested Beria in June 1953 and shot him in December of that year. They also arrested Beria's leading aides, including General Pavel Sudoplatov, who would spend years in Soviet prisons. The master killer was now gone, but with Khrushchev gaining more strength in Moscow than ever before, the task of hunting down Bandera was passed on to the new generation of intelligence officers. Stashinsky became the most recent addition to the ongoing KGB operation against the Ukrainian émigrés in Central Europe.

Stashinsky's road to Germany went through Poland. The car carrying the secret agent crossed the Soviet-Polish border just west of Lviv. Alerted by their commanders, the border guards left the border open for almost an hour. They lifted the crossing barrier and stopped checking traffic on both sides of the border until the car with Stashinsky and his control officer inside had passed the checkpoint. They drove across Poland toward the former German city of Stettin, now Polish Szczecin in the former East Prussia, which had been divided between Poland and the Soviet Union after the Potsdam Conference of 1945. They finally stopped in the city of Stargard, a medieval town whose center had been all but destroyed by the Allied bombing in the last years of World War II. Its German residents had been driven out and replaced by Poles, as well as by Ukrainians deported from the areas along the new Soviet-Polish border, so as to deprive the Ukrainian Insurgent Army of popular support.

In Stargard, Stashinsky was given a new identity. In Kyiv he had lived under the name of Moroz; now he became Bronisław Kaczor. He was put up with a member of the Polish secret police and for five months studied the invented biography of the person whose identity he was to assume once in Germany. His new name was Josef Lehmann, born to a German-Polish family in eastern Poland on November 4, 1930. His birthday remained the same, November 4—he just became one year older. Lehmann supposedly had a checkered past, and he had lived in Ukraine and Poland before making his way to East Germany. That was supposed to explain his accented German. In Poland, Stashinsky even visited the places where Lehmann had allegedly lived. Once he had mastered Lehmann's biography, Stashinsky's KGB handler brought him to the new Polish-German border on the Oder. They crossed the river by night, walking across the bridge. Stashinsky turned in his documents in the name of Bronisław Kaczor and became Josef Lehmann.

Stashinsky first met his new handler there at the border, First Lieutenant Sergei Aleksandrovich Damon. Or so he was introduced to Stashinsky. Damon was in his mid-forties, with brown, slightly curly hair that he combed back, a youngish face with a pointed nose, and a pleasant, disarming smile. Behind it was the toughness of a battle-hardened counterinsurgency operative. He came from Ukraine, had fought with the nationalist insurgency there, and spoke the language. From now on, they would be a team.[2]

From the border, Damon brought Stashinsky to East Berlin. It was the first time that Stashinsky had visited Karlshorst (Karl's Nest), the heavily guarded compound in an East Berlin suburb that served as the center of the Soviet military administration in Germany and of its intelligence services—the KGB and the GRU (military intelligence). An area of about one square mile was surrounded by a three-meter-high fence and guarded by a special KGB detachment. The top Soviet military commanders, civilian administrators, and spies not only worked in Karlshorst but also lived there. So did some top East German officials, who found the guarded territory of Karlshorst a much safer place to live and raise their families than the unprotected areas around it.

In 1954, divided Berlin was ground zero in the Cold War and the only loophole in the Iron Curtain dividing Europe's east and west. Officially, the city was still occupied by the four victorious powers—the Americans, Soviets, British, and French—but the significant division was the one between the Western and Soviet zones, which were not yet separated either by barbed wire or by the concrete of the Berlin Wall. From Berlin, which was in the middle of East Germany, but connected by a highway to West Germany, the Soviets sent hundreds of officers and agents on secret missions all over the West. They also used their Berlin base to provide support for Soviet espionage activity in the United States and other parts of the world. From East Berlin one could easily get to Tempelhof Airport in the western part of the city and, from there, proceed to anywhere in the world.

The Berlin loophole was not a one-way street. If you could get easily from East Berlin to the West, you could do the same in the opposite direction as well. There were dozens—even hundreds and thousands—of Western intelligence officers and their agents using the loophole to go east and spy on Soviet and East German military and industrial installations. "It was as easy to travel from East to West Berlin and back as from Hammersmith to Piccadilly," wrote the British double agent and prized Soviet spy George Blake. "Although there were checkpoints on main streets, people could cross freely in both directions. On the Underground there was no check at all. All this made Berlin an ideal centre for intelligence activities, and the opportunities it offered in this respect were exploited to the full. . . . One had an impression that at least every second adult Berliner was working for some intelligence organization or other and many for several at the same time."[3]

Bogdan Stashinsky lived in Karlshorst for about a month before being allowed to settle in the city. The German he had learned in Kyiv turned out to be insufficient for living independently: he could read the language but did not understand native speakers in conversation. He spent Christmas Day 1954 in an East Berlin hotel. It must have been a lonely holiday for a former village boy in a foreign country who spoke a foreign language. His family was far away. In fact, he had no family to speak of, and his adopted KGB family was on vacation.

Stashinsky spent the first months of 1955 studying the German language and way of life. By April, his handler, Sergei Damon, considered him ready to step into his new identity. Stashinsky was sent to Zwickau to work for a joint Soviet–East German venture. It was originally planned that he would do office work, but his German was not good enough for that, so they made him a laborer. Josef Lehmann had now become a real person with a first real job, first work record, and first genuine stamp in his papers. In the summer of 1955, the KGB awarded Stashinsky for his hard work with a vacation on the Black Sea coast. In the fall he was back in East Berlin. He rented a room in the city, introducing himself as Josef Lehmann, an employee of the East German Ministry of Foreign Trade. East Berlin became his base of operations, but his ultimate destination was West Germany, especially Munich, the headquarters of Stepan Bandera and other leaders of the Ukrainian nationalist movement.

In early 1956, Sergei Damon sent Stashinsky to Munich to meet a KGB agent known as "Nadiychyn," a code name derived from the Ukrainian word for "hope." Nadiychyn's real name was Ivan Bysaga. Born in 1919 to a Ukrainian peasant family in Transcarpathia, which had just become a province of the newly minted Czechoslovak state, but would transfer in 1945 under the Soviet control, Bysaga had been trained as a spy in Kyiv after the war. In 1953 he showed up in Austria as a refugee. In 1954, the year Stashinsky began his training as Josef Lehmann in Poland, Bysaga moved to Munich. His early attempts to establish contact with the Bandera people failed, as they suspected him (like anyone else coming from Ukraine after 1945) of working for the KGB. Bysaga was more successful in gaining the trust of Bandera's opponents, who organized themselves around a newspaper, the *Ukrainian Independentist*, edited by a forty-four-year-old lawyer turned political activist and journalist, Lev Rebet.[4]

Lev Rebet lived in Munich with his wife, Daria, who was also a political activist and journalist, and their children, Andrii and Oksana. Lev and Daria were leaders of the opposition within the ranks of the Organization of Ukrainian Nationalists. The Bandera people accused Rebet and his supporters of being CIA stooges. Sergei Damon, Stashinsky's KGB handler, characterized Rebet as an intellectual leader of the Ukrainian nationalists whose writing tarnished the international image of the Soviet Union and dissuaded Ukrainian émigrés from ceasing their hostile activities and returning to Soviet Ukraine. Stashinsky began working as a courier between Karlshorst and Bysaga, a supporting player in the KGB's plan to kidnap

Rebet and take him to East Berlin for use in a propaganda campaign against the West, as had been done with some other "defectors."

On orders from his Karlshorst bosses, Stashinsky suggested that Bysaga put a chemical substance in Rebet's food that would incapacitate him temporarily and make the kidnapping easier. Bysaga never refused outright, but was reluctant to take this risky step. He told Stashinsky that he was not close enough to Rebet and that it would be all but impossible for him to do the job. Lev Rebet's son, Andrii, remembered later that when he, then a thirteen-year-old boy, visited his father at the newspaper office with his four-year-old sister, Oksana, Bysaga showed special affection for little Oksana. That probably appealed to Rebet, but his strong-willed wife, Daria, was suspicious of Bysaga, and he never became a family friend.[5]

Stashinsky's task was not only to supply Bysaga with money and transport his written reports back to Karlshorst, but also to provide moral support for the agent. As far as the KGB was concerned, Bysaga was having other problems apart from his inability to get close to Rebet. He was clearly cracking under pressure and believed that both Bandera's security people and the West German and American counterintelligence services were after him. Eventually Stashinsky helped Bysaga return to East Berlin. As always in such cases, the KGB used the withdrawal of its agent from the West for propaganda purposes. The Soviet media published Bysaga's "defection" letter, denouncing the leaders of the Ukrainian emigration and their subversive activities against the Soviet Union.[6]

Bysaga was gone, but Rebet was still there, and it soon became apparent to Stashinsky that he had inherited Bysaga's object of surveillance. In the early spring of 1957, Sergei Damon showed Stashinsky a photo of a bald man in round glasses. It was Lev Rebet. Damon knew where Rebet worked in downtown Munich, but he wanted Stashinsky to verify Rebet's home address. In April, Stashinsky went to Tempelhof Airport in West Berlin and boarded a flight to Munich.

At the Grünwald Hotel in Munich he filled out a registration card. It read: "Siegfried Dräger, resident of Essen-Haarzopf, born August 29, 1930, in Rehbrücke near Potsdam." The document was forged, but the forgery,

Damon assured Stashinsky, was of the highest quality. The real Siegfried Dräger indeed lived in Essen, so before going to Munich, Stashinsky had visited Essen to familiarize himself with the city and look at the house of the man whose identity he had just assumed. The trip was a precaution. If he was detained and police asked questions about the city or street he allegedly lived on, he would be able to provide credible answers.

To an outside observer, the newly minted Herr Dräger would have clearly seemed to be a fan of Munich architecture and an outdoor enthusiast. He spent hours in the downtown area, observing buildings and people. It also appeared that he loved Schwabing, Munich's northern borough. According to KGB files, it was there that Rebet lived with his family. The address that Stashinsky had been given in Karlshorst was Franz-Joseph-Strasse 47. The entrance to the building was not locked, and Stashinsky visited every floor, looking at the nametags on the doors. Rebet's surname was nowhere to be found. Stashinsky spent the next few days trying to figure out whether Rebet actually lived there. He would observe the building and the adjacent street from 7:00 to 10:00 a.m., then again during lunch hours and between 3:00 and 5:00 in the afternoon. There was no trace of Rebet. Stashinsky went to the Sunday service at the Ukrainian Catholic Church—the church of the majority of the Ukrainian émigrés in Munich, hoping to spot Rebet there, but Rebet made no appearance.

Stashinsky moved his observation post to downtown Munich. He especially liked to frequent one of Munich's most famous landmarks, Karlsplatz. His other favorite spot was the beginning of Munich's longest street, Dachauerstrasse. According to KGB sources, Rebet had offices in both locations. Stashinsky had more luck with Karlsplatz than with Dachauerstrasse. One day he spotted the balding man from the photograph leaving building no. 8 on Karlsplatz square. Lev Rebet headed for a tram stop and boarded a tram. Stashinsky followed him onto the car. When it moved, he realized that it was heading for Schwabing, the area he knew so well. Stashinsky positioned himself immediately behind his target. He tried to calm his nerves, but it was a difficult task. He could not figure out which ticket to buy. The price depended on distance traveled, and he did not know how far

Rebet was going—he had a tram pass and did not have to buy a ticket. What if he bought a ticket for 25 pfennigs and Rebet traveled to the next zone? After vacillating for a moment, he bought a ticket for 30 pfennigs. Then he noticed that he was the only person in the tram wearing sunglasses. Per his KGB training, he had put them on in order to blend into the background. It was a sunny day, and sunglasses were appropriate, but no one in the tram was wearing them. He removed his.

Stashinsky then got the feeling that he was being followed. Was he right? He moved farther away from Rebet to be safe. When the tram reached the Münchner Freiheit station, not far from one of the entrances to the English Garden, Rebet stepped off. Stashinsky did not dare follow him and stayed on the tram. The next day he left Munich for Berlin. His orders were not to stay in the city longer than ten days, and he had already reached that point. But his time in Munich had not been wasted. The old residential address that the KGB had in its files could now be discarded, and the new area of Rebet's residence established. The KGB officers now knew which tram he took to work and back home.

In June 1957, Stashinsky went back to Munich to learn more about his target. Once again he checked into the Grünwald Hotel, but this time he asked for a room looking onto Dachauerstrasse, the location of one of Rebet's offices. Now Rebet would pass under Stashinsky's window as he walked to work in the morning. It was easy to follow him from one workplace to another, and eventually to his home. One day Stashinsky followed him on a tram to the Münchner Freiheit stop, and then to nearby Occamstrasse. On this trip he traveled on a different tram car, and he did not wear sunglasses. Still, his nerves were on edge; he believed that he had been uncovered. Upon reaching Occamstrasse, Rebet turned into an archway on the right side of the street leading to a cinema. Stashinsky followed him into the archway and, to his surprise, found Rebet standing there, apparently looking at the movie posters. Rebet left the archway the moment Stashinsky appeared.

Back on the main street, he saw Rebet entering one of the corner buildings. He followed him and, passing the building, saw Rebet's nametag on the entrance. The next day he returned to the area, waited until Rebet left for work, and then went to his building and took pictures of the residents' nametags. The KGB officers in Karlshorst were more than pleased with the results: the young agent who was going by the name of Siegfried Dräger had managed to locate Rebet's residence and fully establish his route to work and back. In July, Stashinsky was sent back to Munich to confirm his earlier findings and to see if the entrance hall in Lev Rebet's building had any mailboxes.

Stashinsky did not know what the KGB's plans were for Rebet, and, knowing the KGB rules, he never asked. He knew that his old contact in Munich, Ivan Bysaga, had been asked to help with the kidnapping of Rebet, but Bysaga was now back in the Soviet Union. Meanwhile, Stashinsky was given a new mission—to follow the publisher of the same *Ukrainian Independentist* newspaper that Rebet worked for. It seemed that, at least for him, the Rebet saga was over.[7]

6

WONDER WEAPON

Bogdan Stashinsky led a relatively comfortable, if not stress-free, life as a spy. He followed Ukrainian émigrés on his numerous trips to Munich; stuffed dead drops (hiding items such as money or instructions for recipients to later come and pick up, thereby avoiding the need for personal contact); and spied on American and West German military installations. He had a routine. That routine, however, came to an end in September 1957, when Sergei Damon invited him to a meeting at the KGB safe house in Karlshorst. They were about to meet an important guest from Moscow, Damon told him. The time had come, he added significantly. Stashinsky remained unsure of what was going on until the moment their unnamed guest took something from his pocket: it was a metal cylinder, eight inches long and less than an inch in diameter, with a safety catch and a trigger attached to it.

The guest from Moscow told Stashinsky that it was a weapon and went on to explain how it worked. The cylinder contained an ampoule with liquid, said the Moscow guest. When the trigger was pressed, a striker set off by a gunpowder charge hit the ampoule with poison, spraying the contents from the cylinder. The cylinder would have to be aimed at the other person's face or chest for him to breathe in the gas and the liquid poison. The poison caused unconsciousness and then death; the contents would evaporate

almost immediately after the discharge, leaving no trace. Damon explained
that the first effect was the same as suffocation. Death by cardiac arrest, continued the guest from Moscow, would follow within two to three minutes.
He went on: "Once the liquid evaporates, it leaves no trace; a minute after
death the veins return to their previous state, making it impossible to establish violent death." Damon added that the weapon was 100 percent
foolproof.[1]

This turn of events took Stashinsky by surprise. They clearly wanted
him to become an assassin, or they would never have shown him the secret
weapon, let alone explained its workings. Stashinsky also understood that
he would not be the first to use the spray cylinder. He couldn't have known,
but the weapon was in all probability a Soviet improvement on the German
World War II–era liquid poison gun.

The guest from Moscow wanted to demonstrate his 100 percent foolproof weapon, and loaded the pistol with an ampoule of water. He then released the firing pin and pressed the trigger. Stashinsky heard a sound like
that of hands clapping. The pistol shot water onto a towel pinned to the
wall approximately one meter away. The water left a stain on the towel
about 20 centimeters in diameter. The guest explained that the ampoule of
poison would shoot half a meter farther, and the area of impact would be
larger from farther away, as the poison was lighter than water. He took a
wrench out of his case, unscrewed the bolts of the cylinder, cleaned the
weapon, and reloaded it. He would shoot it a few more times. He then used
a broom to collect small pieces of glass from the broken ampoules, which
had fallen to the floor. They were no more than a millimeter in diameter.

Before he left, the guest from Moscow explained to Stashinsky that the
person shooting the pistol was also in danger of breathing in the poisonous
fumes, but two ways had been found to make the procedure safe. The first
was to take a pill between sixty and ninety minutes before the shooting. It
would prevent the constriction of blood vessels and was effective for four
to five hours. The other option was to use an antidote contained in a special
ampoule immediately after the shooting. Stashinsky would have to crush
the ampoule in a piece of fabric and breathe in the gases evaporating from

it. The antidote was so strong, continued the expert, that if it was administered to the object of the attack within one minute, that person could be
revived. The safest way was to use the pill before the shooting and the antidote after it. The man from Moscow also suggested that it would be useful
for Stashinsky to see the spray pistol at work loaded with poison, not water.
Damon agreed. They decided to try the weapon on a dog, and said they
would let Stashinsky know when everything was ready for the experiment.
With that, the meeting was over.[2]

Damon volunteered to drive Stashinsky out of Karlshorst into the city.
He was excited, and congratulated Stashinsky on the honor that was being
bestowed on him with such a high-clearance assignment. When Stashinsky
showed little emotion and remained mostly silent, Damon asked whether
he fully understood how much trust the authorities were placing in him.
Stashinsky remembered later that Damon behaved as if the two of them
were saviors of the nation. Stashinsky was confused. He was not a novice in
the game of betrayal, and he had experienced brutal life-and-death
skirmishes with the insurgents in the woods and mountains of the Carpathians. But he simply could not imagine himself killing an unarmed person. He had been raised a Christian, and some of the values his parents had
taught him had stayed with him. At the same time, he was equally convinced that he could not turn down the assignment. Once again he felt
trapped—increasingly so as time passed. He spent days and nights trying
to find a solution to his moral dilemma. He failed to find one.

The trial of a fully loaded spray pistol on a dog a few days later did
nothing to assuage his mental torment: if anything, it increased his anxiety.
Damon and the mysterious guest from Moscow bought a small mongrel at
the local market and then picked up Stashinsky in the city. They drove to a
wooded area near Müggelsee Lake outside of East Berlin. There the poison
expert from Moscow gave Stashinsky a pill. They tied the dog to a tree and
waited the requisite sixty minutes for the pill to start working. Stashinsky
had no way of telling whether it had taken effect. The man from Moscow
handed him a loaded cylinder. Stashinsky could not bear to look at the dog.
He felt sorry for the small creature. When he approached with the pistol,

the dog tried to lick his hand. Stashinsky turned his head away and pressed the trigger. The spray hit the dog's muzzle. The dog fell, its legs moving jerkily. A few minutes later it was dead. "My first victim," Stashinsky thought to himself. He knew there would be others to follow. Someone crushed an ampoule containing the antidote, and the three men all breathed in the evaporating gases. They got into the car and drove back to East Berlin. The experiment was declared a success.[3]

Stashinsky had no doubt who was supposed to be his next victim. When he was called in for the first meeting with the man from Moscow, Damon had mentioned that it would concern his old "acquaintance." The name of that "acquaintance" was never mentioned explicitly during the meeting, but Stashinsky was sure it was Lev Rebet. With Bysaga gone, and no other person close to Rebet in sight, the KGB had decided to kill the troublesome journalist instead of kidnapping him. Despite assurances that the pistol had been successfully used before, the KGB officers were far from certain that the weapon would remain undetected. In fact, they were fairly sure that the assassination would be recognized immediately, and that the blame would fall on Rebet's archenemies from the Bandera camp. Like Stalin, who had ordered the assassination of Konovalets, his successors counted on the murder of Rebet to deepen differences and provoke conflicts among the leaders of the Ukrainian emigration.

Talk of "eliminating" leaders of the Ukrainian émigrés—who were allegedly preventing their followers from achieving reconciliation with the Soviet regime and returning to their homeland—was commonplace in Karlshorst's émigré department, but Stashinsky had never thought—or, rather, did not wish to think—that it meant much in practice. Now he remembered Damon's words, which he had initially dismissed as idle talk. When he had described to his handler how close he had stayed to Rebet while following him for the first time on the tram to Schwabing, Damon had said that striking Rebet with a pin would solve the whole issue. There was now no doubt that he was talking about a poison pin. It was also becoming clear why Damon had wanted Stashinsky to find out whether there were mailboxes in the foyer of Rebet's building. The KGB had probably also discussed the possibility of using a parcel bomb to eliminate the Ukrainian journalist. There were no mailboxes in Rebet's building, Stashinsky had reported to Damon, probably sealing his own fate as the one who would have to carry out Plan B.[4]

Stashinsky was torn. He did not want to kill anyone. But neither could he imagine not following orders. The consequences of insubordination were clear to him. During his first months in Germany, after reading in the newspapers about the defection of a KGB assassin named Nikolai Khokhlov, Stashinsky had asked Damon who Khokhlov was and what position he had held in the KGB. Damon had responded that Khokhlov was an adventurist and a morally fallen man. Then he added something that etched itself in Stashinsky's memory: "We'll get him sooner or later." They did. The man from Moscow who had brought the spray pistol had probably been involved in another scientific "experiment"—the failed assassination attempt on Khokhlov, who had been poisoned with radioactive thallium in Frankfurt that same month. The KGB kept its word and hunted down rogue assassins wherever they were. Khokhlov had refused to kill his target and escaped to the West, and now he was a hunted man.

Stashinsky eventually found a solution to his moral conundrum, taking refuge in a political rationalization of what he was about to do: he would kill one person to help many others find their way back to their homeland. It was a rationale Sergei Damon had suggested, and Stashinsky latched on to the idea, burying his qualms down deep.[5]

7

GREETINGS FROM MOSCOW

On the afternoon of October 9, 1957, Air France attendants at Tempelhof Airport in West Berlin checked in a young man on his way to Munich carrying documents in the name of West German citizen Siegfried Dräger. In his pocket he had another document issued in the name of Josef Lehmann, a resident of East Germany born on November 4, 1930, in the Lublin province of Poland. Dräger/Lehmann was carrying more than a thousand West German marks, and there were two cans of Frankfurt sausages in his luggage. He seemed ready for any eventuality, including a sudden East German takeover of West Germany and the disappearance of food supplies from West German stores.

The documents, money, and sausages had been given to Stashinsky at Karlshorst. They told him to use his Western passport for the flight to West Germany, and the East German one thereafter. If he was caught, he should declare himself an East German citizen, which would presumably improve his chances of returning to the Eastern bloc. The most incriminating piece of evidence in his luggage were the sausages. He had two tins of them, but only one actually contained sausages. The other had been opened and redesigned by KGB technicians at Karlshorst to conceal his weapon: the spray pistol. The weapon was wrapped in cotton wool and placed in a metal cylinder. The cylinder was then placed in the tin, which was filled with water. Both the weapon and the cylinder were made of aluminum, and the weight of the fake tin was the same as that of the real one, with a special mark on the fake tin to distinguish it. Other than that, they looked identical.

The original plan had been to smuggle the weapon into West Germany through diplomatic channels. A member of one of the East European diplomatic corps was supposed to bring the weapon to Munich and pass it to Stashinsky there. Diplomats were not checked by customs officers, and the KGB planners thought that this would ensure safe passage of the secret weapon across the border. The plan was dropped, however, when someone pointed out that a diplomat might be followed by West German counterintelligence, leading its agents to Stashinsky, who would then be caught with the weapon in his possession. It was ultimately decided that Stashinsky would take the weapon with him on his flight to Munich. If he was caught with the fake tin in his luggage, he was supposed to tell investigators a story about meeting a man in East Germany who had paid him to bring both tins to Munich and pass them on to a woman at Maxim's Bar. If he was caught with the weapon on him after using it, he was to say that he had just found it on the stairs.

Stashinsky was not checked at the border. He reached Munich safely late in the afternoon of Wednesday, October 9. His instructions were to carry out the act in the office building at Karlsplatz 8. If that should prove difficult, he had a free hand to choose the office building on Dachauerstrasse or the residential one on Occamstrasse. He took the first antidote pill around 8:00 a.m. on Thursday, October 10. He had ten pills and two ampoules—a supply that would last him the ten days allotted for his mission. Everything was now ready, the weapon in his pocket. He wrapped it in newspaper and made a hole in the wrapper so he could operate the safety catch and trigger. He discarded the tin that had contained the weapon in a garbage container in the English Garden.

By 8:30 a.m. he was on the street, observing the entrance to building no. 8 on Karlsplatz square. It contained numerous professional offices, including those of doctors. If he was caught in the act, he was supposed to say that he was an East German tourist who had suddenly gotten a toothache while admiring Munich's architectural marvels, and was visiting a dentist in the building. If he was surprised by someone immediately after the act, he was to pretend that he had just found the victim lying on the floor and was trying to help him. That day he waited until 10:30 a.m., but Rebet did not appear. Nor was he in evidence that afternoon. He was also a no-show on Thursday, October 10, and Friday, the 11th. On each particular occasion it was a relief, but of the kind that increased his overall anxiety. Stashinsky felt it on awakening every morning. The psychological stress would reach its peak in the morning hours designated for the killing of his victim. As morning passed and afternoon approached, Stashinsky would feel some relief. He would walk the streets of the city to try and forget his deep, moral unease, but the next morning it would be back. The only way to get rid of the stress and put his life back on track seemed to be to carry out the order, but he felt that it was beyond his capacity. It was a vicious circle.[1]

Lev Rebet did not usually go to his office on weekends, but did his customary reading and writing at home. On Saturday, October 12, he decided to make an exception. The previous night he had stayed up late reading Alexander Dovzhenko's recently published autobiographical novel *The Enchanted Desna*. It was the last work produced by the famous filmmaker, who had died in Moscow the previous year. Dovzhenko had long been prohibited by Stalin from living and working in his native Ukraine, and his last novel was full of nostalgia for his childhood days in the picturesque surroundings of the Ukrainian countryside. This was a subject with which Lev Rebet, a native of the Ukrainian village and a longtime émigré himself, could easily identify, despite all the ideological differences between him, a committed nationalist, and Dovzhenko, a Soviet filmmaker and communist convert.

On the morning of October 12, Rebet, who generally was reluctant to display his softer side to his children, showed interest for the first time in many months in the piano exercise performed by his teenage son, Andrii. He even patted him on the head. When his wife, Daria, shouted to him from the kitchen not to stay at work too long and not to be late for lunch, he told her not to worry. He joked that he wasn't sure if he would even make it to his office. The family members later believed that Lev Rebet had had a premonition of what would happen to him that day.[2]

That Saturday, Stashinsky was at his observation post at Karlsplatz soon after 9:00 a.m. It was a pleasant, sunny day. He had left his coat in the hotel and was walking around in his suit. As always, he was nervous. He took a sedative as well as his antidote pill. The sedative did not work. His anxiety only continued to grow as he waited on tenterhooks for his target to materialize. The pressure peaked sometime after 9:00 a.m. and then began to subside. It was already close to 10:00, and Rebet was nowhere in sight— Stashinsky began to relax. Suddenly he spotted the figure that by now he could distinguish from thousands of others. Rebet had gotten off the tram and was walking directly toward his hunter. Stashinsky turned around and walked toward the entrance to Karlsplatz 8. It all unfolded as in a dream. "Before and at the time I felt as though I were only half awake," he remembered later. "My surroundings, people, traffic in the street did not seem to penetrate my conscious mind. It was all in shadow, as if only reaching my subconscious mind." Whether it was the effect of the pill he had been given at Karlshorst (the chemical experts would later claim that instead of an antidote he was given an anti-anxiety drug) or the desire to rid himself of the burden that had been oppressing him for so many days, Stashinsky was determined to carry out his orders. Before entering the building he took out the cylinder rolled up in newspaper and disappeared into the doorway, the weapon in his right hand.

He went upstairs to the second-floor landing and stopped there. He released the safety catch, fingering it through the hole in the newspaper, and got ready to face his victim. When he heard the door opening downstairs, he began his descent, keeping to the left so Rebet would be forced to pass by his right side. He soon saw a man coming up the other side—it was Rebet. As they were about to pass each other, Stashinsky raised his hand with the rolled-up newspaper and pressed the trigger. He tried not to look in his victim's direction. Still, he could not help noticing out of the corner of his eye that the man he had targeted slumped forward. Stashinsky did not see what happened to his victim after that. He put the cylinder back in his pocket, took out the antidote ampoule as instructed at Karlshorst, crushed it in a piece of gauze, and inhaled the fumes. He felt like he was about to faint.

Stashinsky exited the building and turned left, then left once again. It took about ten to fifteen minutes after exiting the building for his mind to return to normal. "My surroundings made an impression upon me again and penetrated my conscious mind," he remembered later. Eventually he made his way to one of Munich's busiest streets, Ludwigstrasse, crossed it, and found himself in the Hofgarten, a public (formerly royal) garden established in the early seventeenth century by Elector Maximilian I of Bavaria. Heading for the edge of the garden, he stood on a bridge across the Kögelmühlbach, a stream that flowed through the garden, and dumped the spray pistol in the water. So far he had followed to the letter the instructions received at Karlshorst, down to the stream where he disposed of his weapon.

After leaving the Hofgarten, Stashinsky began to return to his hotel before realizing that perhaps a dog might be used to trace his scent. Instead he took a tram and rode it aimlessly for a few stops before heading back. Years later he would remember every detail of the route he had taken from the Hofgarten. He could not help but follow a subconscious urge to revisit the scene of his crime. The building no. 8 on Karlsplatz was surrounded by a crowd of people and police. Stashinsky turned his eyes away and hurried to his hotel. He packed up his belongings, which no longer included Frankfurt sausages, placed the West German ID in the name of Siegfried Dräger in his pocket, paid the hotel bill, and headed for the Hauptbahnhof. His instructions were to leave the city immediately upon fulfilling his mission. He followed them exactly.[3]

Lev Rebet was found on the stairs of his office building sometime between 10:20 and 10:45 a.m. He died after managing to reach the second-floor platform. The cleaning lady who heard his screams (despite the assurances of the weapon expert from Moscow, the poison pistol failed to make a victim unconscious right away) found him lying on the floor and alerted others in the building. They called an ambulance and then the police. Patrol officers received a call soon after 11:00 a.m.: "Some man has fallen on the staircase," was the message. One minute later they were informed that he had died. Dr. Waldemar Fischer, who was called to the scene, estimated that death had taken place at approximately ten minutes to eleven. The cause of death was cardiac arrest. There was no way to call Lev Rebet's wife and children, as the Rebets did not have a home telephone. But one of their Ukrainian neighbors did, and people in Rebet's office knew that number. They called the neighbor, who happened to be at home, and he broke the news to Mrs. Rebet. The neighbor also volunteered to drive her to Karlsplatz.

Daria Rebet was shocked, not least because her husband had never complained of any heart condition. But the autopsy conducted two days later by Dr. Wolfgang Spann of the Institute of Forensic Medicine at Munich University confirmed Dr. Fischer's diagnosis. One of Lev Rebet's arteries was significantly narrowed, and the University of Munich experts found no reason to believe that death had occurred as a result of anything other than natural causes. Rebet's family and friends had no choice but to accept the diagnosis. Deep down they hoped that it was not what they thought it might be: the start of a KGB operation to eliminate them all.[4]

On the afternoon of October 12, 1957, as the police, doctors, and family tried to figure out what had happened to Lev Rebet, a receptionist at the Continental Hotel in Frankfurt registered a new visitor: Siegfried Dräger. The next day, Stashinsky, as Dräger, took a flight to Tempelhof Airport in Berlin, crossed the border into East Berlin, and went home to Marienstrasse in the city center, where he was renting a furnished room from an elderly woman named Frau Stranek. She knew her tenant as Josef Lehmann, a *Volksdeutscher* (ethnic German) from the East—one could tell that from his accented German. Josef Lehmann paid his rent on time and did not cause any trouble. He was quiet and polite—an ideal tenant for any landlady. Lehmann told Frau Stranek that he worked as an interpreter for the East German Ministry of Trade and had to go on business trips from time to time. It appeared as if he had just returned from another trip that Sunday afternoon. On Monday morning he left for work as usual.

Stashinsky's first order of business that Monday was to call Karlshorst. He told his case officer, Sergei Damon, that he was back. Damon asked whether everything was all right and whether the trip had been successful. Stashinsky answered in the affirmative. They agreed to meet in the city, whereupon, apart from an oral report, Stashinsky filed two written ones. The first gave the dates of his trip, the places he had visited, the hotels he had stayed in, and the airlines he had taken. The second was of a different nature. "On Saturday," went the report, "I met the person in question in a town that I know well. I greeted him, and I am sure that the greeting was satisfactory."

Damon explained to Stashinsky that this report would never be typed— there would exist one copy, and one copy only. Unbeknown to Stashinsky, on November 15, 1957, the chief of the KGB intelligence directorate, Aleksandr Sakharovsky, sent the Soviet leader, Nikita Khrushchev, a secret report "on measures taken in Germany." The report was written by hand and produced in a single copy, for Khrushchev's eyes only.

Stashinsky truly hoped that he would never again have to "pass greetings" to anyone on behalf of the KGB. As the shock associated with the assassination wore off, he felt a new burden on his soul—he had killed a man against his own convictions. "Now, after what had happened," he remembered later, "it seemed to me that I was lost in every respect. Later, once a good deal of time had passed, I tried to tell myself that it had happened once, it would not happen again; perhaps there had been other reasons for this assignment that were unknown to me." Once again he started looking for justification of what he had done. Sergei Damon and other KGB officers he met at Karlshorst were eager to help. They often told him that if émigré leaders did not understand the demands of the time, they should be "eliminated." He also found solace in the fact that the killing was not violent. "The weapon I was given," he recalled later, "was constructed in such a way that it required no exertion, nor the use of force to bring about someone's death." There was no need to take aim or look at the target. "I did not see the act of killing, only the act of pressing the trigger."[5]

PART II
PERFECT MURDER

8

RED SQUARE

Bogdan Stashinsky was moving up in the world. In April 1959, Sergei Damon told him that he was being summoned to Moscow, possibly to meet the head of the KGB himself. Why such an honor was being bestowed on him Stashinsky did not know, but later that month he received a ticket and travel documents and boarded the train to Moscow.

In Moscow he was met by a KGB man who provided him with Soviet currency and registered him at the Hotel Ukraine, one of the "seven sisters," the seven Moscow high-rises commissioned by Joseph Stalin. The Hotel Ukraine (known today as Radisson Royal Hotel, Moscow) was a brand-new building. Its construction had begun in 1953, the year of the dictator's death, and had been completed four years later. At about the same time, Khrushchev, Stalin's longtime viceroy in the Ukrainian Soviet Socialist Republic, had fully consolidated his hold on power. When the hotel officially opened to guests in May 1957, it had been heralded by the Soviet press as the largest hotel in Europe. It was certainly the tallest, measuring 650 feet from its foundations to the top of its spire. Its façade and outside walls were decorated with symbols of Soviet power: stars, hammers and sickles. The hotel stood at the head of the new, glamorous (by Soviet standards) Kutuzov Avenue—which was lined with the residences of the most famous and powerful citizens in the Soviet capital.[1]

The day after Stashinsky arrived, the KGB officer showed up at his suite with a man who introduced himself only by his first name and patronymic: Georgii Avksentievich. Stashinsky never learned his surname or his exact rank and position in the KGB. "The practice in the KGB," he recalled later, "is that when you speak with some colleague, you never know exactly what position he holds." Was he the head of the secret police? The answer to that question remained unclear. Stashinsky remembered later, however, that Damon had said "the head of the KGB himself" would speak with him. Whoever he was, the man made a strong impression on Stashinsky. He seemed to be in his mid-forties and was unlike any KGB officer Stashinsky had met before. "I looked upon him the whole time as an aristocrat; he was so calm and, as he sat beside me, he expressed his thoughts in such an un-wavering tone that contradicting him was unthinkable. In highly self-confident fashion. . . . One could easily see that he was used to giving orders; that he occupied one of the top posts in the KGB."[2]

According to declassified biographies of KGB officials, Georgii Avksen-tievich's last name was Ishchenko. At the time of their meeting, Colonel Ishchenko was a few months short of his fiftieth birthday, but with his dark hair combed back, he apparently looked younger than his age. There was nothing aristocratic about his background. He had been born in 1910 into the family of a manual laborer in the village of Krymskaia in the Kuban re-gion of the Russian Empire. He claimed to be a Russian despite his Ukrainian surname—probably the result of the drastic change in Soviet na-tionality policy in the early 1930s, when Stalin ordered the closing of all Ukrainian publications and educational institutions in the Kuban in the wake of the Great Ukrainian Famine of 1932–1933, when all Ukrainians in the region were reregistered as Russians. Ishchenko began his career in the party apparatus and switched to the secret police in the wake of Stalin's great purge of 1937. In the last years of Stalin's rule, Ishchenko headed the NKVD apparatus in his home Kuban region. After the dictator's death he was sent to Hungary to run the NKVD; later he served as liaison with the Hungarian security services. He took an active part in the suppression of the Hungarian Revolution in the fall of 1956. At that time he worked closely with the head of the KGB, General Ivan Serov, who had been dispatched to Budapest.[3]

Sitting at the table in Stashinsky's hotel room, Colonel Ishchenko asked him about his latest assignment: a successful mission to track down Stepan Bandera, the leader of the largest and, as the Soviets believed, most dangerous group of Ukrainian émigrés in the West. Stashinsky obliged, and told Ishchenko what he knew about Bandera.

In the spring of 1958, Sergei Damon had asked Stashinsky to go to a West Berlin bookstore and look for anything published by an author called Popel. It was the first time that Stashinsky had heard the name. In fact, the only book that would have had that name on the cover was one that had been published in Lviv in 1943. It was *A Chess Player's Beginnings* by Stepan Popel, a Ukrainian chess player. After the war, Popel had won numerous Paris championships, and after moving to the United States in the 1950s he had held the Michigan state championship for three consecutive years. Not surprisingly, the bookshop Stashinsky visited in West Berlin in the summer of 1958 did not have Popel's Ukrainian-language book from fifteen years prior. Stashinsky told his case officer that he had seen no books by such an author, and Damon had dropped the issue.[4]

Popel's name would soon come up again in Stashinsky's life. In May 1958, Ukrainian émigrés in Europe marked the fiftieth anniversary of the assassination of the founder of the Organization of Ukrainian Nationalists, Colonel Yevhen Konovalets, who had been killed on Stalin's personal orders by Pavel Sudoplatov. The KGB officers decided to use the commemoration of Konovalets's death to start plotting their assassination attempt on his successor. The commemorative ceremony on May 25, 1958, took place at the Crooswijk Cemetery in Rotterdam, where Konovalets was buried, and brought together Ukrainian nationalist leaders from around the world. Both Stepan Bandera and Andrii Melnyk, the leaders of the two rival factions of the OUN, attended the ceremony. Damon wanted his agent to see and identify in person the man he would later be ordered to kill. But he of course did not reveal his true motives to Stashinsky. Instead, Damon asked him to attend the ceremony with his camera and take a few pictures of the nationalist leaders. Stashinsky was off to Rotterdam.[5]

Despite the tight security, Stashinsky managed not only to make his way to the cemetery, but also to take pictures of people in the commemorative procession. He got close enough to Konovalets's tombstone to see the speakers delivering eulogies. One of the speakers, whom he had never seen before, received more attention than the others. His speech was the longest. He mourned Konovalets and lashed out against his killers. "Today, as before, we can say that the enemy of God, Ukraine, and all freedom-loving humanity has not managed to destroy the OUN and the Ukrainian liberation movement by killing its founder and leader," declared the speaker. "But at the same time we realize that this is a great, irreparable loss, one that we have not been able to overcome in twenty years."[6]

Stashinsky did not know who the speaker was, but he noticed his car—the dark blue Opel Kapitan. Upon his return from Rotterdam, Sergei Damon showed him a newspaper with the texts of speeches delivered at the ceremony. The longest of them was attributed to Stepan Bandera. It was then that Stashinsky realized who the speaker was and to whom the Opel Kapitan belonged.

Damon was interested not only in Stashinsky's pictures and the people he had seen in Rotterdam, but also in his description of the cemetery and the area around Konovalets's grave. He asked whether something could be hidden there. Stashinsky responded in the affirmative. But when he realized that Damon had in mind another bomb, not in a box of chocolates this time but in Konovalets's grave, he changed his answer and said that it would be hard to do something like that. He also suggested that, given the congested space, the victims of such an attack would include not only nationalist leaders but also women and children. Damon dropped the subject at the time, but the assassination of Bandera was evidently very much on his mind.[7]

It was in early January 1959 that Damon gave Stashinsky his next assignment: go to Munich and find out where Bandera lived. Damon told him that Bandera most likely was living under the name Stefan Popel. He was possibly still at the address the KGB had on file, but they wanted that information either confirmed or updated. Stashinsky flew to Munich, using new West German documents issued in the name of Hans Joachim Budeit. It did not take long for him to confirm that the man whom he had seen in Rotterdam did not live at the address they had given him at Karlshorst. Where he lived now was anyone's guess.

The assignment was over. Stashinsky could return to Berlin and report on his findings. But at the last moment he decided on a whim to check the Munich telephone book. And there he was, Stefan Popel, with his telephone number and residential address, Kreittmayrstrasse 7. Was this the right Herr Popel? The next morning Stashinsky was at Kreittmayrstrasse. In the archway leading to the courtyard at building no. 7, he saw the familiar Opel Kapitan and the speaker from Rotterdam working on his car. The list of residents near the entrance to the building included the name Stefan Popel. Later that morning Stashinsky saw the same Opel Kapitan parked near the headquarters of the local Ukrainian organizations on Zeppelinstrasse. There was no doubt that Stefan Popel of Kreittmayrstrasse 7 was none other than Stepan Bandera. Stashinsky was a good agent. Not for nothing had he abandoned the guerrilla hideouts of Western Ukraine and made it all the way to the coveted posting in Berlin. Damon could not believe his ears when he heard the report. "We have finally managed to pick up Bandera's trail," he told Stashinsky euphorically.

After attentively listening to Stashinsky's story about tracking down Bandera in Munich, Colonel Ishchenko told him that the decision had been made to "liquidate" his target in the same manner as Rebet. Alarmed, Stashinsky voiced his reservations: unlike Rebet, Bandera was armed and had a bodyguard. The KGB colonel told the assassin that the weapon he was about to receive was an improved model with two barrels. If necessary, Stashinsky could kill the bodyguard as well. "He paid no attention whatever to my objections," remembered Stashinsky later. "I was to carry it out, exactly how was my business; he said that my attempt would be successful." They got a bottle of Soviet champagne and drank to the success of the mission. "It made me think of a Russian film I had once seen," recalled

Stashinsky. "It was about the 'heroic deed' of a spy, and the officer who sent the spy on a mission behind enemy lines took leave of him with champagne."[8]

Colonel Ishchenko told Stashinsky that it would be a shame for him to know Western Europe, but not to get acquainted with Moscow. He wanted him to see the Soviet capital. It was standard KGB practice to show their agents and assassins the holy places of the Soviet Union before they were dispatched abroad. Lenin's mausoleum and Red Square were by far the most venerated ones. Ishchenko gave Stashinsky a special pass to the grandstand at Red Square to attend the May Day military parade and demonstration. Stashinsky had seen parades before in Lviv and Kyiv, but those couldn't compare to this grand display. Stashinsky was especially impressed with the new military equipment showcased at the parade. As he watched the demonstration of Soviet might, he could look directly across the square at Nikita Khrushchev, the man who had never forgotten about Bandera. Now fate and circumstances had brought them together, united in a single purpose: kill Bandera.[9]

9

HERR POPEL

Before leaving Moscow, Stashinsky received a new, improved spray pistol. This one had two barrels so that the assassin could kill two targets without reloading—in this case Bandera and his bodyguard. Colonel Ishchenko, the KGB officer with aristocratic manners, told Stashinsky to go back to East Berlin and await orders. Stashinsky went back to his apartment on East Berlin's Marienstrasse, and he began drinking heavily. His orders came during the second week of May 1959: Moscow wanted Bandera dead as soon as possible. Stashinsky got documents from Sergei Damon, a new weapon, and the antidote pills and ampoules. He also received a set of keys to open the entrance door to Bandera's apartment building. The hallway was the ideal place in which to carry out the killing, he was told in Moscow. But if circumstances were right, he could do so in the courtyard of the building as well. He could use his own judgment.

After arriving in Munich, Stashinsky followed the same routine for a few days. He started his days loitering near Bandera's apartment building, and by 11:00 a.m. he would move to Zeppelinstrasse, where Bandera had his office. He saw Bandera on a number of occasions, mostly in the company of his bodyguard. One day he spotted Bandera returning home alone. Bandera went by in his Opel Kapitan on Kreittmayrstrasse near the entrance to his apartment building. The car turned into the archway, heading toward the courtyard and garages. Stashinsky took his weapon out of his pocket and prepared to carry out his assignment, but changed his mind at the last moment. In order to make it impossible to go back, he fired the spray pistol into the ground and then dropped it from a bridge into the same stream in the Hofgarten where he had dumped the weapon he had used to assassinate Lev Rebet a year and a half earlier.

Stashinsky may have felt relieved after refusing to follow the order to kill Bandera. But there was also a reason for concern: he would have to explain to Sergei Damon back in Karlshorst why he had failed to carry out the assignment. For all he knew, he might well have been followed by another KGB agent who would have seen him dropping the pistol into the water. The only thing Stashinsky knew for certain was that whoever followed him could not possibly have seen what actually happened in the courtyard of Bandera's building. Stashinsky decided to tell Damon that he had seen someone in the courtyard near Bandera's garage and had been forced to abort the attempt. He also went the extra mile to show that he had tried hard to get into the apartment building—the KGB's first choice for the site of the assassination. As he tried to open the entrance door, he had broken a couple of keys. He had then tried his own key and broken it as well. Stashinsky was going to show Damon the broken key as evidence that he had done his best to carry out the assignment.

Sergei Damon was not pleased to hear the news, but there was little he could do. In August, Stashinsky went to the Soviet Union to take a short vacation. It was only after his return that Damon told him Moscow had ordered another try. Stashinsky flew to Munich on October 14, carrying the loaded pistol, the antidote pills, and a set of new keys to Bandera's apartment building. He expected to spend anywhere between seven and ten days in Munich—as was standard. After ten days, the KGB wanted him back whether he fulfilled the assignment or not.

October 15 was supposed to be Stashinsky's first "working day," and he didn't expect to accomplish much, hoping only to begin his observations. Even so, he took his antidote pill in the morning and put the spray gun, wrapped in newspaper, into the inside pocket of his jacket. It was too late to find Bandera at home, so he went to the Ukrainian offices on Zeppelin-strasse. His observation point was on the Ludwig Bridge, near the Deutsches Museum and the tram stop. It was there that visitors to the museum and tram passengers might have noticed a man in his late twenties loitering with no obvious purpose, taking quick looks from time to time in the direction of Zeppelinstrasse. First he spotted Bandera's car parked near building no. 67. Then, around noon, he saw a man and a woman leave the building, get into the car, and drive away.

It seemed that Stashinsky's working hours were over. Bandera was in someone's company, so there was no chance to get him that day. But Stash-insky decided to take a tram and go to Bandera's apartment building, if only to prove to his handlers, if they were watching, that he was doing all he could to complete his mission. After arriving at Bandera's street and not seeing him or his car, Stashinsky decided to set a time when he could leave the area without raising any watcher's suspicion that he had not tried hard enough. He decided on 1:00 p.m. as a cutoff point. As he was checking his watch for the magic moment, he suddenly saw a car coming in his direction. It was Bandera's Opel Kapitan, and he was alone. The woman Stashinsky had seen an hour earlier from the Ludwig Bridge was gone.

When the Opel Kapitan turned into the archway, Stashinsky moved in that direction as well. The car was in front of an open garage, and the driver was busy unlading things from the back. Stashinsky used his new set of Karlshorst-made keys to open the main entrance. He was now in the hallway of the building, the place where his bosses wanted him to do his job. Everything was falling into place, until he heard a woman's voice a few stories above. Stashinsky turned toward the elevator and waited until the woman passed him on her way out. He then returned to his previous position behind the first turn of the stairs, where he could not be seen by anyone entering. Stashinsky was back in control. He heard someone trying to open the main door. He knew this was Bandera. He began to go down the stairs, the pistol wrapped in newspaper in his right hand. He would shoot Bandera as he had shot Rebet, once they were on the same level. But there was a problem with the original plan. Bandera was carrying a bag of vegetables and, with only one hand free, was struggling to open the door: his key was stuck in the lock. Holding the bag in his right hand, Bandera tried to push the door with his foot while using his left hand to withdraw the key. It was not working. Stashinsky bent down, ostensibly to fix his shoelace, while he waited for Bandera to figure out the door.

Stashinsky began to have second thoughts—perhaps it was not the right time to carry out his plan. But he kept going. After asking Bandera what was wrong with the lock, and receiving an answer that everything was in order, he raised the weapon, still rolled up in the newspaper, and fired it in Bandera's face. He later admitted that he had been nervous and fired both barrels, not just one. There followed a pop. Stashinsky stepped out, closed the door behind his back, and turned left, walking along Erzgiessereis-trasse. He then headed toward the city center. He unrolled the newspaper, hid the eight-inch cylinder in his pocket, and took out a handkerchief and sniffed it, holding it to his mouth and nose. In two hours he was aboard an express train to Frankfurt.[1]

Stashinsky wanted to get out of West Germany as soon as possible, but by the time he reached Frankfurt, the last flight to West Berlin had already left. He ordered a ticket for the next day and registered at the Hotel Wiesbaden, room 53. Today the hotel, which still stands, is advertised as being located only ten minutes from the city center and fifteen minutes from the airport. Stashinsky was interested in the latter. When he arrived at the airport the next day, the newsstands were full of papers reporting the mysterious death of Stepan Bandera, known to his neighbors as Stefan Popel. This was Stashinsky's first real confirmation that his target had died. Upon arrival in Berlin, he called Sergei Damon. The KGB handler already knew about the outcome of the operation and congratulated Stashinsky on a job well done. They met at the Café Warsaw in the eastern part of the city, and Stashinsky told Damon the details. He again filed two reports—the first on the places he had visited and the time he had spent there, and the second, as after the killing of Rebet, pertaining to greetings to an "acquaintance." He reported that the greetings had been delivered successfully.[2]

10

DEAD ON ARRIVAL

In her third-floor apartment at Kreittmayrstrasse 7, Yaroslava Bandera, known to her neighbors as Frau Popel, was waiting for her husband to come home for his usual lunch. When she heard the sound of his car in the courtyard, she looked down from the balcony, saw the Opel Kapitan in front of the garage, and went to open the door to the apartment. Mrs. Bandera, a forty-two-year-old housewife and mother of three children, was bracing herself for what might be a highly unpleasant continuation of the fight they had begun that morning. They had argued about a woman.

For years she had suspected him of infidelity and fought it every way she could. According to Bandera's bodyguards, she obsessively called him at work, checking to see if he was in his office or had already left for home. She got rid of the maids who helped run the household because she believed that he was trying to seduce them. Eventually she banned all female guests at home and only barely tolerated male guests, as her husband would volunteer to drive them home and then disappear for hours. However, many who knew Mrs. Bandera believed that she loved her husband dearly, despite the unhappiness in her marriage.

Stepan Bandera avoided being at home on weekdays. He would come to work earlier than anyone else and leave the office last, often after 10:00 p.m. It was true that he had a soft spot for women, especially younger ones. His friends and colleagues knew that for years he had been meeting with a woman more than ten years his junior, and that he had not broken off the liaison even after she married. Now Mrs. Bandera suspected him of trying to seduce a young maid. A trained nurse, the maid looked after the three children of the Weiner family, who lived on the first floor of the apartment building. Those who knew Stepan Bandera well believed that he was smitten—he took every opportunity to meet with the maid, either in front of the building or as she entered or exited the apartment where she worked. Mrs. Bandera sensed the danger and shot the young woman dirty looks every time she saw her in the building. She also demanded an explanation from her husband. That was what they had been arguing about that morning. Stepan Bandera was distressed and left the apartment earlier than usual. The last words he heard from his wife were: "Just wait until you come back for lunch, and I'll let you have the rest of my 'prayer.'"

Mrs. Bandera was waiting expectantly for her husband to climb the stairs to their apartment and continue their exchange. But when she opened the door, she heard a terrible scream from below and the voice of her first-floor neighbor, Mrs. Chaya Gamse: "My God!" Chaya and her husband, Melach, were survivors of the Nazi concentration camps and in poor health. Mrs. Bandera thought that something might have happened to one of them. Then she saw Herr Gamse coming upstairs and asked whether he needed to use her telephone, but he asked her instead to come down: her husband was lying on the first-floor landing. She got the keys to her apartment and ran downstairs. There, lying between the elevator door and the entrance to the Weiner apartment, was her husband. There was blood coming from his mouth, nose, and ears, but he was alive, able to open and close his eyes. A hoarse sound was coming from his throat.

Magdalena Winklmann, the maid from the Weiners' apartment, with whom Mrs. Bandera believed her husband was having an affair, was next to him, cleaning blood from his face, and it seemed that he was tightly holding her hand in his. There were other people around, including Herr and Frau Gamse, whose apartment was across the hall from the Weiners'. The Gamses had been getting ready to eat lunch when they had heard the sound of heavy footsteps on the stairs, and then something resembling a scream. Frau Gamse was the first to come out of her apartment and see the man they knew as Stefan Popel lying on the floor. Together with Magdalena, who had emerged from the Weiners' apartment, she placed Bandera on his side so that he would not choke on the blood coming from his mouth. Frau Gamse had learned that technique in the concentration camps.

Mrs. Bandera screamed. She sat on the floor, took her husband's head in her hands, and tapped it, speaking to him in Ukrainian: "Stepan, what happened? Stepan, say what happened." Herr Gamse had already called for an ambulance, which arrived a few minutes later. Mrs. Bandera suspected a stroke. She called her husband's office to let his aides on Zeppelinstrasse know that there had been an accident: her husband had fallen on the stairs and needed medical attention. She was obviously under extreme stress. The man who took her phone call remembered a few days later that "she talked without making any sense. All I could understand was something about a fall, about lying on the steps." He promised to come right away. Mrs. Bandera accompanied her husband to the hospital on Lazarettstrasse, which was only minutes away.[1]

Stepan Bandera's associates from Zeppelinstrasse arrived when the ambulance had already left. They talked to Bandera's teenage daughter, who told them that her father had apparently had a stroke. They wanted to know details and then talked to the Gamses. They could see blood on the floor near the entrance and by the elevator. They also saw the bag of tomatoes that Bandera had been carrying when he was assassinated, which he seemed to have placed carefully on the floor before he fell. Once Bandera's visibly distressed associates had left the building, Frau Gamse and Magdalena Winklmann returned to the ground-floor platform with a broom, mop, and bucket of water. They thoroughly cleaned the floor. A few minutes later, there was no sign that anything had happened. The bag of tomatoes was taken away by Herr Gamse.[2]

Stepan Bandera was pronounced dead on arrival. The doctor on duty inspected the body and agreed that the cause of death was a stroke. Bandera's fall on the stairs had bruised his skull, causing the bleeding from his nose, mouth, and ears. There was no sign of foul play and no reason to suspect anything but an unfortunate incident. Bandera's associates, however, seemed to think differently. One of them asked whether Bandera could still be revived, perhaps by injections or by administering oxygen. After receiving a negative answer, the associate asked whether the doctor thought the accidental-looking death might be an assassination. The doctor did not think so: stairs were a tricky thing, and a trip and fall that took place as the result of a stroke could easily be fatal. Bandera's associates had no choice but to accept the conclusions of the doctor who signed the death certificate: it had been a stroke.[3]

Bandera's associates returned to their headquarters and began their own investigation of what had happened that day. The morning of October 15 at Zeppelinstrasse 67, the building occupied by numerous branches of Bandera's covert organization, had begun like any other. Stepan Bandera had arrived sometime after 8:00 a.m. in the company of his bodyguard, Vasyl Ninovsky. He had proceeded to his office while Ninovsky had gone to the print shop of the organization's newspaper *Shliakh peremohy* (The Way to Victory), located on the first floor of the building.

Bandera's aides and office employees had begun to arrive at about 9:00 a.m. Bandera had been in meetings that morning with three of his associates, all of whom were later investigated by police and the Bandera organization's internal security service. Around 11:30 a.m., Bandera had left his office and descended one floor to the newspaper offices, where his old acquaintance Eugenia, known to the German authorities as Eugenia Mak, had her work station. He asked whether she would like to accompany him to the market to buy some fruit, but she declined. "She refused three times, stating that she wasn't in the mood," recalled the witnesses. "And that she didn't need anything." According to the same report, "Bandera insisted, stating that she should at least go to keep him company. She agreed to go only after other employees kept urging her."

They began to leave for the ground floor, but Bandera suddenly remembered that he had left his beret in his office. After a moment's hesitation, he told Eugenia that he would get it after lunch. Bandera usually lunched at home, and he decided to pick up some fruit and vegetables at Munich's famous market, the Grossmarkthalle. Known to his circle as a "hands-on" head of his household, Bandera loved to run errands; he personally bought food products for his family, and he enjoyed eating well. His other passion was his car, which he took care of personally, spending hours keeping it clean and running properly. He would fix minor engine problems himself instead of going to a mechanic. Bandera and Eugenia left the building, got into Bandera's dark blue Opel Kapitan, and drove off to the Grossmarkthalle, located southwest of Zeppelinstrasse on the other side of the Isar River.

At the market, Bandera purchased some grapes and plums, as well as tomatoes, apparently for pickling. Their shopping done, the two put their bags in Bandera's car and drove back to Zeppelinstrasse. He dropped Eugenia not far from the office building. She wanted to take the bag of walnuts she had bought at the market, but Bandera promised to bring them to her after lunch—they were buried under his own purchases in the trunk of the car. He was in a hurry. "Wait a moment. I'll tell Vasyl Ninovsky to escort you home," suggested Eugenia, referring to Bandera's bodyguard. But Bandera, who was known for not following his security team's instructions, would not listen. "By the time Ninovsky comes down, I'll be home," he told his secretary. "I'll be seeing you." Bandera's associates could learn no more about their leader's last hours.[4]

It was a matter of routine rather than any particular suspicion about the cause of death that made the medical personnel call the Munich Kripo (Kriminalpolizei), a police unit responsible for criminal investigations. While examining the body, the doctor had found a gunbelt under Bandera's right arm containing a Walther 765 PKK, a relatively small pistol, easy to conceal, originally designed for the German police force. It was unusual—indeed, illegal—to carry a gun in Germany, and the medical personnel were under instructions to report every such case to the authorities. The police originally were not terribly interested: the medical examination had shown no sign of violent death. Eventually it was decided that Bandera's body would be taken to the Institute of Forensic Medicine at the Ludwig Maximilian University for an autopsy. The postmortem was scheduled for the following day, so the police investigation would have to wait until then. The two detectives assigned to the case, Hermann Schmidt and Oberkommissar Adrian Fuchs, felt no reason to rush.

The postmortem investigation took place on Friday, October 16. It was conducted by a group of doctors, who were led by the director of the Institute of Forensic Medicine, Professor Wolfgang Laves, a balding, bespectacled sixty-year-old medical doctor and scientist who had headed the institute since 1945. Laves was assisted by a younger colleague, Dr. Wolfgang Spann, a physician who later conducted the postmortem examination of Hitler's right-hand man Rudolf Hess. Bandera's autopsy lasted two hours. Its findings took the police by surprise. The head of the homicide unit, Hermann Schmidt, returned to police headquarters visibly shocked and pale. When questioned by journalists, he responded brusquely, "You will not learn anything from me!" He then called in his staff and phoned the Bavarian branch of the Federal Office for the Protection of the Constitution (Bundesamt für Verfassungsschutz). He spent considerable time on the phone with representatives of the office, which was also in charge of West German counterintellegence. The news that Schmidt did not want to share with the journalists made the protectors of the West German constitution very concerned.

With Hermann Schmidt silent, the journalists turned for comment to the head of the city police, Anton Heigel. They did not get very far. Heigel told them: "I have not yet received any report, and the whole matter does not interest me at all." The police chief's comment was disappointing but also intriguing. The only statement that the police had issued so far, before the results of the autopsy were released, had confirmed what journalists already knew from their own sources: Stefan Popel was not the man he claimed to be. "Death resulting from an unfortunate accident," read the press release. "About lunchtime on 15 October 1959 the 50-year-old stateless journalist Stefan Popel, called Bandera, fell down the stairwell of his residence in the western part of the city. He died of his wounds while being taken to hospital. An investigation has begun into the course of the unfortunate accident."

The name "Bandera" was first mentioned in connection with Popel at about 10:00 p.m. on October 15, when the Munich-based Bayerischer Rundfunk (Bavarian Broadcasting) transmitted the following bulletin: "One of the leaders of the Ukrainian émigrés, the 50-year-old Stepan Bandera, lost his life in Munich today. It is said that he suffered such an unfortunate fall on the stairs of his building that he died while being taken to hospital. The police still do not know anything about the precise circumstances of his death." The announcer concluded with the following statement on Bandera's background: "As a Ukrainian nationalist, before and during the Second World War he was incarcerated in Polish and German prisons or concentration camps." Bandera, whom many knew by name but had never seen in person, was one of the most mysterious and reclusive leaders of the anti-Soviet Ukrainian movement in the West. The media knew that his organization had influence over tens of thousands of recent émigrés in Germany, Britain, the United States, Canada, and several other countries.

The journalists hounding the police for answers had good reason to be impatient—the latter were clearly hiding something from the press. The Munich tabloid *Abendzeitung* explained the flurry of media interest: "Munich has become a playground for agents, spies, and emigrants, mainly from the East. The unwitting resident generally knows nothing about the activity of these people from the shadows, which is shrouded in secrecy. Only once in a while is the curtain raised on such sinister doings—when a crime is committed against one of those to whom the Federal Republic has granted political asylum." The weekend issues of other Munich newspapers would also publish stories about Bandera's mysterious death, but no conclusive evidence on whether it was anything more than a stroke and an accident.[5]

On Monday, October 19, the Munich Kripo homicide unit issued a press release. It quickly became apparent why Hermann Schmidt, the head of the unit, had looked so harried and secretive the previous Friday. The release stated that the autopsy of Stepan Bandera, which had begun on Friday, had continued into Saturday. "The investigation carried out on October 17 at the

Institute of Forensic Medicine to establish the cause of death revealed that Bandera died of cyanide poisoning," detailed the report. "The homicide commission is now investigating whether this was a suicide or a criminal act."

On Friday, Professor Laves's young assistant Wolfgang Spann had detected a faint smell of almonds from the corpse's dissected brain. Further investigation had found traces of cyanide in the stomach—the result of both barrels of the weapon being fired simultaneously. There were no remains of a capsule, and there was not enough residual cyanide to kill a person, but there was no doubt that cyanide was involved and had somehow entered the deceased man's stomach. The police decided to release the news of cyanide poisoning without going into much detail. The results of a full investigation into the chemical particles found in Bandera's stomach would not be forthcoming until much later. The news was picked up and broadcast the same day by Reuters and other international news agencies. German newspapers published the news on October 20, the day of Bandera's funeral.[6]

The news that Stepan Bandera had died of poison came as a shock not only to those who assumed that he had died of natural causes but also to those among his entourage who believed that he had been assassinated. Cyanide poisoning with no indication of violence pointed to suicide rather than murder, but Bandera's colleagues preferred to paint him as a martyr for the cause rather than a depressed and disillusioned individual who, for whatever reason, had taken his own life. Yet the latter explanation was the one gaining traction among the medical doctors who conducted the autopsy and the police investigators. Professor Laves had little doubt about it. He assured Frau Popel, who was now being called Frau Bandera, and her husband's associates that he had significant experience with suicides of "freedom fighters," as he had conducted autopsies of seven or eight such individuals. "Freedom fighters," he argued, were under constant pressure, and they often were inclined to choose death over life.

Professor Laves had considerable experience indeed, although most of it concerned suicides in general, not necessarily those of "freedom fighters." His most famous former patient, Adolf Hitler, had committed suicide back in April 1945. In his conversations with Mrs. Bandera, Professor Laves explained to the distressed widow that for someone like her husband, suicide was little more than an occupational hazard. A "freedom fighter" might voluntarily choose to kill himself when faced with overwhelming pressure from an enemy intent on breaking him psychologically, or blackmailing him and threatening his family and friends. Any or all of these scenarios might have led Stepan Bandera to commit suicide by swallowing cyanide.

Laves concluded that the poison in Bandera's stomach had been orally ingested no more than three hours before his death. When Frau Bandera and her husband's associates continued to argue that suicide was hardly possible, given the character of the deceased, Dr. Laves lost his temper. "Then who killed him? A ghost?" he asked his interlocutors, not without condescension. The case seemed closed.[7]

11

FUNERAL

Stepan Bandera's interment was expected to be attended by dozens, if not hundreds, of "freedom fighters" from all over the world, and the Munich police, along with the Office for the Protection of the Constitution, accordingly took extra precautions to guard the funeral procession and the funeral itself. They feared possible assassination attempts by the communist authorities behind the Iron Curtain from whose embrace the freedom fighters were trying to liberate their nations.

There were hundreds of plainclothes police officers hiding behind the trees of Waldfriedhof Cemetery—the "Paradise Garden" designed in the early twentieth century—on the gloomy, cold afternoon of October 20. Some of them, armed with cameras, were videotaping and documenting the event. They were not alone in doing so. There were also cameramen from the East, primarily from East Germany, as well as representatives of the Soviet Union. In attendance, apart from diplomats and journalists, were leaders of a Soviet Ukrainian folk ensemble that had just begun its schedule of performances in Munich. Many in Bandera's organization regarded the "easterners" with utmost suspicion, thinking that Bandera's killer could be a member of the ensemble.

Close to 2,000 mourners gathered for Bandera's interment. It had all the trappings of a state funeral, although the deceased was a leader of a stateless nation. At the head of the procession was a middle-aged man carrying a large cross. He was followed by numerous priests and a church choir. Then came standard-bearers with the blue and yellow national flags of Ukraine and the red and black flags of Bandera's organization. Walking solemnly behind them were two men, each accompanied by two assistants. They carried two small urns on red pillows. One contained soil from Ukraine, the other water from the Black Sea. The symbolism was obvious to most of the mourners—Bandera had lived and died fighting not only for the independence of his country, but also for its integrity and territorial unity, from his native Carpathians to the faraway Black Sea. The salt water in the urn had been brought to Munich by one of Bandera's associates from Turkey, the only country on the Black Sea not cut off from the rest of the world by the Iron Curtain.[1]

Bandera's oak coffin was carried by six of his closest associates—all men of his age and background who had been with him since the early days of resistance in Ukraine. Behind the coffin walked Bandera's widow, Yaroslava, and the couple's three children. When the procession reached the burial site, the first to speak was the Ukrainian Catholic priest, himself a recent immigrant from Ukraine. "The life of Stepan Bandera of blessed memory followed a thorny course," said the priest to the mourners. "He spent almost a quarter of his adulthood in prisons, jails, and concentration camps of foreign states that sought to enslave our fatherland."

It was not only Ukrainians who came to mourn Bandera. There were also "Caucasians, Georgians and Belarusians, Hungarians and Lithuanians," wrote the correspondent of the *Frankfurter Allgemeine Zeitung*, "a cross-section of the whole Eastern emigration." Some of them, especially those on the left, had set themselves against Bandera when he was alive. Nevertheless, they came now to show solidarity with their political opponent: an attack on him was an attack on all of them. They were all vulnerable. Many of those gathered at the cemetery wondered who would be next. "Assassination literally hung in the air," wrote a reporter for the German newspaper *Das Grüne Blatt*.[2]

The events of October 15 were not just a major emotional and political blow to Bandera's followers but also a terrifying and unprecedented breach of security. Fingers were pointed at members of the Bandera security team who had failed to do their job. After Myron Matviyeyko had been parachuted into Ukraine in May 1951, his job as head of Bandera's security service had gone to his second-in-command, Ivan Kashuba, and Kashuba's intelligence chief, Stepan Mudryk, both experienced intelligence hands. The security people, in turn, blamed Bandera himself. "More than once, I warned my leader and his entourage about threats to their security," Mudryk told the German police. "But my warnings were not always heeded, and I can only say that my leader behaved quite carelessly. If he had listened to me, I think it would not have come to that."

They weren't wrong. After successfully turning the nationalist underground into a largely terrorist outfit in the early 1930s, Bandera had believed that he could manage security issues on his own. After years of living undercover, he had become inured to the sense of danger—so much so that when he lived outside of Munich, he would often pick up unknown passengers on his way to the city. Aside from ignoring the rules that his security service tried to impose on him, Bandera had also tended to treat his bodyguards very badly, leading many of them to leave both him and the organization. Finally, Bandera had decided that he would manage his own security. In the fall of 1959, the security staff consisted of a single person— his bodyguard, driver, and courier Vasyl Ninovsky, a former guerrilla fighter in Soviet-occupied Western Ukraine.[3]

Two weeks before the assassination, disturbing news had reached Bandera's security service that had forced him to consider paying more attention to his security and even changing his cover name. By that time, he had been using the name Stefan Popel for almost a decade. On October 2, 1959, Stepan Mudryk, Bandera's chief of intelligence, called Bandera's headquarters in Munich from Düsseldorf, where he was on a business trip, and demanded that an extraordinary meeting of the organization's leadership be called for the next morning, when he was to return to Munich. Mudryk barely slept on the night train to the city because he was so troubled by the news that he was about to deliver.

The next morning, everyone was waiting for Mudryk in Bandera's office. The leader was at his desk; his assistants were around the table. Disheveled and tired after a rough night on the train, Mudryk sat in front of his bosses and told them of an encounter he had had in Düsseldorf. On October 2, he had had a routine meeting with a double agent, someone who worked for the KGB while keeping Mudryk informed of his activities. The agent had just returned from East Berlin, where he had met with his KGB handlers, and told Mudryk that in Moscow the decision had been made at the highest level to liquidate Bandera and his close associates. "All the arrangements have been made with regard to Bandera," declared the double agent. "The hit may take place any day. Remember that a decision has been made to do away with you; there are technical resources involved of which the world is as yet unaware. You will not be able to withstand them." The double agent wanted money in exchange for further information. Mudryk did not have money to give him, but believed that the information was solid. He wanted Bandera to leave Munich, possibly for Spain, where General Francisco Franco's dictatorship made it hard for the KGB to operate with impunity.

Bandera refused to follow his intelligence chief's advice. He said that they were in a state of war, danger was a given, and they simply had to carry on. But a few days later he took a brief vacation in the Alps, while Mudryk was ordered to go to Bonn to produce new documents for Bandera and his family. Stepan Bandera was about to turn into someone else, throwing off possible KGB assassins. Mudryk once again boarded a night train and, early in the morning of October 15, began his secret mission in the West German capital. During the lunch break he called Munich to report on his progress, but he had missed Bandera by a few minutes. Shortly before noon on October 15, 1959, Bandera had left the office for lunch at home. In the register for security personnel he had noted that he did not need any lunch-hour protection that week, as he intended to have lunch at work. The next morning, Mudryk called home and learned from his wife that his mission in Bonn was obsolete: Bandera was dead.[4]

Mudryk and his colleagues now faced the outrage of members of their own organization who demanded an explanation for the security breach. For years Mudryk would be at pains to defend his role as chief of intelligence in his memoirs, private correspondence, and interviews. He argued that he had done all he could to prevent the assassination, and many years after the event he still wondered whether Bandera had remembered his warning in the last moments of his life. Vasyl Ninovsky, Bandera's part-time bodyguard, whose services Bandera had rejected on the day he was murdered, was psychologically destroyed by what had happened on his watch. Decades after the assassination, his wife was still telling Ninovsky's relatives stories that cleared her husband of responsibility. According to her, on October 15, Vasyl Ninovsky was in the hospital, having saved his leader from a previous attack in which an unidentified automobile had crashed into Bandera's car. If Ninovsky had been on duty that day, Bandera would still be alive, went the family legend.[5]

Ivan Kashuba, the chief of Bandera's counterintelligence service and the man directly responsible for his security, would tell anyone willing to listen that Bandera had killed himself over his unrequited love for the maid who looked after his neighbor's children. "Stepan Bandera was in love with that German woman and spent more than one night sleepless over her," Kashuba told one of his acquaintances. "He would take every opportunity to meet with her, either in front of the building or at her door, to speak with her. It is also possible that he met with her in the evenings in secret from his wife and from that maid's employers." Kashuba argued that Bandera had deliberately chosen to commit suicide in front of the apartment where his beloved was working that day—she was the last person to hold his hand before he stopped breathing. Kashuba maintained that Bandera's love for the German maid was known to other leaders of the organization. It was anyone's guess whether Kashuba truly believed the theory of love-lorn suicide; perhaps he advanced it only to ward off allegations of his own security failure.[6]

As early autumn darkness fell on Waldfriedhof Cemetery, and people started to become almost indistinguishable from the rows of crosses and surrounding trees, the last mourners left. Also gone were the cameramen from East Germany. The newsreel about Bandera's funeral would be ready for distribution before the end of the month. The Munich police could congratulate themselves on a job well done. The funeral had gone on without a hitch, with no shootings or unexpected collapses. The police detachment hidden in the courtyard of the cemetery chapel dispersed soon after the mourners. As far as they were concerned, they were done with the death of Stepan Bandera.

12

CIA TELEGRAM

The chief of the CIA base in Munich reported the news of Bandera's death to Washington on the day it happened. The priority telegram was addressed to the director of the CIA, Allen Dulles. It was marked as "Redwood," indicating an action alert for the agency's Soviet Russia division, and "Lcimprove," meaning that the information it contained dealt with the activities of Soviet intelligence worldwide. The telegram was sent close to midnight Munich time, and its contents were cryptic indeed: "15 Oct[ober] subj[ect] reported Stefan Bandera dead. Details when available. End of message."[1]

Although addressing the telegram to the director of the CIA did not mean that he would actually read it, the odds were that that one would reach its addressee. William Hood, the thirty-nine-year-old chief of the Munich base, knew Allen Dulles personally. At the end of the war, he had served under Dulles's supervision in the Office of Strategic Services—the predecessor of the CIA—in Bern, Switzerland. Back then, Dulles and his staff had been busy establishing links with the SS commander in Italy, General Karl Wolff, in hopes of securing the surrender of German troops on the Apennine Peninsula. News of Dulles's dealings with the Nazis had reached Joseph Stalin and caused an international scandal, the precursor of Cold War espionage rivalry. William Hood had joined the CIA in 1949, the same year the agency was established. His foreign assignments had included a stint as deputy chief of the CIA station in Vienna, where he had been involved in recruiting and handling the CIA double agent Major Petr Popov of Soviet military intelligence. In Munich, Hood then took over the local CIA base. The CIA station responsible for covert operations throughout Germany was in Frankfurt, but Munich was a very important hub of CIA activity in Germany, second only to West Berlin where Hood was transferred in December 1959.[2]

At the end of the war, Munich had fallen into American hands. The city center was almost entirely destroyed by Allied bombing. The roof of Munich's main tourist attraction, the Gothic Frauenkirche, a Catholic cathedral, had collapsed, and one of its onion-dome towers had been severely damaged. On April 30, 1945, the soldiers of the US 42nd Infantry Division, who had liberated the Dachau concentration camp in the vicinity on the previous day, made their way to the center of Munich through the rubble of bombed-out and ruined buildings. There was no resistance. The surviving citizens, whose beer halls had given birth to the Nazi movement back in the 1920s, were eager to surrender to the Americans. At Marienplatz, the city's main square, German police officers turned in their weapons in exchange for a receipt provided by an American GI. The alternative—retreat to the east to be captured by the Soviets—was much worse.[3]

Under American military administration, Munich became a safe haven and a destination of choice for displaced persons—refugees from the East who wanted to stay in the West. The Soviets demanded their return, calling them traitors to the motherland. They generally denied the charges by claiming that the places they had left did not belong to the Soviet motherland, but had been unjustly conquered in the course of the war: the Baltics; Western Ukraine and Belarus, which had belonged to Poland before the war; Bukovyna and Bessarabia, which were parts of interwar Romania; and Transcarpathia, which was part of Czechoslovakia. After initially repatriating some of them by force, the Americans let the rest stay. As time passed, most of them would move to the United States, Britain, Canada, and Australia. Some claimed to be stateless and remained in Germany. In the late 1950s, there were close to 80,000 refugees from the East still living in

Munich. By far the largest contingent was the one made up of Ukrainian refugees from interwar Poland.[4]

Stepan Bandera was hardly unknown to the CIA officers in Munich. Immediately after the end of the war, the US Army Counterintelligence Corps, or CIC, which was responsible for security in the American zone of occupation, and in many ways a forerunner of the CIA, cooperated with Bandera's group to root out suspected Soviet spies in the displaced persons' camps in the American zone. But the Americans soon developed serious reservations about Bandera and his people. Bandera, it was believed, used heavy-handed tactics, intimidation, and violence to secure both his own position in the organization and his organization's dominant role among the Ukrainian refugees. Bandera and his followers were staunchly anti-Russian and anticommunist, but those characteristics carried much less weight immediately after the end of World War II than they would a few years later, with the start of the Cold War.

The operational benefits that the Bandera group could provide the CIC and then the CIA seemed limited as well. The Bandera faction of the Organization of Ukrainian Nationalists, a highly centralized and disciplined group run by a narrow circle of professional conspirators seasoned in partisan warfare against the Germans and the Soviets, was difficult for US counterintelligence officers to use, let alone control, as they had little experience in dealing with East European guerrilla fighters. The Bandera people made contacts with the CIC, but they hardly ever conveyed any kind of reliable information, unless it had to do with possible Soviet penetration of Ukrainian refugee camps. They kept their secrets close, while engaging in all sorts of illegal activities. They eliminated those whom they suspected of treason, or who did not follow the party line. To fund their operations, they used counterfeit American dollars.

The Soviets had demanded the extradition of Stepan Bandera, who was the recognized symbol of anti-Soviet struggle in Ukraine. They had sent officers and agents into the American zone to kidnap Bandera, but he had gone into hiding, changing his name and the places where he stayed. The Americans were prepared to cooperate with their wartime ally. The officers of the Strategic Services Unit, in fact, saw the Soviet request as an opportunity to get rid of an inconvenient and, indeed, dangerous leader. But no matter how they tried, they could not deliver Bandera. The US intelligence network was infiltrated by Bandera supporters, who gave false or misleading information about their leader's whereabouts. He was also just incredibly lucky. Once, while riding in his car, he had been stopped by an American officer, but the officer had allowed him to continue because Bandera had a press ID. Bandera, who was indeed directly involved in publishing his organization's newspaper, would continue to use the journalist's cover up to the end of his life. The search was eventually called off. Soon afterward, Soviet-American relations deteriorated to the point where any cooperation between them became impossible. Bandera would stay in Bavaria.[5]

In 1949, the newly created Central Intelligence Agency took over primary responsibility for the refugees and their networks in Germany from the Army Counterintelligence Corps, and although they never tried to capture or extradite Bandera, they also stayed clear of him and any intelligence opportunities that his organization could offer. Bandera, whose main base of operations remained the US occupation zone, instead began cooperating with MI6—section 6 of British Military Intelligence, responsible for foreign operations. The British had more expertise in dealing with European nationalities than the Americans and were less scrupulous when it came to the ideological inclinations and operational tactics of their clients. A contemporary British report described Bandera as "a professional underground worker with a terrorist background and ruthless notions about the rules of the game." The British also believed that of all the organizations of Russian and East European provenance, Bandera's people had the largest and best-established network, and that it could be used for intelligence gathering in the Soviet Union.[6]

The Americans had their doubts in that regard, believing that Bandera's networks were thoroughly penetrated by the Soviet secret police. Instead of Bandera, the CIA made an alliance with his rivals in the Ukrainian nationalist camp. By 1947, the Bandera branch of the Organization of Ukrainian

Nationalists had split. The rival group was led by Mykola Lebed, the former head of the OUN Security Service and the man who took over the leadership of the organization after Bandera's arrest by the Germans in July 1941. He was responsible for its survival and its heroic struggle against the Nazis. But it was also on his watch that the OUN units began their massacres of Poles in Volhynia, which resulted in tens of thousands of victims. In 1944, with the Soviets advancing into Ukraine, Lebed was sent to the West to represent the Ukrainian nationalist cause among the Allied powers. He clashed with Bandera over control of organization and his links to Western intelligence services. Bandera allegedly ordered a hit on Lebed, but the former security chief escaped to the United States with the help of the CIA. From there he ran his own organization, called the Foreign Representation of the Supreme Ukrainian Liberation Council. Lev Rebet, assassinated by Stashinsky in October 1957, was one of the émigré Ukrainian intellectual leaders in Lebed's milieu.

While Bandera's Foreign Units of the OUN worked with the British, Lebed's Foreign Representation supplied cadres for CIA covert operations in the USSR. In May 1951, the two intelligence services, the CIA and MI6, coordinated an airdrop of their agents on Soviet territory. The British group, led by Myron Matviyeyko, was seen off by Bandera, while the American one received blessings from Lebed. Group after group was dropped by parachute into the Ukrainian forests. The first news was more than encouraging: the groups were able to avoid capture and establish radio contact. But eventually both the Americans and the British began to suspect that the indications were too good to be true. The grim reality was that most of the people parachuted into Ukraine soon fell into the hands of the KGB and—like Matviyeyko—worked under their control. After years of losing agents, the Americans and the British decided to stop the airdrops. The CIA began to use Lebed's people for psychological warfare against the USSR instead. By 1954, MI6 had severed relations with Bandera and his group. One point on which the Western services agreed was that, as a British cable put it, "despite our unanimous desire to 'quiet' Bandera, precautions must be taken to see that the Soviets are not allowed to kidnap or kill him. . . . [U]nder no circumstances must Bandera be allowed to become a martyr."[7]

With William Hood's cryptic telegram to Washington, there was little doubt that both security services had failed. If it was indeed the Soviets who had finally killed Bandera, then he might become a more significant figure in death than he had been during his lifetime. The Munich base sent a more substantial message the following day. "Bandera dead on arrival hospital," read the cable of October 16. "Undetermined whether top of head damage caused by fall. Bandera people suspect foul play." On Sunday, October 18, before the results of the autopsy became public, the Munich officers had to cable Washington again, delivering the latest news from one of his agents inside the German security services: "Prelim[inary] autopsy findings indicate Bandera did not die natural causes. Indications he [was] poisoned." The Munich base chief wrote nothing about the possibility of suicide. He suspected murder.[8]

13

UPSWING

In the days following Bandera's assassination, the CIA officers in Munich scrambled to figure out who had killed the Ukrainian leader and why. There were no obvious answers.

Back in March 1958, CIA headquarters at Langley had cabled the CIA Munich base, requesting information on the latest activities of Stepan Bandera. The request originated in the US Congress and reached Langley through the State Department. Someone of significant influence in the American capital wanted Bandera to come to the United States. The CIA officers in Munich checked their files and found nothing new on Bandera's activities that would preclude his entering the United States. They also checked with the US consulate in Munich and found out that Bandera had not applied for a visa, apparently awaiting the results of his supporters' lobbying in the United States. For a while, however, William Hood and his subordinates showed little interest, either, in supporting Bandera's application. The CIA's own people among the Ukrainian émigré circles—the Lebed group—were vehemently against Bandera's presence on their turf, the United States and Canada. Bandera stayed in Munich.[1]

But in the months leading up to his death Bandera showed up at the US consulate in Munich to officially ask for a visitor's visa to the United States. He hoped to be able to travel there in the spring of 1959, but, as he informed one of his old friends in New York, he was not sure whether he would be allowed to do so. In the documents he submitted to acquire the three-month visa, he identified himself as Stefan Popel, but he used the Bandera surname for his wife and children. Popel/Bandera was interviewed by Kermit S. Midthun, a young consular official whose earlier career had been with the Federal Bureau of Investigation. Midthun was more than suspicious of Bandera's request. He had serious doubts that Bandera's organization, whose full name was Foreign Units of the Organization of Ukrainian Nationalists, fully embraced the principles of democracy that underlined American policy in postwar Europe.[2]

Bandera did little to dispel Midthun's misgivings. After the German invasion of the Soviet Union, some of the members of Bandera's organization had joined the German-run police and, in its ranks, participated in the Holocaust. But Jews were not at the top of the Ukrainian nationalists' hierarchy of foes. For them, Poles and "turncoat" Ukrainians figured as the main enemies of Ukrainian statehood. Terror remained a popular weapon in their arsenal not only before and during World War II but also in its aftermath. After the war, it was directed primarily against the Soviets and their "collaborators"—Ukrainians who, finding themselves between two fires, NKVD troops and nationalist guerrillas, refused to support the nationalist cause.[3]

When the FBI officer asked Bandera how his organization would establish and preserve democracy once it came to power in Ukraine, he gave an answer that left Midthun highly dissatisfied. Democracy, claimed Bandera, would naturally accompany national self-realization. He promised to send Midthun literature produced by his organization so that he could make up his own mind about its democratic credentials. Eight brochures soon arrived at the consulate. They offered a critique of the decisions of the latest Soviet Communist Party congress and of the Gulag system of prison camps, while promoting the Ukrainian struggle for independence and setting forth the programmatic documents of Bandera's organization. Midthun did not have the time or inclination to read the brochures, which were eventually sent to the Intelligence Collection and Distribution

Section. In the end, it was not up to Midthun alone to decide whether Bandera would get an entry visa. The CIA had its say, too. [4]

On October 5, 1959, a mere ten days before Bandera's death, Hood wrote to his superiors at Langley, asking them to consider helping Bandera get an entry visa to the United States—the same visa that the consular officials in Munich had denied him for months. The Munich chief of the base's memo accompanied a more detailed request from a CIA contact in the German security services code-named "Herdahl." The CIA officers had assured Herdahl that "headquarters are very interested in the matter, especially as regards indications that Bandera has 'reformed' and ideas concerning his future operational usefulness." It was believed that Bandera had abandoned the heavy-handed tactics he had once used to keep his organization and the entire Ukrainian émigré community under control, and which had made the US consulate so nervous.

Officially, Bandera had applied for a three-month visa to the United States to see his relatives. The real reason was different. He planned to see and reenergize his followers in the United States; according to German estimates, there were between 300,000 and 400,000 of them there. North America was also a major source of financial support for Bandera and his activities. The Germans estimated that from Canada alone the organization had received $900,000 over the course of the five years ending in 1958. Bandera also wanted to meet with officials in the US government to discuss possible cooperation. "In principle," as Hood summarized the agent's argument, "Bandera has more to offer operationally than most if not all other Russian émigré groups in the West today." The operations Hood had in mind were espionage activities behind the Iron Curtain— the land of desire and terra incognita for Western intelligence services. Hood believed it was in the CIA's best interest to accommodate the request of someone who could potentially share a great deal of useful information with the agency. "If the visa can be granted," wrote Hood to his superiors, "we would be very well informed on the future collaboration between Upswing and Bandera. If the visa is not granted, it seems likely that Herdahl will slam the door on this aspect of Upswing operational activities in a bit of a huff." William Hood was still awaiting a response from Langley when the disturbing news of Bandera's death reached the Munich base.[5]

Herdahl's real name was Heinz Danko Herre. He was a senior official in the Federal Intelligence Service, or BND (Bundesnachrichtendienst). The BND was formally created on April Fool's Day of 1956 and placed under the direct supervision of the Office of the Chancellor, Konrad Adenauer. The BND was his joint brainchild with the CIA, which for ten years had funded and run its predecessor, known as the Gehlen Organization, or simply Org, after its chief, General Reinhard Gehlen, who had been in charge of spying on the Red Army during the war. In CIA traffic of the late 1950s, the BND came to be known under the code name "Upswing," later to be changed to "Uphill." Its creation was indeed a dramatic upswing for the CIA, which maintained close ties with the new organization but was no longer responsible for its funding or day-to-day business. It was also a major upswing for General Gehlen, who became president of the BND and ran it for the next twenty-two years.[6]

It was the "legalization" of the Gehlen Organization in the form of the BND that brought Stepan Bandera and his people, who were previously shunned by the British and Americans, back into the spotlight in the intelligence war between East and West. Negotiations between Bandera and the Gehlen associates began in March 1956, even before the BND was officially launched. The Americans warned their junior West German partners against using Bandera's agents in Ukraine, believing that his networks had been penetrated by the KGB. The BND took that advice and stopped the negotiations. But they would return to the idea of cooperation with Bandera a few years later. There were a number of reasons for them to reconsider it. The BND was a young intelligence organization looking for ways to prove itself, and for Reinhard Gehlen there was no easier way to do so than to use their old World War II connections. Bandera, one of Gehlen's associates wrote to William Hood, "has been known to us for about 20 years." The CIA objections could only hold them off for so long.

Heinz Danko Herre was William Hood's main source of information about Bandera, his death, and the investigation into his possible murder. In the BND hierarchy, Herre was directly responsible for contacts with Bandera and his followers. Herre also happened to be the main liaison between the BND and the CIA. An expert on Russia and Eastern Europe, he had attracted Gehlen's attention during the war. In April 1942, Gehlen had taken him under his wing and arranged a transfer from the front lines to the Intelligence section of the General Staff. There Herre had launched a successful psychological warfare campaign, code-named "Silver Lining," whose goal was to convince Red Army soldiers to desert. At the end of the war, Herre was one of the few officers Gehlen chose to accompany him in his defection to the Americans. In 1957, a year after the BND went "public," Herre was appointed head of the division responsible for intelligence operations against communist countries. For an old Russia hand, this felt like a homecoming.[7]

Herre's new responsibilities corresponded well with the main interests of the CIA in the region. James H. Critchfield, the head of the CIA base in Pullach, a suburb of Munich where the headquarters of the Gehlen Organization were located, referred to Herre as the CIA's "key man in Gehlen's inner circle." Decades later, remembering his years at Pullach, Critchfield wrote that Herre was "the one who, when the going got tough, was able to deal with both sides, keep communications open, and lead the search for compromises." Herre worked hard to secure the position of "go-to man" for the Americans. "He became an expert on American baseball and off the top of his head could quote batting averages and league standings," recalled Critchfield.[8]

After Bandera's unexpected death, Herre kept William Hood well informed about the Kripo investigation into its circumstances. He also briefed the CIA chief on the lunch meeting he had had with Bandera and his associates on the afternoon of October 14, less than twenty-four hours before the Ukrainian leader's death. The lunch, which had taken place at the Ewige Lampe restaurant in Munich, had lasted from 10:00 a.m. to 2:00 p.m. Bandera had been accompanied by two associates who had later described the meeting to the police, placing special emphasis on the food that had been served, as they suspected that one of the dishes could have been poisoned. One Ukrainian participant told the police that one of the Germans had picked up the bill, but none of those interrogated would say what had been discussed at the meeting.

Herre was less conspiratorial with his CIA contact. "Lunch [was] devoted primarily discussion Upswing support mounting further ops into USSR," cabled Hood to Langley. "Also discussed status present ops group which has not reported over weeks and at last report had not crossed into USSR." In July 1959, Herre had sent a group of Bandera cadres to the USSR across the Czechoslovakian border. Herre had held a meeting with Stepan Bandera and one of his associates on April 9, 1959, to discuss the operation. By the time they met again at the restaurant in the Bayerischer Hof Hotel on October 14, even though the group that had been sent through Czechoslovakia had not yet reported back, Herre was prepared to expand the BND's cooperation with Bandera and his people. The CIA would eventually learn more about the business discussed at the Herre-Bandera lunch from its sources in the Ukrainian émigré community. "The Germans accepted all the suggestions made by Zch/OUN [Foreign Units of the Organization of Ukrainian Nationalists] and promised all sorts of aid. Stepan Bandera was very satisfied with the results of the talks," read a report. Indeed, that day Bandera came home in a good mood. He told his wife that the meeting had gone well and that he had liked the food. The partridge was particularly good.[9]

Stepan Bandera's aides suspected that their leader could have been poisoned during the lunch with Herre and alerted the CIA to that possibility. But there was no doubt in the minds of the CIA officers in Munich that neither Gehlen nor Herre was involved in Bandera's death. Rather, they suspected the Soviets. On October 19, four days after Bandera fell dead on the steps of his apartment building, the chief of the CIA Munich station sent the CIA director a cable in which he asked headquarters to pass on to the BND "info re[ferring to] RIS [Russian Intelligence Services] use [of] specific poison in past." He felt that this information "would be particularly helpful since [it] appears to date that sufficient quantity poison [was] not found [while] autopsy makes it certain Bandera poisoned." Hood believed that information from one of the cases investigated by the CIA in the past could "point to specific type poison that may have been used, that difficult [to] detect, and that could have been administered considerably in advance Bandera's death."[10]

14

PRIME SUSPECT

Agents at CIA headquarters at Langley were not just collecting information from Munich; they were also trying to help the investigation by providing leads, one of which was cabled to Munich on November 5, 1959. The telegram read as follows: "Aecasowarry 2 says wife Aecavatina 11 with him just prior death."[1]

Only people with access to the agency's code books could make sense of the message. Along with the "Redwood" action marker, which referred to the CIA's Soviet Russia Division, the cable had another cryptonym in its upper right-hand corner, "Aerodynamic." It stood for the agency's operations in support of the activities of the Foreign Representation of the Supreme Ukrainian Liberation Council, the group of Ukrainian nationalists led by Mykola Lebed, who had broken with the Bandera faction in the late 1940s and since then had closely cooperated with the CIA. CIA officers used the prefix "ae" (Aerodynamic) and other code names to identify operations and individuals engaged in intelligence activities against the Soviet Union. Aecassowary 2 and Aecavatina 11 clearly belonged to that group. Cassowaries—large and colorful but flightless birds from New Guinea— were used as code names for members of the Lebed group involved in "Aerodynamic," including the agents parachuted into the USSR. "Cavatina" was a term borrowed not from zoology but from the world of classical music, in which it means a short, simple song. It was used for the members of the Bandera organization.

Thanks to the fairly recent release of select cryptonyms used by the CIA during the Cold War, we now know who those members of the Lebed and Bandera groups were. The code name "Aecassowary-1" was reserved for the Lebed group as a whole; "Aecassowary-2" was the group's leader, Mykola Lebed. They used a slightly different system for the Bandera group, whose leader was code-named "Aecavatina-1." The code name "Aecavatina 11" stood for his former head of security, Myron Matviyeyko.[2]

Thus CIA headquarters wanted its agents in Munich to know that Mykola Lebed had informed the agency that one of the last people in contact with Bandera before his death had been the wife of his former security chief, Myron Matviyeyko: Eugenia. The secretary in Bandera's headquarters who accompanied him to the Munich market before his death and was known to the German police as Eugenia Mak was in fact Eugenia Matviyeyko, the wife of an operative long behind Soviet lines. Eugenia had been born in Lviv in 1916. She was forty-three years old in 1959 and was known to her friends, colleagues, and associates under a variety of surnames, including Mak, Sczyhol, and Koshulynska. When her husband had been chosen for a dangerous mission in Ukraine, she had stayed behind in Munich, where they had made their home soon after the war. Eugenia had then gone to work for her husband's boss, Stepan Bandera, at Zeppelinstrasse 67.

Shortly before noon on October 15, 1959, Eugenia Mak had left the office with Bandera and accompanied him on at least part of what turned out to be his last car ride. She was now a person of interest to the police, as well as to the many other investigators of Bandera's death. The Munich police and Bavarian counterintelligence office thought she might be an accomplice in what everyone now agreed was a murder. The police informer within the Bandera organization and the medical report all pointed in the same direction: the poison had been administered by someone close to Bandera. Eugenia Mak found herself at the top of that list. Many pointed to the tug of war between Eugenia and Bandera's wife, and some suggested that Bandera and Eugenia were secretly lovers. Besides, if Bandera had been poisoned while tasting fruit at the market, it was impossible to imagine that Eugenia was not involved. Although, according to the CIA report, no one "was able to determine how the poison was put in the fruit in front of Bandera. There is little chance that the fruit could have been prepared in advance, as the trip was apparently spontaneous, so no one knew in advance that the two were going shopping."[3]

The CIA and its informers in the Ukrainian emigration did not exclude the possibility that Eugenia may have acted on behalf of her husband, Myron Matviyeyko. It was widely assumed that Matviyeyko, who had "miraculously" avoided capture by the Soviets for more than eight years, was in fact acting under Soviet control. A few days before Matviyeyko had parachuted into Ukraine, a similar group recruited from Lebed's people had been dropped as part of a CIA-run operation. After the airdrop, Matviyeyko and his associates had easily established radio contact with the British and Bandera. The CIA group, for its part, had been ambushed, and its leader had been captured by the Soviets. Matviyeyko had been looked at with suspicion ever since. If Matviyeyko was in fact working for the KGB, then one had to consider a connection between Eugenia, her husband, Bandera's death, and the KGB.[4]

While under Soviet control, Matviyeyko, we now know, tried to stay loyal to his cause, if not to his former boss, Stepan Bandera. On the night of June 16, 1952, slightly more than a year after his capture, Matviyeyko suddenly disappeared from the heavily guarded Lviv villa where he had conducted his radio game with the West. The loss of a major asset in the radio game, which had begun so successfully and promised so much, shook the Soviet security establishment. The USSR minister of state security ordered the arrest of Colonel Ivan Shorubalka, who was in charge of the radio game and had been given an award only two years earlier for his role in eliminating the commander in chief of the Ukrainian Insurgent Army. The investigation into Matviyeyko's escape was conducted by Roman Rudenko, the chief Soviet prosecutor at the Nuremberg Trials.

In the morning after his escape, as the entire KGB machine mobilized to search for him, Matviyeyko frantically checked his old contacts and safe houses. He was in for a major disappointment. The people he had known during the war were all gone, either killed or arrested by the Soviets. Matviyeyko was forced to come to terms with a new reality. For once, Soviet propaganda was not lying: the resistance really was limited to small, isolated groups deep in the mountain forests. It was doomed, and so, thought Matviyeyko, was he—he would be captured sooner or later. He had nowhere to turn. In desperation, Matviyeyko prepared handwritten leaflets explaining who he was, what had happened to him, and under whose control he was working. He began dropping them on random city streets in the hopes that one of them would make its way to the underground, and then, eventually, abroad. As for his own fate, Matviyeyko came to the conclusion that his only chance of survival was to return to captivity.

On the evening of June 17, after less than twenty-four hours of freedom, Matviyeyko headed for the main Lviv railway station. There he approached a passing sergeant and asked whether he worked for the secret police. When the sergeant said that he did, Matviyeyko declared that he was armed and wanted to surrender to the security services. He then admitted who he was. Matviyeyko was flown to Moscow, where the conditions of his imprisonment were nothing like those in Lviv.

It was only after Stalin's death in March 1953 that Matviyeyko was returned to the custody of his old handlers in Munich. His brief freedom and the subsequent time he had spent in Moscow remained unknown to British intelligence and the Bandera people in Ukraine. For eight long years, Matviyeyko and his radio messages remained the voice of the OUN "leadership" in Ukraine. Matviyeyko managed to make his way back into the trust of his captors. In June 1958, seven years after his capture and six years after his bizarre escape, Bandera's security chief was pardoned for his nationalist activities by a secret decree of the Supreme Soviet in Moscow. By that time he was officially married to a female KGB agent who was spying on him for her bosses.[5]

Only a few months before his death, Bandera had begun to doubt the bona fides of his emissary in Ukraine. In the early summer of 1959, the Munich Ukrainians received what they knew to be completely false information from Matviyeyko. Bandera and his people became worried. Had the inevitable happened, and had Matviyeyko finally fallen into the hands of the enemy and begun working under the enemy's control? Through the usual channels, Bandera sent Matviyeyko a new message, giving him the opportunity to secretly and safely indicate whether he was working under KGB control. If he was, then he was to use the word *borshch* (Ukrainian beet soup) in his reply. Matviyeyko responded in late September, making no reference to the dish.

Bandera was relieved. He was planning a major conference of nationalist organizations for November 1959, and he needed Matviyeyko's help and support. Apart from assessing the state of the resistance movement in Ukraine and agreeing on its future tasks, the conference was supposed to resolve once and for all who truly represented "fighting Ukraine," Bandera or Lebed. Matviyeyko was supposed to lead key participants from Ukraine to Germany, giving Bandera high hopes that he would emerge victorious from the long and exhausting émigré dispute. But Matviyeyko informed his boss that he would not be able to arrange the arrival of the delegation from Ukraine that fall. He was, however, fairly sure that he could come himself and bring the other delegates a year later. When Bandera and Eugenia Mak went shopping at the Munich Grossmarkthalle less than an hour before Bandera's death, Bandera was happy to tell her that her husband would be back in the country the next year. Bandera died not knowing that his Ukrainian emissary had betrayed him long before that.[6]

Stepan Bandera and Eugenia Mak seemed to be the last believers in the miracle that Myron Matviyeyko could have avoided KGB arrest for eight long years. The CIA agents looking into the circumstances of Bandera's death were much less optimistic. They assumed that Matviyeyko was working under Soviet control, and they were confused about why Moscow would decide to eliminate Bandera when they could have continued to manipulate him through Matviyeyko. The only explanation the CIA could come up with was that perhaps the Soviets wanted to get rid of Bandera before the planned conference took place, fearing that Bandera might still suspect Matviyeyko of working for the KGB and, on confronting him in

Munich, might force a confession out of him. In that scenario, the Soviets would have preferred to send Matviyeyko to Germany for a conference only after a weaker leader replaced Bandera.[7]

Neither the Munich Kripo nor the counterintelligence office truly suspected that Eugenia had poisoned Stepan Bandera. "Eugenia Matviyeyko-Mak is capable of anything," wrote the author of the CIA report on the investigation into Bandera's death. "But I do not believe that she personally fed cyanide to Bandera. The German police are of the same opinion." As of November 12, 1959, the leading theory, according the CIA cable sent that day to Langley, was that "the poison was administered by force after Bandera entered his apartment house." According to that theory, Eugenia could have "tipped off the killers when Bandera would be coming home." They would have been "hiding in the elevator that was stopped at one of the upper floors."[8]

The investigators believed that Bandera had tried to resist. "When he was found," read the CIA cable, "Bandera was lying on his face in the hallway of the building with his left arm doubled under him and his left hand clutching at his right shoulder. Questioning of Bandera's associates revealed that Bandera was left-handed and carried a pistol in a shoulder holster on his right side." The investigators believed that in the last moments of his life, Bandera was about to shoot someone. Their major regret was that the bloodstains on the ground floor, where Bandera had died, had been removed by an unidentified "janitress" before they could be examined by police.[9]

15

ACTIVE MEASURES

Sergei Damon was the first KGB officer to congratulate Stashinsky on a job well done upon his return to Berlin on October 16, 1959, after killing Bandera. In a celebratory mood, Damon called his agent a hero. Stashinsky had filed two reports, just as he had after killing Rebet. The first listed the localities in West Germany that he had visited on his secret trip. The second stated that he had met a person known to his superiors and passed on their greetings.[1]

The news was reported to the very top of the Karlshorst KGB pyramid and from there to the KGB headquarters in Moscow. Major General Aleksandr Korotkov, a forty-nine-year-old spymaster in charge of the KGB apparatus in Karlshorst, had reason to celebrate. Korotkov held one of the most important positions in KGB intelligence operations abroad. He had first come to Berlin under diplomatic cover on the eve of the German invasion of the Soviet Union in June 1941. At that time, registered officially as third secretary of the Soviet embassy, he was running the illegal Soviet spy network in Germany. He had left Berlin after the invasion but returned in April 1945. Korotkov had attended the German surrender ceremony, which happened to take place at Karlshorst, and then stayed in the compound to become the first Soviet intelligence chief in postwar Germany. He had been called back to Moscow in January 1946, but had returned to

Karlshorst ten years later with the rank of major general and the cover of councilor of the Soviet embassy in East Berlin. His real job was to liaise with the East German security services and manage the KGB apparatus in Karlshorst.[2]

Korotkov's subordinates were responsible for operations not only in Germany, but also in the rest of Western Europe, and they provided support for clandestine activities in North America as well. Korotkov's apparatus consisted of officers working for various KGB departments. By far the largest KGB department at Karlshorst was the one dealing with support for illegal operatives in West Germany and the West in general. Somewhat less numerous in personnel was the department dealing with operations against the Soviet émigrés abroad, a category that also included Western Ukrainians and Balts who were never Soviet citizens but came from lands occupied by the USSR during the war.[3]

In January 1959, KGB headquarters in Moscow created a new department within the foreign intelligence directorate. Its responsibility was "active measures," a euphemism for disinformation campaigns abroad. The chief of the department, conveniently labeled "D" for "disinformation," was Ivan Agaiants, the same officer who had welcomed Pavel Sudoplatov to Paris in May 1938 after his assassination of Colonel Konovalets. Now Agaiants's main target was West Germany. His task was to portray the country as a hotbed of anti-Semitism. Agaiants first tried his hand on Russian soil: KGB officers were sent to a Jewish cemetery in the Russian countryside at night to desecrate tombstones. They soon learned that while most of the villagers were reacting negatively to this act of vandalism and anti-Semitism, a small group of youths had become inspired by the "active measure" and were carrying out similar assaults on their own. East German agents were then sent to West Germany to vandalize Jewish cemeteries there. The operation was a success, causing a spike in anti-Semitic acts all over the country.[4]

Meanwhile, the Central Intelligence Agency wanted to know what was going on behind the high fences of the Soviet security compound. They tried to recruit East Germans working in the Karlshorst, used double agents to identify the KGB officers and their locations in the compound, and used listening devices to pick up on their conversations. In June 1958, the US secretary of state, Christian Herter, surprised the Soviet foreign minister, Andrei Gromyko, with a CIA-prepared exposé of subversive Soviet activities in Berlin that included a surprisingly detailed description of the Karlshorst compound.

Korotkov was well aware of Western efforts to penetrate his lines of defense. His technical counterintelligence officers had even discovered a microphone concealed in his own office. When they reported their find to Korotkov, he wanted to keep the microphone in place for a while so that he could tell the Americans in no uncertain terms, using the full power of the Russian language, what he thought of them. He was dissuaded: there was too great a risk that the microphones would pick up not only the words he intended to be heard but also those he did not. Much of what was discussed in Korotkov's office went far beyond the "legitimate" activities of any intelligence service. The Karlshorst staff was busy not only supplying Moscow with intelligence information but also "removing" those whom the Kremlin considered undesirable.[5]

Bandera's assassination presented the Karlshorst disinformation specialists with a new challenge and a new opportunity. Unlike the death of Lev Rebet, that of Bandera was almost immediately identified as a murder. The KGB officials could either maintain that it had been cardiac arrest or suicide, or blame it on someone else, as they had planned to do after the killing of Rebet. They chose the second option. This time, the plan was to blame not a rival faction of Ukrainian émigrés, however, but the political establishment of West Germany itself—a much more desirable target. The campaign began immediately after KGB operatives in Karlshorst learned that the mission had been a success.

On October 16, the day after Bandera's death, the East German Information Agency (Allgemeiner Deutscher Nachrichtendienst) broadcast a news piece associating Theodor Oberländer, West German federal minister for refugees and displaced persons, with Bandera and suggesting that the minister was involved in the death of the Ukrainian leader. "Bandera, who was the leader of a Ukrainian group of fascist terrorists, bears part of the responsibility for vicious crimes against the Ukrainian and Polish population," said the agency, referring to events of World War II and, as usual, branding any anticommunist group as fascist. "Some of those crimes were committed by units for which Oberländer was directly responsible. After being appointed minister, Oberländer did everything in his power to rid himself of his compromising ties with Bandera. It is said that one of the consequences of those efforts was that Bandera received only inadequate funding for his work from the Bonn government. Hence some people assumed that Bandera had publicly reminded the Bonn minister of their common past."[6]

Neues Deutschland, the newspaper of the Central Committee of East Germany, added more detail to the information agency's version of events in its issue of October 19: "During the Nazi period Bandera was a murderer in league with the current minister, Oberländer, at the time of the Nachtigall battalion's bloody butchery in Lviv. He was now to appear as the chief witness in the course of the investigation of an accusation against Oberländer. The main witness has been eliminated." The article was accompanied by a cartoon that depicted Oberländer commenting on Bandera's death: "I'm sorry for him. He was such a good Nazi, but he just knew too much about me." More details were soon provided by *Berliner Zeitung*, another East German newspaper. Its correspondents suggested that Bandera had been killed on Oberländer's orders by the operatives of Reinhard Gehlen, the head of the West German Federal Intelligence Service (BND). The Soviet media took the same line as their East German counterparts, and one of the leading Soviet newspapers, *Komsomol'skaia pravda* (Truth of the Communist Youth League) even reprinted the Oberländer cartoon.[7]

Oberländer, who had served in June and July 1941 as a liaison officer between the German command and the Ukrainian Nachtigall battalion—recruited from among Bandera's followers—was a thorn in Moscow's side as a minister directly opposing the recognition of postwar borders. In August 1959, the Union of Persecutees of the Nazi Regime filed charges against Oberländer in a West German court because of his connection to

Nachtigall. The Federal Prosecutor's Office ordered an investigation into the matter and turned to the *Bundesminister* for explanations. Oberländer denied the charges. Nachtigall, he claimed, had taken no part in either executions of Polish intellectuals or in the pogrom of Jews in Lviv. On the contrary, said Oberländer, the battalion, which entered Lviv ahead of regular units of the German Army early in the morning of June 30, 1941, had discovered hundreds of bodies of inmates of Soviet prisons who had been massacred by the Soviet secret police before they left the city. They were uncovering the war crimes of the other side, not committing crimes of their own. And indeed, later research would demonstrate that as a military unit, the battalion had no role in the Jewish pogrom, which was conducted by nationalistic mobs with the support of the German authorities.[8]

The West German media seemed to be on Oberländer's side, especially given the fact that the Union of Persecutees of the Nazi Regime was widely perceived as a communist front working on orders from the East. It was despised by the Christian Democrats and shunned by the Social Democrats and leaders of Jewish organizations alike. But then came Bandera's mysterious death, and the whole story took a new turn. Had Oberländer committed a new crime in his efforts to cover up the crimes of his past? His East German critics claimed that he had. On October 22, three days after Bandera's funeral, Professor Albert Norden, the head of the East German Committee for German Unity, called a press conference in East Berlin in which he directly linked the murder of Bandera to Oberländer. Professor Norden was more than a leader of the Committee for German Unity. He was also secretary of the Central Committee of the ruling Socialist Unity Party, a member of its Politburo, and the man responsible for its information gathering, propaganda, and relations with the West.

Albert Norden's press conference and the statements that he and other participants made regarding Oberländer's involvement in the Lviv massacres put the story on a different political level. It was no longer individual journalists who were making damaging accusations against a powerful West German minister, but the chief propagandist of the East German state. Later that month, the East German documentary film company

DEFA issued a newsreel in which a thirty-two-minute report on Norden's press conference was followed by a twenty-five-minute item on Bandera's funeral. It presented Bandera as Oberländer's underling in the Nachtigall battalion, responsible for the Lviv massacres.[9]

The film made an unexpected impression on Bogdan Stashinsky, who watched it in one of East Berlin's cinemas. He was especially affected by the images of Bandera lying in his coffin surrounded by family members, including his three children. As the narrator announced that the Ukrainian nationalist leader had been murdered in cold blood by paid assassins working for the United States, the word "murder" reverberated in Stashinsky's head. He rushed out of the cinema. "Bandera has a wife and children," he later told Sergei Damon. "I have done it. I'm a murderer." But Damon did not seem to share his concerns. With a smile on his face, he told his agent: "You don't need to worry yourself about that. Bandera's children will later be grateful to you for having done it, when they are able to see things in perspective." Stashinsky was anything but persuaded. The KGB's "active measure" had produced the opposite effect.[10]

PART III

MOSCOW NIGHTS

16

HIGH HOPES

In early November 1959, Sergei Damon picked up Bogdan Stashinsky in the city and brought him by car to the KGB compound in Karlshorst. He told his prized agent that he was about to meet his ultimate boss, the general in charge of the KGB apparatus at Karlshorst. Although Stashinsky was never given the general's name, there was only one general and one boss of the KGB operations in Karlshorst. His name was Aleksandr Korotkov.[1]

The general played the welcoming host, launching into small talk. According to the memoirs of General Pavel Sudoplatov, Korotkov had no qualms about what was called "wet work" in criminal parlance. He had been twenty-nine when he had planned and helped execute his first murder. In the late 1930s, he had traveled to France at the head of a group of assassins who had hunted down and killed two political enemies of the regime. One of them was an associate of Stalin's archenemy Leon Trotsky, the other a former member of the Soviet intelligence network in Istanbul. The latter's defection had led to the arrest of hundreds of Soviet agents in the Middle East. Korotkov had not only planned but also taken part in both killings. The bodies of both victims, one of them decapitated, had been stuffed into suitcases and dumped into the water. One of those suitcases had later been found in the Seine by the Paris police, and Korotkov and his assassins had fled France.[2]

One of the first "wet" jobs that Korotkov must have overseen after his return to Berlin in the spring of 1957 was the failed assassination attempt of a former agent who had gone rogue. His name was Nikolai Khokhlov. An experienced Soviet intelligence officer whose heroic wartime exploits had served as an inspiration for the 1947 Soviet blockbuster *A Scout's Exploit*, Khokhlov had decided to jump ship while on assignment in Germany. One day in March 1954, instead of killing Georgii Okolovich, a leader of the émigré National Alliance of Russian Solidarists, he had gone to Okolovich's apartment in Frankfurt and confessed. Khokhlov later claimed that he had read literature produced by Okolovich that appealed to his sense of Russian patriotism. Once in CIA custody, he was persuaded to give a press conference exposing the Soviet plot to assassinate leading figures of the Russian emigration in the West. The next day, the KGB arrested his wife in Moscow, who was sentenced to five years of internal exile. Khokhlov became a hunted man.

By that time General Korotkov was already in complete command of his Karlshorst apparatus. The assassination attempt in 1957 took place during Khokhlov's first public appearance on returning to Europe after extensive debriefing in the United States. He was a speaker at a Russian émigré conference in Frankfurt, the city where he had refused to be an assassin. After delivering his remarks, Khokhlov went to the porch to breathe some fresh air and enjoy the view—the conference hall was situated in the Palmengarten, the largest garden in Germany. Someone offered him a cup of coffee. Khokhlov drank, as he later remembered, half a cup. Instead of being refreshed and reenergized by the drink, he began to feel exhausted and tired.

He soon lost consciousness. Khokhlov's associates, including Georgii Okolovich, whose life he had saved three and a half years earlier, drove him to the hospital. His face was covered with red and blue spots, and he could not see, as his eyes were producing some kind of sticky liquid. His hair was starting to fall out. The German doctors treated him for food poisoning, but things were only getting worse, and they did not know what to do. They transferred him to the US Army hospital, where the American doctors concluded that he had been poisoned with thallium. Khokhlov overheard one of the doctors saying that there was also some other foreign element in his system—but they wouldn't know more until after the autopsy. It never came to that. Khokhlov survived to learn the results of the medical analysis of the poison used against him. It was radioactive thallium prepared in a special laboratory, which many believed could only have been sponsored by the KGB.[3]

If Khokhlov had finished drinking his coffee, General Korotkov and his subordinates at Karlshorst would probably have achieved their purpose. His luck, and the work of the US military doctors, saved his life. The whole operation turned out to be yet another embarrassment for the KGB.[4]

But in October 1957, a month after the unsuccessful attempt on Khokhlov's life, Bogdan Stashinsky assassinated Lev Rebet. Now he had succeeded in killing the most important Ukrainian figure of all, Stepan Bandera. During his years at Karlshorst, Korotkov had developed a habit of meeting with his agents personally. He had learned from them not only about émigré leaders and their contacts with Western intelligence services, but also about political life and developments in West Germany. It was almost a nostalgic experience for the former operative, who could no longer "work" in the field. Korotkov had not met his star assassin after his first success, but he was delighted to see him now. There was good news from Moscow, from the very top of the Soviet pyramid, that he wanted to share with Karlshorst's new top agent. [5]

Korotkov began by asking Stashinsky about his impressions of Munich. The conversation went on for about fifteen minutes until the general ushered his guests into an adjacent room, where dinner was served. They were going to celebrate their success and discuss plans for the future. Korotkov offered cognac to his guests before breaking the big news. It gave him great pleasure, he told Stashinsky, to inform him that the Presidium of the Supreme Soviet of the USSR had awarded him the Order of the Red Banner of Valor. It was the oldest Soviet military decoration—indeed, the only one that existed in the first years of Soviet rule to recognize heroism in combat and acts of military valor. It was second only to the Gold Star of Hero of the

Soviet Union, which was introduced much later. Korotkov explained to Stashinsky that it was extremely rare to be awarded the Order of the Red Banner of Valor in peacetime. It was a clear indication of how important the young agent's assignment had been to the Soviet government.[6]

Bogdan Stashinsky had not expected such an award. Moral struggles aside, he was clearly pleased. For completing his previous assignment, the killing of Lev Rebet, he had been given a Contax camera. Now it was a prestigious state award. Its importance was underscored by the fact that he would go personally to Moscow to receive it, Korotkov told him. The general also spoke of the future. For now, Stashinsky would have to disappear from Berlin—the assassination of Bandera, unlike that of Lev Rebet, had raised an uproar in the West, and he could not return until the dust had settled. Instead of wasting time in East Berlin, he would be better off going to Moscow for a year of additional training. Judging by the general's words, the award marked a turning point in Stashinsky's career. He was moving up in life. His case officer, Sergei Damon, suggested that after training in Moscow he would be sent either to West Germany or to another Western European country. One day, Damon told Stashinsky only half-jokingly, he would replace his case officer in Karlshorst.[7]

On November 20, 1959, Stashinsky boarded a train to Moscow. As was always the case on his trips to the Soviet Union, he used a Soviet passport in the name of Aleksandr Antonovich Krylov. Compared to his previous trip to Moscow in April, he had significantly heavier luggage—his bosses expected him to stay at least until summer. The border guards and customs officers usually did thorough searches of passengers, looking for coffee and other smuggled goods that were in short supply or of poor quality in the Soviet Union, but they did not bother Comrade Krylov. His travel documents had a seal with the number of a Soviet Army military unit that border officials knew better than to investigate. The post office box number 42601 stood for the KGB.[8]

For Stashinsky, the trip to Moscow opened new horizons. Even before the meeting with Korotkov, he had heard from Damon about the possibility of working for the KGB in Western Europe, but now it became much more real. Moving up the KGB ladder meant learning to carry out tasks other than assassinations, which Stashinsky was determined not to repeat. Training in Moscow would allow him to leave that stage of his life behind without jeopardizing his career in the secret service. He also knew that he could not leave of his own free will: like the Mafia, the KGB did not allow agents to resign. There was also little else in life that he knew how to do. Given all this, he had high hopes for the meetings he was about to attend in Moscow. There was also an important question of a personal nature that only Moscow could decide.

17

MAN AT THE TOP

In Moscow, news of the assassination of Stepan Bandera was met with great jubilation. Notices of his death were buried discreetly in the middle pages of major newspapers, but those holding the Kremlin's top offices were clearly pleased.

On November 3, 1959, less than three weeks after the assassination, the Presidium of the Central Committee of the Communist Party of the USSR, under the leadership of Nikita Khrushchev, approved the draft of a secret decree of the Supreme Soviet of the USSR awarding Bogdan Stashinsky the Order of the Red Banner of Valor. The decision was made on the basis of a KGB report that credited Stashinsky with carrying out "several responsible assignments involving risk to his life." The Presidium, knowing who had been assassinated and why the award was being proposed, voted to recognize the man who had risked his life abroad. Three days later, Marshal Kliment Voroshilov, a member of the Presidium of the Central Committee and head of the Presidium of the Supreme Soviet of the USSR—the formal head of the Soviet state—signed the decree. The decision to award Stashinsky with a military order had been made at the highest levels and in record time.[1]

There could be only one explanation for that breathtaking speed—the deep satisfaction that the news had brought the man at the very top of the Soviet power pyramid, Nikita Khrushchev. The Ukrainian resistance movement had been a thorn in Khrushchev's flesh during his years as Stalin's prefect in Ukraine. Khrushchev's major regret was that in September 1939, when the Red Army had crossed the Polish border under the terms of the Molotov-Ribbentrop Pact and taken over Western Ukraine and Belarus, Bandera had been able to escape his Polish prison. After years of fighting the "Banderites" in Ukraine, Khrushchev wanted Bandera dead.

General Pavel Sudoplatov, head of the secret police directorate responsible for sabotage and the assassination of Colonel Yevhen Konovalets—Bandera's predecessor at the helm of the Organization of Ukrainian Nationalists—recalled that after Stalin's death in 1953, Khrushchev had demanded that the security chief, Lavrentiy Beria, immediately intensify efforts to kill Bandera. At Khrushchev's request, Beria summoned to Moscow two of Bandera's sisters, who were serving sentences in the Gulag because they were members of his family. The goal was to convince them to establish contact with their brother and persuade him to meet with an NKVD agent in Germany. The plan failed. Khrushchev did not give up on the idea of having Bandera assassinated after he removed Beria from power in July 1953. Meeting with Sudoplatov in the presence of other party officials soon after Beria's arrest, Khrushchev allegedly told the top NKVD assassin: "You will shortly be asked to prepare a plan for liquidating the Bandera leadership of the Ukrainian fascist movement in western Ukraine, which is arrogantly insulting the leadership of the Soviet Union."[2]

Sudoplatov was soon arrested and spent years in Soviet prisons. He believed that this was the result of a fatal mistake he had made while meeting with Khrushchev and other party officials after Beria's arrest. When they had asked him to list the assassinations undertaken by his department on Beria's orders, he had provided a list that began with his assassination of Colonel Konovalets and included "wet work" approved not only by Stalin and Beria—one safely dead, the other in prison—but also by people present in the room, including Viacheslav Molotov, Nikolai Bulganin, and Nikita Khrushchev. Sudoplatov had merely been trying to shield himself from accusations of having conspired with Beria, but he incurred the wrath of party bosses who wanted no witnesses of their complicity in Stalin's crimes.[3]

Khrushchev's enthusiasm for solving his political problems at home and abroad by means of secret-police assassinations was not shared by many people in the secret services, including, apparently, Beria himself. Sometime in the spring of 1953, General Sudoplatov overheard his boss talking with Khrushchev by telephone. "Look," Beria allegedly told Khrushchev, "you asked me to find a way to liquidate Bandera, and at the same time your petty crooks in Kyiv and Lviv are preventing real work against real opponents." Beria's comments reflected the growing feeling among secret-police officials that Bandera was becoming less and less relevant to what was going on in Ukraine, and that assassinating nationalist leaders would not resolve the military struggle that had been going on in Western Ukraine for more than eight years. The KGB wanted to focus on convincing the nationalist leaders to cooperate with the regime and put an end to the guerrilla struggle. But Khrushchev was not amenable to that strategy, even if people he trusted were suggesting it.

General Tymofii Strokach, the Ukrainian minister of the interior, once tried to convince Khrushchev to spare the life of the last leader of the Ukrainian Insurgent Army, Vasyl Kuk (nom de guerre "Lemish"), whom the NKVD had caught in 1954, when Khrushchev was busily consolidating power in Moscow after Stalin's death. It was a difficult task. One of Strokach's subordinates recalled his words:

> "I told Nikita Sergeevich that I had promised those people not only freedom but also the normal life of a Soviet citizen. I had promised them high official awards. And he said to me: We make a lot of promises for the sake of our enterprise and our goals. It should be clear to you that Lemish and everyone associated with him are sworn enemies of Soviet Ukraine; the noose is begging for his neck, but you ask that they be pardoned. I said to him: Nikita Sergeevich, there are thousands of Lemish's political sympathizers standing behind him, and we need to work on them."

Kuk's life was saved, according to Strokach, only because of the interven-
tion of Ukrainian party officials. When Khrushchev was approached by his
close political ally Oleksii Kyrychenko, the first secretary of the Ukrainian
Central Committee, he eventually backed down and changed his mind.[4]

Bandera was a different matter. There Khrushchev and Kyrychenko
seemed to be in complete agreement. In the summer of 1953, immediately
after taking over as party boss of Ukraine, Kyrychenko insisted at a conference of secret-police officers that Bandera be eliminated. According to one
account, he told the gathering: "That enemy of Soviet rule, Bandera, is still
alive and active in the West. Believe me, once Bandera is gone, that will be
the end of the OUN movement." Kyrychenko brought those same sympa-
thies with him when he was transferred to Moscow by his boss and patron,
Nikita Khrushchev, in December 1957. He became the second-most powerful man in the Soviet Union after Khrushchev himself. Kyrychenko oversaw the activities of the KGB on behalf of the Central Committee.

In May 1959, Kyrychenko addressed a major conference of KGB offi-
cers. The purpose of the conference was to discuss how to coordinate KGB
activities with the new party line. "I would consider it one of the main tasks
to activize work on the liquidation of foreign centers," Kyrychenko told the
KGB brass, referring to émigré groups. He then listed the leaders of the
Ukrainian and Russian émigré organizations: "Bandera, Melnyk, Poremsky,
Okolovich, and many others must be actively unmasked." He went on:
"Who is Bandera? He was an agent of Hitlerite espionage, then of English,
Italian, and a number of other services; he leads a corrupt way of life and is
greedy for money. You Chekists are aware of all that and know how that
same Bandera can be compromised."[5]

Although Kyrychenko spoke euphemistically, some of the KGB officers in the audience were well aware that the Central Committee wanted
them not to "compromise" but to kill Bandera. KGB officers who were
working on the problem of Ukrainian insurgents argued against assassinating Bandera. Like their Western counterparts, they believed that killing Bandera, who by then had little influence on developments in
Ukraine, would turn him into a martyr. But their voices were not heard

by those at the top of the KGB, which was run in 1959 by Khrushchev's handpicked man, Aleksandr Shelepin. He was remembered by those who worked under him in the KGB as a leader who was very demanding of his underlings, but extremely accommodating when it came to his superiors, especially Khrushchev.[6]

Shelepin was only forty years old when, in December 1958, Khrushchev appointed him to the most sensitive position in the country, that of KGB chairman. His main task was to get rid of Stalin-era people and traditions. Shelepin originally refused to take the position. His political experience until that point had been limited to the Central Committee of the Young Communist League—the youth branch of the party—which he had led since 1952, when he was appointed to that position by Stalin. Before the fateful conversation with Khrushchev, he had spent only a few months as a department head in the Central Committee of the Communist Party. Khrushchev told Shelepin that he had his full confidence and promised to help. Shelepin agreed. The leader of state then asked the new head of the KGB to do everything in his power to prevent the wiretapping of Khrushchev himself—a clear indication that he did not fully trust his own security officials.

Shelepin took the place of Khrushchev's longtime ally, the "pacifier" of Budapest, General Ivan Serov. The general was transferred to a politically much less sensitive position at the head of military intelligence. Khrushchev wanted to curb the power of the KGB and drastically reduce the number of its officers and agents. Serov, who had joined the secret police in the days of Joseph Stalin, clearly had been the wrong man for the job. Shelepin, by contrast, had no reservations about paring down the KGB. He was also eager to switch the main thrust of its operations from the home front to the international arena. There, he believed, the KGB had to focus much more on achieving the foreign-policy goals of the Soviet government. One of his innovations in the sphere of intelligence was the creation of the disinformation department. West Germany became one of the testing grounds of its techniques, and Theodor Oberländer, the West German minister accused not only of Nazi-era crimes but also of killing Bandera, became one of its first targets.[7]

Now Shelepin could add to his record of achievement the killing of an archenemy of Soviet rule who had also long been considered a personal enemy of Nikita Khrushchev. Things were looking very good for Aleksandr Shelepin. He was prepared to take full credit for what had happened in Munich, and personally present a high award to the man who had made it possible.

18

PRIVATE MATTER

B ogdan Stashinsky arrived in Moscow on November 22, 1959. At the Belarus train station he was picked up by a KGB officer he first met in Karlshorst. Stashinsky knew him by his first name and patronymic, Arkadii Andreevich, but in Germany he used the alias "Avramenko." Avramenko was in fact Arkadii Andreevich Fabrichnikov. He checked Stashinsky into the Hotel Leningrad, which, like the Hotel Ukraine, Stashinsky's earlier hangout in Moscow, was one of "seven sisters," a group of neo-Gothic skyscrapers built during the late Stalin period.[1]

The next day, in another hotel, the Moscow—built in the 1930s in the constructivist style—a senior KGB officer greeted Stashinsky and introduced himself as Aleksei Alekseevich. According to declassified biographies of KGB senior officers, it was none other than General Aleksei Krokhin. He had served in the Soviet counterintelligence directorate during the war and had begun working for foreign intelligence in 1946, at the outset of the Cold War. In 1950, Krokhin was sent to Paris under the name "Ognev" and the cover of a diplomatic position to assume responsibility for KGB operations in France. He returned to Moscow in 1954 to serve as a deputy head of the First Main Directorate. For a while he also headed the division responsible for running the KGB illegals, the agents who worked abroad under false names and without diplomatic cover. In the central apparatus he replaced General Aleksandr Korotkov, who was now running KGB operations at Karlshorst. General Krokhin's meeting with Stashinsky indicated that he had been transferred from the émigré department to the one overseeing the activities of illegal agents.[2]

Krokhin spelled out the coming changes in Stashinsky's life and career to which General Korotkov in Karlshorst had only alluded. Stashinsky would stay in Moscow to receive training for his future work abroad. He would improve his German and learn English. In the future, he would no longer be based on Soviet-controlled territory; instead, following the training, he would settle in a Western European country. That assignment was expected to last for three to five years, and Stashinsky, who was looking forward to a longer stay in the West, must have been pleased with what he heard. But then, to his disappointment, Krokhin told Stashinsky that despite the change of his base of operations, he would be continuing the work he had done before—assassinating enemies of the Soviet regime. The general added that his other assignments might include running a group of illegal agents. Krokhin stressed that Stashinsky was no longer a common agent but would be joining the KGB elite.[3]

Stashinsky kept silent on the matter of future assassinations. But he raised the question that his handler, Sergei Damon, had told him could only be decided in Moscow. Karlshorst's star agent was in love. He had an East German girlfriend and wanted to marry her before coming to Moscow for a year. Her name was Inge Pohl, and Stashinsky had met her in April 1957, the month in which he had first traveled to Munich to track down Lev Rebet. They had spotted each other at the Casino dance hall, part of the famous Berlin landmark Friedrichstadt-Palast.

The Casino was the place to go if one wanted a good time in East Berlin. The venue was extremely popular, the main attraction being the music. Back in the 1920s, when the famous actor and director Max Reinhardt had bought and rebuilt the Friedrichstadt-Palast, it had welcomed such performers as Marlene Dietrich. Different performers and tunes were in fashion by the late 1950s. In April 1957, Elvis Presley's single "All Shook Up" climbed to the top of the US pop charts and stayed there for eight weeks.

The Casino had a night bar and a dance hall that were open from 10:00 p.m. to 4:00 a.m. The entrance stairs led to an impressive space reminiscent of a temple, with ceilings fifteen meters high. The yellow walls were decorated with gypsum sculptures. The Casino had a ten-meter-long bar and a podium for the orchestra. The place badly needed renovation: its old tables and chairs, greasy from years of use, were covered with red and yellow plastic. But the visitors were prepared to overlook its numerous imperfections. The admission price was quite reasonable: 2 marks.

Single, with some Western currency to spare (he was paid 800 German marks per month, plus per diem when traveling), Stashinsky was well known to the staff and patrons of the establishment. The woman whom Stashinsky met at the Casino and eventually fell in love with was by no means a striking beauty. Inge Pohl had bluish eyes, a round face with a large pointed nose, and small dimples when she smiled. Her brown hair, with a reddish tinge, was cut in the latest Berlin fashion. She was of medium height, about five foot eight, and people tended to comment on her well-formed legs. She lived in Dallgow, an East German town, and worked in the Rechholz hair salon in Siemensstadt, located in West Berlin on the border with Spandau. She fell in love with Stashinsky the first time she saw him. "He had a very good appearance and actually looked very, very, nice," she remembered later. She liked his black hair and his smile, which showed snow-white teeth, and the way he dressed: he seemed to prefer dark suits.

Inge did her best to learn as much as possible about her new dance partner. He clearly had an accent in German, and at first she thought he was a Czech. But the Casino porter, who knew Stashinsky as a regular visitor, told her that he was a Pole working for the Polish embassy in East Berlin. Inge did not particularly like the idea of dating a Pole, but in Stashinsky's case she decided to make an exception. She needn't have worried, as Stashinsky soon told her that he was neither a Czech nor a Pole but a Volksdeutscher, a German from the East who was working for the East German Ministry of International Trade. His name was Joseph Lehmann, Stashinsky told his new acquaintance and future girlfriend. Inge was relieved and happy.

Inge loved her "Joschi." True, his German grammar was not always correct, but it was improving and was not bad for a German who had been born in Poland and had grown up hearing only corrupt German, if any at all. American GIs, who had much more pocket money than did local Germans, were especially popular among German girls in those days. Joschi was no worse than those Americans—he always had Western money. But as far as Inge was concerned, that was not all that important. Her own earnings in Western currency were the black-market equivalent of the salary of a highly placed East German official, and she saw in Joschi someone who was doing equally well in life. Well-dressed, polite, and intelligent, he was a great catch for a village girl who had become a hairdresser in the big city.

Stashinsky also felt attracted to his new acquaintance. Following KGB protocol, he informed Sergei Damon of his new passion. With the help of its East German underlings, the KGB checked the girl's background and found no criminal record or possible connections to Western intelligence services. Stashinsky was allowed to date her. However, the KGB warned Stashinsky to bear in mind that even though Inge and her family lived in East Germany, her father, Fritz Pohl, was a "capitalist." He owned an auto shop, where he "exploited" three workers.

Stashinsky and Inge shared the same birthday—November 4—but she was five years younger than he was. She had been born in 1936 in the Berlin suburb of Spandau. Relations between her parents were less than cordial, and by the time Inge met Stashinsky, she was already living on her own, renting a room from a lady a few houses away from her father's home. Stashinsky was not the first man with whom Inge had fallen in love. She had been involved with a young man who worked as a driver for the East German minister of justice, Hilde Benjamin, who was widely known as "Bloody Hilde" or the "Red Guillotine" for the death sentences she handed down at show trials in the late 1940s and early 1950s as vice president of the East German Supreme Court. Stashinsky seemed a much more attractive choice. But not unlike her first love, Stashinsky presented some ideological issues of his own to be sorted out.

Inge found her boyfriend too devoted to Moscow. "He said that the government circles in the Soviet zone did not answer to his conception of what they should be—he found them too militarist—but he praised everything connected with Russia and the communist ideology," remembered Inge later. The KGB agent had to put up not only with the anticommunist and anti-Russian attitudes of Inge's father but also with Inge's less firmly held but fundamentally similar attitudes. Inge did not agree with everything her father told her. But she did not accept everything her boyfriend said to her, either. Quite often they argued, failing to find common ground and remaining loyal to their original beliefs. "I did not share his convictions and enthusiasm for Russia," recalled Inge. "I would bring up points of argument, but he always had a counterargument ready."

They spent their free time walking together through the streets of East and West Berlin and going to the movies or to the Casino dance hall. Over time, Inge began to notice some strange things about her boyfriend's behavior. He was surprisingly careful about protecting his papers. Once, at the Casino, when Stashinsky's wallet fell out of his jacket pocket and Inge picked it up, Stashinsky immediately seized the documents. He did not seem to have regular work hours, and he would sometimes disappear for weeks at a time, saying that he was going abroad, mostly to Poland, on assignment for the Ministry of Trade. Once he was away for a whole month, telling Inge that he had attended the Leipzig Trade Fair. In fact, he was on one of his KGB assignments in Munich. Inge rightfully grew suspicious.

In the spring of 1959, two years after they had begun dating, Inge secretly followed Stashinsky to his rented room in East Berlin, thinking that he might be seeing someone else. She found nothing but a surprised boyfriend. Inge voiced her suspicions, threatening to end the relationship, but Stashinsky assured her that he was not involved with anyone else. He loved her; more than that, he wanted to marry her. Stashinsky proposed, and Inge happily accepted. They bought their rings in the Gesundbrunnen district of Berlin, part of the Western occupation zone. The rings were larger than the ones they could get in the East. They were happy. Despite their political differences, they clearly loved each other. "Personally, we understood each other very well," remembered Inge later. She was not particularly cultured or educated, but she possessed a strong character and an independent mind. Most important, she remained loyal to Stashinsky, who found in her a kind of resolve that he believed he lacked himself, a steadying moral influence that he needed badly in his life. Their political disagreements were secondary. Their love for each other came first.[4]

Stashinsky did not immediately tell his KGB handlers about the engagement. But after his meeting with General Korotkov, who informed Stashinsky about his transfer to Moscow, he could no longer keep the attachment secret. What would happen to Inge, Stashinsky asked Damon. He told Damon that he wanted to marry his fiancée. The KGB officer was unimpressed. She was a poor match for him, said the handler—of lower social status and a German. Marriage to a German woman would impede Stashinsky's career, which was showing so much promise. Damon believed that a transfer to Moscow would present a good opportunity to break up with Inge. To make the whole thing easier, he could offer her a cash settlement. The KGB was willing to help by chipping in a few thousand deutschmarks. That was not what Stashinsky wanted to hear. He insisted that he was in love and wanted to marry Inge, no matter what Damon said. Damon decided to play for time. He told his agent that he would have to raise the question of marriage with the higher-ups in Moscow. Stashinsky agreed.[5]

Now he raised the question of marriage to Inge before the highest KGB official he had ever encountered, General Krokhin. Like Stashinsky's superiors in Karlshorst, Krokhin was against Stashinsky's marriage. He told Stashinsky that KGB men did not marry foreigners. Besides, he could not do so for the simple reason that his days as Josef Lehmann were over. He would soon assume a different name and learn a different life story, or "legend." The general suggested that Stashinsky marry a Soviet woman who would be a KGB employee. Then both of them could receive appropriate training and be dispatched to the West. That would boost Stashinsky's chances of success and his career prospects with the KGB. Stashinsky would not budge. He tried to come up with a counterargument. Marriage to an ethnic German woman would benefit his KGB career, as it would make it easier for him to establish himself in the West, he told the general. But Krokhin would not listen. He wanted Stashinsky to forget about Inge. Sergei Damon had merely delayed giving Stashinsky the official line: in Moscow, they were as strongly opposed to his plans for marriage as his handlers were at Karlshorst.[6]

Before leaving, General Krokhin told Stashinsky to consider well what he had told him about Inge. "In a few days, once you've given the matter some thought, let me know: I'll be glad to come and see you, and we'll discuss it once again," he told Stashinsky. Stashinsky knew what that meant. The general expected him to accept his proposal to drop Inge and find himself a wife among the female KGB employees. Stashinsky had only a few days to make up his mind.[7]

19

AWARD

As always, the first week of December was a busy time in Moscow. December 5, 1959 was a holiday, Constitution Day. The newspapers reported on Soviet economic achievements, and the cinemas of Moscow, Leningrad, Kyiv, and other republican capitals treated their viewers to a documentary on Nikita Khrushchev's visit to the United States. "It is a joy to witness the fine fruits of the peace-loving foreign policy of the Soviet state," wrote the Communist Party's mouthpiece, *Pravda*, on the premiere of the film, which showed Khrushchev rubbing elbows with US President Dwight Eisenhower. One day earlier, the Soviet Ministry of Foreign Affairs had presented the United Nations Organization in New York with two impressive gifts: a statue called *Swords into Plowshares*, produced by the leading Soviet sculptor, Yevgenii Vuchetich; and a model of Sputnik—the world's first artificial satellite, which the Soviets had launched in October 1957. The sculpture of a muscular naked man striking a broken sword with a hammer was meant to symbolize the Soviet desire for peace. Sputnik, on the other hand, served as a symbol of Soviet technological achievement and a reminder that Soviet missiles could now reach American shores.[1]

It was around Constitution Day that Bogdan Stashinsky was finally admitted to the inner sanctum of the world of the secret police—the KGB headquarters at Lubianka Square in downtown Moscow. Approaching the building he had heard so much about, Stashinsky could not help noticing the most recent addition to its courtyard—a brand-new monument to Felix Dzerzhinsky, the Polish-born founder of the Soviet secret police. The Dzerzhinsky monument symbolized an attempt by the new leadership of the KGB to clean up its image, which had been badly stained by the Stalin era, and to link it to the mythologized past of Lenin and the Bolshevik founders of the Soviet secret service.

After clearing security at the entrance, Stashinsky was met by his old acquaintance Colonel Georgii Ishchenko, the head of the émigré department of the KGB intelligence directorate. During Stashinsky's previous visit to Moscow in April 1959, it was Ishchenko who had given him the order to kill Bandera. Now, Ishchenko would accompany his star agent to the office of the chairman of the secret police, Aleksandr Shelepin. When they were shown in by the duty officer, Stashinsky saw a short man in his early forties with a receding hairline, a high forehead, a sharp nose, and inquisitive eyes. In Shelepin's office, Stashinsky also saw his new boss, General Aleksei Krokhin.

The KGB chief rose from his chair, took a few steps toward Stashinsky, and greeted him with a smile. After welcoming Stashinsky, Shelepin reached for a file on his desk to which an enlarged photo of Stashinsky was clipped. He took out a citation from the file and read its text aloud. The decree, signed by the chairman of the Presidium of the Supreme Soviet of the USSR, Marshal Kliment Voroshilov, on November 6, 1959, invested Bogdan Nikolaevich Stashinsky with the combat Order of the Red Banner "for carrying out an important official assignment in extraordinarily difficult circumstances." Having read out the citation, Shelepin took a case containing the medal from his desk and handed it over to Stashinsky, then shook his hand and congratulated him on the award. The KGB officers present at the investiture stood at attention. "It was solemn," remembered Stashinsky later. Stashinsky received the award but not the citation, which went back into his KGB file—its content remained secret. Shelepin told Stashinsky that there would be no announcement of his award in the press. "You know that such things are not written about," he said.[2]

Shelepin was eager to talk to his prized agent and hear a firsthand account of Stashinsky's secret mission. The KGB head was interested in every detail, starting with Stashinsky's first travels abroad to track down Bandera. He showed particular interest in the details of the assassination itself. He wanted to know where Stashinsky had stood and where Bandera was at the time of the shooting. He even asked about the color of the tomatoes that Bandera was carrying: red or green? The media had reported that Bandera was carrying a bag of green tomatoes, but Stashinsky claimed that they were red. If asked about what had happened to Bandera by his own boss, Nikita Khrushchev, Shelepin had to be able to fill him in on the details, the smallest particulars of the act.[3]

Then, having listened to his lengthy description of the Bandera assassination, Shelepin told the young agent what he already knew from Korotkov and Krokhin: for the time being he would stay in Moscow to get additional training. But once the stir created by the assassination had subsided, he would be sent back to continue his same work in the West. "Using a good deal of political and propaganda padding," remembered Stashinsky later, "he said that what was expected of me was difficult but honorable." Stashinsky agreed, and then seized the opportunity to raise the matter that was at the top of his personal agenda. He told the KGB chairman that he wanted to marry Inge Pohl.

Shelepin, who was Stashinsky's last hope for permission to marry his fiancée, had already been briefed on his agent's love affair. Like his subordinates, he was against the marriage. "Isn't it a bit early?" he asked. He then used the same argument that Stashinsky had already heard. "You know that it's not done for a KGB operative to marry a foreigner," said Shelepin. Stashinsky responded that in the three years he had known Inge, he had become convinced that she was the right woman for him. "I described her as a decent, hard-working girl with whom I got on well and who was by no means wholly unreceptive to Soviet ideas," said Stashinsky later. He was lying through his teeth. He knew that Inge was anything but sympathetic toward Russia and communism, but had decided to risk everything. "I lied to Shelepin to attain my goal," he recalled later.

General Krokhin gave him a few days to consider the matter further, and Stashinsky did just that. His bosses' reservations aside, he had doubts of his own. Going through with the marriage meant dragging the woman he loved into the nightmare of his past and present relations with the KGB. But the alternative—leaving her and marrying a KGB employee—was one that he refused to entertain. "Renouncing her would mean, to say no more, leaving her alone and abandoning her," he remembered later. "That was something I did not want to do and could not do." The man who had made treason his profession and betrayed his family was not prepared to betray Inge Pohl.

It was more, however, than love and fear of betrayal that informed his decision. "I had no high opinion of myself," said Stashinsky, recalling his state of mind after the assassinations. He needed someone who could understand and forgive him. "My soul was at stake," he remarked on another occasion. "I already abominated what I had done. Had I not married Inge Pohl, I should probably have become again a faithful party-line communist and KGB man." That was the fate that awaited him if he married a KGB woman, as his bosses suggested. And that was what Stashinsky wanted to avoid at all costs. He was trying to save his soul. Inge was his means of salvation, the rock on which he could lean to lift himself out of the quagmire.

But Shelepin pressed on. "You now have great accomplishments behind you," he told Stashinsky, trying to use the career card. Nor was he above playing the matchmaker. "We also have pretty women. Look at this one, for instance," continued the KGB chief, pointing to a photo of an attractive young woman in his file. "Beauty is not the point," replied Stashinsky. "When you've known someone for a long time and know that it will be good to go on living with her, that's exactly what you need." It was then that Shelepin gave up his attempts to persuade Stashinsky to marry a Soviet citizen. If Stashinsky insisted and was confident of his fiancée's positive attitude toward the Soviet Union, they would try to make an exception in his case. There was a catch, however. They could not make such an exception while Inge was a citizen of an East European country: she would have to acquire Soviet citizenship. Inge would also have to agree to help him in his KGB work.

The KGB's logic was simple. If Stashinsky would not marry a Soviet woman in service to the KGB, then his German wife would have to become a Soviet citizen and join the KGB. Her willingness to do so was a prerequisite to their marriage. William Hood, the head of the CIA station in Munich on whose "watch" Stashinsky had killed Bandera, later wrote that the Soviets' extremely cautious attitudes toward their agents' romantic liaisons probably stemmed from the 1931 defection of Georgii Agabekov. Agabekov, the USSR's chief of intelligence in Turkey, had fallen in love with the young Englishwoman whom he had hired to be his language teacher. It was believed that their romance had contributed to his decision to abandon his post and turn over key intelligence about the Soviet spy networks in the Middle East. The memory of Agabekov's defection was very fresh for the KGB brass. It was, after all, Stashinsky's boss at Karlshorst, General Aleksandr Korotkov, who had "liquidated" the traitor and helped stuff his body into a suitcase to be thrown into the Seine.[4]

Stashinsky was taken aback by Shelepin's proposal—these conditions would make the marriage a trap for him and his fiancée, not a psychological escape from the embrace of the KGB. Nevertheless, it was the best he could get under the circumstances, and he was not going to let it slip through his fingers. Stashinsky suggested that he go back to East Berlin at the end of the month and propose. But General Krokhin had other ideas. He wanted Stashinsky to start training as soon as possible and wait until spring or early summer to go to Berlin for the wedding. Until then, Stashinsky and Inge could correspond only. "I did not agree to that," remembered Stashinsky later. "It was clear to me that he wanted to use the time to interfere with my plans."

Stashinsky quickly came up with a new line of argument. He told Shelepin and Krokhin that it would be difficult for him to live in a state of uncertainty for so long. He would prefer to settle his family matters before starting his training and taking on new assignments. That seemed reasonable to Shelepin. He told Stashinsky that they would do a check on Inge in Berlin. "We have good relations with our friends in the German Democratic Republic. If that is what she's like [i.e., as you describe her], then we have nothing against it." Shelepin suggested that before Stashinsky disclosed his KGB employment to Inge and proposed to her, he bring her to Moscow for a few weeks to familiarize her with life in the USSR. There, of course, the KGB could size up Stashinsky's fiancée for itself. They agreed that Stashinsky would travel to East Berlin for Christmas and then bring Inge back to Moscow.[5]

20

PROPOSAL

On the evening after his audience with Shelepin, Bogdan Stashin-sky celebrated his award with Major Arkadii Fabrichnikov and a certain Nikolai Nikolaevich, another KGB officer assigned to take care of him in Moscow. Judging by the declassified biographies of the KGB officers, his full name was Nikolai Nikolaevich Kravchenko. He was a lieutenant colonel in the KGB and served as the assistant to the head of the KGB émigré department, Colonel Ishchenko.

Fabrichnikov, an ethnic Russian, had fought the Germans as a Red Army soldier and joined the NKVD after the war. One of his first assignments had been to help root out the Polish underground in Ukraine. He then switched to working against Ukrainian émigré groups, first in Czechoslovakia and then in Germany. There his targets had included the Munich-based and US-funded stations Radio Liberty and Radio Free Europe, which broadcast across the Iron Curtain. Fabrichnikov had first gone to Berlin in February 1954, and by 1957 had been identified by the CIA Berlin station as a KGB officer.

Fabrichnikov left for Moscow in October 1959, the same month in which Stashinsky assassinated Bandera. A rumor making its way through the Karlshorst KGB offices said that Major Fabrichnikov, who was considered one of the leading experts on the emigration, had opposed the assassination of Bandera on the grounds that it would only turn him into a martyr. Whatever Fabrichnikov's thoughts on the subject, he said nothing about it to Stashinsky. The successful assassination meant awards and promotions not only for Stashinsky but also for the KGB officers involved in the operation. Nikolai Kravchenko, the man with whom Fabrichnikov and Stashinsky celebrated the occasion, was awarded the highest KGB decoration, "Distinguished Member of the KGB," on the same day that Stashinsky got his own order. The chances are good that he was a key figure coordinating the assassination of Bandera from Moscow.[1]

Stashinsky had good reason to celebrate. The road to marriage with Inge Pohl was all but open. In the following days, Stashinsky had a detailed discussion with Kravchenko about how to deal with Inge and her family in Berlin. Before inviting Inge to Moscow, he was supposed to tell her that he was in fact working not for the East German Ministry of Trade, as he had led her to believe, but for the Stasi—the East German Ministry of State Security. His bosses were happy with his work and wanted to give him additional training for work in West Germany. He wanted her to join him in training for that important assignment; then they would go to the West together to work for world peace. The plan was to recruit Inge not only on personal grounds, exploiting her feelings for Stashinsky and her desire to marry him, but also on ideological ones—that is where the idea of struggling for peace came in handy. If Inge agreed to join him in working for the Stasi, he would invite her to Moscow, where he would tell her the truth—or, rather, part of the truth—about their joint future service to the KGB. Stashinsky signed on to the plan.[2]

Inge was happy to see her Joschi back. He had not planned to return before summer, but he had unexpectedly managed to get a few days off for Christmas break, he told her. It was a pleasant surprise. So far she had received just one letter from him, which had been mailed, as far as she could tell, from Warsaw—the city where he had told her he was going when he actually went to Moscow. (He had sent two, but the first letter, which he had turned over to his handlers in Moscow to be mailed from Warsaw, mysteriously disappeared and never reached Berlin.) Stashinsky picked up

Inge after work at the hairdresser's salon, and they spent Christmas Eve in the company of her family in her native village of Dallgow on the border with West Berlin. Everyone at the table was interested in hearing about Joschi's experiences in Warsaw, but he preferred to discuss other topics.

After the holiday dinner, Stashinsky and Inge walked to the house where she was renting a room. On the way he asked her whether anyone had approached her in the past few days and asked her to hold onto a package for safekeeping. Stashinsky was relieved when she said no. He suspected that the KGB would try to trick her into taking a recording machine so that Stashinsky's handlers could spy on the conversation. Sergei Damon had even asked him to tape the conversation he was about to have with Inge. "He explained the reason why he wanted to do that," remembered Stashinsky later, and had said it was "not because they did not trust me." Damon told Stashinsky that if there was a recording, they could help him understand what Inge really thought: "Given my close relations with my fiancée, I might not always understand her responses correctly, while he would understand them well." But clearly, the KGB did not entirely trust its star agent.[3]

William Hood, the Munich CIA station chief at the time of the Bandera assassination, later wrote that the task of handlers everywhere was to maneuver their agent "into a position where there is nothing that he can hold back—not the slightest scrap of information, nor the most intimate detail of his personal life." "Whatever his motives may be," he wrote, "the role of a spy is to betray trust. A man who has volunteered, or been tapped, to commit treason cannot logically ever be trusted again. . . . Whatever reservations an agent may have when he signs on, the fact is that when an intelligence service buys a spy, it buys him *in toto*. No espionage service can tolerate the merest whiff of independence or reserve on the part of an agent. For the spy, espionage is a one-way street."[4]

Stashinsky's KGB bosses were clearly following the international espionage handbook, but their star agent would not go along. In the course of his years with the KGB, Stashinsky had learned how to deal with his handlers. The best way to say no, in his experience, was to agree enthusiastically with the proposal in principle but then raise objective factors that made it difficult or impossible to carry out a particular assignment. With Damon, Stashinsky enthusiastically embraced the idea of taping his conversation with Inge, but then pointed out that unfortunately the signal from the listening device could be picked up at a distance no greater than two hundred meters. To make the plan work, a van with listening equipment would have to be parked near the Pohl family home, which was at a significant distance from other buildings. That would be sure to arouse suspicion. Damon had to agree with Stashinsky's reasoning. His conversation with Inge would not be taped.

Stashinsky started with a personal confession. He told Inge that he had been deceiving her about his identity. He was not Josef Lehmann, he said. In fact, he was not even German. He was a Russian. She was shocked and perplexed. He would later say that she reacted as if she had "fallen out of the sky." He recalled: "I tried to soften the blow by saying that I was not actually Russian but Ukrainian." It was a calculated move. Many Germans saw the Russians as traditional enemies and now occupiers, but they saw the Ukrainians as one of the East European peoples held captive by the Soviets. By now he was in clear violation of all the instructions he had received from the KGB both in Moscow and at Karlshorst. He had blown the Lehmann cover and revealed his true identity. Instead of giving her the Stasi story, Stashinsky told Inge that he was working for the KGB and had come to Berlin not from Warsaw but from Moscow. There he had seen the head of the KGB himself, who had given his approval for their marriage. She was the first non-Soviet woman to be allowed to marry a KGB agent. The catch was that she would have to join the KGB.[5]

Inge burst into tears. Her wartime experiences had made her anything but friendly to the Russians, or to Soviets in general, for that matter. Her father, Fritz Pohl, had been drafted into the German Army, and in early 1945, fearing the coming Soviet attack on Berlin, Inge and her mother had moved to the town of Feldberg in Mecklenburg, northeast of the capital. Feldberg ended up in the Soviet sphere of occupation. The new Soviet-appointed mayor of the city was the renowned antifascist German writer

Hans Fallada, who praised the Soviet occupation and the new regime in his novels. The Soviets loved to quote one of his complimentary remarks: "I was astounded by the Russian people. . . . Where and when has a conquering army ever been known to be so kind and generous to a conquered people?"

The actual situation was very different from its portrayal in Fallada's novels. Inge remembered the mass rape of women in Feldberg by soldiers of the victorious Red Army. "The worst were the Mongols," she recalled later, "who wore Cossack hats and had little whips in their hands." She was probably referring to Soviet soldiers recruited from the Central Asian steppes and southern Siberia—the "Asiatics," who were portrayed as subhuman in Nazi propaganda. Now it seemed that they were doing their best to prove Joseph Goebbels right. Inge's mother had been raped three times. "No woman was spared," remembered Inge. Many women took their own lives. But Inge and her mother had survived the ordeal. On Christmas Eve 1945, Fritz Pohl came home. He had been released from a British POW camp. But he was in for a surprise: earlier that year, Inge's mother had given birth to a son, also named Fritz. The elder Fritz's war experiences had done little to turn him into a supporter of the new regime. "The Pohl family were by no means Russophiles but rather viewed the Russian occupation as hostile," recalled Stashinsky later. Inge's father made no secret of his feelings, especially when he got drunk. His views became public when he was mentioned by name in one of the local newspapers. He did not seem to care very much. "He always carried the newspaper cutting about with him and showed it with great pride when conversation was on that subject," remembered Stashinsky.[6]

After listening to Stashinsky, Inge was not only shocked—she was horrified. She did not care that these were the "words and conditions" of his superiors, and not what he himself wanted. She told Stashinsky immediately that he must be out of his mind to propose such things, being perfectly well aware of her attitude toward the communist system. "That's fine," answered Stashinsky. "But if we are going to live together, come what may, you have to do this. You have to act as if you accept their proposals and agree to cooperate." Inge was not prepared to give up on him or the prospect of their marriage, but neither was she about to join the KGB.

She had a better plan for both of them: they should flee immediately to the West. With Dallgow a few miles away from West Berlin, that seemed a reasonable thing to suggest. But Stashinsky refused to go along. "I told her," he remembered later, "that I could not do it now, but that possibility remained open to us in the future. We should play for time." Stashinsky believed that the training he was about to get in Moscow would greatly help him when it came time to establish their life in the West. "I knew that after the new training I would again be sent to West Germany or to another West European country," he said, recalling his thoughts at the time. He told Inge that his future assignment in the West had already been decided.

It was a long talk. Inge eventually calmed down. Stashinsky told her that she would not become a true KGB employee and that he would do everything in his power to shield her from taking on any KGB assignments. All that was required was that she play a role. He told her a good deal about himself, but nothing about the nature of his work for the KGB or the assassinations he had carried out. He was not concerned that she would inadvertently betray him, but he thought it best for her own safety that she know nothing about the assassinations. Eventually Inge agreed to play the role he had assigned her for their forthcoming trip to Moscow—that of a Soviet sympathizer willing to help her future husband in his difficult but honorable work on behalf of world peace.

"So we came to an agreement," remembered Stashinsky, "and I warned her that everything we had discussed must be between ourselves. I told her she must not only say nothing in Moscow about what we had discussed but that for the present she mustn't say anything to her parents—we must keep to the old 'legend.' She agreed to this."[7]

21

INTRODUCING THE BRIDE

On January 9, 1960, Stashinsky and Inge boarded a train to Moscow. In their pockets were Soviet passports provided by Sergei Damon. A few days earlier, Damon had asked Inge for a photo, and now she had in her purse a brand-new Soviet passport issued in the name of Inga Fedorovna Krylova. Stashinsky, as always, traveled on the passport of Aleksandr Antonovich Krylov. While Stashinsky and Inge were not yet married, the Krylovs were. In Moscow a KGB officer picked them up and took them to the Hotel Ukraine, where Stashinsky had stayed during his first visit to Moscow in April 1959. But he was not supposed to show familiarity with the hotel or the city. His KGB bosses wanted him to tell Inge that he was in Moscow for the first time and that the trip was a reward for his good work for East German intelligence.

Stashinsky's KGB bosses were working hard to assess his fiancée. Arkadii Fabrichnikov, the KGB officer who escorted the couple on their sightseeing and shopping tours in the city, wanted to know what she thought about Moscow and Soviet life in general. He asked her opinion about everything she saw. Inge was not supposed to know that he was a KGB man, although it was hard not to guess his identity, given his constant presence. She played the role of an excited tourist rather well, but privately she asked Stashinsky from time to time whether she was supposed to show familiarity with a particular detail or not. The KGB tried to keep tabs on the couple whenever their officially assigned escort was not around. Their belongings in the Hotel Ukraine were searched. Stashinsky also suspected that the room in the Hotel Moscow—to which they had moved from the Hotel Ukraine at the KGB's insistence—had been bugged. In Stashinsky's presence, Fabrichnikov had quarreled for a while with a hotel clerk who wanted to give the couple the "wrong" room.[1]

Inge, who was reluctant to travel in the first place, was anything but impressed by the reception they received. In fact, she was terrified by what she saw around her. At the railway station in Warsaw, where the train stopped on the way to Moscow, she already felt trapped, betrayed, and all but sold into slavery. That feeling only grew stronger in Moscow. Stashinsky and his KGB handlers showed her masterpieces of tsarist architecture and marble decorations in the Soviet subway stations, but she was shocked by the contrast between the magnificent decor of the buildings and the poorly dressed people inside of them. Images of impoverished women wearing thick headscarves, calico coats, and felt boots, carrying bags full of bread on their backs, became forever engraved in her memory. Then there were the drunks, who seemed to be everywhere, often congregating in subway stations and taking refuge from the cold in the marble halls of the buildings. Those who did not make it there lay unattended in the snow in freezing temperatures.

Inge found the sanitary conditions in the Soviet capital utterly appalling. The trash cans were full and always dirty, so one had to be careful not to brush against them. People would spit everywhere. She called the toilets a "public tragedy." Some of them were nothing more than holes in the ground, surrounded by filth, emitting a terrible smell. "I cannot think about toilets. Terrible!" she would confide to a journalist a few years later. The KGB handlers' efforts to charm her and make her appreciate Moscow and the Soviet way of life were futile. She found both Arkadii Fabrichnikov, whom she knew as "Alexander," and his wife (or the woman who pretended to be his wife), whom she called a "German-hater," pretentious. At an expensive restaurant dinner to which Stashinsky and Inge were invited, Mrs.

Fabrichnikov seemed barely to touch a plate full of caviar and other delicacies, saying that people generally believed Russian women to be overweight because they ate too much. It seemed that nothing could please Inge. Even the local children looked unattractive to her. She was depressed and often cried.[2]

Stashinsky and Inge spent two months in the USSR, mostly in Moscow, with a two-week trip to Leningrad, and had plenty of opportunities to compare the realities of Soviet life with the image presented by official propaganda. A few days after their arrival in Moscow, Nikita Khrushchev delivered a long address to the Soviet parliament in which he boasted about Soviet economic achievements compared to those of the United States. Between 1953 and 1959, he pointed out, Soviet production of pig iron and steel had grown by 57 percent, while American production had dropped by 16 percent. This "achievement" actually indicated that the Soviet Union was stuck in pre–World War II economic thinking. To Khrushchev, however, it was evidence of Soviet superiority.

Sputnik and the other Soviet successes in outer space were regarded as further proof that the Soviets were winning the technological race with the United States. This was the point that Khrushchev tried to make in July 1959 in his "kitchen debate" with the American vice president, Richard Nixon, who visited Moscow to open an American exhibition there. The debate took place on the exhibition grounds in a kitchen fully equipped with new American appliances. Khrushchev told Nixon that the Soviet Union was more technologically advanced than the United States and that the US advantage in the production of consumer goods would be obliterated in seven years. The debate was shown on television more than once in the United States, but only once, very late at night, in the Soviet Union. The Soviet authorities did not want the viewers to see the head of their country admitting that it was behind the capitalist West in anything.[3]

It is unlikely that Inge ever heard of the kitchen debate, which took place six months before her arrival in Moscow. There can be little doubt, however, that she took anything Khrushchev said on the subject with a hefty grain of salt. When she was alone with Stashinsky, she was not shy about noting the yawning gap between official pronouncements and the realities of Soviet life. Earlier in their relationship, Stashinsky had taken to defending the official Soviet line, but by now he was running out of arguments. "You will come to your senses," she used to tell him. "It's all quite different from what you have beaten into your head." He knew that she was right.

Before Stashinsky received final approval to speak with Inge about his involvement with the KGB, his bosses had made a last attempt to persuade him to drop her. The task was taken on by Colonel Georgii Ishchenko, the head of the émigré department of the KGB foreign intelligence directorate. Ishchenko asked Stashinsky whether he still wanted to marry Inge. Upon Stashinsky's positive response, he told him, "Take care that in future you do not regret having made such a decision." He then told Stashinsky that he could now talk to Inge about his involvement—and subsequently, hers— with the KGB. In Moscow, as previously in East Berlin, the KGB wanted to listen in on the conversation. Ishchenko asked Stashinsky to talk to Inge in the room in which they were conversing, where no one would eavesdrop. Stashinsky knew that the room was bugged. He later told his KGB handlers that he had been forced to have the conversation elsewhere. But Inge, he reported happily, had been informed about his involvement with the KGB and was ready to help him in his work.[4]

Inge's agreement to cooperate, which Stashinsky relayed to his bosses in late February, was supposed to clear the way for their return to East Berlin and eventual marriage. But there were nerve-wracking delays. The KGB ordered Stashinsky to return the tickets he had already bought for Berlin and extended the term of their exit visas. Stashinsky and Inge began to worry. Had the KGB figured out what they were up to? At Inge's urging, Stashinsky finally decided that they would have to leave Moscow without KGB approval. But as soon as he began to inquire about air tickets to Berlin, permission to leave Moscow was granted. On the eve of March 8, International Women's Day, which was widely and lavishly celebrated in the Soviet Union, Arkadii Fabrichnikov showed up in Stashinsky's suite in the company of another senior officer, who handed Inge a box of sweets and greeted her on the occasion of the holiday. The officer also told her they had been granted permission to marry. The ceremony would take place in East Germany. There was, however, one further condition: the couple would have to come back to Moscow for Stashinsky to undergo a year of further training. Inge wept.[5]

The couple returned to Berlin on March 9, 1960, two months to the day after their arrival in the Soviet capital. They had played their parts admirably and achieved their goal. The wedding took place on April 23, 1960. They first registered their marriage at the East Berlin central records office, and then, against KGB advice and without the knowledge of Stashinsky's Karlshorst handlers, had a religious wedding at the Golgotha Evangelical Church on Borsigstrasse—a late nineteenth-century red brick Gothic-style building that had miraculously survived the Allied bombing of Berlin. In Moscow, the KGB officials had told him to proceed with the religious ceremony only if a refusal would lead to a breach with his in-laws. But he never tried to dissuade Inge from a church wedding. "I wanted everything to be as it should be," he remembered later. "I knew, too, that it would make my very religious parents happy." Stashinsky was keeping a growing number of secrets from his KGB controllers.

At the reception that followed, Inge wore a white dress and a wedding headpiece with a veil. Stashinsky was dressed in a black suit with a white shirt and white tie. In the photo taken at the wedding table, they both looked content, if less than exuberant. Inge had accidentally closed her eyes, as if recalling the stressful events of the last few months. Stashinsky looked straight at the camera, appearing more resolute and determined than happy. Inge's grandmother had died on that day, but her relatives postponed sending a telegram. They wanted her to be happy on her wedding day.[6]

22

MONTH OF THE SPY

Stashinsky and Inge left Berlin for Moscow on May 9, 1960, the fifteenth anniversary of the Nazi surrender at Karlshorst. Inge later recalled that instead of going on a honeymoon, they traveled to the Soviet Union—the greatest nightmare she could imagine. They made a stopover in Warsaw, where they had told Inge's relatives they were going to live. An officer from the local KGB station supplied Stashinsky with Polish postcards and stamps, as well as with a price list of products and consumer goods. Inge's thirteen-year-old brother, Fritz, had asked for the postcards and stamps. The prices were needed to convincingly lie to Inge's relatives about everyday life in Warsaw. The couple would use a Warsaw address provided by the KGB—the letters were to be picked up there and delivered to Moscow. Inge and Stashinsky's letters to Berlin would be sent in envelopes with Warsaw postmarks. They told her unsuspecting relatives that they would be back in a year.

At the Warsaw railway station in Moscow, Stashinsky and Inge were met by the ever-present and polite Arkadii Fabrichnikov, who introduced them to their new case officer, Sergei Bogdanovich Sarkisov. The KGB was kind enough to provide them with an apartment, but Inge saw it as anything but a gift. The apartment was in a new construction complex with no paved road leading to it, or even a pathway. Whenever it rained, their shoes, socks, and clothes were covered with mud. The apartment was, at best, a work in progress. The parquet floor was installed in a way that made tar come up between the pieces of wood; traces of tar also covered the tiles in the washroom. The floors were uneven, making the table, chairs, and cabinets wiggle; the toilet pipe was not properly adjusted; the door to the kitchen would not move; and a window did not close properly, allowing water to seep over to the ceiling when it rained. Last but not least, Inge hated the wallpaper. "The wallpaper you see in Russia makes you dizzy," she remembered later.

What Inge saw when she left her apartment depressed her as much as the interior. In the hallways, she would try to avoid stepping on the fish and chicken heads scattered all over the place. Sunflower seeds were everywhere, and no one ever tried to sweep or mop the common areas. It seemed that everyone in the apartment building had a cat, and the cats would all be let out at night to start their wailing, which made it hard for Inge to sleep. If it wasn't the cats, then it was the neighbors, who threw raucous parties late into the night, shaking the light fixtures in her apartment. Life became an endless nightmare, and Inge seemed to be reaching the end of her rope. She was not shy about making her displeasure known to Stashinsky and his KGB handlers alike. They tried to save the situation by moving the couple into a different apartment, this time in a well-established area close to the city center. It was a positive change but came too late to alter Inge's overall attitude toward the Soviet way of life.[1]

The Stashinskys' new home was located in the northern subdivision of Ostankino, which was inhabited predominantly by blue-collar workers and their families. In the mid-1960s, a monument to the Conquerors of the Cosmos was erected in the area, and many of its streets were given cosmos-related names. One was renamed Star Avenue (Zvezdnyi bulvar), while another was named for Sergei Korolev, the chief designer of Sputnik and the first Soviet rockets, and yet another for Friedrich Zander, a pioneer of rocket science. By the end of the 1960s, the area was also home to the Ostankino Television Center and tower, which for some time was the tallest free-standing structure in the world.[2]

Stashinsky and Inge could get home from downtown Moscow by taking the subway to the Exhibition of the Achievements of the Soviet Economy station. The nearby exhibition, with its fountain surrounded by statues of young women dressed in national costumes and representing the union of Soviet republics, was a showcase not only of the Soviet "friendship of peoples," but also of Soviet technological progress. Soviet and foreign visitors alike could judge for themselves how accurately the innovations displayed at the exhibition represented the realities of everyday Soviet life. Inge had learned from her first visit to Moscow that the difference was enormous. The Russian dissident writer Aleksandr Zinoviev would later dwell on the gap between propaganda and reality in his novel *The Yawning Heights*, a satire on the "shining heights" of Soviet propaganda campaigns.

Stashinsky's days as an employee of the émigré department were over. He was now officially under the auspices of the illegals department. Inge found his new handler, Sergei Sarkisov, a KGB operative in his early thirties, much more affable than Fabrichnikov. Sarkisov also spoke better German, which he had allegedly picked up from talking to a West German capitalist friend. Sarkisov explained to Stashinsky that his training would include individual lessons with a tutor of German and English, going over the German school curriculum, and reading the latest Western literature so as to blend into his new environment successfully. He would also take radio and photography classes. The training of candidates for illegal work abroad was a task that the KGB took very seriously. "The Soviet investment in each illegal agent is immense," wrote the onetime Munich CIA base chief William Hood. According to Hood, the KGB used illegals to "handle agents too sensitive to risk placing in contact with case officers under legal cover in an embassy. Other illegals serve[d] primarily as communications experts, conduits for information being funneled to Moscow from agents in place."

That was indeed one of the tasks that Stashinsky's boss, General Aleksei Krokhin, had suggested that he would perform in the future. But he also told his star agent that he would continue to carry out assassinations. Stashinsky was learning to become an illegal of a sort unknown to Hood—an

assassin in deep cover living in a Western country who could strike on relatively short notice whenever and wherever his KGB bosses and their Kremlin overlords deemed appropriate. It was decided that he would be trained
as a barber so that the two of them, Stashinsky and Inge, could open a bar-
bershop as a cover for their espionage activities. Stashinsky was offered a
choice of two countries for his future work: Switzerland or England. He decided on Switzerland. Inge did not care where they went, as long as she
could escape her virtual imprisonment in Moscow.[3]

In May 1960, the month Stashinsky and Inge arrived in Moscow for
their training, Soviet rocket scientists finally caught up with American
technology. On May 1, International Workers' Day, the Soviet high-altitude
S-75 Dvina rocket, fired by a missile battery near the city of Sverdlovsk
(Ekaterinburg) in the Ural Mountains, downed an American Lockheed
U-2 high-altitude reconnaissance aircraft piloted by thirty-two-year-old
Captain Francis Gary Powers of the CIA special air force unit. Powers survived the ordeal, but so did the parts of the plane that contained high-
resolution cameras and the photos they had taken. The Soviets captured
the downed pilot and collected what was left of the plane.

The Americans had been caught red-handed spying on the Soviet
Union, although they were not immediately aware of it. President Dwight
Eisenhower initially believed that Powers had died in the incident; he authorized a statement denying Soviet accusations of espionage and claiming
that the lost aircraft was a weather research plane. Khrushchev, under
growing pressure at home for being soft on the Americans, felt that he had
no choice but to cancel his participation in the forthcoming Paris summit
on the status of Berlin. He also withdrew the invitation that he had earlier
issued to Eisenhower to visit the USSR in June, causing an international
scandal of unprecedented proportions.[4]

In the aftermath of the canceled summit and the humiliating U-2 incident, the White House and the CIA launched a damage-control campaign,
trying to prove to the world that spying was a normal aspect of international relations: the Soviet nuclear arsenal could not be left unassessed and
unchecked. They also claimed that the Soviet Union was more guilty of

spying than the United States was. Secretary of State Christian A. Herter told Congress that there were approximately 300,000 Soviet agents working in twenty-seven countries around the world. Between 10,000 and 12,000 of them were so-called "master agents." The authorities in the Federal Republic of Germany provided their own statistics on the matter. In eight years they had made 18,300 arrests in connection with Soviet espionage activities, declared the West Germans in the wake of the U-2 scandal.[5]

In May, Soviet newspapers were preoccupied not only with the international crisis caused by the downing of the U-2 airplane but also with the East German trial of the West German federal minister Theodor Oberländer, whom Soviet and East European sources were linking to the Bandera assassination. On April 28, 1960, Oberländer was sentenced in absentia to life imprisonment for his alleged participation in the murders of Jewish citizens of Lviv in June 1941. The next month he resigned his post in the West German government. Despite earlier Soviet and East German assertions, the killing of Stepan Bandera was not mentioned among his alleged crimes.

The KGB left it to their counterparts in the West to speculate on the forces behind the murder. In the media frenzy following the U-2 incident, the West German government claimed publicly that a KGB officer visiting West Germany had bragged that his organization was the one responsible for killing Bandera. The KGB misinformation department was silent. Moscow seemed to have lost all interest in the topic.[6]

23

GOING IN CIRCLES

s Bogdan Stashinsky undertook his training in Moscow, the murder he had committed in Munich on October 15, 1959, was rapidly turning into a cold case. By the end of the year, Oberkommissar Adrian Fuchs of the Munich Kripo had interviewed close to a hundred individuals who might know something about the circumstances of Bandera's death, but he was as far from cracking the case as he had been in mid-October.

There was no shortage of theories, but evidence was lacking to prove any of them. In December 1959, Professor Wolfgang Laves of Munich University and his associates came up with the final autopsy results concerning the individual they were still calling Stefan Popel. The new results were as inconclusive as those produced in October. There were traces of cyanide in Bandera's stomach, but no certainty about whether he had ingested an amount sufficient to kill him. One hypothesis was that Bandera could have been killed by one poison, while another (cyanide) might have been applied later to throw the investigation off track. In February 1960, CIA and BND experts were still arguing about the kind of poison involved.[1]

On May 2, 1960, the chief of the CIA base in Munich dispatched a long-delayed report on the CIA investigation into Bandera's death to headquarters in Langley. It was compiled by Father Michael (Mykhailo) Korzhan, the principal CIA agent dealing with Ukrainian émigré circles in

Europe from 1947 to 1961. He had come to Munich at the invitation not only of the CIA but also of his former disciple in the art of espionage, Ivan Kashuba, now the Bandera organization's security chief.

In the hierarchy of Ukrainian nationalist security cadres, Father Korzhan, an ordained Orthodox priest from Galicia, was second to none. Myron Matviyeyko, Bandera's security chief, had taken his first steps in counterintelligence training under Korzhan's supervision back in 1940. He later characterized his former chief to KGB interrogators as "a highly experienced agent." Korzhan was respected and trusted on both sides of the nationalist divide. A longtime member of the Organization of Ukrainian Nationalists, he was officially part of the Bandera faction but refused to take sides in the struggle between Bandera and Lebed. Many believed that, if anything, he was closer to the opposition than to Bandera's people. At the same time, rumor had it that he was so close to Ivan Kashuba that he drafted Kashuba's reports to the OUN leadership.[2]

In Munich, Kashuba offered Father Korzhan all the intelligence support he and his people could provide. He knew that Korzhan had extensive connections in the intelligence world and was probably working for the BND. Kashuba was equally sure that whatever conclusions Korzhan drew from his investigation would be shared with his American handlers, who were suspicious of Kashuba's motives and actions. Indeed, when Korzhan came to Munich, he arrived with a mandate from the CIA to draft a report on the investigation he was about to conduct.

As the CIA's man in charge of contacts with the Ukrainian community, Korzhan collected information about the community at large, gathered intelligence about the USSR, and worked to prevent Soviet penetration of émigré organizations and churches. He had his own budget and a number of "spotters" who identified possible contacts among Ukrainian émigrés traveling to the Soviet Union or living with relatives there. The number of code names that the CIA created and used to identify Father Korzhan was impressive, attesting to the role he played in a whole series of agency projects: Capelin 1, Aecapelin 1, Aebath 1, Aecassowary 29, and Petroclus were among those names. His Gehlen Organization numbers were V 9460.9 and V-13611.[3]

Korzhan arrived in the Bavarian capital sometime in early November 1959—he wrote in his CIA report that he was on the spot less than a month after Bandera's death—and he stayed there until January 1960 before returning to Paris. While in Munich, Korzhan interviewed many leaders and rank-and-file members of the Bandera group and had two meetings with Oberkommissar Fuchs, the primary investigator of Bandera's death. The report was prepared in Ukrainian and then translated into English. The main report is dated December 23, 1959, but Korzhan supplied a number of additions and amendments to it in January 1960 before leaving for France.[4]

In the report, entitled "Delving Behind the Scenes of the Death of Stepan Bandera," Korzhan not only presented the facts he managed to uncover and the rumors he heard in Munich but also provided a thorough analysis. Of all the accounts of Bandera's death that he heard in Munich, he found five "more or less logical." He discussed all five in detail, listing pros and cons in his report. The first version blamed the death of Bandera on Bundesminister Theodor Oberländer and Reinhard Gehlen's people; the second suggested that he had been killed by the KGB for his continuing involvement in the nationalist insurgency in Ukraine; the third pointed a finger at Bandera's former chief of security, Myron Matviyeyko; the fourth blamed Mykola Lebed, the head of the anti-Bandera forces in the OUN; and the fifth suggested that Bandera had committed suicide by taking cyanide. "Each of these versions had some plausibility," wrote Korzhan, "and at first there was so much basis for each one that it was possible to accept any of the versions as true."[5]

Korzhan believed that the version being touted in East Germany's newspapers, implicating Oberländer, was nonsense. The Soviet-backed campaign in East Germany accusing Oberländer of complicity in the Lviv massacres and then in Bandera's murder was likely retaliation for the minister's resistance to Soviet requests that West Germany grant diplomatic recognition to the communist governments of Poland and Czechoslovakia. Also, Oberländer simply had no real motive. "The Soviet version is primitive," wrote Korzhan, "and does not stand up against criticism because: If Bandera was a participant in the Lviv murders, or more specifically the

Nachtigall, which was organized at his request, then it is clear that he could only have defended Prof. Oberländer in order to protect himself."[6]

Among those investigating the case, there were two versions of the theory that Bandera had been assassinated by KGB agents. According to the first, poison had been administered to Bandera by force in the hall of his apartment building; the second posited that it had been slipped to Bandera by someone close to him. The first scenario was favored by Bandera loyalists, who claimed that two strangers had been seen in his apartment building prior to his death. The strangers had allegedly followed Bandera in the days leading up to his death, shadowing him even on his trip to the mountains to pick mushrooms, and on October 15 they had hidden in the elevator, awaiting their victim there. The Kripo investigation, wrote Korzhan, found that the original reports of two people in the building before Bandera's death were unsubstantiated and could not be confirmed by neighbors, who heard no sound in the hallway from anyone other than Bandera himself. The rumors about the two strangers had been disseminated by the Banderites themselves, as they helped to glorify the story of their leader's heroic death.

The Kripo investigators paid much more attention to the theory that the poison had been administered by someone close to Bandera who was secretly a Soviet agent—a version staunchly rejected by the Banderites, who tried to prevent Fuchs from talking to members of their organization, and encouraged him to focus his investigation on finding an outside murderer. Korzhan, who had much better access to members of the organization than Fuchs, was able to reconstruct the last day of Bandera's life minute by minute. Eugenia Mak (Matviyeyko) was at the top of both Fuchs's and Korzhan's list of "insider" suspects, but neither of them believed that she had administered the poison. With the original reports about the sighting of two men in Bandera's apartment building dismissed, it was hard to imagine who could have been using her to finger the victim.

Korzhan did not exclude the possibility that the Soviets might have been putting pressure on Eugenia through her husband, Myron Matviyeyko, but he found no evidence that Matviyeyko had visited Munich before Bandera's death. The theory of Soviet involvement in Bandera's death in any of its versions made no sense to him. Neither did that of Lebed's involvement. Korzhan, who knew the Lebed people in Munich very well, argued that there was simply no one in place to successfully undertake such a mission.

With four hypotheses about Bandera's death dismissed, Korzhan focused on the fifth—that Bandera had committed suicide. That theory was advocated by Korzhan's Munich host, Ivan Kashuba, and Korzhan agreed that it was the most logical of the lot. But Korzhan had his own theories about Bandera's motive for suicide. While Kashuba believed, or at least argued, that Bandera had been driven to suicide by unrequited love, Korzhan suggested that the cause was the unbearable psychological situation at home.

"As a result of some very difficult experience in her life, and for fear of constant surveillance, Bandera's wife had practically lost all her senses," wrote Korzhan:

> If it weren't for the fact that she was the wife of the leader . . . she would have been in an insane asylum a year ago. All of Bandera's friends knew about her situation. . . . Bandera's wife purposefully compromised his every move. She made him appear without any character, a despot, a sadist, a liar amoral and dishonorable. . . . Bandera, who considered himself a hero, and perhaps was one, and an individual who enjoyed the respect of the members of his organization and to whom he was a "god," had to bear the slander and accusations made by his wife, who saw him only as a human being, her husband and the father of her children. This was more than he could stand. The people who were acquainted with this situation felt that these tortures (for which he often was personally to blame) were so horrible that any normal individual would have committed suicide long ago.

Korzhan suggested that Bandera had committed suicide by taking potassium cyanide, purposefully choosing a time that might enhance his image as a folk hero. By committing suicide when a Soviet choir was performing in Munich, and his own security service was concerned about Moscow's plans to eliminate him, Bandera made it almost inevitable that his death would be blamed on the Soviets. The information in support of this "most logical" version of Bandera's death, as Korzhan termed it, came from Ivan Kashuba, who knew Bandera's family situation firsthand.

Korzhan was so certain of his hypothesis that he put his reputation, and, indeed, his intelligence career, on the line when he wrote in his report: "If anyone proves to me that the situation was other than that which I have summarized above, I shall never again take any interest in either political or intelligence work. However, I am certain that no one will prove me wrong. I think that the German Commission which is composed of professional individuals will come to the same conclusion, even though all the information that was available to me will not be available to them."[7]

Despite Korzhan's best efforts to convince his CIA bosses that Bandera had committed suicide, the CIA believed that Bandera had been killed by the Soviets. Both the Gehlen Organization people and their CIA counterparts now considered not only Korzhan's theories, but also Korzhan himself, highly suspicious. The former felt that his "reporting on Bandera's death amounted to deliberate whitewash." The latter had "various reservations about his bona fides" and dropped Korzhan as their agent in 1961. The firing of Korzhan had little effect on the case. The investigation into Bandera's death remained stalled. It looked as if Bogdan Stashinsky had added one more name to the Soviet Union's list of clandestine achievements that would successfully remain secret. And in his line of work, keeping a secret was no less important than getting the job done.[8]

PART IV

ESCAPE FROM PARADISE

24

MOSCOW BUGS

Bogdan Stashinsky's stay in Moscow led to a personal awakening, but not the kind that the KGB had been hoping for. Among the books given to him for translation as part of his language lessons, one left a strong impression on him. "It was a book intended for Germans resettling elsewhere—I don't recall its title now—that summarized information about living conditions in North and South America, Africa, and Europe as well," he recalled later. "I translated it, and that became my first rather detailed acquaintance with living conditions in other countries: on the other hand, I knew living conditions in Moscow, made comparisons, and always calculated how much workers made there and here. First and foremost, I paid attention not to money but to political and economic structure. I saw the socialist and capitalist systems before me but could hear nothing of people's poverty and suffering, which I knew from experience in Moscow." Now he was able to compare them firsthand, and communism was coming up short.[1]

Moscow enjoyed special status and was much better supplied with consumer goods than other parts of the country. But even there, waiting in long lines for essential food supplies and goods was part of everyday life. The year 1960 was relatively good for Soviet industry, but also the second straight year of poor harvests. In 1958 the government had received close to 42 million tons of wheat from the collective farms, but in 1959 the figure was close to 34 million tons and, in 1960, less than 31 million tons. Food shortages became endemic in the USSR around 1960. Robert W. Gibson of the *Los Angeles Times*, who lived in Moscow in the late 1950s, remembered that when he left the Soviet capital in January 1960, "cabbage, frostbitten potatoes, garlic and bread represented winter's staples. An orange or a chunk of meat created an occasion. Life offered few treats."

Many of Gibson's Soviet acquaintances had privileged status, given the fact that they were allowed to deal with foreigners, but they still spent hours in food lines. "And they yearned deeply for material comfort," wrote Gibson later. "Like most Russians, they had suffered much from war, Josef Stalin's terror, and everlasting priorities during peacetime for steel, machine tools and still more weapons. Cynicism saturated their outlook. At times, vodka did, too." The cynicism grew partly out of the enormous gap between the promises given to ordinary Soviet citizens by party propaganda and the hardships of everyday life. "While I was a correspondent [in Moscow]," recalled Gibson, "Khrushchev frequently boasted that the Soviet Union would overtake the United States in industrial production by 1970, surpass it overall by 1980 and leave it in the dust ever after. The Soviet lead in space established by Sputnik and the Lunik moon probes offered credibility."[2]

In 1961 the Soviet Union began buying grain abroad, especially from Canada, to alleviate the food shortage at home. In the following year, food shortages and rising prices for meat and milk caused mass strikes all over the country. In the city of Novocherkassk in southern Russia, workers' strikes turned into riots. Khrushchev dispatched a high-powered delegation that included Aleksandr Shelepin, who had left the KGB the previous year to become a secretary of the party's Central Committee, but the party and state officials failed to alleviate tensions. After the Novocherkassk workers chased the Moscow delegation out of local party headquarters, the army opened fire, killing more than twenty protesters. Khrushchev was anything but lenient toward those who survived. Hundreds were arrested and imprisoned, and seven sentenced to death and executed. The disturbance was keep quiet;

the rest of the country and the world would not learn what had happened in Novocherkassk until the last days of the Soviet Union.[3]

As time passed, Inge began to behave more independently and erratically. She refused to attend lessons in spycraft and became increasingly bold in expressing her dissatisfaction with Soviet conditions. She complained to her husband about the lack of basic foods, including potatoes. Her anti-Soviet sentiments aside, she had to prepare the couple's meals, and there were constant shortages. The empty shelves in Moscow stores and long lines for bare necessities spoke for themselves. She would remember for years how she was unable to reliably obtain the kind of meat she wanted—and was prepared to pay for—in a Soviet grocery store. Moscow lagged embarrassingly behind not only West Berlin, where Inge had worked, but also East Germany, where she had lived.

Inge told Stashinsky that she was puzzled about how a clever person such as he could fall so easily for Soviet propaganda tricks. "One day you will wake up," she said, "and find yourself cured." The cure was a process rather than a onetime event and would come in stages. Reading a German-language book on the life of Admiral Wilhelm Canaris, the chief of Hitler's military intelligence, given to him by his KGB handlers, Stashinsky was forced to conclude that the communist secret police were no better than the Nazi secret police they despised. As he later recalled, "In conversations with my wife, we reached the conclusion that, generally speaking, there was no difference between the Gestapo and what was going on here."[4]

The KGB certainly would not have appreciated such a comparison. Luckily, Stashinsky did everything in his power to keep his conversations with Inge private. Immediately after they moved into the KGB-provided apartment, he checked it for listening devices. He looked in every corner and checked the light fixture but found nothing. Still, he never felt truly secure in his own home. That very month the whole world was reminded of Soviet proficiency at placing bugs in the most unexpected places. In late May 1960, seeking to counter Soviet propaganda in the wake of the downing of the U-2, the US representative to the United Nations, Henry Cabot Lodge, proudly showed members of the Security Council a bug discovered in a wooden replica of the Great Seal of the United States that had been presented to the American ambassador to the USSR back in 1946. The seal had hung in the ambassador's private office at Spaso House—the ambassadorial residence in Moscow—for fourteen years before the bug was discovered by the embassy's security officials. Lodge claimed that more than a hundred similar microphones had been found in official US residences in the Soviet Union and Eastern Europe.[5]

Stashinsky needed no reminder about the KGB's ability to eavesdrop on persons of interest, but he was not a specialist. As he later suggested, he and Inge only found hidden bugs by accident. In late July 1960, for example, soon after he and Inge moved into their second apartment provided by the KGB, Inge took a systematic approach to eradicating the rooms of fleas. After cleaning everything they had, she asked Stashinsky to lift a picture hanging on the wall of one of the rooms. It was a great idea: beneath it they found the fleas' main nest. They also found two wires under the paper coming from different directions and leading through a hole in the wall to the neighboring apartment. Stashinsky immediately recognized that they were being bugged. Inge cried. Fleas were the least of their problems.

"Of course, I was completely stunned by that discovery, but I couldn't do anything about it," remembered Stashinsky later. "My wife just looked at me with sympathy. I kept silent and said nothing at all." Stashinsky and Inge were cautious enough not to betray their discovery by commenting on it immediately. Throughout their stay in Moscow, they tried to discuss politically sensitive matters outside their apartment. But not every conversation could be held outdoors (to do so anyways would arouse suspicion), so they freely exchanged their views on the shortages of food and goods, as well as on the generally dismal situation in the Soviet Union. "It would have been best to return to Berlin, but that was a thought not expressed in words," said Stashinsky, recalling his thoughts of the moment.

Even so, he hoped that what he had found was not what he thought it was. "I discovered a wire, I told myself," remembered Stashinsky later. "But perhaps there was no microphone there; perhaps those were just apprehensions. I didn't want it to be so!" When they were next visited by

Stashinsky's case officer, Sergei Sarkisov, Inge asked him the purpose of the wire in their apartment. Since Stashinsky was bound by the quasi-military discipline of the KGB, they had decided that Inge would be the one to ask the inconvenient questions. Sarkisov had no answer. Wide-eyed, he said that he did not know, but that it could be a telephone wire. He promised to make inquiries and report back to Stashinsky on his findings. He never did. When Inge confronted him with the same question the next time around, Sarkisov said that the person who might know the details was on vacation—they would have to wait.

Stashinsky and Inge could not wait. They were extremely anxious to find out what the KGB knew about their private conversations and wanted the answer as soon as possible. Stashinsky showed the wire to electricians who were making repairs to the building, but they were of no help. So he decided to do his own detection. To find the location of the microphone, he connected one end of the wire to his tape recorder and spoke into it as he walked around the room. Playing back the recording, he could hear his own voice with varying degrees of clarity but was unable to locate the microphone. The KGB technicians were clearly more adept at this aspect of spycraft than he was. And their bosses clearly wanted to continue listening to what was going on in the apartment.

Sarkisov eventually came up with an improbable excuse for the wire in their apartment: the flat had allegedly previously belonged to a shady character, and the bug had been installed in order to keep him under surveillance. Inge later recalled that, according to Sarkisov, that individual had since been arrested. This story, fake or not, was not comforting. Was that the fate in store for her and Stashinsky as well? Stashinsky soon obtained clear evidence that he and Inge were being listened to. One day his handlers told him that instead of Stashinsky reeducating Inge, she was reeducating him. "Now I realized perfectly well with whom I was collaborating," he recalled later. The day Inge had been dreaming of, when Stashinsky would wake up and be cured of his illusions, had finally arrived. But it had come too late and in the wrong city, as far as both of them were concerned.[6]

25

FAMILY

The KGB messenger was in a good mood and asked Inge to dance. It was an old Russian custom that the postman could ask the recipient of a letter for a dance as payment for delivery. The messenger had brought Inge letters from her family, who thought that she and her husband were living in Poland. Her relatives addressed the letters they wrote to her to a Warsaw address controlled by the KGB. Inge was supposed to be pleased and do a couple of pirouettes, but she refused. She was not familiar with the custom and was in no mood to dance. Stashinsky asked the surprised messenger to hand over the letters without the usual dance. The messenger produced the letters—the envelopes had already been opened— and told the Stashinskys that he had had no time to read and translate them. He instead asked the couple to tell him what the letters were about. Now it was Stashinsky's turn to experience culture shock. The KGB was reading their correspondence and not even trying to hide the fact from them.

"My wife and I were angry," recalled Stashinsky later. "I could not contain myself and asked him sharply what this was supposed to mean. Those were our letters, after all. He said that he had not opened the letters; they had come from Poland in that condition. I said that if this kept up, I would have to take measures of some kind. The war had been over for fifteen

years, and I could not allow anyone to open my letters." Stashinsky threatened to complain to his superiors. The KGB messenger was quite taken
aback. What he had done by asking them to tell him the content of the letters, instead of reading them himself, was a breach of KGB protocol and a
clear sign that he trusted them. They obviously did not take it that way.
First there were the wires in their apartment, and now their letters were
being opened. They were outraged and complained to Stashinsky's contacts
in the KGB.

Stashinsky's case officer, Sergei Sarkisov, tried to calm the couple down
once he was briefed on the incident. But his explanations and assurances
were contradictory, at best. On the one hand, he said that the KGB completely trusted Stashinsky; on the other, he admitted that the letters had
been opened in Poland on KGB orders. He told Stashinsky and Inge that
anyone corresponding with foreigners was subject to censorship, and he
himself would not be treated any differently if he were to correspond with
someone in Europe. He was certainly right on that point. The KGB trusted
no one and, like any other intelligence service, tried to keep its agents under complete control. After that, the Stashinskys received their letters in
sealed envelopes. But the people reading them were definitely sloppy, or
simply did not know German well enough. Stashinsky and Inge could not
help noticing that sometimes the letters arrived in the wrong envelopes.
Sarkisov blamed those incidents on the German and Polish authorities,
over whom the KGB allegedly had no control.[1]

With their apartment bugged and their letters opened by their KGB
handlers, Stashinsky and Inge were happy to take a break and leave Moscow for a vacation in the countryside, away from the KGB and its eavesdropping equipment. In late August, they decided to travel to Stashinsky's
home village of Borshchovychi, not far from Lviv in Western Ukraine.
Stashinsky wanted to introduce his young wife to his family: his father,
mother, and two sisters, who still lived in the village. It was easier said than
done. Stashinsky's Moscow handlers did not want Inge to meet Stashinsky's
family or learn his real name. Stashinsky ignored the KGB's advice and insisted on the trip.

They spent almost a month in Borshchovychi, returning to Moscow in late September. Stashinsky told his parents and neighbors that he had met Inge in Moscow, where she was allegedly a university student studying abroad. They had fallen in love and married. Inge made a strong impression on the local women, who envied the well-dressed foreigner from the capital for having won the heart of their handsome neighbor. "The German woman was tall and slender, with her hair cut short," remembered one of the local girls years later. "I see her as if it were yesterday, wearing her polka-dot dress with a broad belt and metal buckle. She was interested in everything but understood nothing; Bogdan translated everything."[2]

Stashinsky's family had never fully forgiven him for his betrayal back in 1950. It had been a shock to the family and their neighbors when Stashinsky had started openly working for the secret police. As the authorities began arresting people in the village linked to the nationalist underground, suspicion naturally fell on Stashinsky. He was accused of killing his sister's fiancé, Ivan Laba, the local underground commander. He had denied the accusations, but it did not help. The relatives of those who were arrested had blamed not only Stashinsky but his entire family for their tragedy. Once popular in the village, the Stashinskys became outcasts. The relatives of those arrested grew increasingly hostile, until the family did not dare to go out after dark and boarded up their windows to prevent break-ins. Stashinsky, whose secret police career had taken him first to Lviv and then to Kyiv, Berlin, and Moscow, could do little to help his family.

In any case, they did not want his help. They did not want to see him. From 1951 to 1954 Stashinsky had no contact with his family. Eventually he managed to restore relations to some extent through his older sister, Iryna. She told him that he could come home. But he would not dare to do so without getting his father's approval first. Stashinsky's father agreed to meet him and gave him permission to return—and only then did he risk showing up in his native village. "Relations changed after all," remembered Stashinsky later. "It was not entirely pleasant." News of the assassination of Stepan Bandera had reached the village of Borshchovychi through Western broadcasts and rumors, but no one in the family could imagine that the person responsible for the death of the symbol of their resistance to the Soviets was their own Bogdan.[3]

Stashinsky's neighbors in Borshchovychi remembered that during their visit to the village, Stashinsky and Inge spent a lot of time walking in the garden. They also traveled to neighboring Lviv for sightseeing. Inge must have felt more at home in Lviv than she did in Moscow, as the city's architecture resembled that of her native Germany. Founded by a Rus' prince in the early thirteenth century, the city fell under Polish control in the fifteenth century and became part of the Habsburg Empire in the eighteenth. Lviv was governed for centuries according to the German town rules, and it was centered on a city hall and a market square around it, like any German town. Its buildings were a mixture of major European architectural styles, from Renaissance to Baroque and Classical. Dominated again by the Poles after the fall of Austria-Hungary in 1918, Lviv, known then as Lwów, was claimed by Stalin at the Yalta Conference for the Soviet Union. By the late 1950s, with the Jews of Lviv exterminated in the Holocaust and the Poles resettled to formerly German areas, Ukrainians became the city's main ethnic group.

Tour guides on the streets of downtown Lviv and in its numerous museums emphasized the Rus' roots of the city, its Ukrainian past, and its allegedly strong links with Russia. They noted brief visits to the city by Tsar Peter I of Russia in the early eighteenth century, when he negotiated with Polish notables in an attempt to build an alliance against Charles XII of Sweden. While Ukrainians indeed had deep roots in the city, most of those whom Inge saw on its streets in August and September 1960 were relatively recent arrivals who had come from nearby villages after the war. Stashinsky was one of the tens of thousands of those who had migrated to Lviv in search of education and better job prospects. It was the city of his youth—he had begun his studies there in a teachers' college back in the late 1940s. Two of his victims had also spent much of their youth there: Stepan Bandera studied agriculture, while Lev Rebet and his wife, Daria, studied law. Stashinsky had no way of knowing that, and, if he had known, he would not have told Inge, who still had no idea what services he had performed for the KGB.[4]

Among the many subjects that Stashinsky and Inge must have discussed while walking the streets of the ancient city and the gardens of Borshcho-vychi, away from KGB listening devices, was their future as a family. Inge was pregnant—a fact that the couple was hiding from the KGB. But once Stashinsky and Inge returned to Moscow in late September, they learned that the KGB wires were clearly doing their job and had betrayed at least that secret to their superiors.

On the day after the Stashinskys returned from Ukraine, Sarkisov raised the subject. He began indirectly, saying that people in their situation should have no secrets from their superiors, even if they concerned personal mat-ters. Stashinsky got the message: the KGB knew about the pregnancy. He quickly "volunteered" that information to Sarkisov. The KGB officer did not look surprised. When Inge asked Sarkisov how he knew that she was pregnant, he told her: "There are no secrets from the KGB." He told the couple that giving birth to a child would delay or derail altogether the plans that the KGB had made for them. He asked whether the Stashinskys wanted to keep the baby or have an abortion. It was an easy and routine thing to do in the Soviet Union, he explained to Inge.

Both Stashinsky and Inge told their handler that they were keeping the baby. He did not argue with them, but that was not the end of the matter. Sarkisov soon came back and insisted on the abortion. "Although it was not formulated as an order, he said quite clearly that it would be better if my wife consented to an abortion." Stashinsky and Inge would not budge, but this time Stashinsky took the lead in saying no to the KGB. As he had be-fore, he came up with an explanation for why a KGB suggestion was good in principle but impossible in practice. Inge had had difficulties with child-bearing before, he said, and a doctor had told her that she would require an operation to be able to give birth in the future. Her current pregnancy was nothing short of miraculous, and they were very glad that it had happened without an operation. They could not risk an abortion under those circumstances.

Sarkisov gave up on the idea of abortion but soon came back with a new proposal—that Inge put the newborn child into a foster home. She protested vehemently, but he told her that it was an honor to give a child to the country and the community. Inge collapsed, and Stashinsky exploded. Sarkisov realized that he had crossed the line. The KGB eventually relented, and the Stashinskys were allowed to have their baby. Furthermore, to make amends, the KGB unexpectedly gave Stashinsky a 20,000-ruble bonus—a major sum by the standards of the time—to buy furniture. Sarkisov escorted Stashinsky to a bank to withdraw the money and then to a furniture store, where he used his KGB connections to secure the purchases.[5]

26

CHANGE OF PLANS

Everything changed for Stashinsky after he and Inge decided to keep the baby. His language lessons came to a halt—Elvira Mikhailovna, the KGB star teacher of German who had also been lecturing Stashinsky on German history, geography, and etiquette, suddenly disappeared. Sarkisov explained that she had been sent on assignment to the West. Stashinsky was left with little to do but work on the few translations commissioned to him by the KGB. It was suggested that he would soon start training as a barber. But the conversations that he had constantly been having with Sarkisov about their future life in the West, the name they were going to use there, and their cover story came to an end as well.

Stashinsky learned that his status within the KGB had changed on December 3, 1960, slightly less than a year after his all-important meeting with the KGB chief, Aleksandr Shelepin. On that date, Stashinsky's case officer brought him to meet with another important official, who was introduced to him as Vladimir Yakovlevich, a department head at KGB headquarters on Lubianka Square. According to declassified biographies of senior KGB officers, the stocky and somewhat below-average-height man who greeted Stashinsky on that day was Vladimir Yakovlevich Baryshnikov, the deputy head of Directorate C of the KGB foreign intelligence branch. Created in 1957, the directorate was in charge of illegals and their support abroad. Its first head was Stashinsky's acquaintance at Karlshorst, General Aleksandr Korotkov.

Baryshnikov had turned sixty in July. A graduate of a German commercial school in St. Petersburg before the revolution, he joined the secret police in the late 1920s and made a name for himself during the war as the architect of radio games with the German military intelligence—a deception tactic made possible by advances in radio technology. Before assuming his current position at Directorate C, he had served under Korotkov at Karlshorst, where he was second-in-command. Stashinsky's assassination of Lev Rebet had taken place on his watch. In KGB circles, Baryshnikov was a well-respected senior officer known as a scholarly type. His subordinates remembered him constantly bending over his paper-strewn desk—he was nearsighted and refused to wear glasses.[1]

After greeting Stashinsky, Baryshnikov began the conversation in his usual soft-spoken manner. He inquired about Inge, asking how she was coping with her new living conditions and occasional shortages of products. Stashinsky, who knew where those questions were coming from, put on a brave face and denied that any such problem had ever existed in his family. He assured Baryshnikov that both he and Inge loved living in Moscow and had learned to replace goods to which they were accustomed in Germany with those locally available. Baryshnikov dropped the subject. He took a different approach, telling Stashinsky that, given the impending changes in his family, certain things would have to be rearranged when it came to his work with the KGB.

"You have long led the life of a gadabout, never having a permanent base," he told Stashinsky. "Now you are married, you will have a child, and, naturally, once there is a child, you should have a permanent residence where you can hang your hat." It did not take Stashinsky long to grasp what Baryshnikov was driving at. The KGB had either postponed or canceled plans to send him and Inge abroad. Moscow was about to become their permanent home. The Americans and West Germans, said Baryshnikov, had opened an investigation into both of the murders Stashinsky had committed. It would be dangerous for him to travel to East Berlin. In fact, he would have to stay in the Soviet Union for at least another seven years. Stashinsky would never need to worry about money—the KGB would pay him a salary of 2,500 rubles per month—and he would be given an opportunity to continue his education, Baryshnikov assured him.

Stashinsky reacted calmly at first, but then the conversation took another bad turn. Baryshnikov raised the matter of the Stashinskys' plans to spend Christmas in East Germany with Inge's family. Everything was ready for their departure; Stashinsky and his KGB handler had already bought gifts for the family and ordered tickets. Arrangements had also been made for the couple to spend some time in Warsaw to allow Inge to familiarize herself with the Polish capital and be ready to answer questions about their alleged life there at the family gathering. Stashinsky had expected to receive the final go-ahead for the trip at the meeting with Baryshnikov. Now Baryshnikov was telling him that "we promised your wife that she could travel without difficulty and could also spend some time in Warsaw. But we cannot let you go to Berlin."

Stashinsky was shocked. His worst fears had come true. Before the meeting, he had fretted that the KGB had learned too much about his and Inge's attitudes toward the Soviet regime and probably would not let them both go to Berlin. He did not mention his fears to Inge and hoped that they would prove groundless, or that he could talk his way out of the situation if it turned difficult. But Baryshnikov made it impossible to get around the decision. According to the general, Stashinsky was in serious danger of being exposed if he went to Berlin. Of course, in the future he could go to West Germany by bypassing Berlin, said Baryshnikov. But he could do so only if he was not accompanied by his wife; if he traveled with Inge, she would naturally want to see her parents in Berlin and thus expose Stashinsky to danger. "He wanted to separate us," remembered Stashinsky. "The whole situation changed."[2]

The meeting was over. The stunned Stashinsky had much to think about. Baryshnikov's words made it clear that the KGB wanted one of them, either Stashinsky or Inge, to stay in Moscow as a hostage. They were letting Inge go to Berlin and counting on her love for Stashinsky to bring her back to him. They were also prepared to let Stashinsky go to the West after the child was born, counting on his love for his family to keep him from deserting the USSR. Baryshnikov was trying to turn the KGB's problems with Stashinsky—his love for Inge and desire to have a child—from an impediment into an advantage. This realization led to an equally disturbing thought: they no longer trusted him. He was not only a perpetrator but also a witness to the crimes they had committed on foreign soil, and he knew what the KGB could do with unwanted witnesses. Were he and Inge now under suspicion? Were their lives in danger?

"I had to reckon with the possibility," remembered Stashinsky later, "that something might happen to us both. After the talk with General [Vladimir] Yakovlevich I felt I must warn my wife that she might one day meet with a fatal accident. The same might also happen to me." He had to do something. "I understood," recalled Stashinsky later, "that I could no longer vacillate as to my intentions. I must clearly decide what to do. There was no other way out for me." But what exactly could he do under the circumstances? Should he try to repair his relations with the KGB, or flee to the West? Stashinsky's growing fears about his and his wife's safety made the first choice rather unrealistic. And with the KGB's new rules against traveling as a couple, the second possibility was not much of an option. It was a dead end.[3]

27

NEW YEAR

On the last day of 1960, Stashinsky and Inge prepared to ring in the new year, and wondered what it would bring them, two KGB pawns trying to escape from a tightly closed trap.

Inge could not understand at first why the KGB refused to let Stashinsky visit her parents in Berlin, and he finally decided to tell her the whole truth, including the kind of work he had done for the KGB in West Germany. It was not an easy decision. Not only did he truly believe that she would be safer if she knew nothing about them, but he simply could not bring himself to make the confession to her. As he said later, "It is not so easy to tell such things to the person you want to live with." But now the situation had changed dramatically. After his meeting with General Baryshnikov, Stashinsky believed that Inge's life was already in danger, even though she knew nothing about what he had done in West Germany. Psychological pressure was also mounting. Stashinsky had borne the burden of guilt alone for too long, and now he believed that if he told Inge the truth, she would not only understand but also help him.[1]

Inge was shocked—in fact, she fainted—but Stashinsky had read her correctly. Despite her deep religious beliefs and strong sense of morality, she did not turn her back on him. He felt great relief at not having to bear the secret (and the accompanying guilt) alone any longer. Usually when

Stashinsky and Inge needed to discuss matters that they wanted to keep secret from the KGB, they would take their conversation outdoors, but it was a cold winter in Moscow, and Inge was approaching her sixth month of pregnancy. They devised a different method of communication. "In our room we picked up notebooks and expressed our thoughts in written form," recalled Stashinsky. "We considered our plans for the future." The only future they could imagine at that point was in the West, but to get there they would have to circumvent the KGB and find their way out of a country that had closed itself off behind two Iron Curtains, not one. The second was between the Soviet Union and the countries of Eastern Europe, to which the access of Soviet citizens was almost as limited as to the West.[2]

For the moment, Inge refused to go to Berlin on her own. The immediate plan was to pressure the KGB into allowing them to go together, so they decided to play for time. Unable to spend Christmas with Inge's family in East Germany, Stashinsky and Inge spent it with Stashinsky's family in Ukraine—the second trip there in less than four months. Like all Eastern-rite Christians, the Stashinskys celebrated Christmas on January 7, following the ancient Julian calendar. For them, Christmas 1960 came in 1961. For Stashinsky, this trip home was very different from the one he had taken a year ago, soon after receiving the official award from Aleksandr Shelepin. Back then, while haunted by the sins he had committed, he had also been full of optimism—not only was his career with the KGB taking a turn for the better, but he had also received approval to marry the woman he loved. Now they were married and Inge was expecting their first child, but dark clouds were obscuring Stashinsky's career and their life together.

For Stashinsky, that Christmas at home carried a special weight. If his and Inge's plans came to fruition and they successfully escaped to the West, this would be his last holiday with his family. Stashinsky and Inge would leave Ukraine and the Soviet Union forever, taking refuge in the West and cutting all communication with his family to avoid being tracked down by KGB assassins. Stashinsky took photographs of his wife surrounded by members of his family. There was also a picture of his two sisters, Maria and Iryna, with the elongated faces and prominent noses of the Stashinsky clan. Both were unsure of themselves. Iryna was smiling somewhat artificially, while Maria was more reserved. They were wearing what appeared to be identical dresses—a result of fabric shortages.[3]

As they had done a few months earlier, Stashinsky and Inge used their stay in the village, blissfully away from KGB ears, to discuss their plans for the future. They considered applying to the East German embassy in Moscow for an exit visa, but had to abandon the idea; it was the KGB, not the East Germans, who controlled the Soviet border. Ultimately they devised a different, much riskier plan. Stashinsky hoped that he could appeal directly to his acquaintance Aleksandr Shelepin, the head of the KGB, and ask for permission to follow Inge to East Berlin. From there they would cross to West Berlin and then to West Germany. Stashinsky would use his alias of the East German Josef Lehmann to apply for political asylum. That was one reason why both he and Inge insisted on keeping the old alias when the KGB wanted to create a new identity for the Stashinskys. At first, Inge raised objections to the "Shelepin plan." "My wife considered it unethical," recalled Stashinsky later. "She said: we will go to him, he will give us permission, and we will disappear. He will have difficulties." Stashinsky brushed aside her objections, telling Inge that they had to treat the KGB as it was treating them. Inge eventually agreed.[4]

Back in Moscow, they went to the KGB's Lubianka headquarters to see Shelepin, but they got no farther than the duty officer. Stashinsky explained his situation to the officer and asked for a personal audience with the KGB chairman. He was taken instead to a room with a mailbox for letters addressed personally to Shelepin. The trip was a total failure. Not only did the Stashinskys fail to meet with Shelepin, but they also complicated relations with Stashinsky's KGB handlers, who had been kept in the dark regarding the visit.

Given the situation, the Stashinskys decided to change tactics. Inge would agree to go to Berlin on her own. The KGB had originally approved a short visit to her parents, but the couple secretly agreed that she would stay long enough to give birth to their child, for whom they wanted East German citizenship. Ideally, she and the child would never come back to

Moscow. Once Stashinsky found a way to join them in Berlin, all three of them would go to the West. Their plan required several steps. First, Inge would prolong her stay in East Germany by claiming difficulties with the pregnancy. An accident in Moscow helped them devise a credible cover. Shortly before leaving for East Berlin, Inge had to see a doctor: she had lifted a heavy object and felt sick afterward. The KGB knew of the visit and its purpose. Now the Stashinskys decided that soon after arriving in East Germany, Inge would go to a doctor and, citing complications from the Moscow accident, ask for a note advising her against traveling long distances.

Inge would then embark on the second stage of the plan, which involved bringing Stashinsky to help her with the newborn child in Berlin. Once again, they pinned their hopes on Shelepin. Inge was supposed to write a personal letter to the KGB chief and send it to him through the Soviet embassy in East Berlin—correspondence from abroad, the couple guessed correctly, would receive more attention than domestic mail. If Shelepin turned them down—and Stashinsky realistically thought that would be the most likely outcome—Inge would go in a different direction and try to contact the Americans with the help of Frau Schade, a friend of her father's. As Stashinsky recalled later, "She was to tell them that I was an undercover KGB worker who had morally dissociated himself from his employers and wanted to go to the West. She was to ask the Americans to help me in this. She would say that when I had succeeded in reaching the West I would give them details of my work for the KGB."[5]

For better or worse, Bogdan Stashinsky had made up his mind. If Shelepin did not help him, and if it proved impossible to ask for political asylum using his Josef Lehmann identity, he would turn to the KGB's archenemies, the CIA, and reveal Soviet secrets in exchange for safety and cover. This would be an act of treason, but Stashinsky felt no loyalty to his KGB masters. The couple decided on the place and time of day when the Americans were to contact Stashinsky in Moscow if they accepted the overture. The exact day of the meeting would be agreed upon by Inge and the American agents with whom she would get in touch. If she failed to contact the Americans, for whatever reason, she was to return to Moscow. "In that case," remembered Stashinsky, "I had decided that on the next occasion when I was given a KGB assignment to carry out in the West I should make contact with the Americans or with German intelligence."

They also devised a secret code to help them correspond through the mail, which they knew would be read by the KGB. Shelepin would be called "dear God" in their correspondence. Once Inge sent Shelepin a letter pleading that he allow her husband to join her in Berlin, she was to write in a letter to Stashinsky that she had cut her finger. If that "blood sacrifice" to "dear God" brought no results, Stashinsky would give Inge his go-ahead to make contact with the Americans by advising her to see a seamstress. Altogether there were about twenty code words that they agreed upon to let each other know what was going on in Berlin and Moscow, including such eventualities as Stashinsky being pressured by the KGB or being forced to move to another apartment. Once they were ready, they told Stashinsky's case officer that Inge had agreed to travel to Berlin on her own. The Stashinskys' KGB handlers were relieved, believing that the couple had finally realized that there was no alternative to complying with the KGB's advice and rules.

The pregnant Inge boarded a plane to East Berlin on January 31, 1961. In her two suitcases she carried almost all their belongings. Stashinsky was left in Moscow with only essential items and the hope that he would soon follow Inge to the city with no visible borders.[6]

28

BACK TO SCHOOL

It was around the date of Inge's departure for Berlin that Bogdan Stashinsky obtained his first genuine Soviet document in years. A passport issued by the Moscow police on January 26, 1961, gave his real name, as well as the place and date of his birth: Bogdan Nikolaevich Stashinsky, born on November 4, 1931, in the village of Borshchovychi in the Lviv region of Ukraine. The passport would allow him to enroll as a student in the Moscow State Pedagogical Institute of Foreign Languages, where he was supposed to study German and then English.

The KGB provided Stashinsky with the required letter of reference as well. Issued in the fake name of the director of an equally fake secret research institute, it stated that Stashinsky had been in their employ from March 1951—the year he officially entered the KGB service—to December 1960. He was characterized as an "honest and conscientious worker." It was also mentioned that he had been awarded the Order of the Red Banner by decree of the Presidium of the Supreme Soviet of the USSR "for successful work on an important problem." The information about Stashinsky's award, which had been considered a state secret when he was preparing for a new mission abroad, was now regarded as confidential at most: the institute officials who admitted him as a student in the middle of the academic year knew perfectly well that he was a KGB agent.

Stashinsky entered the language training institute in March 1961 without taking the obligatory entrance exams, which were waived at the KGB's request. He did so in midsemester, joining a student cohort that was already concluding its second year of study. Stashinsky had earlier studied German at individual meetings with a highly qualified teacher and listened to tape recordings of radio announcers from western and northern Germany, but he was now expected to master the language as one of a relatively large group of students. Some of their professors had never visited the country in whose language they were supposed to be experts. Stashinsky's studies progressed slowly. Luckily, the KGB's primary purpose was not language training, but simply pacifying one of their agents with a university degree. Stashinsky was no longer training for illegal assignment in the West. The KGB's new plans for Stashinsky were less exciting. In recognition of his past service to the secret police and, indeed, to the state, they wanted to help him settle in the USSR, which he was never supposed to leave.[1]

Stashinsky, of course, had altogether different plans. Shortly after Inge's arrival in East Germany, she sent a letter informing Stashinsky about alleged problems with her pregnancy. As they had agreed before her departure, she saw a doctor and received a note prohibiting her from long-distance travel. Stashinsky duly reported the news to Sarkisov, telling him that Inge had not felt well before leaving for East Germany and probably would be unable to travel before the birth of their child. By the end of February, Inge wrote to Stashinsky that she had cut her finger, meaning that she had written to the KGB chief, Aleksandr Shelepin, requesting permission for Stashinsky to join her in East Berlin. The letter to "dear God," as Shelepin was code-named in their correspondence, had been sent through the Soviet embassy. It probably arrived before Inge's letter to Stashinsky, but there was no response from the KGB boss for some time.

Meanwhile, the KGB read the letter and discussed the matter. A rumor at KGB headquarters had it that General Aleksandr Korotkov himself was the deciding voice against Stashinsky and Inge's plans. "Stashinsky cannot be released to the West. Optimal living conditions should be created for him, and a country house should be built for him in whichever part of the

Soviet Union he desires," suggested the general. By the end of March, the response was ready. Sergei Sarkisov informed Stashinsky that Inge had written to Shelepin asking him to let Stashinsky go to East Berlin. The request was denied. Moreover, Sarkisov asked Stashinsky to write to his wife, telling her to stop bothering the KGB chief with her letters. Stashinsky had to agree.[2]

The only positive development was that the KGB decided it was time to change Stashinsky's case officer. His relations with Sarkisov were clearly strained, and the trust that was supposed to exist between agent and handler had failed to develop. Moreover, Stashinsky was no longer being trained for illegal work abroad. Stashinsky was given a new handler and most likely transferred to a different KGB unit entirely.

Lieutenant Colonel Yurii Aleksandrov was assigned to handle the disillusioned Stashinsky. Aleksandrov was senior to Sarkisov and had much more power than his predecessor, and he tried to be as honest with Stashinsky as could be expected under the circumstances. He told Stashinsky that he "had learned of strained relations and misunderstandings that had arisen, and that he had been authorized to clear up those misunderstandings in order to ensure good cooperation in future." He was also direct in letting Stashinsky know that establishing good relations was in his interest as well. "You know as well as I do," he told Stashinsky, "that we are now permanently associated 'like needle and thread,' as the Russian proverb has it."

Stashinsky welcomed the change of case officer. He told Aleksandrov that he was unhappy about the eavesdropping, the opening of personal correspondence, and the obvious distrust toward him—this after all that he had done for the KGB. Aleksandrov agreed with him and promised to help. He also wanted Stashinsky to write to Inge, encouraging her to come back to Moscow as soon as possible. Aleksandrov even offered to supply her with genuine new documents for her return to the Soviet Union. As with Stashinsky, the KGB saw no reason to go on concealing Inge's identity. Stashinsky liked his new handler but suspected that the KGB was being so good to him for a reason: they wanted Inge back as soon as possible. He wrote to his wife and, instead of encouraging her to return, advised her to go the seamstress.[3]

Inge began to put their plan into action. She soon wrote to her husband:

> My dear Bogdan, as we agreed, I am getting ready for your arrival. I must do a great deal myself. Yesterday I was at the seamstress's. Everything is in order. She is making everything as planned. You should see how bright these little baby shirts are. I just don't know which color I should choose. Light blue, I think. But I sense that you have no need of these foolish ideas of women. Wait for our meeting. All in all, I love you. Oh yes, Aunt Klara wanted me to tell you that the thing you asked about is definitely working out. Actually, when I visit my relatives, I am always in such a good mood that I have no fear at all about our future.

The latter reference was to Frau Schade, the friend of Inge's father who was supposed to become a go-between for Inge in her dealings with the CIA. It seemed that she had agreed to perform that role.[4]

But then Inge received a sudden call from Moscow. Stashinsky had been stressed for days after sending his wife to contact the CIA. What if the KGB had her followed and found out about the contact? How would the CIA respond to her overture? If CIA officers decided to meet with him in Moscow, would they not also be followed by the KGB? There were more questions than answers. After agonizing over the right course of action and going back and forth on his original decision, Stashinsky eventually decided to call off the whole enterprise. He panicked. In violation of the security protocol he had devised for communicating with his wife, he called her on an open line from Moscow and told her not to go to the seamstress. They aborted the plan.

The next news Stashinsky received from Berlin was of a much happier nature. On March 31, 1961, Inge gave birth to their son, Peter. That was the happiest day of Inge's life. Stashinsky learned of the birth the same day via telegram. Perhaps because of the cumulative stress that Inge had experienced in Moscow, the birth was a month premature, and Stashinsky decided to take advantage of that circumstance to request permission to see his wife and newborn son in Berlin. He turned to his new case officer, Lieutenant Colonel Aleksandrov, for help, but the request was denied. Inge's telegram said that both she and the child were well, and besides, the KGB wanted them back in Moscow, not Stashinsky traveling to Berlin.

As spring gave way to summer, Stashinsky's letters to Inge became more and more disconsolate. Inge realized that she had no choice but to go back to Moscow. There was no chance that her husband's handlers would allow him to join her in Berlin. "My minders from Karlshorst, with whom I had to maintain constant contact," recalled Inge later, "were very glad to hear of my decision and notified Moscow of it the very same day." In early August she began preparing to fly back to Moscow. Whatever plans she and Stashinsky had made for life in the West would have to be postponed, if not completely abandoned. They should stay together as a family. So Moscow was the only option.[5]

29

TELEPHONE CALL

On the evening of Tuesday, August 8, 1961, Stashinsky received an unexpected visit from Lieutenant Colonel Nikolai Kravchenko, an assistant to the head of the KGB émigré department and one of the two men with whom he had celebrated his award back in November 1959. Kravchenko dropped by Stashinsky's apartment to tell him that he should call his wife in Berlin. He did not give a reason, but Stashinsky assumed it was to discuss the details of Inge's forthcoming return to Moscow.

Private telephones were a luxury in Moscow in 1961. When calling someone in another city, the usual procedure was to send a telegram asking the person to go to a post office or telephone station at a certain time and await the call. Kravchenko asked Stashinsky to invite Inge for a telephone conversation at 7:00 p.m. Central European time, which was 10:00 p.m. Moscow time. Stashinsky agreed. At the time indicated by Kravchenko, the two were on the phone and Stashinsky's world had turned upside down.[1]

Stashinsky could not believe his ears. Their son, Peter—the healthy boy born four months earlier—was dead. He had fallen ill and developed a high fever by the time they took him to a hospital. Inge was disconsolate and wanted him to come to Berlin. She was demanding that from her contacts at Karlshorst as well. All Stashinsky could tell her was that he would talk to his bosses. It was a terrible night for him. He had never seen his son, and now the baby might be buried without him. He couldn't contact his case officer, Lieutenant Colonel Yurii Aleksandrov, until the next morning. But Aleksandrov was already aware of Peter's death. The KGB had wanted Stashinsky to hear the news firsthand from his wife, Aleksandrov explained to Stashinsky.

Aleksandrov sounded genuinely compassionate on the phone. He asked Stashinsky whether there was anything he could do to help him. "I can do nothing other than go to Berlin and help my wife," responded Stashinsky. During the sleepless night following Inge's call, Stashinsky had devised a strategy that might bring him to Berlin after all, capitalizing on Inge's precarious condition after the loss of her child. He told Aleksandrov that "in her present state of mind she might do something in despair that would be harmful to the KGB," such as turning to the German authorities and demanding his arrival in Berlin. That could blow his cover. Aleksandrov responded hotly that Inge herself was responsible for Peter's death—things would have turned out differently if she had not delayed her return to Moscow. But he promised to talk to the higher-ups.[2]

When Stashinsky called Aleksandrov a few hours later, the case officer had good news for him—permission to travel to Berlin had finally been granted. The KGB did not want Inge causing scandals in a city that was only partly under their control. The decision was apparently made at the highest level, possibly by Aleksandr Shelepin himself. (Years later, his successor at the helm of the KGB, Vladimir Semichastny, would blame Shelepin for going soft on Stashinsky and letting him leave the country.) Stashinsky could not wait to pass on the good news to Inge, with whom he spoke by phone later that day—they would see each other either tomorrow or the day after, he told his anxious wife.

That evening, Aleksandrov told Stashinsky that everything was ready for his departure. He would go to Germany on a military plane that was flying there the next morning, and would need to be ready by 5:00 a.m. Aleksandrov would collect him near his apartment building. He asked Stashinsky to turn in all his KGB-issued documents and passes before leaving for Germany, keeping his travel document only. It was issued, as always, in the name of Aleksandr Krylov. Stashinsky had only one night to collect his thoughts and pack his belongings for the trip he had dreamt of for so long, and which was now taking place under such tragic circumstances. Stashinsky was shocked and overwhelmed by the death of the son he had never met, and concerned about Inge trying to cope with the tragedy on her own. But he was not going to lose the opportunity presented by this unexpected trip. Stashinsky would not bring Inge back to Moscow—they would escape to the West.

Stashinsky had always wanted to use his old documents, issued in the name of Josef Lehmann, for that purpose. Now, in direct violation of Aleksandrov's instructions, he took the Lehmann identity card with him, which was good until April 1970, and a driver's license in the same name. He also pocketed his Soviet passport and a Foreign Languages Institute student identity card, both issued in his real name. To these, he added the letter of reference that the KGB had provided for his enrollment at the institute. The letter mentioned the Order of the Red Banner—proof of the importance of the tasks he had carried out for the KGB. Stashinsky was ready not just to go to the West and request asylum, but to turn himself in and disclose his real name and the work he had done for the KGB.

Shortly before 5:00 a.m. on August 10, Stashinsky was waiting near his apartment building to be picked up by Aleksandrov. Before leaving, he put his household effects in order and destroyed the list of code phrases that he and Inge had used in their correspondence. The only incriminating evidence remaining was what he carried on him—the identification papers and documents he was taking to Berlin against the orders of his case officer. If they were discovered, the KGB would have no doubt about his real intentions. He was risking his life.

Aleksandrov showed up on time, all dressed up—he was clearly happy to get out of Moscow for a trip to Berlin. He had a lot of friends there. Until recently he had served at Karlshorst, where he was widely known and respected not only among fellow KGB officers but also among Soviet diplomats. The head of the KGB apparatus, General Aleksandr Korotkov, had attended informal gatherings at his apartment. Besides, the trip to Berlin came with a per diem in foreign currency, and the opportunity to bring back highly valued gifts and merchandise that could not be found in the Soviet capital. When Stashinsky learned that Aleksandrov would accompany him on the trip to Berlin, his heart sank. His chances of escape had just diminished, while the risk of being caught had increased dramatically. He turned over to Aleksandrov the envelope with his identification papers and passes. Aleksandrov did not ask about the missing Lehmann and Stashinsky documents.

They drove to the military airport on the outskirts of Moscow and spent a few hours waiting for their flight. It was there that Aleksandrov dropped another bombshell on Stashinsky. He told him that the KGB had considered two possible scenarios to explain Peter's death. The first was the involvement of American or West German intelligence services, which might have killed the baby to lure Stashinsky to Berlin and seize him there. The second possibility, said Aleksandrov, was that Inge was somehow involved in the death of their son, possibly in an attempt to bring Stashinsky to Berlin after all her other attempts had failed.

Stashinsky was appalled. "After all that I had experienced with the KGB, this conversation was the last straw," he remembered later. "Those people really thought that a mother was capable of murdering her child in order to gratify her wishes." Stashinsky exploded and told Aleksandrov with indignation: "You can't be saying that my wife murdered her child!" The KGB officer tried to calm him down. They were professional intelligence officers, which meant being vigilant and taking every possibility into account. They would soon learn what had really happened. For now, they had little information to go on, and they had to be cautious in order to prevent anything untoward. "He told me," recalled Stashinsky, "that, given both possibilities, it was necessary that I be protected at all times, and that he had ordered a car with KGB personnel for that purpose." Either scenario conveniently gave the KGB sufficient excuse to keep Stashinsky under constant watch during his stay in Berlin. His chances of escape were diminishing by the hour.

Stashinsky had a lot to think about on the flight from Moscow to Spremberg, ninety miles southeast of Berlin. There, as expected, he and Aleksandrov were met by KGB officers. One of them, a gray-haired man whose name Stashinsky never learned, was responsible for liaison with Inge. He was unhappy to learn that Stashinsky had already called Inge from Moscow and let her know of his impending arrival—that, he told Stashinsky, was premature. Stashinsky was required to stay at Karlshorst for the duration of his visit, and, if he wanted to spend his nights with Inge, she would have to come there as well. The gray-haired man spoke about the rapidly deteriorating situation in Berlin. The city had become a "seething den of vice," he told Stashinsky. Besides, some suspicious people had been making inquiries about him, corroborating General Baryshnikov's story about the Western intelligence services allegedly being on Stashinsky's trail. And the murky circumstances of Peter's death only complicated the situation. For his own safety, Stashinsky could not stay in the village of Dallgow with his wife.

Stashinsky reconciled himself to the circumstances but would not wait until the KGB declared the situation safe enough for him to see Inge. He wanted to call and see her right away. Was that not the reason they had let him come to Berlin? The man with the gray hair had to agree. On the night of August 10, they got into a car and drove to Dallgow.[3]

30

BERLIN

On Thursday, August 10, 1961, the day Bogdan Stashinsky flew from Moscow to Spremberg, Muscovites were eager to get their hands on the morning newspapers. The print media reported on the festive reception that had been given to Major Gherman Titov, the Soviet cosmonaut, the previous day. Political leaders and ordinary citizens had gathered on Red Square to welcome him home. Titov had become the second Soviet cosmonaut to orbit the earth in a space capsule. The first to do so, four months earlier, had been Major Yurii Gagarin, who had spent less than two hours in outer space on April 12. Titov was in orbit for twenty-five hours on August 6 and 7, circling the earth seventeen times—a new record that made the Soviets proud.

Nikita Khrushchev was on Red Square to greet Titov and congratulate him. The Soviets were ahead of the Americans, who would not put a man into orbit until February 1962. Khrushchev proudly emphasized the peaceful nature of the Soviet space program, telling the jubilant crowd that "the spaceship Vostok 2 had no atomic bombs or any other death-dealing weapons on board. Like other Soviet artificial earth satellites and spaceships, it was equipped with scientific instruments for peaceful use." At the same time, however, Titov's report, published in the Communist Party mouthpiece *Pravda*, ended with words that, if read carefully, might send a chill through the capitals of the West: "I am prepared to carry out any assignment of the party and the state." It was up to the Soviet leaders to decide whether the next assignment would involve "instruments for peaceful use" or nuclear bombs.[1]

It was Khrushchev's second major speech in less than three days. On August 7 he had given a much longer and more bellicose speech as a response to an address given two weeks earlier by John F. Kennedy, who was then completing his sixth month as president. Kennedy's speech focused on the growing security crisis in and around Berlin. He told his American audience that he recognized the legitimacy of Soviet security concerns in Central Europe and was open to talks on Berlin, but he rejected the language of ultimatums, which Khrushchev was continuing to use in his efforts to force Western powers to abandon West Berlin.

Kennedy was taking a firm stance, clearly indicating that he would not be pushed around. In his July 25 speech, Kennedy had declared that he would ask the US Congress for more than $3 billion in additional defense spending and was adding eight more divisions to the US armed forces. "We seek peace, but we shall not surrender," declared the president. He was eager to counter the widespread impression in his own country that he was weak and indecisive; earlier that year, when he refused to provide air support for the Cuban exiles' invasion of Fidel Castro's "island of freedom," the venture had ended in a fiasco.

Khrushchev was enraged by Kennedy's speech. In his own televised response, he compared Berlin to Sarajevo in 1914, suggesting that the growing Berlin crisis could lead to a new world war. He also used imagery and examples from World War II, suggesting that Soviet divisions could be moved to the western frontiers of the Eastern bloc countries to counter the American threat. He referenced a recent meeting of the political leaders of the Warsaw Pact, the Eastern bloc's military organization, who had unanimously voiced support for the Soviet's demands that the Western military leave West Berlin and allow it to be incorporated into a "free city" in East Germany. What he did not mention was that the meeting, which had ended in Moscow a few days earlier, had also given the go-ahead for the construction of a wall that would cut Berlin in two and turn it into a permanently divided city.

While Khrushchev was delivering his August 7 speech, Walter Ulbricht, the communist leader of East Germany, was busy finalizing his plans to divide Berlin with barbed wire and, eventually, concrete blocks. He had admitted to Khrushchev long before that he saw no other way to stop the flight of his citizens to the West. Khrushchev agreed. He told the Eastern bloc leaders gathered in Moscow in early August that the continued existence of the German Democratic Republic was at stake, and, by extension, the existence of their own regimes as well. The leaders had reluctantly given their support to Ulbricht's initiative. Their main concern was possible Western retaliation in the form of economic sanctions or even military action. Khrushchev was more optimistic in that regard. If he had correctly read the messages sent to him by President Kennedy, the Americans would not intervene. Either way, he was prepared to take the risk. They agreed on a date for the closing of the border—the night of Saturday, August 12.[2]

The preparations to close the border were made with the uttermost secrecy. Nothing that Bogdan Stashinsky saw on the streets of Berlin on the night of August 10 indicated that a major operation to seal off East Berlin from the western part of the city was only two days away. The KGB car carrying Stashinsky left East Berlin and headed for the village of Dallgow, where Inge was staying with her family. So much had happened since Stashinsky had bid her farewell seven months ago, and there was so much for them to talk about. But with the KGB men around, they had very little privacy. By 11:00 p.m., the minders had driven the couple to Karlshorst, where they were placed in a KGB-run safe house. They could not talk there, either. Like their KGB flat in Moscow, it was certainly bugged. Stashinsky and Inge would not take any more risks. The next morning, Stashinsky discovered that they had been under observation throughout the night. From his window he saw a car with a diplomatic license plate parked near the house in which they were staying, which soon swapped places with a

Soviet-made Volga sedan. After that, a third car showed up. Its occupants were Lieutenant Colonel Yurii Aleksandrov and the gray-haired man from the day before.

Aleksandrov told Stashinsky that they were still suspicious about the cause of Peter's death, and a KGB crew would stay close to Stashinsky and Inge throughout the day to protect them against any threats. He wanted Stashinsky to go to the hospital where Peter had died and inquire about the cause of his death. They were given a car and driver for the day, and instructions to rendezvous with Aleksandrov at 4:00 p.m. at the Café Budapest in downtown East Berlin.

Stashinsky and Inge asked the driver to first take them back to Dallgow. As the Volga drove up to the Pohl family home, Stashinsky noticed a car conspicuously parked with a clear view of the house and the whole street. Although the Stashinskys were observed from outside, they were fairly sure that there were no bugs in the house, so they decided to talk freely for the first time since they had left Berlin more than a year earlier. First and foremost, they needed to agree on a plan. It was Friday, August 11. Peter's funeral was scheduled for Sunday, the 13th. They decided to flee to West Berlin immediately after the funeral. "My wife left the decision up to me," said Stashinsky, recalling their conversation later. "She said that she would follow wherever I went."

The KGB car took Stashinsky and Inge from her parents' house to the hospital, where Stashinsky was told that his son had died of pneumonia, which made sense, given the high fever Inge had told him about. That diagnosis, he hoped, would put the suspicions to rest about Inge or Western intelligence services playing a role in Peter's death. The two then drove to the cemetery, where Stashinsky first saw his son's now lifeless body in a chapel. By 4:00 p.m. they were at the Café Budapest. Aleksandrov already knew the cause of Peter's death and had probably known it even before he sent Stashinsky to the hospital. They agreed that Stashinsky and Inge would spend the rest of the day in the city, and the car would pick them up in front of the same café at 11:00 that night to take them back to their

Karlshorst safe house. They were virtual prisoners, but they had a few hours to talk freely. The couple walked the streets of Berlin, discussing all that had happened since their parting in January. They noticed that even though the KGB had now verified the completely innocuous cause of Peter's death, they were still being followed by secret-police minders.[3]

31

DOWN TO THE WIRE

It was only on the morning of August 12 that Lieutenant Colonel Yurii Aleksandrov implied that their KGB "protection" would be removed while they planned the funeral for their son. He drove them to Dallgow and left them there to make arrangements for the next day. They would be picked up at the Pohl family home at 10:00 p.m. and taken back to Karlshorst, said Aleksandrov. Stashinsky and Inge spent the morning of August 12 at her family's home. In the afternoon they decided to go to her rented room just down the street to pick up some items. It was a difficult walk—Inge had spent the previous four months there with her newborn, and now the room brought back painful memories. Stashinsky experienced a different kind of pain. On the way to the apartment, he noticed that despite what Aleksandrov had said, the KGB "protection squad" was still there.

On the street, Stashinsky noticed the same parked Volkswagen that he had earlier seen at the railway station. It was part of the KGB fleet that had followed Stashinsky and Inge the previous day. The KGB was doing a poor job of hiding their tracks: cars with foreign-looking men stood out in a neighborhood with little if any traffic. When Inge's fifteen-year-old brother, Fritz, asked Stashinsky who the people in the cars were, he had sarcastically responded that they were there to protect him. But they were clearly still under surveillance, meaning that they would probably have no freedom of movement after the funeral on Sunday. Until 10:00 p.m. that night, however, they would be watched, but not fully controlled. If they wanted to go to the West, they had to act immediately, he realized. Tomorrow, after the funeral, it would be too late.

Stashinsky shared his thoughts with Inge. "I was very much afraid she would not be able to bring herself to do this," he remembered later. "But she realized that it was vital to do so and that we could be of no further use to our son even if we did attend the funeral." Inge steeled herself to follow his advice. It was hard to keep their plans secret from Inge's family: Fritz realized that something was wrong when Inge told him that he would have to take her and "Joschi's" wreaths to the funeral. He did not object when she told him that the three of them were now going for a walk. If anything, he was excited.

Before they left the house, Stashinsky asked Fritz, who had just come in with the funeral wreaths, what he had seen on the street. Fritz replied that an East German Wartburg sedan, which he had seen previously in the neighborhood, had just passed in the direction of the railway bridge. Stashinsky concluded that the car had not yet returned. He, Inge, and Fritz left the house, turned right, and walked along the fence toward the building where Inge had rented her room. They did not look back. After a few minutes, Stashinsky sent Fritz ahead to check for cars. There were none: the fugitives crossed the street and entered the house where Inge's rented room was located.

Stashinsky and Inge knew that they would not be returning to Inge's family home and had to prepare for a trip whose outcome was unknown. Stashinsky changed his shirt and packed his raincoat. Inge changed her dress. Stashinsky later remembered: "We could not take much, as we had to be inconspicuous and allow for being challenged in the course of our flight." But when Inge asked whether she could take the quilt she had used to swaddle Peter, he let her do so. They left the house from a side entrance. "Our flight to West Berlin really was a flight," recalled Inge later. "There was no other way out for us, though with all the strain and stress and emotional burden of the last few days we were not really fully aware of the consequences of our step."[1]

On a map of Berlin and its environs, the trip from Dallgow to the western part of the city seems easy. Dallgow, located west of Berlin, bordered a section of the city that had been occupied by the Western Allies in 1945. Until 1951, the Soviets and then the East Germans had maintained a checkpoint there to control automobile traffic heading for West Berlin. The easiest way to get from Dallgow to West Berlin was to take a train heading east. In two stops, they would reach the relative safety of the western sector. But they did not dare show up at Dallgow railway station, where the KGB would certainly have agents posted. Fritz also told Stashinsky and Inge the alarming news he had heard from a friend: the police were checking passengers' documents at the station in Staaken, the last city before the border with West Berlin. By a quirk of fate, the eastern part of Staaken had become part of West Berlin, while its western part was assigned to East Germany. Now the East German police were turning back many East German passengers bound for West Berlin.

The East German authorities were desperate to slow down, if not completely stop, the flood of refugees to the West. That day alone, close to 2,000 East Germans had applied for political asylum in West Berlin. More than twenty charter flights had left West Berlin, taking the asylum seekers to various destinations throughout West Germany. Refugee facilities in West Berlin were full to capacity, and the West Berlin authorities had been forced to ask the US Army to help with food rations. In one sense, the East German policemen turning people back at East German railway stations were helping their West Berlin counterparts keep the situation under control.[2]

One way or another, the direct route to West Berlin through Staaken was closed to the Stashinskys. If they were detained, no cover story could possibly convince the KGB that Stashinsky was not defecting to the West. Another route had to be found. Ultimately, Stashinsky decided that they would head for the nearby village of Falkensee, about three miles north of Dallgow, and try their luck there. Stashinsky, Inge, and Fritz took the back entrance through the garden. Hidden by high shrubs, they walked to

Falkensee. If they were stopped, they would say that they had decided to go to Falkensee to have some ice cream. Fritz would serve as proof that they were engaged in nothing more than a family outing. Luckily, they were never stopped. The walk took them about forty-five minutes.

In Falkensee, Stashinsky decided to avoid the train and instead take a taxi. They found a taxi driver on a side street who agreed to take the three of them to East Berlin. He drove along the Berliner Ring Road, circling the city from the north. As they crossed the border between East Germany and East Berlin, which were both under Soviet occupation, they were asked for documents. Stashinsky told the guards that he was returning home to East Berlin and produced an identity card in the name of Josef Lehmann. Had the card been found on Stashinsky by his KGB "protectors," it could have cost him his life. But now, the guards waved them through.[3]

On their way downtown, they passed through the East Berlin suburb of Pankow, home to many of the East German political elite. It was past 6:00 p.m., and some of the most prominent inhabitants of Pankow were not at home. That evening, the East German supreme leader, Walter Ulbricht, was throwing a garden party about twenty-five miles north of Berlin. In the middle of the party, Ulbricht invited his already tipsy guests to congregate for an announcement that sobered up many of them in a split second. In three hours, Ulbricht told his ministers, the "still open border between so-cialist and capitalist Europe" would be closed. Everything was ready for the final move to seal East Berlin from the western part of the city and stop the flow of refugees that was bleeding the East German economy dry. Ulbricht then told his guests that for security reasons no one would be allowed to leave the premises until the operation was over. Only now did some of them realize why they had seen more than the usual number of troops in the woods surrounding the villa. No one was foolish enough to raise any objections, even if they had them. They went back to eating and drinking. The party went on late into the night.[4]

Like Ulbricht's guests, Stashinsky and Inge were surprised to see more than the usual number of soldiers as their taxi made its way downtown. Inge even thought she saw military maneuvers going on. They got out of the taxi on the corner of Friedrichstrasse and Reinhardstrasse. In case the police interrogated the taxi driver, he had no way of knowing where the group was heading from there—east or west. Stashinsky and Inge decided that the time had come to say goodbye to Fritz as well. Fritz wanted to go with them, but they refused. Inge gave Fritz 300 East German marks to cover the funeral expenses and told him that they probably would not see each other for a while. If he was asked at home where the two had gone, he was to say that they were visiting relatives in Berlin. Fritz made his way to the S-Bahn station and bought a ticket to Staaken through West Berlin.

With Fritz gone, Stashinsky and Inge went to Schönhauser Allee, where they boarded the S-Bahn. Their route was designed in such a way that if the police or KGB stopped them, Stashinsky could say that he was heading for his old rented room, where he had left his shoes. But their cover story was valid only up to a point: the old rented room was, after all, in East, not West Berlin. Then they noticed that the East German police were checking documents in the neighboring train car. If they reached Stashinsky and Inge's car, there was no telling what would happen. With their East German documents, they had no business going to West Berlin and could easily be turned back or even detained. But their luck held—the police did not get to their car. They got off the S-Bahn at Gesundbrunnen, the first station in West Berlin.

There was no time to savor the moment. Stashinsky and Inge grabbed a taxi and asked the driver to take them to the apartment of Inge's aunt, who lived in West Berlin. But Inge's relatives were not at home. Stashinsky returned and asked the taxi driver to take them farther north, to Berlin-Lübars, where Inge's other aunt lived. It was getting dark. At the East German army headquarters thirty kilometers east of Berlin, General Heinz Hoffmann, the East German minister of defense, was gathering his senior officers and handing them sealed envelopes with their marching orders. Precisely at midnight they were instructed to start moving troops and equipment into place to seal off East Berlin completely. At this point, Stashinsky and Inge would have been happy to see the border securely closed.

They could no longer be stopped by East German police, but the border remained open to KGB agents who might already be on their trail.

Luckily, Inge's second aunt was at home—in fact, both aunts and their families were spending the evening together. Stashinsky and Inge were now off the street and in relative safety—and completely out of cash. "Uncle Heinz," said Stashinsky to the husband of one of Inge's aunts, "pay for the taxi. We have to go to the police, the American secret police, as soon as possible." Heinz Villwok, a fifty-one-year-old municipal employee, could see that Stashinsky, whom he knew as Joschi (as did all members of Inge's family), was under great stress. "He was highly agitated," remembered Villwok, "just like my niece; they looked very poorly and were exhausted." Stashinsky and Inge spent no more than half an hour at her aunt's apartment and then went to the police station near Tempelhof, the airport from which Stashinsky had flown to Munich so many times. Back then, he had wanted to avoid the police at all costs; now he believed that they were his only hope of salvation.

But the policemen were in no hurry. A Soviet intelligence officer wanting to turn himself in to the Americans? Was that for real? Heinz Villwok, who negotiated the surrender, had to wait twenty minutes to talk to an officer. Then he waited again. After that, he spoke with police officials together with Inge. Finally they persuaded the police to call the Americans. It was already past 9:00 p.m., less than an hour before Aleksandrov would be certain to discover the Stashinskys' disappearance, and three hours before the East German Army and police started unrolling their barbed wire.[5]

PART V
PUBLICITY BOMB

32

SHOCK WAVE

I t was a strange funeral. More KGB agents and officers of the East German Ministry of Security came to say farewell to the four-month-old Peter than the Rohrbeck Evangelical Cemetery in Dallgow had ever seen. Despite the absence of Peter's parents, the funeral went as planned. A record in the parish registry indicates that Peter Lehmann—the last name was a product of the KGB officers' imagination—was buried there on August 13, 1961.[1]

Also absent from the funeral was Fritz Pohl, Inge's brother. He had not brought the promised funeral wreath, and the 300 East German marks that Fritz had been asked to bring home to cover the cost of the funeral had disappeared as well. Fritz had resolved to follow Inge and her husband to the West. He had indeed boarded a train to Dallgow, but then he had changed his mind, turned back, and made his way to the house of his aunt, Grete Villwok, in West Berlin. On the day of his nephew's funeral, he applied for asylum in West Berlin.[2]

Georgii Sannikov, a thirty-two-year-old KGB officer then working in Berlin under diplomatic cover, later described the shock felt by his KGB colleagues and superiors once they realized that Bogdan Stashinsky had defected. "The KGB operatives present at the child's funeral were puzzled by the parents' absence," wrote Sannikov. "By the end of the day on 13 August 1961 it was clear that the Stashinskys had gone to the West. Everyone who knew what tasks the agent had carried out in Munich in 1957 and 1959 and what could happen if Stashinsky were to talk was in shock." The KGB officers immediately started recalling agents whom Stashinsky knew or might have known from the West. Every measure was taken to find the defector and silence him before he could talk to the Americans.

A few days after the funeral, Sannikov was summoned to Karlshorst and ordered to accompany another KGB officer, Colonel Aleksandr Sviatogorov, on a special mission. The two took up positions a hundred meters away from the entrance to the Central Intelligence Agency building on Clayallee in West Berlin. "We kept watch for two days," remembered Sannikov. "Sviatogorov hoped for a miracle. On the first day, taking his chosen position, he told me, 'Georgii, I have a pistol with me. If we see Bogdan, go away; I'll shoot. I have nothing to lose. I'll kill Bogdan and myself.'"[3]

Sviatogorov, the KGB officer who was prepared to sacrifice his life in order to kill Stashinsky, was a seasoned forty-four-year-old intelligence veteran. He had carried out a number of daring commando-style operations behind the German lines during World War II, then received additional training in Kyiv in order to work diplomatic cover, first in Czechoslovakia and then as an illegal in West Germany. An ethnic Ukrainian, he was an expert on Ukrainian émigré circles and the art of "special operations." Since 1956 he had been stationed at Karlshorst, where he worked under the cover of a Soviet army colonel. His area of responsibility was clandestine operations, and he ran dozens of agents through a number of "residents." Sviatogorov had doubted Stashinsky's loyalty when he had become engaged to Inge and then married her, but Stashinsky was soon out of Berlin. He had become someone else's responsibility.[4]

With Stashinsky back in Berlin for his son's funeral, Sviatogorov's suspicions had returned. He had warned his commanding general that Stashinsky could not be trusted and asked for increased surveillance of the couple. Sviatogorov's warnings were ignored. Stashinsky's handler, Yurii Aleksandrov, had complete trust in his agent. "How could you?" he asked Sviatogorov. "Distrust such a heroic man who has done so much for our county?" Now, with Stashinsky gone, Sviatogorov felt that his career was on the line.

Sannikov, who had been chosen for the operation because he had diplomatic immunity and could recognize Stashinsky, whom he had once seen during his KGB training in Kyiv, did not believe that they had any chance of locating the defector. He assumed that the Americans had already whisked Stashinsky out of Berlin. But Sviatogorov insisted on continuing the surveillance, still hoping to get Stashinsky, and ready to give his life in the process. "I would not have allowed the German police to take me alive," Sviatogorov remembered later. "As far as I was concerned, I decided that if something were to happen, I would shoot myself in the head."[5]

The KGB general who had ignored Sviatogorov's warnings was by all accounts Aleksei Krokhin, the former deputy chief of the KGB Foreign Intelligence Directorate. Krokhin had been present in Aleksandr Shelepin's office when the KGB chief had awarded Stashinsky the Order of the Red Banner of Valor. He had been sent to Berlin after Korotkov's unexpected death in June 1961. Shelepin, who was slowly purging the agency of supporters of his predecessor, Ivan Serov, did not mourn Korotkov's death. His passing had come as a shock to everyone who knew the young, healthy-looking general, but the KGB brass was unmoved. On learning the news, the head of East German intelligence, Markus Wolf, and his colleagues flew to Moscow to attend the funeral, only to be surprised that Shelepin was ignoring the event.[6]

With Korotkov out of the picture and Krokhin now in place at Karlshorst, it would be his responsibility to deal with the consequences of Stashinsky's escape. To save his own career, he had to pass blame along to his subordinates. The first to go was Lieutenant Colonel Yurii Aleksandrov, Stashinsky's case officer, who had trusted his agent too much. On the evening Stashinsky and Inge escaped to West Berlin, Aleksandrov was partying with old friends at Karlshorst. Once the special commission to investigate the incident arrived in Berlin, Aleksandrov was sent back to Moscow, where he was soon arrested.

What had happened in Berlin was a major blow not only to Soviet intelligence operations but also to the international prestige of the Soviet Union and Khrushchev himself. The Western media were about to have a field day turning Khrushchev, a self-styled man of peace, into the assassin in chief. It

was not just that a Soviet spy had been caught: this was an assassin who
had taken orders and received awards from the top echelon of the KGB.
"Khrushchev was very angry: they say he tore papers and threw things,"
Sviatogorov recalled later. "Anyone at all who had had anything to do with
the matter was removed from his post, fired, and put on trial."[7]

According to later reports, a total of seventeen KGB officers were sent
packing or reprimanded, some of them dismissed from the service altogether. Aleksandr Sviatogorov, who never got a chance to kill either Stashinsky or himself, was arrested, put behind bars in the infamous Lefortovo
Prison in Moscow, and tried by the Military Branch of the Supreme Court.
He was cleared of criminal responsibility but demoted in rank and dismissed
from the KGB without a pension. He expected Krokhin, whom he had apparently asked to increase surveillance of Stashinsky, to vouch for him, but
the general did nothing: Krokhin had to look after himself. Among those recalled to Moscow was Vadim Goncharov, who was responsible for eavesdropping on Stashinsky and Inge. He later claimed that he had caught them
discussing their escape and reported the news to the top, but his warning had
been ignored. It seemed that every KGB officer recalled from Berlin had
warned his superiors about the threat presented by Stashinsky.[8]

One person who received no punishment at all was Stashinsky's old case
officer, Sergei Damon. When Stashinsky and Inge had returned from Moscow to Berlin to get married in April 1961, they had learned that Damon had
been transferred to Kyiv. It was about that time that a man called Aleksei
Daimon appeared at KGB headquarters in Kyiv and was put in charge of the
émigré department of the local intelligence directorate. Born in 1912, he was
the same age as Sergei Damon. According to his personal file, preserved in
the Kyiv archives, Daimon came from the Donbas region in eastern Ukraine
and was recruited to the secret police in 1939, while working as an engineer
at one of the mines in that region. His responsibility was economic sabotage.
During the German-Soviet war, he was in Stalingrad, where he was in charge
of training individual spies and commando groups and sending them behind
the German lines. From a counterintelligence officer he became an intelligence specialist and remained a member of the intelligence department of

the Ukrainian branch of the Soviet secret services after the war. From Kyiv, his new base of operations, they would dispatch him to Poland and Czechoslovakia. An ethnic Ukrainian, he was fluent in Ukrainian and Russian but struggled with German. He was married but had no children. His mother was killed by the Germans in the spring of 1942.

Daimon was promoted and awarded for his work against the Bandera faction and its rivals among the Ukrainian nationalists. His superiors considered him an energetic, effective, and imaginative operative, well-acquainted with the inner workings of the Ukrainian nationalist organizations. In September 1954, Daimon was transferred to Berlin to head the Ukrainian division of the KGB émigré department at Karlshorst. Stashinsky became his first agent, whom he would groom, train, and handle on his own. The murders of Rebet and Bandera became their joint "achievements." Daimon was awarded the order of Distinguished Member of the KGB on November 3, 1959, the same day as Voroshilov signed his decree awarding Stashinsky for the killing of Bandera. On the very next day, Daimon was promoted to full colonel ahead of schedule in recognition of "successes achieved in work with the anti-Soviet emigration." His awards and rank remained intact.[9]

Meanwhile, the KGB tried to figure out where they had gone wrong with Stashinsky. The KGB commission sent from Moscow reached different conclusions. The KGB brass believed that Stashinsky had originally been a reliable, ideologically motivated agent dedicated to the Soviet cause. It was his strong-willed anti-Soviet wife who had led him astray after becoming convinced that the KGB was going to kill them both. The KGB was not prepared to admit its own mistake in either selecting or handling an agent. As for Nikita Khrushchev, who was behind the entire operation, he was infuriated by the assassin's escape, but apparently had no second thoughts about the killings themselves. In May 1963, he would advise the young communist leader Fidel Castro to work harder in order to penetrate Cuban émigré circles and, if necessary, kill his opponents. "There are times when the security services should physically eliminate the leaders of the counterrevolution in exile," Khrushchev told his Cuban guest.[10]

33

DEFECTOR

s Aleksandr Sviatogorov and Georgii Sannikov watched the entrance to CIA headquarters in Berlin, CIA Berlin base officers were
recovering from the shock of learning about the newly constructed
Berlin Wall. A few days earlier, John Dimmer, the deputy chief of the base,
had spoken at a meeting of the Berlin Watch Committee, an interagency
intelligence group in West Berlin, where he dismissed intelligence reports
about Soviet plans to seal off East Berlin and said that putting up a wall
would be tantamount to Walter Ulbricht's political suicide. On the morning of August 13, 1961, it became clear that if anyone had committed political suicide, it was Dimmer, not Ulbricht.

On August 13, the Soviet defector was the last thing on the mind of the
chief of the CIA base, William Graver. He was trying to figure out what
could be done if the Soviets crossed the border and took over West Berlin.
He asked for evacuation plans, but was told that no evacuation was possible: the Soviet armed forces had Berlin completely surrounded, and the
Western Allies had few forces at their disposal to prevent an invasion. David Cornwell, who was then serving as a British intelligence officer in the
West German capital of Bonn—and later became known under his pen-
name, John le Carré—remembered later that the British embassy personnel had discussed evacuation in secret conclave but failed to develop a

plausible plan: "Where do you evacuate to when the world is about to end?" The CIA officers in West Berlin began to activate emergency links with their agents on the other side of the rapidly rising wall. They also monitored the situation on the ground in West Berlin, where the locals were growing angry at the lack of Western response to Soviet actions. But once the initial panic at the CIA Berlin base was over, Bogdan Stashinsky was transferred from besieged West Berlin to Frankfurt, where he would spend the rest of the month in CIA custody.[1]

As attested by CIA veteran William Hood, the CIA tried to transfer defectors promptly from places where the Soviets could get at them. "When possible," wrote Hood about his experience in Vienna—which, like West Berlin, was deep inside Soviet-controlled territory until 1955—"defectors were hustled out of Vienna as soon as plans could be made for their reception in West Germany. No matter how long a defector may have brooded over his plan, the actual break always unleashes emotional demons, among which acute anxiety and depression are the most common." Hood wrote that "the most that could be done in Austria was to make sure the person was who he claimed to be, to assess the strategic intelligence he might be able to impart, and try to siphon off any perishable information he might have on the security of the American forces in Austria."[2]

Bogdan Stashinsky was flown to Frankfurt on August 13, 1961, while Inge was interrogated separately by the West German authorities. Stashinsky would be housed in a block of buildings used by the CIA and US Army personnel, and there he would be interrogated repeatedly by CIA officers. The first of the many problems that CIA interrogators faced in dealing with Stashinsky's testimony, both in Berlin and then at the CIA interrogation center in Frankfurt, was that they could not establish his identity. The many documents he produced had three different names on them: Bogdan Stashinsky, Joseph Lehmann, and Aleksandr Krylov. The CIA officers did not know which of them, if any, was authentic. The CIA also had no way to verify Stashinsky's career with the KGB, or his surprisingly candid claims that he had killed Stepan Bandera and Lev Rebet. Besides, no one thought that Rebet had been assassinated, and what Stashinsky was telling the interrogators about Bandera ran counter to all the evidence they had collected so far and all the theories developed on the basis of it. The documents assembled in the CIA's Bandera file suggested that he had been poisoned by someone close to him, not by a lone killer wandering the streets of Munich with a strange tube in his pocket.[3]

The most likely scenario—a theory the CIA kept strictly classified—came from the report of a CIA source inside Polish intelligence, Lieutenant Colonel Michał Goleniewski. Goleniewski had first reported to the CIA on what he claimed to know about the KGB's role in Bandera's death in the fall of 1959. Two years later, on January 4, 1961, Goleniewski and his East German mistress had taken a taxi to the American consulate on Clayallee in West Berlin and asked for asylum. During questioning, Goleniewski did not provide any additional information on Bandera's demise, but his accurate information on Soviet spies in the West had forced the CIA to reconsider his original report and take it seriously.[4]

On August 24, 1961, as Stashinsky was being interrogated in Frankfurt, the chief of the Soviet Russia section at CIA headquarters received a memorandum summarizing Goleniewski's old report on the Bandera murder. According to the report, an unsuspected KGB agent in Bandera's circle had convinced him to meet with an alleged Soviet defector who was in fact another KGB agent. During the meeting, that agent had dropped delayed-action poison into Bandera's coffee. The death of Bandera had allegedly cleared the way for another KGB agent to climb to the top of the Bandera organization. To the CIA agents, this seemed like the most reliable information they had at the time of Stashinsky's defection. His stories about spray pistols and stalking Bandera around the streets of Munich not only sounded suspicious but made no sense at all.[5]

The CIA officers in Frankfurt decided to let Stashinsky be someone else's problem. As far as they were concerned, he posed too many risks and offered too little benefit. "After initial Agency interrogation of Stashinsky in Frankfurt on Main in August 1961," reads a later CIA report, "the conclusion was drawn that he would not be valuable operationally as a double agent, that he was not a bona fide defector and the individual he purported to be." Interrogations of bona fide defectors in Frankfurt lasted months; such individuals were typically debriefed on the political situation in the Soviet Union, popular attitudes toward the Soviet regime, the effect of Western radio broadcasts on the popular mood, and the spread of Ukrainian nationalism, among other topics. But since Stashinsky was not considered a genuine defector, his interrogation was over in less than three weeks. The CIA decided to dump him on their West German hosts.[6]

Stashinsky's hopes for security and freedom in the United States, nourished during long and lonely months in Moscow, were dashed. The information he was offering them, and for which the Soviets were ready to kill him, was deemed fake—the Americans would not be saving him. Had he and Inge made a mistake in risking their lives and fleeing to the West? Stashinsky's shock and despair must have turned to horror when the CIA told him that they were going to turn him over to the West German authorities to stand trial for the crimes he claimed to have committed. But he had no choice but to accept the new reality. "Stashinsky told the Agency officials," reads a CIA report, "that at the time he came to the West, he did not feel his past actions were criminal. They were patriotic acts committed in the name of the state. He said he now realized that the German law took a different view. He said that although he did not want to go to jail, he would have to suffer the consequences."[7]

Stashinsky did not trust the West Germans, and he had not wanted to deal with them in the first place. To make matters worse, the Americans were transferring him not in order to make a deal like the one he had been planning with the CIA—exchanging information for security and protection—but to prosecute him for crimes to which he had voluntarily confessed. Stashinsky must have felt trapped. He could not rescind his confession. If he was dumped by the Americans and acquitted by the Germans, he would have nowhere to go but back into the hands of the Soviets, and he could only imagine what awaited him there. In many ways, a German prison seemed like the safest place available under the circumstances.

On September 1, 1961, Stashinsky was officially turned over to the West German authorities. Interrogations began immediately, and once again, his main task and challenge would be to prove that he was guilty, not innocent. There is no indication that throughout those weeks he was allowed to get in touch with Inge. They were now both in the West, but Inge would live there in freedom, while Stashinsky would be confined to a prison cell.[8]

34

INVESTIGATION

Friday, September 22, 1961, was a warm and sunny day in Munich. The West German newspapers were reporting on an unexpected visit by General Lucius Clay of the United States to Steinstücken, an isolated enclave of West Berlin that had found itself cut off from the American zone of the city after the construction of the Berlin Wall. Steinstücken was in many ways a miniature model of West Berlin. West Berlin was linked to West Germany by a single road controlled by the Soviets and their East German clients; Steinstücken was linked to West Berlin by a road passing through the Soviet sector of the city. Once the Berlin Wall was built, President Kennedy ordered a column of US troops to march along the only highway linking West Germany to West Berlin to demonstrate American resolve to stay in the city. General Clay's visit to Steinstücken showed his determination to defend the tiniest piece of Western territory if the East Germans and Soviets decided to annex it.

As German newspapers discussed Clay's symbolic visit to the enclave, which had a population of only forty-two families, Clay ordered a small detachment of US Military Police to take up permanent residence there. A month later he would send American tanks to Checkpoint Charlie in the center of Berlin to reaffirm the American right to travel in the eastern part of the city. The world was careening toward one of the most dangerous conflicts in modern history, but for the moment, everyone in Germany seemed excited about General Clay's cowboy tactics. The message was clear. The Americans would not retreat: they were there to stay and fight if need be. That same day, the US Congress passed a bill creating the US Peace Corps, allocating $40 million to send American college graduates to Third World countries to make friends, mark the territory, and stop the spread of communism.[1]

The fine weather that day reminded Bogdan Stashinsky of another warm autumn day he had spent in Munich: October 12, 1957, the day he killed Lev Rebet. Stashinsky mentioned that to one of the eight agents who accompanied him on a tour of his crime scenes. It was the first time he had seen the streets of Munich since his assassination of Stepan Bandera two years earlier. Among the agents and officials supervising Stashinsky on his return to Munich was Oberkommissar Adrian Fuchs of the Munich Kripo, who, after months of going around in circles in search of Bandera's killer, was thrilled to finally have his man. Fuchs, a stocky forty-year-old Bavarian police officer, held a microphone in his hand and kept reminding Stashinsky that he was not supposed to mention any names while describing details of the killings he had committed.

They traveled to both crime scenes, at Karlsplatz 8, where Stashinsky had killed Rebet, and Kreittmayrstrasse 7, where he had assassinated Bandera. Stashinsky not only described how he had done so but also reenacted both crimes, walking the same routes and climbing the same stairs for the benefit of a police camera. The photos taken that day show a lean, erect young man with black hair cut short, wearing a black shirt without a tie, a jacket slightly lighter in color, and even lighter pressed pants. At Karlsplatz, Stashinsky was asked to go to the second floor and then walk down toward an agent who was going up. He was told to aim at the agent with a rolled-up newspaper once they reached the same level and, after the virtual pistol shot, to hide the newspaper in the inside pocket of his jacket. In the hallway of Bandera's apartment building on Kreittmayrstrasse, Stashinsky was asked, among other things, to bend down and pretend to fix his shoelaces. The photograph captured his black slip-on shoes and white socks. Stashinsky's face showed no expression on either photo: he looked calm and detached and resigned to his fate. The crowd of accompanying agents was needed to protect rather than guard him. He had nowhere to run.[2]

The chief investigating officer at the scene was Inspector Vanhauer of the Federal Criminal Police Office (Bundeskriminalamt). He became the first German official to interrogate Stashinsky once the latter was in West German custody. Had the CIA discerned any operational value in Stashinsky or his information, he would have been handed over not to the criminal police but to one of the CIA's West German partners—the BND (foreign intelligence) or the BfV, the Federal Office for the Protection of the Constitution, or Bundesamt für Verfassungsschutz (counterintelligence). Interrogations began on the day of his transfer, September 1, and continued the following day. Like the CIA interrogators, Vanhauer found it difficult to believe Stashinsky's testimony. "At first I treated the matter skeptically, as this was the first we had heard of both murders," remembered Vanhauer later. "After the interrogation, we discussed the case late into the night, weighing the 'pros and cons.' Later we inclined ever more to the conviction that Stashinsky's account was genuine."

The investigators would leave no stone unturned in checking his story. On September 11, Oberkommissar Fuchs was asked to go back to Munich and check the automatic lock of the entrance door at Kreittmayrstrasse 7. Stashinsky had claimed that he had twice broken his keys trying to open the door. Sure enough, Fuchs found metal parts of the broken keys in the lock. Stashinsky's testimony on the dates of his travel and hotel stays matched the records unearthed by Fuchs and his assistants. On September 11, the authorities interviewed Inge Pohl, who confirmed and further corroborated her husband's testimony. The Americans, they concluded, were wrong: Stashinsky was not lying.

The final turning point in the interrogation came on September 12, 1961. Present in the interrogation chamber along with Vanhauer were the chief police commissioner and a number of security officers. A report filed by those present stated that "Stashinsky's quiet, sure and precise statements with regard to events preceding the assassination, the lapse of time, and the description of the localities and the execution of the deeds led to the general conclusion that Stashinsky could, in fact, be the murderer of Rebet and Bandera." The information he then provided upon visiting both crime scenes on September 22 added further credibility to his story.[3]

In late September and early October 1961, Stashinsky was questioned once again by agents of the Federal Criminal Police Office (Bundeskriminalamt, or BKA), who concluded once and for all that he was telling the truth. To make certain, they brought along an interpreter who could interrogate Stashinsky in his mother tongue. Whatever doubts the German investigators had about Stashinsky's story were now gone. The suspect seemed as genuine and as distressed as a person could be under such circumstances. "His behavior made it apparent," recalled Inspector Vanhauer, "that he wanted to tell all that was weighing on him and have it recorded in the minutes with all the details."

Stashinsky must have been relieved that this time the investigators believed him. At Vanhauer's request, he prepared a map of his native village and made drawings of his apartment building and apartment in Moscow, as well as of the weapons he had used to kill both his victims. But it did not come easily to him. He probably suffered from insomnia, as he had in the past. Vanhauer also noticed signs of depression. "On some days he was very downcast, and it was apparent that he was seriously remorseful about having carried out the assassinations."[4]

By late September the CIA came to the realization that Stashinsky, to whom the CIA officers referred using the code name "Aeskewer 1," was actually a gold mine of information. The Americans were putting pressure on the West German authorities to go public with Stashinsky's testimony. But the West Germans were hesitant.

The federal elections that took place on September 17, 1961, left West Germany without a strong government. Chancellor Konrad Adenauer struggled to create a coalition in the new parliament and stay in power. No one in the interim government wanted to take responsibility for releasing explosive information that could cause another crisis in relations with the Soviet Union. Moreover, the Federal Prosecutor's Office was not prepared to say anything publicly about the investigation before its indictment was ready. The Germans offered to publish the story in the United States rather than at home, but the CIA turned them down, as the case lay outside American territory.[5]

Stashinsky continued to be questioned into November. "My present attitude to both deeds is fundamentally different," said Stashinsky to his interrogators:

This is explained by the change which I have undergone since November 1959. The reason for my flight to the West is to be found in this change. I wanted to unburden my conscience and wanted to give world-wide publicity to the way in which "peaceful coexistence" really works in practice. I did not want to go on being used on murder assignments. I wanted to warn all those who live in danger of being liquidated, as were Rebet and Bandera, to take precautions. I hope that my flight to the West will be seen as lessening my guilt, for I have brought a great deal upon myself through my flight. The fate of my parents and relatives will come to pass, or may already have come to pass, as I have described it. My flight has already resulted in my father-in-law, who still lives in the Soviet Zone, being kept in custody for seven weeks by the Soviet authorities. It is by no means certain that he will not be subject to more serious measures when my case becomes known in its entirety. My wife and I will always live in the fear that we shall one day be overtaken by retribution from the East. Quite apart from that, we are certainly without means here in the West. Nevertheless I have decided in favor of the West, because I believe that this step was absolutely necessary for the world at large.[6]

Bogdan Stashinsky was fighting for his life. His strategy was not to hide what he had done but to explain why he had done it and why he now regretted his actions. He was also prepared to go public with his revelations. Publicity was never part of Stashinsky's original plan, and it is hard to say whether this idea came to him independently or was suggested by the interrogators, but he was ready to play along. He had accepted the prospect that both his family and Inge's would probably become victims of any such publicity. For his interrogators, this was a chance to unmask Soviet actions on the international scene. Stashinsky's statements were beginning to have international repercussions, whether he wanted them to or not.

35

PRESS CONFERENCE

While the West Germans debated whether to publicize Stashinsky's statements, the Soviets decided to beat them to the punch and tell their version first. On Friday, October 13, 1961, Kurt Blecha, the head of the East German government press service, called a press conference in East Berlin to announce their cover story. "Today we will become acquainted with the criminal intrigues of the Bonn Federal Intelligence Service, which is subordinate to [Director of the Federal Chancellery Hans] Globke . . . and which is headed by [Reinhard] Gehlen, the former general of the Nazi Secret Service," Blecha told the journalists. He referred to Globke as "the murderer of Jews."

Globke had been involved in the implementation of the Nuremberg Laws, which stripped German Jews of their citizenship, while Gehlen had worked in the Wehrmacht intelligence. Blecha was now suggesting that Globke and Gehlen—now in prominent roles in the West German government—had continued their criminal activities long after the end of the war, and he had evidence to prove it. "Herr Lippolz," continued Blecha, referring to a man he was about to introduce to the reporters, "by using concrete examples will acquaint us with the methods of these political murderers. And in this way, we will help the German public and the whole world take notice of the criminal intrigues of the Bonn 'ultras' and their political methods, which include the murder of individual people as well as mass murder."[1]

Stefan Lippolz, a balding, bespectacled man in his early fifties, began with an apology for his limited command of German. Lippolz had been born in 1907 to a family of German colonists in the Volhynia region of Ukraine, which then belonged to the Russian Empire. As the Soviet Union took over Volhynia in 1939 after the signing of the Molotov-Ribbentrop Pact, Lippolz claimed the status of *Volksdeutcher* and was resettled in the Third Reich. He was soon drafted into the army and sent to intelligence school; after graduating, he served as an interpreter for various military intelligence units, including one under Gehlen's general command. He was briefly imprisoned by the Soviets in 1945. Until 1951 he lived in East Germany, after which he moved to the West using the Berlin loophole. Settling in Munich, he opened a restaurant and befriended fellow Ukrainians, many of whom belonged to the Bandera organization. According to CIA records, he had been in Soviet employ since 1929 and was sent to Munich with a supply of poison and the order to kill Bandera. Instead he turned himself in and confessed to the officers of the US Counter Intelligence Corps, who in 1954 passed him to the CIA as a double agent. The KGB recalled him to the East soon after Stashinsky's defection.[2]

Now Lippolz claimed that while in Munich, he was approached by a certain Dr. Weber, a representative of Gehlen's BND, who asked him to collect intelligence about Stepan Bandera. Soon thereafter he was ordered to kill the émigré leader by mixing a poisonous powder into his food. The Gehlen people wanted Bandera out of the picture because he had decided to cooperate with British intelligence rather than the West Germans. Lippolz failed to carry out the assignment. He told Dr. Weber that he did not have adequate access to Bandera and advised him to recruit someone who was better placed.

Lippolz claimed that Dr. Weber had found such a man in his friend Dmytro Myskiw, a confidant of Bandera's. Believing that Gehlen's operatives were about to kill him, Lippolz fled West Germany, only returning to visit Myskiw in late December 1959. He found his friend terribly distraught: Myskiw told Lippolz that he had assassinated Bandera by putting poison into his food at lunch on the day of his death. Myskiw also said that Bandera's security people were looking for him. Lippolz left West Germany again, this time hiding in Norway. It was there that he learned about Myskiw's unexpected death in March 1960. "You can well imagine the impression all this created on me," Lippolz told the reporters. "I was just as uneasy, depressed and intimidated as Dmytro Myskiw was a few months ago. . . . Realizing that there was no other way to escape the secret murderers of the Gehlen Intelligence, I crossed the border to the GDR and surrendered myself to the authorities."

The statement was followed by a question-and-answer period in which Lippolz did his best to link his testimony to the allegations against Theodor Oberländer that had been advanced earlier by the East German and Soviet press. Bandera, suggested Lippolz, was killed because he stood in the way of Bundesminister Oberländer, who was afraid that the Ukrainian leader would testify against him at the trial concerning Oberländer's participation in the Lviv pogroms in June and July 1941. According to Lippolz, Myskiw had confessed to him that the Gehlen operative who had ordered him to kill Bandera had said the following: "Bandera should finally shut his mouth, as certain respectable people in the CDU [Christian Democratic Union] also have an interest in that," clearly referencing Oberländer. The press conference included a statement by a representative of the East German Ministry of State Security (Stasi), who attacked former Nazis holding senior positions in Gehlen's BND and stressed the links between Bandera's people and Oberländer. He promised a full investigation into the circumstances of Bandera's death.[3]

With the wealth of Nazi archives at their disposal, the East German Security Ministry and the KGB were uniquely positioned to track down and expose former Nazis in the West German security services. They also were known to blackmail former SS men into working for Soviet intelligence in exchange for keeping their past hidden. The CIA believed that it was from one such ex-Nazi that the Soviets had learned that Stashinsky was talking to the West Germans. The name of the former SS officer and now Soviet spy in the ranks of Gehlen's service was Heinz Felfe. A former SS Obersturmführer, Felfe had joined the Gehlen Organization in 1951 and quickly rose through the ranks, becoming head of the counterintelligence department. Catching

Soviet spies was his daytime job, providing the perfect cover for his own covert activities. He supplied the KGB with huge quantities of information on BND and CIA agents in the East.

The information that Felfe provided on Stashinsky's testimony was one of the last messages he sent to his KGB handlers. Felfe was placed under surveillance after the CIA triple agent Michał Goleniewski helped to identify him as a KGB spy after escaping to East Berlin in January 1961. On October 20, 1961, the authorities intercepted a radio message from the East addressed to Felfe: "Inform promptly whether it is advisable to ask Busch about reaction to Lippolz's press conference of 13.10. [1961]." Another message on that subject followed a week later: "Inform promptly whether it is advisable to continue the explanatory campaign. Your opinion of the question put to Busch on 20.10. [1961]." Friedrich Busch was a BND officer responsible for efforts to counter the KGB deception campaign against the BND. The KGB was eager to know whether its disinformation campaign was working. New requests with regard to the impact of the Lippolz press conference were sent to Felfe on October 28, and again on November 4. It was that last request, mailed to Felfe by one of his accomplices, that provided legal grounds for Felfe's arrest on November 6, 1961.[4]

Lippolz's press conference was sponsored by the Stasi. But the public spectacle, which was supposed to control the damage, failed to accomplish its purpose. It was soon revealed that Dmytro Myskiw, who had allegedly confessed to the murder of Bandera, could not possibly have been the assassin: on the day of Bandera's death he had attended a major Ukrainian church gathering in Rome. The Bandera organization was quick to offer proof of this alibi, thus discrediting KGB allegations that Bandera had been killed by one of his own before the theory could gain any traction in the Western media.[5]

Despite its promise at the press conference, the East German Security Ministry never reported on the outcome of its investigation into Lippolz's accusations. On November 10, 1961, the ministry held another press conference accusing Gehlen and the BND of political murder, but provided no new information about the killing of Bandera. On April 2, 1962, they held yet another press conference in East Berlin, this time featuring another of their operatives, whom they recalled from Munich: a former agent of the Abwehr (Nazi military intelligence), Osyp Verhun. Verhun claimed that Stashinsky was not an agent of the KGB but in fact a loyal member of the Ukrainian underground who had killed Bandera on orders from the rival nationalist faction. Immediately after the press conference, the KGB sent a request to its counterpart organizations in the Eastern bloc countries, asking them to use their clandestine channels to publish the conference materials in the West. The goal was not only to exonerate the KGB of the murder of Bandera but also to drive a wedge between Western intelligence services: Verhun also claimed that General Gehlen's BND was recruiting agents among Ukrainian nationalists to spy on the United States.[6]

In Kyiv, the KGB was getting ready to deal with a possible backlash from the remnants of the nationalist underground as a reaction to Stashinsky's revelations. They reckoned with the possibility of terrorism in retaliation for the assassination of Bandera. In November 1961, the head of the Ukrainian KGB, Vitalii Nikitchenko, sent a memo to regional KGB offices warning them that "a provocational fabrication is being disseminated in the foreign press and radio to the effect that the death of one of the heads of the foreign Ukrainian nationalist centers, Bandera, supposedly resulted from measures taken by state security agencies of the Soviet Union." He advised his underlings to deny everything: "If reports concerning that matter are received from agents, the operative should tell the agent that this is one more provocation."

In February 1962, the heads of regional KGB branches in Ukraine received a new memo from their chief in Kyiv. Nikitchenko called on them to be vigilant with regard to published materials associating the KGB with Bandera's death that were being sent to Ukraine from the West by regular mail. Ironically, the memo warning KGB officers about "provocational reports on the involvement of Soviet intelligence in the death of Stepan Bandera" was prepared for Nikitchenko's signature by none other than Colonel Daimon, Stashinsky's control officer, now safely in Kyiv. As always, he was particularly careful. The words "death of Stepan Bandera" were inserted in the document by hand—the typist was not supposed to know the key element of the memo that she typed.[7]

36

HIGH POLITICS

The West German response to the Soviet disinformation campaign came on Friday, November 17, 1961. On that day, with the personal approval of Chancellor Konrad Adenauer, the Federal Prosecutor's Office stated that it had taken custody of a Soviet citizen, Bogdan Stashinsky, who had been arrested on charges of "maintaining contacts intended to carry out treason to the state." The authorities announced that Stashinsky had been convinced to defect by his young East German wife. He believed that he would be assassinated as an unwanted witness if he remained in Russia and, despite the murders he had committed, believed defection was his only chance to remain alive.[1]

By the time the statement was released, Heinz Felfe, the BND officer and KGB agent who had informed Moscow about the results of Stashinsky's interrogations, was already in a West German prison. The West German governing coalition had finally solidified after the indecisive September elections, and Chancellor Adenauer felt confident in releasing the information that Stashinsky had revealed about Bandera's death. He dropped this public relations bombshell right before leaving for Washington to meet with President Kennedy to discuss the state of East-West relations in the shadow of the rising Berlin Wall.[2]

Bonn's disclosure of Stashinsky's testimony included the extremely sensitive information that the chief of the KGB, Aleksandr Shelepin, had personally given him an award for services rendered. Earlier that week, Shelepin had officially left the helm of the KGB to take up his new position as secretary of the Central Committee of the Soviet Communist Party. Many believed that Khrushchev had tapped him as his successor. The promotion of Shelepin raised questions: Was the Soviet leader himself involved in the Stashinsky affair? German government officials were careful not to insinuate as much, but Ukrainian nationalists in Munich were quick to pin the death of their leader on the man at the top of the Soviet hierarchy.

"There is no doubt that plans for the undercover assassination were known to and approved by the head of the USSR Council of Ministers, Nikita Khrushchev, to whom the chief of the KGB is subordinate," read the statement released by the Bandera organization. The Shelepin-Khrushchev connection was picked up and further developed by a number of West European and British newspapers. The *Illustrated London News* suggested that Shelepin's promotion to a crucial post in the Central Committee indicated Khrushchev's knowledge and approval of the assassination. In the ongoing propaganda war, the Western media had scored a coup.[3]

The release of this politically explosive information on the eve of Adenauer's visit to Washington was hardly accidental. For months, the West German leaders in Bonn had been trying in vain to convince the young and inexperienced American president to accept their view of the future of East-West relations in Europe and get tougher on the Soviets. They failed. The Stashinsky revelations also fell on deaf ears in Washington. On November 17, as Adenauer was making his bellicose statements, American newspapers published the text of Kennedy's address of the previous day. Referring to Soviet-American tensions over Berlin, Kennedy had said: "It is a test of our national maturity to accept the fact that negotiations are not a contest spelling victory or defeat."[4]

The CIA operatives in West Germany—the same ones who had dismissed Stashinsky's testimony in August 1961—were eager to use

Stashinsky's revelations for propaganda purposes, but their hands were tied. In West Germany it was up to the Germans to decide what to do with their unexpected catch, and in the United States the CIA was prohibited from engaging in any activities meant to influence American public opinion. There was also a change of guard at Langley. Allen Dulles, the staunchly anti-Soviet director of the Central Intelligence Agency, was already on his way out. He would resign before the end of November, leading to KGB self-congratulation on the success of its anti-CIA campaign.[5]

The first indication that the release of Stashinsky's testimony had made a political impact outside of West Germany came not from the United States but from Canada. In early December 1961, less than three weeks after the publication of Stashinsky's revelations, the forty-two-year-old Arthur Maloney, a member of the Canadian Parliament and one of the principal authors of the Canadian Bill of Rights, visited the General Prosecutor's Office in Karlsruhe—the center of West German jurisprudence and home of its Constitutional and High Criminal courts. A federal prosecutor who met Maloney in Karlsruhe confirmed media reports about Stashinsky's testimony. The distortions and confusions in media coverage were minimal, he told his Canadian visitor. Stashinsky had indeed killed Bandera and Rebet on orders from the KGB in Moscow, using a specially designed spray pistol. The German authorities were gearing up for a trial that they hoped would take place in April 1962. They were still deciding whether to hold it in Munich or Karlsruhe.[6]

Maloney's visit to Karlsruhe, which the Canadian print media covered, was congruent with the tough anti-Soviet stance taken by Canadian prime minister John Diefenbaker. In 1960, Diefenbaker—the leader of a country that was still working on its declaration of formal independence from the British Empire, five years away from the adoption of its own flag, and twenty-two years away from acquiring full control over its constitution—turned the tables on Nikita Khrushchev on the issue of decolonization, which the Soviets habitually used against the Western powers to win friends in former European colonies. Diefenbaker declared that the Soviet Union was in fact a colonial empire in its own right, denying freedom to tens of millions of non-Russians living within Soviet borders. The prime minister developed this theme at an ethnic forum organized on Maloney's initiative in Toronto on November 22, 1961. In front of 8,000 people representing 29 different ethnic groups, Diefenbaker stated that since World War II, 37 countries with a total population of 850 million had acquired independence from noncommunist states, while the Soviets continued to hold captive 96 million non-Russians who were never given a chance to say whether they wanted to remain in the USSR.

Diefenbaker's championing of the "captive nations" in the USSR came naturally to the leader of the Progressive Conservatives, a center-right party that took pride in its anticommunist convictions. But there was also another reason for Diefenbaker and his government to be sensitive to the plight of non-Russians in the USSR. The Progressive Conservatives had been swept into power with strong support from Ukrainian Canadians, who were especially influential in Diefenbaker's power base—the prairie provinces of western Canada. Arthur Maloney was one of many Progressive Conservatives who had been elected to parliament with the help of the Ukrainian vote. His Toronto district of Parkdale included two Ukrainian churches and the headquarters of several Ukrainian organizations. When it came to foreign policy, Ukrainians wanted the Canadian government to support freedom for their homeland. Though divided along political lines, they all regarded the assassination of Bandera as an attack on their cherished dream of Ukrainian independence.[7]

News of the Stashinsky revelations reached North America while the United Nations General Assembly was in the throes of a three-week debate about colonialism. On November 26, 1961, the American ambassador, Adlai E. Stevenson, addressed the assembly and denounced the "Sino-Soviet" bloc as the largest colonial empire in history. The Soviets, he declared, were ruling the non-Russian nations by force. He included Ukraine among those "captive nations." Earlier, in July 1959, President Dwight Eisenhower—who had made the theme of nations enslaved by communism an important part of his foreign-policy rhetoric—had declared the first Captive Nations Week for the third week of the month. With the Stashinsky revelations, and a new president in the Oval Office, the "captive nations" initiative was again squarely in the limelight.

The Soviets protested vehemently against the initiative, and some of Kennedy's advisers suggested that he distance himself from the controversial stance. It de facto endorsed the overthrow of communist regimes in Eastern Europe, complicating relations with Moscow. However, despite the advice of the father of US Soviet policy, George Kennan, President Kennedy continued the tradition Eisenhower had established, reaffirming Captive Nations Week for July. Refugees from Soviet-controlled Eastern Europe—Ukrainians, in particular—stood guard over Eisenhower's legacy.

In January 1962, Dr. Lev Dobriansky, professor of economics at Georgetown, who was the primary author of the congressional resolution on captive nations, chair of the Ukrainian Congress Committee of America, and founding chairman of the National Captive Nations Committee, issued an appeal to US senators and congressmen urging them to support the liberation struggles of all enslaved nations, notably the largest of them—Ukraine. He mentioned the displeasure Adlai Stevenson's UN statement had provoked in the communist camp and then switched to the news from Germany. "The recent testimony of the Moscow agent Bogdan Stashinsky," wrote Dobriansky, "that on Moscow's orders he murdered the patriotic Ukrainian leaders in exile—Dr. Lev Rebet in 1957 and Stepan Bandera in 1959—provide further proof of the Khrushchev regime's terrorism and its fear of Ukrainian nationalism." Stashinsky's testimony was rapidly becoming part of the "captive nations" discourse in the United States.[8]

Appeals to political leaders were only part of the Ukrainian émigré campaign to alert the Western world to the danger of political terrorism conducted by Moscow. The leaders of the Bandera organization began to mobilize their supporters in Ukrainian communities in Germany and North America on November 17, 1961, as soon as the West German government made Stashinsky's statements public. In the next few weeks, they organized more than a hundred demonstrations, close to eighty in Western Europe and Britain and about fifty in the United States and Canada. The media paid special attention to those in front of the Soviet embassy in

London on November 25, 1961, and before the Soviet mission at the United Nations in New York on December 2. One hundred New York policemen protected the Soviet mission from approximately four hundred angry protesters, who began by displaying caricatures of Nikita Khrushchev and ended by breaking the police cordon and burning the Soviet flag. A few days later, the Soviets protested to the US ambassador in Moscow against "hooligans" and "fascists" whose actions threatened the future of cultural cooperation between the two countries. The official protest made no mention of Bandera or Stashinsky.[9]

37

CONGRESSMAN

As politicians from Germany to Canada and to the United States struggled with the impact of Stashinsky's revelations, the culprit himself was undergoing psychiatric evaluation. Professor Joachim Rauch of Heidelberg University observed him from February 12 to March 5, 1962, at the university clinic before concluding that he was fit to stand trial. The investigators and prosecutors got busy working on the indictment. After Chancellor Adenauer made public the main points of Stashinsky's testimony, court officials did their best to stop further disclosures. Nonetheless, the indictment was leaked to the press almost immediately after it was ready. In late April its essentials appeared in *Christ und Welt*, the largest-circulation weekly newspaper in the country, triggering rumors that the trial would begin in late May. But the Senate of the Supreme Court sent the case back to the investigators, pushing the trial date into summer and then autumn. The trial was rescheduled for October 8, 1962.[1]

Bandera's followers used the postponement of the trial as an opportunity to secure the best representation possible for Bandera's widow, Yaroslava. The organization had already begun collecting funds and obtained the services of a Munich attorney, Dr. Hans Neuwirth, but they wanted him to be backed up by additional attorneys with expertise in Ukrainian affairs and international law. The Bandera people turned for help to two

American attorneys. The first, Jaroslav Padoch, a childhood friend of Bandera's who had emigrated to the United States after World War II, would be their expert on Ukrainian affairs. The second, Charles J. Kersten, an attorney from Milwaukee, Wisconsin, was supposed to wield political influence because of his role in the US government. Many in the Bandera organization considered it a major political coup that Kersten had agreed to help represent Bandera's widow at the trial.

Charles J. Kersten had been a powerful figure on the Washington political scene in the 1950s, serving three terms as a congressman. During his days in Washington, he had led the House Select Committee to Investigate Communist Aggression. He had also served as an adviser to President Dwight Eisenhower on psychological warfare. Kersten was not only a Cold War veteran but a founding father of American anticommunism. Wisconsin voters had first sent him to Congress in 1947, the same year Joseph McCarthy was elected to represent that state in the US Senate, and the same year President Harry Truman asked Congress for funds to stop communism in Greece and Turkey. The Truman Doctrine was born; the war on communism at home and abroad had begun.[2]

In Washington, the forty-five-year-old Kersten had also ended up serving on the House Committee on Education and Labor. It was there that he first met two other freshman congressmen, the thirty-four-year-old Richard Nixon of California and the not yet thirty-year-old John F. Kennedy of Massachusetts. Kersten and Kennedy were practicing Catholics and easily made common cause as opponents of communism. In 1948, Kersten was appointed to chair the congressional subcommittee investigating communist penetration of American trade unions. Kennedy was one of its members.[3]

That same year, Nixon began his rise to power as a member of the House Un-American Activities Committee. Kersten was an important contributor to that rise. "He taught me most of what I know about communism," recalled Nixon, speaking of his first encounters with Kersten. Kersten introduced Nixon to his own advisers on communist affairs, the Catholic clergymen Monsignor Fulton J. Sheen and Father John Cronin. It was also Kersten who advised the vacillating Nixon to bring his accusations against the suspected Soviet spy Alger Hiss to John Foster Dulles, the future secretary of state and rising star in the Republican establishment, who had been keeping Hiss under his protection. John Foster Dulles and his younger brother Allen, the future head of the CIA, were persuaded by Nixon's evidence and withdrew their support from Hiss.[4]

Kersten agreed to attend the Stashinsky trial after being approached by his old acquaintances in the Ukrainian Congress Committee of America (UCCA). In the 1950s, the chairman of the UCCA, Professor Lev Dobriansky, had served as a consultant to the Kersten Committee on Communist Aggression. He had helped Kersten find witnesses who were prepared to testify about Soviet nationality policies, and had himself testified before the committee. The now retired congressman did not let his Ukrainian friend down. He not only agreed to come to Germany to participate in the trial, but also volunteered to rally as many of his former Washington colleagues and acquaintances as possible and impress upon them the importance of the trial that was about to start in faraway Germany.[5]

On Monday, October 1, 1962, Kersten made a stopover in Washington on his way from Wisconsin to Germany. Before coming to the nation's capital, Kersten requested a meeting with Robert Kennedy, the US attorney general and younger brother of the sitting president. Unfortunately, the attorney general was too busy. When John F. Kennedy ran for the presidency in 1960 against Richard Nixon, Kersten had thrown his full support behind Nixon. As a consequence, he was now having difficulty in getting a meeting even with Kennedy's younger brother, to say nothing of the president himself. Kersten had to settle for a meeting with Bobby Kennedy's assistants. A copy of his letter of May 18, 1962, to Kennedy, in which he advised the attorney general that he was going to participate in the Stashinsky trial in order to prove the connection between Stashinsky and senior Soviet officials, was forwarded to the FBI.[6]

One door that was always open for Kersten was that of his former junior colleague Thomas J. Dodd, who was now a senator from Connecticut. In 1962, Dodd was serving as the vice chairman of the Senate Subcommittee on Internal Security. Although they belonged to different parties (Kersten was a

Republican, Dodd a Democrat), the two politicians had much in common. Both were Catholics, and they subscribed to the same brand of American patriotism, which included a determination to fight communism at home and abroad. Dodd had made a name for himself as the American executive counsel at the Nuremberg trials of Nazi war criminals. He had cross-examined such prominent Nazis as Wilhelm Keitel and Alfred Rosenberg, and when Supreme Court Justice Robert H. Jackson left Nuremberg in October 1946, returning to Washington, DC, he named Dodd to take his place as acting chief of counsel until the completion of the trials a few months later. Dodd was elected to Congress in 1952, where he served under Kersten on the House Select Committee to Investigate Communist Aggression.[7]

Kersten and Dodd met as old friends. Later that day, in a memo drafted for the senator, Kersten summarized his reasons for going to Germany as follows: "It will be my purpose to bring out as many facts as possible through Stashinsky and possibly others to show that Stashinsky was acting under direct orders of the Kremlin and that murders such as the one perpetrated by Stashinsky are an integral part of Russian Communism." He also stated his main reason for wanting to see Dodd: "I feel there might be some efforts thorough the CIA or other of our Government agencies from people who are unsympathetic to raising the mask of Communist activities, to sabotage publicity from this trial and Stashinsky's operations," wrote Kersten. "Anything you might do through CIA, Tom, to aid in the publicizing of this trial will be much appreciated."[8]

His concern was informed by an experience he had had in 1956, when he had been serving as an attorney for a Romanian exile on trial in Switzerland. Kersten's defendant was one of four anticommunist Romanians who had occupied the Romanian embassy in Berne on February 14, 1955, demanding the release of a number of political prisoners being held in Romania. The "Berne incident," as the armed takeover of the embassy became known in the media, had resulted not only in the disruption of the embassy's activities, but also in the death of one of its employees. The trial, which received extensive coverage in the European media, had helped to attract European attention to human-rights abuses in communist Romania. Not so in the United States. Kersten later remembered, "I recall Radio Free Europe played it down, and I had understood that *Life* magazine had a story on the Romanian trial, but I had heard that it had been killed and I had hoped that this would not happen in the Stashinsky case."[9]

This time the situation was quite different. On September 7, 1962, long before the date of the trial became known to the public, *Life* magazine published a long exposé by the head of its Washington office, John L. Steele, entitled "Assassin Disarmed by Love: The Case of a Soviet Spy Who Defected to the West." The article was most likely based on records that the US government had acquired from its West German partners. It was the fullest account of the Stashinsky story then available. Later, the CIA press office would refer journalists writing on the KGB assassination program to Steele's article. Steele, who had extensive contacts in Washington, was able to recount the tiniest details of the murders Stashinsky had committed. He presented Stashinsky's political "conversion" as a result of his love for Inge.

Kersten found Steele's article quite accurate and recommended it to Senator Dodd during their meeting on October 1. But he was not fully satisfied with the *Life* feature. "I don't know that it brought out sufficiently what I thought was the very important fact that was proved in the trial," he remembered later, "namely, that while at the same time the Soviet government was preaching peaceful coexistence, they were training professional killers very skillfully trained, to go into the free world to kill carefully selected persons whom they believed to be enemies of their policies. . . . [O]ne of the big factors in their preparations was to prevent any attribution of these murders to the Soviet government."[10]

In his memo to Dodd, Kersten also shared with his old ally that "Stashinsky apparently will plead guilty and is willing to cooperate. The German government, I believe, is also sympathetic to the above objective. I understand that the German prosecutor will ask for clemency for Stashinsky if he goes along with this line." As far as Kersten was concerned, Stashinsky and the West German prosecution had made a deal. The trial was going to be a political one. He wanted to be there. On the night of October 1, 1962, Charles Kersten and his wife boarded a plane to Munich.[11]

PART VI

TRIAL

38

KARLSRUHE

Monday, October 8, 1962, was another deadly day in Berlin. East German border guards opened fire on two refugees who were trying to escape to the West by swimming across the Spree River. The two didn't make it. As East German bullets hit the opposite side, West Berlin police returned fire. That same day, the British, French, and American representatives in West Berlin sent a note of protest to the Soviet occupation authorities for barring a British ambulance from reaching a young East German who was shot by border guards while trying to escape. The Soviets refused to accept the note. Willy Brandt, the Social Democratic mayor of West Berlin, who had just returned from a meeting in Washington with President Kennedy, declared at a press conference: "If Khrushchev wants a clash, he can get it."[1]

In Karlsruhe, October 8 was equally full of tension and anxiety. "A fine autumn day, perfect for carefree rest and observation," wrote a reporter for the *Badische neueste Nachrichten*, the city's only daily. "For those going on a late vacation, that is how it may have been, but not for the Karlsruhe security and criminal police. Since yesterday, it has been posted in full force along a one-kilometer perimeter around the Federal Court of Justice in front of the Third Criminal Senate, where, as is well known, the 'trial of trials' has begun—the court proceedings in the case of Bogdan Stashinsky, who is accused of having carried out two murders and of treasonous relations with the Soviet intelligence service."[2]

Indeed, the police presence around the Federal Court of Justice (Bundesgerichtshof) made public access to the building all but impossible. The *London Evening News* reported the presence of up to sixty uniformed and plainclothes policemen. A reporter for the *Badische neueste Nachrichten* rendered the feelings of many who unsuccessfully tried to make their way to the Federal Court: "Policemen seemed to emerge suddenly from beneath the ground in front of passersby who struck them as suspicious; from cars parked in various places, distrustful eyes were trained on everyone who went by them, and we would not be surprised to learn that throughout the whole trial every residence near the Federal Court of Justice, on Herrenstrasse, for instance, concealed officials of the criminal service in order to monitor all that was going on in the vicinity."[3]

Whether that was the case or not, it was easy to imagine a ubiquitous police presence. Average citizens all over Europe were suddenly on the lookout for spies and foreign agents. That day *Der Spiegel*, the leading West German political weekly, published an article exposing the West German Army's unpreparedness for war. The publication led to the arrest of the journalist who had written the story and of the publisher for violating the country's security laws. Two days earlier, on Friday, October 6, *Dr. No*—the first James Bond movie, starring Sean Connery—was released in Britain, grossing more than $800,000 in the first two weeks of its run. Ironically, the action took place in the Caribbean, where at the time of the movie's premiere Soviet engineers were making nuclear missiles operational, unbeknownst to the Americans—the first warheads arrived in Cuba on October 4. It was easy to imagine a spy or a plainclothes police officer around every corner.[4]

The main concern of the Karlsruhe police posted around the Federal Court building was less the protection of the German public as of Bogdan Stashinsky, who was both the defendant and the star witness. They suspected that the KGB would try to silence him by sending one of his former colleagues with some new type of spray pistol or other murder weapon.

Only a few months earlier, Bela Lopusnik, a former official of the Hungarian secret service who had defected to the West, had died under suspicious circumstances in a Vienna hospital. The West German police started taking special precautions with regard to Stashinsky's diet. In the Karlsruhe prison where he waited before the trial, food was prepared for him in the presence of a police official, and at no point was a single guard allowed to enter his cell—only two at a time.[5]

On the day of the trial, the police presence was reinforced not only around the building but inside as well, including within the courtroom. "The entire premises of the court were placed under the strict control of uniformed and plainclothes police," wrote a reporter. "Anyone wishing to enter the chamber is checked twice: everyone must present personal identification and a separate pass issued by the secretariat of the tribunal." The media assumed that the passes were numbered and visitors assigned specific seats so as to allow the police to place their own people in strategic positions around the chamber.

Only half the available seats (of the total ninety-six chairs in the room) were assigned to visitors; the rest were reserved for court officials and participants in the trial. The Bandera people did their best to monopolize the passes for the guest seats, annoying those who failed to get into the room. "German law students fought openly to obtain at least half-day passes to the chamber," according to one reporter. Few of them were successful. The trial attracted unprecedented publicity, and the courtroom simply could not accommodate all those who wanted to attend the proceedings.[6]

"The public that obtained passes for the trial is quite varied," wrote one reporter, describing the atmosphere in the courtroom. "Men predominate, but there are also more than a dozen women. We even see a priest. Conversations take place in German, French, and English. With interest, we take another close look at the chamber. The front wall consists of large triangular gray and yellow stone slabs. The dark cherry robes of the five judges reflect strikingly against this background." It was a rather large, windowless room with greenish walls, fluorescent lighting, and six rows of chairs for the public to the right of the entrance. To the left was the area reserved for participants in the trial.[7]

Closest to the journalists was a long desk behind which sat members of the victims' families and their attorneys. The German law allowed victims to have their own legal representation, and they were eager to use that opportunity. Nearest to the entrance door were Lev Rebet's forty-nine-year-old widow, Daria Rebet, and his twenty-year-old son, Andrii, who had been only sixteen when his father was assassinated. Next was Natalia, the twenty-year-old daughter of Stepan Bandera. Mrs. Bandera did not attend the trial. She was living in Toronto, Canada, along with tens of thousands of other Ukrainian refugees who had moved there a decade earlier. The members of the victims' families were accompanied by their attorneys— one for Rebet's family and three for Bandera's. Charles Kersten sat to the left of Natalia Bandera, Jaroslav Padoch to the right. The West German attorney Hans Neuwirth, whom Kersten and Padoch were supposed to assist, was seated next to Padoch.[8]

Hans Neuwirth's expenses, like those of Charles Kersten and Jaroslav Padoch, were being paid from funds collected by the Bandera faction of the Organization of Ukrainian Nationalists in preparation for the trial. The Rebet family relied on the more limited funds collected by their own branch of the organization and their supporters. Accordingly, the Rebet family was represented by only one lawyer, the Munich attorney Adolf Miehr. Daria Rebet had found him simply by walking into his office, not far from the place where her husband had been killed in October 1959. Miehr had little knowledge or understanding of Ukrainian émigré realities or of international politics, but Daria Rebet didn't know anyone who was better qualified. Nor did Miehr have anyone like Jaroslav Padoch to help him grasp the Ukrainian nuances. Lev Rebet's close colleague Bohdan Kordiuk took a seat next to Miehr, but he was not a lawyer, had no official status at the trial, and was never invited to speak.[9]

The members of the victims' families, the journalists, and the public all waited anxiously for the appearance of the accused. Their first opportunity to see the man they knew so much about and hated so much came at about

9:00 a.m., when a policeman escorted him into the courtroom and seated him on a bench to the left of the main desk reserved for the judges. "So that is he!" wrote a correspondent for the Banderite newspaper *The Way to Victory*. "This young man of medium height, with a slightly pale complexion, hair combed up, lips pursed, and dressed with exaggerated elegance—dark clothing, a dark blue tie—as if he had just come from the barber shop; this is he—the assassin of the Leader of blessed memory; this is the degenerate who will go down in history as a personification of baseness, like Judas!"

A reporter for the *Frankfurter Rundschau*, writing a few days later, was more reserved in his account of Stashinsky's appearance. He noted that the accused was approximately 1.7 meters tall (about five feet five inches) and had "a handsome, intelligent face [and] very fine hands." Everyone in the room noticed how pale Stashinsky was. It was difficult to say whether that was due to how little time he had spent outside over the past year or because he was nervous. After entering the room, Stashinsky was approached by his attorney, Dr. Helmut Seidel. He listened, nodded in acknowledgment of what Seidel had to tell him, and then looked at the audience. He was clearly nervous.[10]

Stashinsky had always been able to rely on Inge's support during the most difficult moments of his life in Moscow, and then during his escape to Berlin, but now he was on his own. For security reasons, Inge was not allowed in the court. According to the *Stern* magazine reporters, she went into hiding after her husband turned himself in to the Americans. She was afraid that she, too, might end up on the KGB death list, or perhaps she would be kidnapped and taken to the East after the Stasi arrested her father. She refused a 20,000 Deutschmark honorarium to tell her story to a West German magazine. As the media learned later, she had moved under a different name to Stuttgart, where she worked as a hairdresser. A reporter for the *Hamburger Abendblatt* tracked Inge down to an apartment on Böblingerstrasse in Stuttgart. The police, alerted that her cover had been blown, then placed Inge in the home of a police officer. She was also in close touch with Dr. Erwin Fischer of the General Prosecutor's Office, who specialized in espionage cases and had prosecuted Heinz Felfe, the best-known KGB spy in the BND. Even so, Inge did not show up at the trial. Both she and her police guardians feared that she might be tracked down by the KGB and eliminated as an unwanted witness. Stashinsky would face the trial alone.[11]

39

LOYALTY AND BETRAYAL

Shortly after 9:00 a.m., everyone in the crowded courtroom rose to acknowledge the panel of judges dressed in crimson robes. According to the German law, they, and not a jury, would decide the fate of the accused. The judges were led by a man in his early fifties wearing glasses with only one lens. Dr. Heinrich Jagusch, the presiding judge, had lost his right eye in the war, in which he had commanded a tank battalion. Jagusch was an experienced judge, and cases of espionage were his specialty. In October 1959, the month when Bogdan Stashinsky assassinated his second victim, Jagusch was appointed president of the Third Senate of the Federal Court of Justice, with jurisdiction in cases of espionage and high treason. Jagusch was very good at sentencing communist spies. Everyone in the courtroom knew that, including Stashinsky. But the statement with which Jagusch opened the proceedings gave Stashinsky a glimmer of hope that this trial might be different.[1]

"Soon after the indictment was prepared in this case, toward the end of April 1962, a serious large-circulation weekly declared the defendant a murderer, publishing its conclusions in a long article, printing his photograph, and depicting the deeds confirmed in the indictment," began Jagusch, referring to the article that had appeared in *Christ und Welt* earlier in the year. He continued: "In recent days numerous dailies have published similar commentaries, also printing photos of the defendant and declaring him a murderer or a political assassin even before the judicial investigation was concluded. . . . As head of these court proceedings, I am obliged to protect the defendant against inadmissible premature verdicts in public opinion."[2]

Then the trial began. The audience first heard the voice of the accused when Judge Jagusch asked Stashinsky whether he understood German and whether he felt well. Stashinsky responded in the affirmative to both. He looked carefully at the panel of judges, studying the expressions of Jagusch and his colleagues. Jagusch asked the accused to tell the court about himself, and Stashinsky began with his place and date of birth. "I was born on 4 November 1931 in Borshchovychi in the Lviv district," he began. "At the time of my birth, Lviv and the whole area were under Polish rule, so I was also a Polish citizen at the time." He spoke in an expressionless monotone, his hands behind his back, in a manner that made many in the audience suspect it was a rehearsed statement.[3]

Prompted by Jagusch, who spoke in a friendly manner and managed to create an atmosphere of relative ease, if not trust, Stashinsky explained to the court how on one of his trips home in the summer of 1950 he had been picked up by the railway police. He was nineteen years old at the time, and, as was often the case, he was riding without a ticket. That day he was released, but a few days later a policeman showed up on his doorstep and invited him for a talk at the offices of the railway police. It was there that he first met Captain Konstantin Sitnikovsky of the Ministry of State Security, a predecessor to the KGB. Sitnikovsky wanted him to become a spy for the secret police.

Stashinsky's story sent a shock wave through the courtroom. Many reporters asked themselves whether the Soviets indeed used such methods to recruit their agents. But Jagusch, after years of presiding over numerous trials of communist spies, had no trouble believing Stashinsky's story. "Was that the real reason?" he pressed Stashinsky, digging into his motivations. "I understood that he already knew about me and my circumstances," came the reply. "Others from the same village who knew even less than I had already been arrested long before, and some had been sent to Siberia, so I realized that what he had said about the intention to arrest us and send my parents to Siberia corresponded to the facts, and that such things also happened. I also saw the futility of the struggle of the Ukrainian underground."

In his testimony Stashinsky showed no attachment to the ideology or goals of the resistance movement that was fighting for Ukrainian independence. He portrayed himself as an outsider with no interest in politics. He was aware of the resistance movement from his family members, and that awareness, as well as the direct involvement of his sisters in the movement, was used to blackmail him.

If anything, Stashinsky's testimony indicated opposition to the ideology and methods of the nationalists. "Not far from our village, at a distance of one or one and a half kilometers, there was a [Polish] settlement that did not belong to our village," said Stashinsky. "One night we heard shots, and we could see flames in that direction. In the morning, when we went there, we saw the results of that action. About twenty to twenty-five Polish buildings in that settlement had been burned, and all the men had been shot." To Jagusch's follow-up question about the cause of the fighting, Stashinsky responded, "It was an old quarrel between Poles and Ukrainians. . . . For the Poles were supposed to disappear from Western Ukraine and go off to Poland. The Poles did the same in retaliatory actions. They surrounded Ukrainian villages and punished the Ukrainian population in the same way."[4]

Jagusch announced the first fifteen-minute break at 10:45 a.m. after probing Stashinsky with further questions on his attitude toward the resistance movement and motives for cooperating with the secret police. For the reporters and members of the public who filled the corridors of the courthouse, heading for restrooms, lighting cigarettes, and exchanging opinions on what they had just heard, there was a lot to digest. Could Stashinsky be trusted? He had made a positive impression on many reporters. "He speaks excellent German with a Slavic accent and has a talent for telling his story without exaggeration," wrote the reporter for the *Frankfurter Rundschau* a few days later. "He behaves with refined politeness. In a word, he impresses one as an intelligent overgrown boy with wonderful manners."[5]

Many of the Ukrainians in the courtroom thought differently. Among them was Borys Vitoshynsky, forty-eight years old, who had long been a close associate of Bandera and was covering the trial for the Bandera organization's newspaper, *Shliakh peremohy* (The Path of Victory). A lawyer by training and a journalist by vocation, he had joined the organization in high school and marked his twenty-first birthday in the notorious Polish concentration camp of Bereza Kartuzka. He had spent most of the war in Auschwitz, where he had witnessed two of Bandera's brothers being killed by Polish guards. Despite the socialist leanings of his youth, he was close to Bandera; at Bandera's funeral, he had been asked to carry a cup of Ukrainian soil in front of the coffin. What Vitoshynsky thought and wrote reflected the thoughts, attitudes, and feelings of quite a few members of the Bandera organization.[6]

"I look at the face of the assassin," wrote Borys Vitoshynsky in his report on the first day of the trial. "He often smiles, almost imperceptibly striving to create a 'sympathetic impression.' But are we Ukrainians the only ones to whom it seems that there is something repulsive about his behavior?" To the question that troubled many in the room—Was Stashinsky a traitor to his own family, or did he sacrifice himself to save it from persecution?—Vitoshynsky had a very clear answer: he was a traitor. "For indeed," wrote the former prisoner of Bereza Kartuzka and Auschwitz, "could his parents and sisters have supposed for a moment that their son and brother would make them the first victims of his betrayal under the lunatic pretext of protecting them from the Bolsheviks?"

Vitoshynsky found support among some of the non-Ukrainian reporters whom he met at the trial. One of them was Dominique Auclères, a correspondent for *Le Figaro* and an expert on Russia and Eastern Europe—she had just published a book in Paris about a woman who claimed to be Princess Anastasia, daughter of the last Russian tsar. "Stashinsky is posing! He behaves as if he were in the theater; moreover, he makes the impression of someone with a weak character," she told Vitoshynsky. On another occasion she said to him: "I would not grant Stashinsky any extenuating circumstances. He is an informer and a coward. He not only killed Bandera but earlier he even betrayed his own family, which he supposedly wanted to protect." Vitoshynsky was glad to quote Dominique Auclères in his reportages.[7]

The court reconvened after the coffee break, and Bogdan Stashinsky was asked to describe his first major assignment with the Soviet secret police. In early 1951, Stashinsky said, Captain Sitnikovsky told him to penetrate the resistance group on which he was reporting. The task was to collect information on someone who had helped assassinate the well-known Ukrainian communist writer Yaroslav Halan.

The audience listened with a mixture of shock and disbelief as Stashinsky described his penetration of the resistance unit led by his own sister's fiancé. He told the court that Mykhailo Stakhur, the killer of Yaroslav Halan whom he tracked down in the forest and betrayed to Sitnikovsky, was killed in action, not caught on the basis of the information supplied by him. The Bandera people in the courtroom knew that he was lying. Since that summer they had had in their possession Soviet reports on the trial, which prominently featured Mykhailo Stakhur as one of the accused—clearly not dead.[8]

As noon was approaching in Karlsruhe, Heinrich Jagusch declared the court adjourned for lunch. The proceedings would resume at 3:00 p.m. Journalists rushed to the telephones to file their first reports on the trial. Among them was Vitoshynsky, whose article appeared in the Banderite *Shliakh peremohy* on October 10. It ended with the following statement: "We apologize for the highly condensed form of this report, but technical conditions oblige us to relay this material to Munich immediately, so that our readers may learn at least in abbreviated form about the first day of the trial." Despite his apology, Vitoshynsky turned out to be the most detailed chronicler of the trial. No other correspondent had as much background knowledge and intimate interest in what was going on in the courtroom.[9]

Stashinsky's attorney, Dr. Helmut Seidel, got a chance to question his client immediately after the lunch break. Seidel was an experienced attorney, and Stashinsky was lucky to have him on his side. "Stashinsky got a defender from the government, a good attorney from Karlsruhe . . . who is not a man of left-wing convictions," wrote Bandera's successor, Stepan Lenkavsky, to Jaroslav Padoch in May 1962. Seidel asked Stashinsky about the motives that had led him to work for the Soviet secret police. Stashinsky responded that he considered the insurgency senseless and doomed. He also said that he was appalled by the atrocities that had been committed by the members of the underground. "I have already spoken of burned homes in our village," noted Stashinsky. "On coming to that settlement with my parents, I was deeply shaken. I could not forget it."

Seidel's next question dealt with the threat to Stashinsky's family. "Did the promise not to punish you and your parents in the event that you helped also apply to your sister, who maintained ties with the resistance movement?" asked the attorney. Stashinsky answered in the affirmative. He was helpless, maneuvered into a situation that left him no choice but to join the secret police. Seidel was looking for mitigating circumstances to convince the judges that Stashinsky had joined the KGB under duress, not of his own free will. In his testimony throughout the day, Stashinsky clearly followed the strategy adopted by his attorney.[10]

The attorneys for Bandera's and Rebet's families had a very different strategy. They questioned Stashinsky's motives and his story, trying to portray him as a traitor both to his family and to his people. During the first day of hearings, only Dr. Adolf Miehr, who represented Daria Rebet, had the opportunity to ask a question. When Stashinsky testified about breaking and then restoring relations with his family, Miehr inquired whether he knew what had happened to Ivan Laba, the commander of the underground unit who had dated his sister and whom he had betrayed. Stashinsky responded that he had died in battle. He did not know exactly when that happened, but he had heard of it from family members shortly before leaving for Poland and Germany in the summer of 1954. That could be true. Laba had been killed by the secret police in 1951. No one in the West knew of this at the time.[11]

Neither Hans Neuwirth nor Charles Kersten nor Jaroslav Padoch got a chance to ask questions during the first day of the proceedings. Led by questions from Jagusch, Stashinsky continued to testify for the rest of the afternoon about his involvement with the Soviet secret services. After graduating from the Kyiv school, he was sent first to Poland and then to East Germany, where he first met his case officer, Sergei Damon. On Damon's orders he traveled to Munich to meet with a Ukrainian émigré whom the KGB wanted to recruit as an agent. He described how he stuffed dead drops and spied on American and West German military installations. "Stashinsky," wrote the ever-present Vitoshynsky, "speaks as if he were not being tried for known and less known murders and other heinous crimes that he had committed, but as if he were telling an interested public about his exploits. He sometimes smiles, probably thinking that by twisting his lips that way, which suggests cynicism and laughter, and with his subdued voice he is presenting himself as a good-hearted and naively innocent type." The nervousness that had been apparent during the morning session seemed all but gone. "He responds to questions with almost unvarying indifferent equanimity; he does not get excited; he does not raise his voice," said another member of the audience in describing Stashinsky's demeanor.[12]

The first day of the trial was nearing its end. It was largely a two-man show: Jagusch and Stashinsky. The first tried to establish the facts and understand the motives, while the second worked hard to convince the judge that he was answering his questions as honestly and completely as possible. It seemed during the first day of the proceedings that Stashinsky's strategy had failed. While Jagusch treated the accused with utmost respect, addressing him almost exclusively as "Herr Stashinsky," he often questioned Stashinsky's motives. When Stashinsky reminded the court about how shocked he had been by the sight of the burned Polish houses, the judge told him: "You were deeply affected by the burned settlement at the end of 1943, when you were twelve years old. You had your conversation with Sitnikovsky at nineteen years of age." It was not looking good for Stashinsky.[13]

40

FIRST MURDER

On the morning of October 9, the second day of the trial, Borys Vitoshynsky, reporter for the Bandera organization's newspaper *Shliakh peremohy*, was at the entrance to the Federal Criminal Court long before the building opened for business. "This morning was again clear, sunny, and pleasantly cool, refreshing the weary faces of journalists who had doubtless spent the night working to prepare articles and information for their papers," he wrote in his report on the trial. "The doors to the building where the trial is going on are still locked, and a very young police officer is walking by them. And those waiting before the doors are constantly growing in number."[1]

Finally, after a thorough document check, journalists and visitors were allowed into the building and then into courtroom 232. At a quarter to nine, the police brought Stashinsky into the courtroom. Five minutes later, Heinrich Jagusch, in his robe and one-lens glasses, entered with the rest of the judges. With all the attorneys—Stashinsky's Dr. Helmut Seidel, Daria Rebet's Dr. Adolf Miehr, and Yaroslava Bandera's Dr. Hans Neuwirth, Charles Kersten, and Jaroslav Padoch—in attendance, the proceedings could begin. It was a day that Daria Rebet and her twenty-year-old son, Andrii, had awaited with particular trepidation: Stashinsky was expected to testify on the killing of their husband and father. Unlike Bandera's

followers, who had close ties with the West German intelligence and counterintelligence services, the Rebets had no inside information about either
the killer or his testimony. As Andrii Rebet remembered later, they only
learned that Lev Rebet had been murdered by a KGB assassin from the
newspapers. According to CIA records, in the months leading up to the
trial, Daria was followed by someone in what her friends believed was an
attempt to scare her and possibly cause a heart attack. She withstood the
pressure and was now ready to face her husband's killer.[2]

Many in the room were curious to learn why the KGB had decided to
kill Lev Rebet at all; he was a journalist who had no known involvement
with the secret services or their clandestine operations in the Soviet Union.
Andrii recalled that with most of his father's political allies leaving for
North America, Lev Rebet had also made plans to emigrate to the United
States. He had even begun taking courses to become a lathe operator, and it
was only his wife's refusal to go overseas that made him stay longer in Germany. In a perverse way, the question of why Rebet was killed two years
earlier than Stepan Bandera also roiled Bandera's followers, who had spent
years trying to prove that they, not Rebet and his circle, were the true threat
to the Soviet regime in Ukraine. More than that, they had long claimed that
Rebet's opposition to Bandera undermined the unity of the nationalist
camp and thus benefited the Soviets. After Stashinsky's revelations were
made public, rumors spread throughout emigré circles that Rebet had been
chosen simply as target practice to prepare the assassin for the real job of
killing Bandera. After trying the spray pistol on a dog, claimed the cynics,
the KGB tried it on a human being, who just happened to be Rebet.[3]

Back in March of that year, Hans Neuwirth had tried to explain the
choice of Rebet as Stashinsky's first target in a memo for the investigating
judge Fritz von Engelbrechten. He wrote that the leaders of the Bandera
faction rejected any suggestions that Stashinsky had been assigned to kill
Rebet merely for practice. They proceeded from the premise that in calcu-
lating outcomes, "the Bolsheviks are too good and sober to run the risk of
being prematurely compromised without a palpable goal and benefit." But
having rejected that theory, the Banderite leadership could not come up

with an alternative. Still believing that Rebet's revolt against Bandera was in the interests of the KGB, they were at a loss to explain the KGB's motive. "Thus," wrote Neuwirth, "there is no palpable motive why the Bolsheviks would liquidate Rebet. On the contrary, he was beneficial to them because of his oppositional activity." The memo eventually got into the hands of Daria Rebet and her circle; it was then published, adding to the already tangible atmosphere of distrust between the two nationalist groups.[4]

Jagusch began by showing Stashinsky a photo of the man whom the accused identified as Dr. Lev Rebet. Jagusch then read aloud a brief biography of the Ukrainian leader that followed Rebet's life story, from his study of law at Lviv (then Polish Lwów) University to heading the nationalist underground in the wake of Bandera's arrest in 1934, and from his participation in the government of independent Ukraine, proclaimed in 1941 against German wishes, to his imprisonment in Auschwitz, his break with Bandera, and his role as editor of the newspaper that became a platform for the democratic opposition in the nationalist camp. After finishing with the biography, Jagusch asked Stashinsky an open-ended question: "What can you say about Rebet?"

What he knew about Rebet, explained Stashinsky, came almost exclusively from his case officer, Sergei Damon. Like other KGB officers at Karlshorst, Damon spoke of Rebet as an ideologue and a newspaper editor. The KGB argued that nationalist newspapers such as Rebet's were spreading anti-Soviet propaganda and preventing émigrés from returning to their homeland. Stashinsky had never read any of Rebet's writings, however; he had taken Damon at his word.[5]

The previous day, when Stashinsky had testified about his contact with Ivan Bysaga, the KGB agent closest to Rebet, Jagusch had made a special effort to find out what Stashinsky himself had thought about the early plans to kidnap Lev Rebet. "Is it true that you saw those goals and that method of kidnapping as Sergei [Damon] presented them to you?" asked Jagusch. Stashinsky confirmed that that was indeed the case. "I worked for the KGB and had to carry out the assignments I was given," he told the judge. Jagusch pressed on: "Did you think it was right?" Stashinsky answered in the affirmative. "There are various kinds of people," responded Jagusch, "who agree to collaborate with the KGB; some even do so gladly. You, Mr. Stashinsky, belong to that category." Stashinsky was silent. He had nothing to say, or at least preferred to say nothing. Those in the audience could see that he was at a loss.[6]

Jagusch moved on to the issue of the murder weapon. "Have you ever seen this device before?" Jagusch asked Stashinsky, showing him a tube approximately eighteen centimeters long that resembled a somewhat oversized pen. "Dead silence prevailed in the chamber," wrote Borys Vitoshynsky in his report. "All eyes turned to Stashinsky." Stashinsky calmly told the judge that the tube had been reconstructed on the basis of a drawing he had made at the request of the police. Jagusch asked whether the object was the same as the one given him by the man from Moscow. After examining the tube, Stashinsky responded that the length was exactly the same, but the replica was heavier than the original.

"He turns it over in his hands, takes it apart and puts it back together, explaining that the 'apparatus' is quite similar 'in principle' to the real one that he used to kill people, but that the replica is still somewhat different," wrote Vitoshynsky. A thought occurred to him: What if the spray pistol brought to Karlshorst by the man from Moscow had been mass-produced? How many of the "heart attacks" suffered by opponents of the Moscow regime were indeed natural? "No one can answer that question," wrote Vitoshynsky. "Perhaps many simply avoid answering the question, reassuring themselves that only the two assassinations to which Stashinsky has confessed are involved." Stashinsky believed that a pistol similar to the one he used to kill Lev Rebet had been used previously to assassinate someone else, but he did not know who the victim was and never dared to ask. When the pistol was presented to him by the "man from Moscow," Stashinsky explained to the court, he had no time to think about anything: the weapons expert began immediately to instruct him in its usage.[7]

Once Stashinsky's confession had become public in the fall of 1961, many in the Ukrainian emigration had hypothesized that the first victim of Moscow's clandestine killing spree had been Danylo Skoropadsky, the hale and hearty fifty-four-year-old son of Pavlo Skoropadsky, who ruled Ukraine in 1918. The Skoropadsky family was the closest thing Ukraine had to its own ruling dynasty in the twentieth century. Pavlo Skoropadsky, a descendant of an eighteenth-century *hetman*—ruler of Cossack Ukraine—and a high-flying officer in the Russian imperial army, had assumed the title of hetman in 1918 and ruled Ukraine under German tutelage for eight months—the longest period of relative stability in Ukraine's turbulent revolutionary history. When the Germans left at the end of 1918, the Bolsheviks forced Hetman Skoropadsky to leave Ukraine. He spent the interwar period in Germany, running a pro-independence movement that served as an alternative to the radical Organization of Ukrainian Nationalists. He died in April 1945 of wounds from a bomb dropped by an American airplane. The old hetman's cause of creating a monarchical, multiethnic Ukrainian state was continued by his son, Danylo, who took over the movement in 1948 at the age of forty-four.

Danylo Skoropadsky had lived in London, traveling from time to time to Germany and then to the United States and Canada to rally his supporters and create a common front with the other Ukrainian organizations, including the nationalists, who by then had divided into three factions. If Bandera and Rebet were "splitters," Skoropadsky was a "unifier." In April 1956, less than a year before his death, Skoropadsky served as a cosponsor of a 10,000-strong Polish-Ukrainian demonstration protesting the visit of Nikita Khrushchev to Britain—one of the Soviet leader's first foreign trips. On February 22, 1957, Skoropadsky went to his favorite restaurant for dinner. He felt sick and went home, and soon he lost consciousness. That night he was taken to a hospital, where he died the next morning. The inscription on his tombstone read: "I am building Ukraine for all and with all." Rumor had it that he was killed by a KGB agent named "Sergei," who allegedly followed him during the last days of his life.[8]

At the end of the day, Stashinsky testified about the beginning of his hunt for Lev Rebet, with the spray pistol wrapped in a newspaper. Jagusch offered him both the replica of the pistol and a newspaper to demonstrate how he had concealed his weapon. "At the request of the president of the senate," wrote one of the Ukrainian journalists present in the courtroom, "Stashinsky demonstrates to the court in the greatest detail, for almost thirty minutes, how the 'apparatus' should be wrapped so as not to raise the slightest suspicion of a passerby. He is very professional, perhaps even too professional with all the explanations and demonstrations. . . . Such is the impression of more than one onlooker in the room. . . . All his attention is keenly focused on the death-dealing weapon—he is like a hunter entranced by the very appearance of his hunting rifle. . . . The audience listened with bated breath to his calm, coldly objective words of explanation." Throughout the rest of the day, Stashinsky kept his cool, showing little, if any, emotion. Perhaps the only exception was his description of the moment when he killed Rebet. "Walking past him, I suddenly raised my hand," he said with a sigh, "and slowly . . . well, like that, I squeezed the trigger and went on." Blood rose to his cheeks, adding color to his otherwise pale face.[9]

41

BIG DAY

On the morning of October 10, 1962, the courtroom was more crowded than ever. On that day the former KGB agent was scheduled to testify about the murder of Stepan Bandera. There were more journalists present than before, and some celebrities showed up at the trial for the first time. Among them was the now retired Bundesminister Theodor Oberländer. He came to witness the confession of the man who had committed the crime for which he himself had been falsely accused. That accusation had helped finish Oberländer's political career. Perhaps the trial would prove to the world that he was innocent.

Oberländer was a popular figure in the courtroom, which was full of East European refugees whose interests he had represented in the government. Borys Vitoshynsky, who, as always, came to the courtroom long before the opening of the proceedings, even had the opportunity to meet the former minister. "There are more people than on previous days; the noise is louder," wrote Vitoshynsky in his reportage for that day. "Almost everyone listening to the trial leafs quickly through the morning papers to scan the reports on the previous day." As always, Vitoshynsky paid close attention to the behavior of the accused, who consulted with his attorney before the proceedings, as he did every day. "And the fact that Stashinsky listens to him very carefully and always nods his head as a sign of agreement shows that the KGB agent does not feel very confident in the environment of the 'corrupt' West," wrote Vitoshynsky, referring to a Soviet propaganda cliché. "But he tries to adjust to that environment at least outwardly—from time to time he smooths the hair on his head, adjusts his tie or his suit, and ogles the young girls sitting in the chamber."

Apart from the young girls, Stashinsky also paid special attention to the ranked members of the Organization of Ukrainian Nationalists. Among them was the man who Stashinsky believed might have been his next target, the former prime minister of the short-lived independent Ukrainian government of 1941, Yaroslav Stetsko, whom the Germans had incarcerated in Sachsenhausen. Now fifty years old, Stetsko was the head of the Anti-Bolshevik Bloc of Nations. The previous day, Stashinsky had told the court that his KGB handlers had ordered him to locate Stetsko's apartment in Munich, which was exactly how they had first put him on the trail of both Rebet and Bandera. For Stetsko, this was the first day of the trial he could attend. He had just returned from Tokyo, where he had attended a conference organized by the Asian People's Anticommunist League. In his address to the conference, Stetsko had referred to the Stashinsky trial as the latest proof of Moscow's desire to control the world.[1]

Soon after 9:00 a.m., Heinrich Jagusch entered the room along with the rest of the judges. He opened the proceedings with a benign-sounding request: "Tell us what happened in the summer of 1958." With Jagusch's help, Stashinsky told the court the story of his travels to Rotterdam and Munich in search of Bandera. When he described the excitement of his control officer, Sergei Damon, over finding Bandera's address in the telephone book, Jagusch did not hide his disbelief. "That does not sound very probable," he told Stashinsky. "They could have known all that— telephone number, address, license plate number." Stashinsky had no answer. Despite its allegedly deep penetration of the Ukrainian nationalist organizations, the KGB was at least a few years behind its targets. In 1957 Stashinsky's KGB contacts had given him Rebet's old home address, and the same thing had happened with Bandera.

"For some time I did not receive any assignments," Stashinsky continued. Then, in late April 1959, he was ordered to go to Moscow. It was there, in a Moscow hotel, that he met a KGB "aristocrat" called Georgii Avksentievich, who told him that the decision had been made to "liquidate" his target in the same manner as Rebet. "Did he express himself as you said, or did he say which agency had adopted that resolution?" asked Jagusch. "He did not speak clearly about that," responded Stashinsky. "It emerged from what he said that the resolution had been adopted by the 'supreme authority.'" Jagusch probed further. Did the expression mean that the order came from the government? Stashinsky said that it did: he became convinced of it when he visited the head of the KGB, Aleksandr Shelepin, later that year to receive his award for a job well done.

This was the first time that the name of Shelepin, by now a secretary of the Central Committee of the Communist Party of the Soviet Union (CC CPSU), had been mentioned by Stashinsky in his testimony, and the first direct reference to top Soviet government officials. A number of journalists immediately rose from their seats and headed for the exit, and then to the telephones. They were rushing to report on the most politically explosive information so far revealed by the accused: Stashinsky had confirmed earlier press reports that the new secretary of the CC CPSU had been personally involved in the plot to assassinate Bandera.

Stashinsky continued his testimony, speaking to an audience riveted by the sheer drama of what he was describing. "I saw Bandera disappear into the garage," testified Stashinsky, recalling his first direct encounter with Bandera and his first, failed attempt to assassinate him. "Then I went out [of the archway of another building where he had been hiding], taking the weapon out of my pocket on the way." He spoke slowly, heightening the tension in the room. "I held the weapon in my right hand, with an ampoule in the left, began walking, and was convinced that I should attempt the assassination now," continued Stashinsky. "When I was directly in front of the archway, I thought for a moment that here he was, standing and doing something around the car, not knowing that I was already on my way, that by the same token his death was very near, that in an instant he would no longer be alive."

These words were met with complete silence. Pale as always, Stashinsky fixed his gaze on Jagusch, while everyone else looked at him. Even the stenographers had stopped typing. "I went into the entrance archway," continued Stashinsky. "The garage was open, the car was in the garage; he was standing on the left side, doing something near the driver's seat. He had just got out of the car. . . . I had already taken two steps in his direction, but then a thought flashed through my mind, and I told myself that I would not do it. I turned and went away." One could almost hear a sigh of relief from the audience. Only Jagusch seemed unaffected by the emotional roller coaster of the story. "Was it a stone or a wooden bridge?" he asked after Stashinsky told the court that in order to make it impossible to change his mind, he fired the spray pistol into the ground, and then dropped it from a bridge into the very stream in the Hofgarten into which he had dumped the pistol he had used to assassinate Lev Rebet a year and a half earlier. Stashinsky responded that this time it was a stone bridge—same stream, different bridge.

When Stashinsky reached the day of the actual killing of Bandera, he recounted how, after seeing the car leaving Zeppelinstrasse, he had hopped on the tram to go to Bandera's apartment building. Jagusch wasted no time in highlighting the inconsistency: "What were you thinking of? You could have said to yourself: now he's driven off; enough for today. Instead of that, you asked yourself where he was going." Stashinsky had no good answer, except that he was just following orders. "I had to take steps of some kind that would make it clear that I was trying to carry out the assignment," he told the judge. When Stashinsky moved on to the description of the actual killing, Jagusch asked another of his characteristically brief questions: "What did you do?" "I understood that I could not refuse to carry out the assassination," responded Stashinsky. "I had to do it!" The tension in the courtroom peaked again. "Some listeners leaned forward, bracing themselves for the impending shock," wrote Vitoshynsky. "No one stirs; there is no whispering to be heard, nor coughing. Five judges in crimson robes, with broad white fronts and bow ties, sit motionless, like sculptures against the background of the front wall, and do not take their eyes off Stashinsky. And he keeps his head down, speaking irregularly, almost in a whisper, and continues his terrible story."

He did not dare to go into the courtyard this time, Stashinsky told the judges. Instead, he walked to the entrance of the building and opened the door with the keys he had received in Karlshorst. He then locked the door from the inside and took the stairs to the ground floor, where he would wait until Bandera entered the hallway. A few minutes later, after avoiding detection by a woman who was leaving the building, Stashinsky saw Stepan Bandera standing in front of him at the main door, struggling with his key, which he was trying to remove from the keyhole. He was carrying some bags under his arm. One of them was open, and Stashinsky said that he could see it contained green tomatoes. "That was not the right situation for carrying out the killing," Stashinsky told the court, which was hanging on his every word. "He would have had to close the door behind him."

It was then that Bandera, hearing the sound of his approaching footsteps, raised his head and saw Stashinsky. "In that moment he saw me; I looked at him," said Stashinsky. To gain time, Stashinsky pretended to be fixing his shoelace. But when he arose, Bandera was still busy with the door. "Then I went on," continued Stashinsky. "I did not know whether to carry out the assassination or not. I was coming down the stairs and already thinking that in a moment I would pass him, and probably nothing would come of all that. On the other hand, I knew that I had to do it. . . . This was already the second attempt, and I should not let it pass, I thought." Stashinsky told the court that he had heard his own voice as if from a distance. He asked Bandera whether anything was wrong with the lock. He knew that this was foolish: his accent could betray him. Bandera responded that everything was in order. Stashinsky held the door with his left hand. Bandera finally got his key out of the lock. Stashinsky paused for a second, not knowing what to do. "I stood there and wanted to close the door behind me," Stashinsky told the court, " . . . [S]uddenly I raised my hand and pressed both triggers, turned instantly, closed the door behind me, and went away."

Borys Vitoshynsky took a look at his watch. It was 11:30 a.m. on October 10, 1962. The truth about the death of his friend and leader was finally out. Theodor Oberländer, the retired federal minister, finally had proof of his own innocence. Yaroslav Stetsko, the no. 3 man on the KGB hit list, had no problem imagining what his own assassination might someday look like.

A few minutes later, Hans Neuwirth, the attorney representing the Bandera family, had his first opportunity to ask a question: "What did you think when you were killing Mr. Stepan Bandera?" It took some time for Stashinsky to come up with an answer. He was clearly nervous when he finally spoke: "I had no personal reason to kill him. I was only carrying out an order." Jagusch adjourned the court for lunch. The members of the audience headed for the exit.[2]

42

DOUBT

Bogdan Stashinsky's confession of double murder in a courtroom full of West German and foreign journalists was as stunning as it was difficult to believe. Why would someone who had committed two murders admit to them so candidly? Was he being manipulated?

The Soviet and East German media vehemently argued that Stashinsky must be a devoted follower of Bandera who had agreed to sacrifice himself in order to implicate Moscow for crimes it had not committed. In early October 1962, before the trial began, the Soviets published an interview with one Mykhailo Davydiak, a member of the Organization of Ukrainian Nationalists who had been sent by Bandera and the West German foreign intelligence on an espionage mission to Ukraine. Davydiak claimed that before he left in the spring of 1959, Bandera had personally met with him and asked him to locate and gather intelligence on the Stashinsky family in Ukraine. Bandera, suggested Davydiak, wanted to send Bogdan Stashinsky, who was an OUN member currently in the West, on a clandestine mission to Ukraine.[1]

Questions about Stashinsky were raised not only in the East but also in the West. There was still widespread doubt about the veracity of Stashinsky's confession on the morning of October 10. Reporters for the *Frankfurter Allgemeine Zeitung*, *Die Welt* (Hamburg), *Deutsche Zeitung* (Cologne), and

Süddeutsche Zeitung (Munich) all questioned his guilt. Part of the media's skepticism was due to the way the presiding judge, Heinrich Jagusch, had conducted the questioning. Concerned by media leaks before the trial, Jagusch had gone out of his way to stress the impartiality of the court in his opening statement. He had lived up to that statement throughout the first few days of the trial. Jagusch was actively seeking evidence to disprove Stashinsky's testimony about his travels to Munich, his meetings with other agents, and details of the assassinations of Rebet and Bandera. His skepticism became contagious.[2]

At the end of the second day of the trial, Jagusch summarized for Stashinsky what he had said so far about his reasons for committing the murder. He asked the accused to correct him if he was wrong. "Your upbringing from 1950 to 1957 and your views were such that once you were given an order, you were to carry it out in the interests of the Soviet Union and take no account of any feelings of fear for yourself as an individual, but to overcome them," suggested the judge. Stashinsky agreed with his statement. Jagusch asked what consequences Stashinsky had thought he might face if he refused to follow the order. Stashinsky told the court that "refusing to carry out the assassination out of humane considerations and because of my own conscientious objection would mean the most severe punishment for me. Since I knew that the assassination was being planned, I would have been isolated from everyone, which would have been equivalent to a death sentence."

Jagusch's summary of Stashinsky's argument was based not only on his testimony before the court but also on the records of his interrogation by the West German investigators. In his testimony before and during the trial, Stashinsky had spoken of Russia and the Soviet Union as equivalents. He appeared to be loyal to that Russia-led union, not to his native Ukraine. He had tried hard to leave his Ukrainian past and identity behind. Had he not done so, he would have found it difficult to consider himself a patriot.

"I gradually became convinced of the rightness of the Soviet regime and became ever more accustomed to the view that I was doing all this for the good of the Soviet people," said Jagusch, quoting from Stashinsky's testimony to the police investigators. "I was a committed communist; I did everything out of political conviction. . . . I regarded [anyone's] refusal to return to the homeland [from the West] as treason. That followed from my communist convictions. On the other hand, I had sympathy for the families of the victims, but when it came to enemies of the Russian people, my communist upbringing commanded me to be firm." To one judge's question of whether he believed in God, Stashinsky responded with a long silence. He told the court that until he killed Lev Rebet, he believed that he had not harmed anyone else, or at least was not directly responsible for anyone else's death. He had grown up in a religious family, but it was not easy for him to say whether he still believed in God after all that had happened to him and all that he had done.

As the discussion of Stashinsky's motives went on, it was Adolf Miehr, the attorney for the Rebet family, who asked most of the questions, while Stashinsky's attorney, Helmut Seidel, stayed silent. Seidel did not add much to the proceedings—he did not have to. It seemed as if Heinrich Jagusch, who had gone after Stashinsky so doggedly the previous day, was doing his job for him, asking questions and suggesting answers that conformed well to Seidel's line of defense: Stashinsky had committed horrible murders, but he had done so after being brainwashed by Soviet propaganda and on orders from above that he could not disobey without putting his own life in danger. Had Stashinsky's testimony managed to convince the judge that he was not hiding anything from the court and that he had genuinely repented? Or was this evidence of the bargain that Charles Kersten had heard about in Washington: In exchange for implicating the Soviet authorities, was Stashinsky getting lenient treatment from the court? There was more than one way to interpret the proceedings.[3]

With regard to Stashinsky's direct culpability for the killings, Jagusch had little solid evidence apart from the word of the defendant. None of the witnesses could place him on the scene at the time of the killings. Crescenzia Huber, the woman who had passed him in the hallway before he killed Bandera, could not positively identify him in court. She actually said that the man she saw near the elevator door had darker hair than the accused.

The rest of the witnesses, who testified during the fifth day of the trial and included Inspector Vanhauer of the Federal Criminal Police and Ober-kommissar Adrian Fuchs of the Munich Criminal Police, could confirm that Stashinsky, or at least a person using his numerous aliases, had indeed traveled to and from Munich on the days specified by the accused and stayed in the hotels in which he claimed to have stayed. But that was it.

The three spray pistols that Stashinsky had allegedly dumped into the stream in the Munich Hofgarten were never found, even though the stream was drained in a search for them. Adrian Fuchs explained that the city cleaned the stream every year, and the pistols had probably already been removed by the cleaners. With no murder weapon and no witnesses, Stash-insky's ability to answer questions in a manner that generated trust in him and his story was crucial to securing his conviction.[4]

The whole case would simply have fallen apart if he had ever changed his story. He did not. His narrative captured the imagination of the audience in the packed courtroom and found many sympathetic ears outside it. The reporter for the *Frankfurter Allgemeine Zeitung* wrote on October 18, 1962: "This individual has qualities not often found in such measure and in such a combination. Stashinsky is extraordinarily intelligent, reacts quickly, is almost incredibly self-confident, sharp, and seems capable of dedicating himself completely to a cause he considers just." The likability of the con-fessed killer presented Bandera's followers with a major problem. They were working hard to turn the criminal trial into a political one and depict the Soviet regime as one that would stop at nothing to eliminate its ene-mies. Now it seemed as if one of the criminals—the only face of commu-nism directly visible to the Western public—was winning the congeniality contest.[5]

Borys Vitoshynsky repeated again and again in his articles that Stashin-sky's testimony was not the plot of a mystery novel or a movie. It was an indictment of the murderer himself and his masters in Moscow. "Stashin-sky's testimony, aside from the feeling of constant distaste that he arouses toward himself with it (we have in mind only critically thinking people), is constantly and extraordinarily interesting and simply sensational, like a thrilling spy novel, to the many who allow themselves to be 'taken in' by the Moscow spy," wrote Vitoshynsky. "Unfortunately, we are not dealing with a novel. This is a narrative of evil deeds by a person who, on the orders of the criminals in the Kremlin, took the path of the greatest crimes: betrayal of all that is one's own and noble; the path of murder, constant lying, and service to evil."[6]

It became the task of the Banderas' attorney, Hans Neuwirth, and the representative of the Rebet family, Adolf Miehr, to change the atmosphere in the courtroom and the tone of the sympathetic newspaper reports by unmasking him as a traitor, a committed communist, and a manipulative KGB spy. Before the trial, the Bandera people had gathered enough background information on the Stashinsky family to prove that Stashinsky had at least ideologically turned on his own kin. The Stashinsky family was indeed active in Ukrainian affairs, and Stashinsky's uncle had even been arrested and executed by the Soviet regime for his support of the Ukrainian underground. Neuwirth and Miehr finally gained an opportunity to use this information during the fifth day of the trial, when both questioned the accused at significant length. They did everything in their power to portray him as a traitor to his people.[7]

Stashinsky turned out to be a difficult nut to crack. To Neuwirth's question of why he had called himself a Russian throughout the course of the trial, he answered that he had used that term to denote his political allegiance, not his ethnic identity. To Neuwirth's question of whether he knew that, according to the Soviet constitution, Ukraine had the right to secede from the Soviet Union, Stashinsky answered that it was a legal question, and he was not a lawyer. But he was clearly lying when he denied any knowledge that his uncle, Petro Stashinsky, had been killed by the Soviets, and he refused to answer whether he would have killed his sister if the KGB had ordered him to do so.

"You used the word 'traitor,'" said Adolf Miehr, referring to Stashinsky's earlier statement, according to which he believed originally that defecting to the West would be a betrayal of his homeland. "Do you, as a Ukrainian, know at least this fact of the Ukrainian liberation struggle, of history, that the liberation struggle has been directed since the beginning of this century, and even earlier, not against any particular regime, not against any particular political order, but against the rule of any foreign nationality in Ukraine and against any occupation?" Stashinsky dodged the question. "I cannot answer that question," he told the court. "You proceed from the assumption that I am almost a historian, and that my sister, who knew how to write, has historical knowledge like that of a professor of history." Miehr was not convinced and asked what Stashinsky's sister was fighting for. "She fought for an independent Ukraine," finally came the answer he was trying to elicit. That was as far as the two German lawyers, who had undergone a crash course on the Ukrainian liberation movement during the previous few days, managed to get in their efforts to present Stashinsky as a traitor to his nation.[8]

Stashinsky's own lawyer, Helmut Seidel, preferred to stay as far away from issues of national identity, family loyalty, and personal betrayal as possible. His line of defense was clear and simple: Stashinsky, whoever he had been before and at the time of the killings, had changed. He had reevaluated his actions and undergone a major moral and psychological transformation. There was no better proof of that than his defection to the West and his confession, which was the most solid piece of evidence that the investigators, and now the trial judges, had to go on. "Why did you admit all this when you came to the West, given that it would have been impossible to learn of it had you not admitted it?" asked Seidel. Stashinsky gave what was most likely a prepared response. "At first I only decided never again to carry out an assassination," he told the court. "My political and ideological transformation took place during my stay in Moscow. All that I lived through in Moscow prompted me to make that decision. I admitted that it was my duty somehow to make up for my misdeed and try to warn people against anything of the kind." This was the main conclusion that Stashinsky and his attorney wanted the court to draw from the lengthy testimony regarding his meeting with Aleksandr Shelepin and his stay in Moscow after his marriage.[9]

Professor Joachim Rauch, a specialist in psychology from Heidelberg University, who observed Stashinsky in February and March 1962, was called as a witness. He suggested that Stashinsky was not someone who could invent stories or try to attract attention to his own personality by resorting to self-accusation. In fact, argued the professor, Stashinsky lacked an active imagination. He also depended excessively on the opinion of others. "As far as will is concerned, Mr. Stashinsky makes the impression of a mild individual," testified Rauch. He later explained what he meant: "For all his intelligence, Mr. Stashinsky . . . is not independent in his thinking." He had tried to decide matters of principle for himself, but once he was married, Stashinsky had relied on his wife's judgment: "His wife's authority took the place of his own. He would probably be unable to renounce the past on his own. . . . He has a tendency to avoid unpleasant problems, not to solve them independently; he wants to push them aside." Seidel must have been thrilled—as harsh as the assessment was, it made it easier for Stashinsky to claim he had been brainwashed by the KGB.[10]

The role of Inge Pohl in his moral conversion was something that Stashinsky mentioned again and again in his testimony about their stay in Moscow and their decision to escape to the West. As always, Heinrich Jagusch tried to check Stashinsky's story. "If your inner transformation took place as you have now described it, didn't you discuss all that in detail with your wife? When the heart is overloaded, a person needs to share his thoughts with someone." Stashinsky agreed. He told the court that he and Inge had most of their conversations outdoors, but not all of them could be arranged that way, and the KGB probably picked up their indoor conversations. As always, the court had to rely on Stashinsky's word and his powers of persuasion.[11]

And his powers of persuasion turned out to be quite substantial. As the trial progressed, fewer and fewer observers doubted his testimony. It was during the third day of the hearings that Jagusch decided to put to rest speculation that Stashinsky was merely a puppet feeding anti-Soviet hysteria. "Did anyone here in the Federal Republic of Germany influence you at any time (leaving aside the investigative agencies) as to what you were to say about this or that point at this trial?" asked Jagusch soon after Stashinsky concluded his testimony about the killing of Bandera. "No, that never happened," responded Stashinsky. The judge probed further: "Was there ever an earlier attempt to prompt you, for one reason or another, to tell us fairy tales here and incriminate yourself?" "Never," answered Stashinsky. "Perhaps someone did that from outside the Federal Republic of Germany?" suggested Jagusch. "No," said Stashinsky. "Are you sure?" insisted the judge. "Yes!" came the answer.[12]

43

PROSECUTION

The last day of the court proceedings fell on October 15, three years to the day after the killing of Stepan Bandera. His followers came to the courtroom dressed in black suits and wearing black ties. That day they attended a liturgy in memory of their murdered leader at St. Stefan's Church in Karlsruhe. Stashinsky noticed the unusual dress code in the courtroom, but it is not clear whether he made the connection with the event three years earlier.[1]

Bandera's followers and mourners were pleased that day with the position taken by the chief public prosecutor, Dr. Albin Kuhn, an older gentleman with a bald head and round glasses who presented the government's case against Bogdan Stashinsky. Kuhn's speech was anything but good news for the defendant. Kuhn said that Stashinsky had known at the time of the murders that the spray pistol would kill his victims. He defined Stashinsky's crime as "murder, namely, treacherous homicide." The prosecutor recognized that Stashinsky had acted on behalf of the KGB and was an instrument in the hands of a state that resorted to killing its political opponents, but he refused to treat the KGB as a military organization and declared its orders illegitimate.

Kuhn concluded his presentation by stating: "The law provides that murder be punished by an absolute penalty, and extenuating circumstances, as represented by the person of the accused, cannot be taken into account in this case." He asked the court to sentence Stashinsky to two life terms for the murders he had committed, and an additional three years for his espionage activities. Whatever rumors of a clemency deal Congressman Charles Kersten had heard in Washington before leaving for the trial appeared to be false. As expected, Stashinsky had implicated the Soviet leaders in organizing political killings abroad, but the prosecutor showed no leniency in return. Things seemed to be working out very badly for Stashinsky.[2]

Next to speak was Hans Neuwirth. Neither Stashinsky nor his lawyer could have expected anything good from Neuwirth, whose line of questioning in the previous days suggested that he was not only skeptical of Stashinsky's conversion story but also well informed about particulars of Soviet and Ukrainian politics and history. Organization of Ukrainian Nationalist members believed that Stashinsky had shown his true colors under such questioning. "Stashinsky's rude behavior toward the lawyers who ask him questions, his floundering and the impolite tone of his answers cast him in an entirely different light," wrote one of Bandera's followers present in the courtroom. "Only now is it apparent what he is really like: submissive and obedient to those on whom he depends; contemptuous of those whom he does not fear. He even mocks such people. It turns out that at heart he remains a KGB operative, a 'Soviet' man."[3]

Reporter Borys Vitoshynsky claimed that Stashinsky was lying not by distorting the facts but by omitting an important part of his life story. He referred to the Stashinsky family's involvement in the nationalist underground and his motivations for betraying his sisters. Other reporters questioned whether Stashinsky had indeed joined the secret police in order to save his family. "There must have been other motives here that Stashinsky deliberately concealed," wrote the Paris-based Ukrainian newspaper *Ukraïns'ke slovo* (Ukrainian Word). The nationalists wanted Stashinsky to say more about his involvement in the suppression of the Ukrainian underground before he had been called to Kyiv for training. Stashinsky refused, answering Neuwirth's question about how often he took part in anti-insurgent operations by saying only that he had done so as often as ordered. They wanted him to say how many insurgents he and his comrades had killed, and who else in the emigration had fallen victim to KGB assassins, but he either did not know or declined to answer those questions. They also wanted him to describe the heroic struggle of their friends in the underground, but he would not.

Finally, Bandera's followers raised questions about his motives for defecting to the West. "Stashinsky fled to the West not because he was a 'repentant' Bolshevik," wrote Vitoshynsky. "He had quite different, selfish reasons for that." Bandera's people laid out how they perceived those true motives in an article they published after the trial. It stated that Stashinsky's defection was "a perfectly logical step after he observed that distrust of him and his wife on the part of the Moscow leadership of the KGB was obviously growing with every passing day. . . . As a longtime KGB operative, he knew that that institution does not long indulge its suspicious personnel or partners who know too much about jointly committed secret crimes." Stashinsky was selfishly fleeing for his life, not because of any change of heart.[4]

The Bandera people had good reason to be skeptical about the confession of a KGB assassin who had become an overnight media darling and a symbol of repentance and frankness. They had every reason to question his claims that he was ignorant about so much of the Ukrainian liberation struggle, given the fact that members of his family were stalwarts of the Ukrainian underground in the village. He certainly knew what had happened to his uncle, whose corpse had been found in a Lviv prison after the Soviets left the city in June 1941.

The belief that Stashinsky had defected not out of repentance but to save his own life was shared by his former bosses in the KGB. Yurii Nosenko, a KGB officer who had defected to the West in 1964, told CIA interrogators that once Stashinsky detected a microphone in his apartment, he must have become afraid that the KGB was going to assassinate him. That, as he knew, happened fairly regularly to agents involved in politically sensitive operations during the Stalin era. Ironically, Bandera's followers and the KGB seemed to agree on one thing: Stashinsky was a turncoat who could not be trusted.[5]

Hans Neuwirth began his final statement by saying that he was not seeking revenge on behalf of the Banderas, a clerical family that had lost three of its sons in the struggle for the liberty of Ukraine. But as Neuwirth called Stashinsky a traitor who had betrayed his sister's trust to penetrate the Ukrainian underground, it sure sounded like revenge. Stashinsky began to shift in his seat, and the public could see blood rising to his face—a rare occurrence during the trial. That was not the end of Neuwirth's insulting comparisons: he went on to say that Stashinsky's KGB masters had trained him like a dog to kill innocent victims. Still, Neuwirth, like Kuhn before him, acknowledged the defense's thesis of Stashinsky's spiritual transformation. "The man was a product of a method of upbringing like the one used to train [Ivan] Pavlov's dogs, but then this woman appears," said Neuwirth, referring to Inge Pohl, "and she is the one who, appealing to his conscience, ultimately justifies our [Western] system."

But that was as far as Neuwirth was prepared to go in showing sympathy for Stashinsky. "Whatever the angle from which we consider this case," continued the attorney, "we have no possibility of granting absolution, as in a confessional. We are sitting in a courtroom. However diligently we may seek something human, there always remains the murder and destruction of two people." Bandera's followers in the room were not overly impressed with Neuwirth's oratorical skills—he was nervous and spoke in a very low voice—but they liked what he said, not only about Stashinsky but also about their struggle for independence. "According to the principles of our Western tradition, such a struggle is sacred," declared Neuwirth. "And it is precisely the Ukrainians who have shown us throughout their difficult historical process that they are prepared to follow the call of that tradition."[6]

As the court recessed for lunch around noon, Stashinsky's prospects looked as bleak as they ever had in the course of the trial. He had done the seemingly impossible in making the judges and the public like him. Even the prosecutor and the victim's attorneys agreed that he had repented and was no longer the man who had committed the murders. But none of that seemed to matter. The prosecution was demanding two life sentences plus three years. Over the course of the day it seemed more and more likely that they would get their wish.

One of the most memorable speeches that day was given by Stepan Bandera's twenty-one-year-old daughter, Natalia. Her statement was a tribute to her father, who, she reminded the court, had been murdered exactly three years earlier. Bandera's death had left a bleeding wound in the hearts of his three children. When Natalia Bandera rose to speak, silence fell on the courtroom. Even the journalists stopped turning pages in their notebooks. She shared with those present some very personal memories of her father, a professional conspirator whose true identity had not been disclosed even to his children. "[I] remember that on one occasion when I was ill with a serious inflammation of the middle ear, I asked my mother who the strange gentleman was who had stood by my bed and stroked my cheek," said Natalia in a voice trembling with emotion. "I had completely forgotten my father." She was referring to the years immediately after the war, when Bandera's family had lived apart from him in a Displaced Persons' camp in Mittenwald.[7]

Even after the family reunited under one roof in the late 1940s, Natalia did not know either her true name or her father's identity for a long time. "At the age of thirteen, I began to read Ukrainian newspapers, and I read a lot about Stepan Bandera," recalled Natalia. "Gradually, and on the strength of my observations regarding the surnames of many people who were frequently together with my father, I began to draw my own conclusions. On one occasion an acquaintance made a slip, and I was then certain that my father was really Stepan Bandera. But even then I realized that I dare not let my little brother and sister into this secret, since it would have been highly dangerous if they had innocently and unknowingly divulged this fact."

Natalia Bandera's speech gave the audience something that had been altogether lacking in the trial testimony until then—a sense of the human tragedy caused by Stashinsky's actions. Dressed in black like her father's associates, Natalia reminded the audience of Stashinsky's testimony in which he said that his case officer, Sergei Damon, had assured him that Bandera's children would be thankful to him for what he had done once they grew up. Natalia said that that would have only happened if the KGB had kidnapped them and subjected them to a reeducation program, as they did with Yurii Shukhevych, the teenage son of the commander in chief of the Ukrainian Insurgent Army. For his children, Bandera was the supreme moral authority in their lives, a hero who had died for God and Ukraine. "He personified this noble ideal," declared Natalia, "and he will continue to be the guiding star of my life, as well as of the life of my brother and sister and of all the youth of Ukraine."[8]

The public and the judges alike were clearly moved by the speech. Stashinsky became even paler than usual, his eyes downcast.

44

DEVIL'S ADVOCATES

Immediately after the lunch break, Heinrich Jagusch called on Adolf Miehr, the attorney for the Rebet family, to speak. Up to this point he had been as tough and aggressive as Neuwirth in questioning Stashinsky. Like Chief Prosecutor Albin Kuhn, Miehr rejected the proposition that Stashinsky had carried out his killings under duress. But Miehr was equally not convinced by the prosecutor's claim that Stashinsky had committed his murders in a perfidious manner. At stake was what type of killing had occurred. In German law, the most severe penalties would be for murder classified as *Meuchelmord*, or treacherous murder, which would mean that Stashinsky knew that his victim was defenseless and unaware of the impending attack. "Was Rebet defenseless? Was he trusting?" Miehr asked the court, and then answered his own questions in the negative: "In the state in which Rebet climbed the stairs, he certainly was not defenseless. The notion of trust is also irrelevant here." Miehr reasoned that Rebet was in good health and that he was quite capable of protecting himself against an assailant. He then stated: "The concept of treacherous murder (*Meuchelmord*), as generally used by nonprofessionals, is . . . inapplicable here." In a surprising move, Miehr's argument undermined a key element of the prosecution's case, which suggested that Stashinsky had killed a defenseless victim whom he had caught by surprise—and therefore should receive the harshest penalties if convicted.

But that was not the end of Miehr's unexpected attack on the prosecution's arguments. He also maintained that it was unreasonable to expect Stashinsky to defect to the West when he first received his criminal orders, given the kind of indoctrination he had undergone in the Soviet Union and his communist convictions. Miehr concluded his surprising speech with a reference to Rebet's widow, Daria, whose interests he represented—and whose interests diverged from that of the other defendants. "Distinguished Senate!" declared Miehr. "In Frau Rebet's name I must assure you once again that she feels not the slightest hatred for Stashinsky but sympathizes with him, and she is right to do so. . . . A light sentence would also be sufficient, for Stashinsky's action means that he will be burdened by his conscience, of which he, being responsible for the deaths of two people, will never rid himself."[1]

What had just happened? Many in the courtroom were stunned by Miehr's speech. Whose side was this attorney on, and why was he requesting clemency for the murderer and questioning the legal grounding of the prosecution's argument? Daria Rebet spoke next, bringing some clarity to the issue. A forty-nine-year-old woman with an open face and thin lips that bespoke strong will and determination, she rose from her seat behind the desk shared by family members of the victims and their lawyers. She then told the court, in her heavily accented German, that, given her difficulty with the language, and wanting to be as precise as possible, she would read a written statement. Andrii Rebet, Daria's twenty-year-old son, who had translated the text from Ukrainian into German, sat next to her, ready to help if required.

"To begin with," said Daria, "I must say that I find it very difficult to appear in the role of co-plaintiff in this trial. For the question naturally arises: Whom am I accusing? And if I am to answer that question precisely and truly, then the answer will be as follows: the accusation is directed against those who gave the orders, the Russian Bolshevik regime, the Soviet system, into which people are fitted ruthlessly and almost fatalistically, and in which they become mechanical components." Like Neuwirth, Daria was attacking the communist system first and foremost. But unlike the Bandera family's attorney, she was prepared to transfer almost all responsibility from the individual who carried out the criminal order to those who had issued it. "I have no feeling of malice or hatred toward the defendant," she declared. "I can also say and affirm the same on behalf of my almost full-grown son; more precisely, on behalf of both my children. From a purely human viewpoint, the defendant may be pitied, and I attach no importance to his being punished severely. I see the Stashinsky case precisely as a case, a phenomenon, that is simultaneously a reflection of the tragic fate of our people."

Andrii Rebet later remembered that his mother's words were met with disbelief in the courtroom. They made a strong impression on Stashinsky, whose demeanor changed visibly for the better. Andrii fully supported his mother's position on the question of Stashinsky's punishment. The Rebets wanted it to be above all a trial of the Soviet regime and its methods of suppressing the Ukrainian national movement. As may be judged from her statement and later writings, Daria was prepared to see Stashinsky not as a perpetrator or a traitor, as Bandera's followers saw him, but as a victim of the Soviet regime. Her hope was that the publicity accompanying the trial would change the West's treatment of Ukrainian émigrés and their cause, and that news of the trial would reach Ukraine to "give deluded people a reason to think seriously."[2]

Later in the day, Stashinsky got help from another unexpected source. It appeared that Charles Kersten, the high-profile and politically powerful attorney on Yaroslava Bandera's legal team, had also switched sides during the course of the trial. Kersten had remained silent through most of the trial. Although he was officially just a consultant to Hans Neuwirth, many regarded him as the senior figure in the triumvirate of lawyers representing the Bandera family. A photo taken during a trial recess showed him walking very confidently, one hand in his pants pocket, between his two colleagues: Hans Neuwirth limping with a cane, and the diminutive Jaroslav Padoch carrying a briefcase. There was no doubt about who was the most influential. The United States ruled the world, and its support was essential for the continuing existence not only of West Berlin but also of West Germany itself. Everyone knew that Kersten was not just any American: he had connections at the highest levels in Washington.

Kersten addressed the court in English, speaking as if to an American courtroom and using his substantial oratorical skills. He would pause after every paragraph, allowing the interpreter to translate his words into German. Like Daria Rebet and her attorney, Kersten was not there to go after Stashinsky. His main task, as he had formulated it in a letter to Senator Thomas Dodd two weeks earlier, was to expose the threat that the Soviet Union presented to the Western world, especially its government's proclivity for killing its political opponents. "If Stashinsky had not defected," said the former congressman, his voice loud and clear, "some stubborn anti-Soviet UN delegate, for example, might one day be found dead in New York, victim of a 'heart attack' produced by this masterpiece of Soviet science." He put the killings of the two émigré leaders into the broader context of Soviet policy toward Ukraine and its liberation movement. He referred to the Great Ukrainian Famine of 1932–1933, the Great Terror of the late 1930s, and the brutal suppression of the Gulag uprising in Kengir, Kazakhstan, in 1954, where a good half of the prisoners were Ukrainians, many of them former soldiers of the Ukrainian Insurgent Army.

Kersten's speech gave Stashinsky renewed hope. "Mrs. Bandera does not seek vengeance but justice for Stashinsky," declared the US congressman, "recognizing that he was not arrested in the course of his crimes but fled to the West and voluntarily told the full story of the Soviet government's crime and his part in it." Kersten believed that the true goal of the trial was to uncover the "real criminals" at the highest levels of Soviet power. "The Council of Ministers of the Soviet Union, in this case, has been proved guilty of murder in the first degree," he told the court. "This Court may not be able to prescribe the punishment for the real culprit. But it can render a historic judgment and declaration finding the Soviet government guilty of murder, a judgment that will hearten a large part of mankind that is afflicted with the Russian Communist conspiracy." For Stashinsky, the session must have been an emotional roller coaster, for Kersten was followed directly by Jaroslav Padoch, who went hard not only after the Soviet leaders in Moscow but also after the assassin himself.[3]

But then came the concluding statement of Stashinsky's own lawyer, Helmut Seidel, and the scales of justice began again to tilt in his favor. Throughout the trial, Stashinsky had stuck to his story: that he had considered the struggle for Ukrainian independence to be futile and had been a true communist believer when he had committed his crimes. It was only after the killings that he had discovered the truth and repented for his actions. Seidel was happy to reinforce this narrative in his own concluding statement to the court. Seidel cut a striking figure and made a strong impression on those in the courtroom. "He speaks in a very calm voice, but confidently, and with extraordinary command of the case," wrote one of Bandera's followers in his report on the trial. "He deftly exploits all the errors and inappropriate expressions of the previous attorneys to diminish the guilt of his client." Volodymyr Stakhiv, a close associate of Daria Rebet who was present in the courtroom, wrote that "Dr. Helmut Seidel's defense speech was composed professionally and delivered brilliantly."[4]

"I defend Stashinsky—a person, such a person as you or I," Seidel told the court, "a peasant's son whom accident and fate placed in a difficult situation: a person with whom I became acquainted, at first somewhat withdrawn and reserved, but later with a gentle and almost happy openness and a phenomenal memory, so that you are simply horrified on seeing the contrast between him and the deeds he carried out." Seidel explained that contrast as a consequence of Stashinsky's upbringing, which instilled in him Marxist ideology, Soviet patriotism, and obedience to superiors. "Before this court there stands a man who has come from a country where completely different ethical and moral concepts prevail. He was told that there is no such thing as individual freedom; that freedom is willing and conscious service to the inevitable. And who can establish the inevitable better than the Council of Ministers of the Soviet Union itself?"

Seidel told the court that he was not going to argue with the prosecution's suggestion that Stashinsky could not have acted under duress, given that the KGB was not a military organization. As far as Seidel was concerned, discipline in the KGB was tougher than in the army. Still, he was not going to base the defense of his client on the "following orders" argument. He argued instead that Stashinsky had killed Rebet in accordance with the ideological dogmas instilled in him by the KGB, and that he had assassinated Bandera out of fear that if he did not do so, he would be next in line. He then formulated his main argument: "What I am about to say is entirely in accord with my profound legal conviction, to wit, that the defendant is not the one who committed the crime but only the accessory to the criminal."

Seidel's speech changed the mood in the courtroom. It seemed that by portraying Stashinsky as a mere accessory to the murder, his attorney had found the perfect formula to both condemn the Soviet Union for what it was doing to its own citizens and its opponents abroad and to punish the assassin, whose confession and testimony had made the world aware of the danger posed by the Soviet regime. Daria Rebet later remembered that Hans Neuwirth, realizing the change of mood among the judges, made a statement declaring that he did not insist on a life sentence for the accused. But Chief Prosecutor Albin Kuhn stuck to his guns, confirming that he wanted a life sentence for each of the two murders committed by the defendant.

Bogdan Stashinsky was the last to speak at the trial that was deciding his fate. "I can only assert," declared Stashinsky, pale as always, "that I have already said everything I could and can say. My testimony is, in fact, at the same time a sign of my repentance. I am aware of my guilt, and I can only ask the distinguished court to be guided more by considerations of mercy than of law." His testimony was indeed the only card he could play in court. He played it well. If Charles Kersten was right, and there was a deal between the authorities and Stashinsky, he was clearly keeping his part of the bargain by delivering the most damning testimony about the Soviet practice of political killings that had ever reached the Western world.

The trial was now over. Heinrich Jagusch announced that the verdict would be made public at 9:00 a.m. on Friday, October 19, 1962. Stashinsky, the families of his victims, and the world at large would have to wait four long days to learn the judgment.[5]

45

VERDICT

The journalists who gathered on the morning of October 19 to hear the verdict in the Stashinsky case were not sure what to expect. On the last day of the trial they had witnessed a "tense legal contest," as Reginald Peck wrote in the *Daily Telegraph*. Not only did the prosecution and the defense define the two murders differently, but the families of the victims seemed to be divided on who was the main perpetrator, Stashinsky or the Soviet regime. A day earlier, the *Berliner Zeitung* of East Berlin had published a long article claiming once again that it was Reinhard Gehlen and his people who had killed Bandera. The newspaper accused Heinrich Jagusch and the court of following orders from the West German government and substituting anticommunist rhetoric for missing evidence. "Whatever the court's verdict," declared the newspaper, "one thing can already be said ahead of time: there will be no truth in the verdict."[1]

Heinrich Jagusch began his reading of the verdict soon after 9:00 a.m. It was a long document. The judge started with the biography of the accused. It took some minutes before he reached the assessment of the arguments presented by the prosecution and the defense. "The Court of Criminal Appeal of the Federal High Court agrees with the indictment, inasmuch as the two crimes constitute murder by poison," declared Jagusch. That was a clear victory for the prosecution. Unfortunately for the Bandera camp, the prosecution might have won the battle but was about to lose the war. "The Court of Criminal Appeal," continued Jagusch, " . . . agrees with the opinion of defense counsel: in neither case was the accused the perpetrator of a murder though he carried out the acts of killing alone, but only a tool and an assistant. The perpetrators, that is to say the murderers, are those persons who were responsible for planning and plotting the murders down to the last detail as regards the victims selected, the place, time and method of murders."

This was the crux of the trial, and Jagusch and the rest of the judges sided with the defense. Jagusch argued against the prosecution's case, according to which "a person who commits a deed entirely on his own must without exception always be condemned as the perpetrator." Why? Because, Jagusch said, as long as there were "states that plan political murders, [and] issue orders," and as long as "they shall . . . ideologically train certain of their subjects" to carry out those orders, the citizens of such states could not be judged according to the same standards as those of other countries. Jagusch brought up the example of Nazi Germany and the impact its state and ideology had had on regular citizens: "Those who morally resist such negative forces stand alone within the masses when confronting them," said the judge, who had lived through the period. "Those who succumb to these forces succumb to a skillful, overpowering, officially controlled mass influence; they do not succumb to incentives that come under the general category of criminology."[2]

If Stashinsky was indeed just an accessory to murder, and the actual perpetrators were in Moscow, what action could be expected from the court? There was little that Jagusch and the German judiciary system could do about Aleksandr Shelepin, to say nothing of Nikita Khrushchev. As Jagusch said, "Since they hold high-ranking offices in their sovereign territory of a foreign power, they are withdrawn from our efforts to ensure that justice is done, although in the long run no one can escape his just punishment." Stashinsky, on the other hand, was subject to the court's jurisdiction. "The sentence pronounced by this court is not intended to destroy the accused," continued Jagusch. "As far as humanly possible, it is to help him atone. The separate sentences for each of the two cases of murder are six years' penal servitude; the sentence for treason is one year's penal servitude. A total sentence of eight years' penal servitude, allowance to be made for imprisonment pending trial, suffices for atonement."[3]

When Jagusch finished reading the verdict, very few people in the room could fully comprehend the importance of what had just happened. A mere eight years for two murders? That was particularly shocking, given that the prosecution had demanded two life sentences. Bandera's followers tried to put up a brave face under the circumstances. They had also sought an indictment of Moscow and international legitimacy for their struggle—those two goals had been achieved. But they lost the fight to see Stashinsky condemned as a traitor to the Ukrainian nation. Daria Rebet and her circle of Ukrainian émigrés had taken a different stand, treating Stashinsky more as a victim than as a perpetrator, and the court's ruling seemed to endorse their position.

Many of Bandera's followers and people sympathetic to the Organization of Ukrainian Nationalists expressed disappointment with the ruling. Among them was Jaroslav Padoch, who had left Karlsruhe before the announcement of the verdict. "News has just arrived of the eight-year prison term for Stashinsky," wrote Padoch from the United States on October 19 to Stepan Lenkavsky, Bandera's successor at the top of OUN, a Munich acquaintance. "Although none of the prosecutors wanted harsh punishment for him, it is still hard to think of it: eight years for two lives. A cheap, very cheap price." He added that in *Svoboda*, a leading Ukrainian-language newspaper in the United States, news of the verdict had appeared next to a story about a death sentence imposed by a Soviet court in Lviv on a person accused of bribery. "Two systems, two standards of humanism," wrote the clearly disappointed Padoch.

Padoch struggled to make sense of the unusually lenient treatment by the West German court. He suspected that the verdict was the result of a deal that Stashinsky had made not with the German prosecutor, as suggested by Kersten, but with the Americans. "He probably paid for it in a different currency," wrote the disheartened Padoch to Lenkavsky on the day the verdict was published. "He probably spent considerable time with our American investigators." This assumption was shared by others. A reporter for United Press International (UPI) finished his article on the verdict with the statement: "He is considered too valuable to Allied intelligence to exhaust himself crushing rock."[4]

The verdict in the Stashinsky trial caused a sensation in Germany. The West German media was divided in its assessment, as shown by the articles appearing in the next few days. "Verdict of the Year—the Killers Are Sitting in Moscow," wrote a reporter for Hamburg's *Bild-Zeitung*. "Mild Sentence—An Invitation to Killers," opined a reporter for the *Rheinische Post*. A reporter for the *Badische Zeitung* wrote that no ordinary person could understand how an assassin could be judged a mere accessory to murder.

The verdict touched on a number of highly sensitive elements of German postwar political history and identity, one of them being the Nazi legacy. Both the chief public prosecutor, Albin Kuhn, and the presiding judge, Heinrich Jagusch, made reference to the recent Nazi past—Kuhn in his legal judgment on the last day of the trial, and Jagusch in the text of the verdict. But the two references were of quite a different nature. Kuhn evoked the Nazi past to make the point that Germany's own experience with totalitarianism should not make German courts more forgiving of crimes committed on behalf of such states. "We Germans have no reason merely to criticize others," stated Kuhn. "For we have not yet done with our own past. Acts of violence are not, however, less serious because they have been committed by others." Jagusch, on the other hand, argued that the Germans themselves knew how difficult it was to withstand concerted brainwashing on the part of the state. Stashinsky, he said, was not a willing or enthusiastic perpetrator, not an "Eichmann type who joyfully obeys the Führer and carries out the orders he receives with even greater emphasis." He claimed that "the accused was at the time in question a poor devil who acted automatically under pressure of commands and was misled and confused ideologically."[5]

Many immediately sensed the danger of setting this precedent. A reporter for the *Frankfurter Rundschau* wrote: "It sounds like a mockery when President Jagusch of the Senate says in his explanation of the sentence that Germans supposedly have a special understanding for such people as Stashinsky—an assassin acting on orders? . . . Does he not see how close his sentence brings him to the principles of a government for which murder is not a crime?" A reader of the Hamburg *Bild-Zeitung* wrote to his newspaper: "Now all the verdicts in cases of murders carried out on Hitler's orders will have to be reviewed."[6]

Since the Nuremberg trial of Nazi war criminals, the West German courts had universally rejected the argument that Nazi perpetrators had simply followed orders. Now the Federal Criminal Court and then the High Court, which approved its ruling, were dramatically reversing that policy. Both courts formally rejected the "acting under duress of orders" defense in the Stashinsky case, but the ruling opened new avenues for the defense of Nazi criminals, as they could now claim that they had only been accessories to murder, while the main perpetrators, including Adolf Hitler, Heinrich Himmler, Hermann Göring, and other top officials of the Third Reich, were long gone.

Few doubted that the verdict was influenced by a broader political agenda directly related to the Cold War. Some welcomed that; others found it deplorable. "The verdict is perfectly correct, for it must be hoped that thanks to this man's confession the beclouded eyes of many people in the West have cleared up with regard to assessing Moscow's policy," wrote a reader of the Hamburg *Bild-Zeitung*. Another disagreed: "This is frightful. Are we a state under the rule of law or lackeys of a policy of assassins?"[7]

The question of the violation of West German sovereignty by the country's powerful Soviet neighbor was another highly sensitive issue for the public and the political elite. Immediately after the publication of the verdict, Karl-Günther von Hase, the chief spokesman for the West German government, made a statement in which he declared: "It is a monstrous fact that a foreign power has deemed it necessary, with complete disregard of all human laws, to pass summary judgments in this country." The media asked whether the government would take real action against the Soviets in response. "And what will Bonn do?" asked a reporter for the Karlsruhe-based

Badische Neueste Nachrichten. "The unconscionable violation of the sovereignty of our federal state is a proven fact. Rebet and Bandera were murdered in Munich on Soviet orders. Criminal and international law were flouted. No one can consider himself safe from Moscow—no state, no individual." But the government was not eager to act. The author of the *Badische Neueste Nachrichten* article was right. No European state, especially West Germany, could feel safe in the face of a rising communist superpower willing to change the rules of the game in order to gain equal status with the Americans.[8]

German parliamentarians began to request an official government response. The first request was made on December 7, 1962. The government dodged it by pointing out that the High Court in Karlsruhe had not yet filed its official judgment. After repeated requests, the government sent an official note to the Soviet embassy in Bonn in April 1964. It read: "As the Federal Court has established, both . . . crimes were committed on orders of Soviet agencies. This leads the Federal Government to bring to the attention of the Government of the Union of Soviet Socialist Republics that such actions are acutely contrary to generally recognized principles of law, especially international law." The note ended with standard assurances of mutual respect: "The Ministry of Foreign Affairs takes this opportunity to assure the embassy of the Union of Soviet Socialist Republics of its great respect." The Soviet authorities ignored the note, and German officials did not press them for a response.[9]

PART VII

DEPARTED

46

UNANSWERED LETTER

On November 7, 1963, a year after the trial, Charles Kersten sat down to write a letter to President John F. Kennedy. The president, with whom Kersten shared not only his Catholic faith but also a record of anticommunist crusading, was his last hope to bring Bogdan Stashinsky, who was now in prison in West Germany, to the United States to testify before a Senate committee investigating the Soviet assassinations abroad.

Kersten considered Stashinsky's testimony to be a matter of state importance. He presented the highlights of Stashinsky's story and noted that "before his defection Stashinsky was being trained for high level killing in England and the United States. There are undoubtedly others in such training." He wanted the president to force the State Department to lift its objections to admitting Stashinsky to the United States. "I think you agree with me," he wrote, "that full exposure of deadly subversive operations is the best way to prevent them." At the end of the letter, Kersten reminded Kennedy of their days as anticommunist crusaders in the US Congress in the late 1940s. He also recalled the time when "the exposure of Communist operations in Milwaukee, Wisconsin in 1947 helped break the hold of the conspiracy on industry in the area." Kersten attached a photograph of the two of them during their trip to Milwaukee to organize hearings on the communist penetration of trade unions.[1]

Kersten had tried to gain as much publicity as possible for the Stashinsky case. Immediately after the trial, he had issued a statement that read: "The verdict of the German Supreme Court is just and is a great victory for truth. It reveals the Russian Communist government as the real killer." Kersten stated that on behalf of Yaroslava Bandera he was going to bring the case against Nikita Khrushchev and the Soviet government before the International Tribunal in the Hague and the Human Rights Commission of the United Nations. While in West Germany, Kersten had even spoken with Professor Hermann Mosler, a renowned authority on international law at Heidelberg University, to discuss the possibility of bringing the case before the United Nations. Upon his return to the United States, Kersten strategized with his Ukrainian friends and visited some foreign representatives to the United Nations, but the project had never gotten off the ground.[2]

Fresh from his visit to Karlsruhe and disappointed with his unsuccessful attempts to bring the case before the United Nations, Charles Kersten joined a campaign to hold hearings on the Stashinsky case on Capitol Hill. It was spearheaded by Professor Lev Dobriansky, the chairman of the National Captive Nations Committee. On February 19, 1963, Kersten wrote to his old ally, Senator Thomas Dodd of Connecticut, the vice chairman of the US Senate Subcommittee on Internal Security, urging him to take part. "I know that you are fully aware that it is not only the launchings of missiles that we fear from Cuba," wrote Kersten, referring to the Cuban crisis of less than six months earlier. "It is also the diabolical subversive tactics that the Communists employ all over the world, and in this case the potential of swift, silent and unattributed murder of even the highest officials in the United States who oppose the Soviets." Kersten wrote a similar letter to the ranking member of the subcommittee, Senator Kenneth Keating of New York. Both responded in March 1963, with Keating referring the matter to Dodd, and Dodd indicating his interest in the idea.

"I agree with you that the case might give us a wedge with which to go into the entire matter of stimulated and induced suicide as practiced by the Soviet terror apparatus," wrote Dodd to Kersten. He promised to discuss the matter further with his colleagues on the committee. Kersten wrote back to his old friend, further encouraging him to go ahead with the hearings. Kersten cited one of the earlier reports of Dodd's committee, which stated that after considering a number of suspected political killings, the committee could not find "ironclad proof that the Kremlin . . . in any of these cases committed murder and dressed it up as a suicide." The Stashinsky trial, wrote Kersten, provided that ironclad proof.[3]

Lev Dobriansky, the main advocate for the hearings, believed that Stashinsky should be brought to the United States to be a star witness. "My feeling was," recalled Dobriansky later, "that we should dramatize all this. In having Stashinsky and numerous others here we would show the interrelationships of the subject of the political murders ordered by Moscow. Especially after the Supreme Court in West Germany indicted and charged not so much Stashinsky as the Russian government in Moscow, this was deemed necessary." But the State Department refused to give its approval. Officials cited logistical difficulties and security concerns, but Dobriansky believed their lack of support was driven by the "whole détente that was supposed to be built up between the United States and the USSR."[4]

By the summer of 1963, relations between the Soviet Union and the United States had changed dramatically, and for the better. The Berlin Wall crisis of the summer and fall of 1961 and the Cuban missile crisis of October 1962 were in the past. In July 1963, American, British, and Soviet negotiators agreed on conditions for a treaty on a partial nuclear test ban—the first major step toward limiting nuclear arsenals. The next month, John Kennedy and Nikita Khrushchev set up a hotline between the White House and the Kremlin to help resolve possible future crises. Kennedy authorized a quarter-billion-dollar deal for the sale of American wheat to the Soviet Union—a measure intended to relieve the severity of Soviet food shortages. On October 7, in the presence of his advisers and congressional leaders, Kennedy signed the agreement on the limitation of nuclear tests. It was a major turn in his relations with Khrushchev and marked the height of the short-lived Soviet-American rapprochement. No one wanted to hear about Stashinsky or political murders carried out on the orders of the same man in the Kremlin who seemed to have finally come to his senses, was eager to buy American wheat, and promised not to test his nuclear weapons.[5]

The letter that Kersten sent President Kennedy, urging him to support the idea of Senate hearings on Soviet assassination tactics, was never answered. On November 22, 1963, two weeks after Kersten sent his letter, the president was assassinated in Dallas. A copy of Kersten's letter was forwarded to the FBI. The FBI suspected that Kersten's prediction that the Soviets might send trained killers from Havana to assassinate anticommunist leaders in the United States was coming true. Lee Harvey Oswald uncannily fitted the image of the Moscow-trained and Havana-directed killer that Kersten had warned against. Were Khrushchev and Aleksandr Shelepin—who now held enormous power as chairman of the Party and State Control Commission, and would soon be named to the Communist Party Presidium—back at work, now ordering the killing of an American president? This supposition terrified many Americans. If that was the case, what should be the response? And could it be anything less than all-out nuclear war?[6]

These were questions over which many American politicians, including people at the very top of the government, lost sleep. Despite Oswald's prolonged stay in the Soviet Union, his Soviet wife, and his ties with Cuban émigrés, government investigators worked hard to promote the lone gunman theory of the assassination. For William Hood, who served as the CIA chief in Munich during the assassination of Bandera, it was another high-profile killing on his watch, but one of much larger significance and greater potential repercussions. Transferred from Germany to Langley at the beginning of the decade, Hood was one of a handful of CIA officers who signed a cable that failed to disclose Oswald's recent arrest for a quarrel with anti-Castro émigrés. He had helped to remove Oswald's name from the FBI watch list a few weeks before the Kennedy assassination. Despite this, Hood would keep his job and would not retire from the CIA until the 1970s. Whether the Soviets were involved or not—and, in 1963, no one could say for sure—few people in power were prepared to go to war with the Soviet Union, even over the assassination of the president.[7]

47

GUEST FROM WASHINGTON

Friday, April 10, 1964, was an usual day in Bogdan Stashinsky's otherwise monotonous and uneventful life behind bars. That morning
he was transferred to the High Criminal Court in Karlsruhe, where
he had stood trial a year and a half earlier. They wanted him to meet a
VIP from overseas. His name was Senator Thomas J. Dodd. Stashinsky was
on his list of people to see, along with the new chancellor of West Germany, Ludwig Erhard; his predecessor, Konrad Adenauer; the chief federal
prosecutor, Ludwig Martin; and the presiding judge in the Stashinsky trial,
Heinrich Jagusch.

The senator later claimed that whomever else he saw on the visit, his
main purpose was first and foremost to meet Mr. Stashinsky. The meeting
took place in the presence of one of the prosecutors at the Stashinsky trial,
Dr. Oberle, and a number of US officials—some of them had come with the
senator all the way from Washington; others were from the American embassy in Bonn. Senator Dodd's trip to Karlsruhe to see Bogdan Stashinsky
had been long in the making.[1]

The murder of John Kennedy had revived interest in the idea of holding
hearings on Capitol Hill to discuss the Soviet use of political assassinations.
In February 1964, the CIA had prepared a report on the "Soviet Use of Assassination and Kidnapping" for the commission investigating Kennedy's

murder, and it included a section on the Stashinsky case. But the problem of bringing him to the United States remained unsolved. In late January, Lev Dobriansky had learned that in order to move the whole thing along, Senator Dodd had decided to go to West Germany himself to interview Stashinsky and the West German officials involved in his case.[2]

Dodd's German agenda was filled with meetings with top West German politicians, both active and retired. His meeting with Konrad Adenauer took place on the morning of April 8, the first full day of Dodd's visit. The chancellor did not hide his criticism of the late President Kennedy and his foreign policy. He considered Kennedy to be too soft on the Soviets during the Cuban missile crisis. In October 1962, soon after the end of the Stashinsky trial, he asked the US ambassador to West Germany to make the transcripts of the trial available for Kennedy to demonstrate what the Soviets were up to and what they were capable of. Now he raised concerns about the growing American trade with the Soviet Union, especially Kennedy's American grain deal with Khrushchev. The irony, Dodd told him, was that if Kennedy were still alive, the Senate would probably have defeated the deal; the president's death had made that a political impossibility.[3]

The next day, Dodd went to Karlsruhe to meet with Dr. Hubert Schrubbers, the head of the Office for the Protection of the Constitution (West German counterintelligence), who briefed him on the Stashinsky case and Soviet espionage in West Germany. The statistics that Schrubbers presented to Dodd were impressive: there had been 222 cases of kidnapping in West Germany in the past few years, most of them in Berlin. In 52 of those cases, force had been used, and in 7 cases the victims had been drugged. The rest were lured to the East by deception. The threat posed by Soviet espionage and the activities of its agents was nowhere as serious as in West Germany.

April 10 was the Stashinsky day on Dodd's schedule. In the morning, the senator discussed the case with Dr. Bruno Heusinger, the president of the Federal Criminal Court. They also talked about the ongoing trial of the former SS men involved in running Auschwitz—Dodd had visited the proceedings the previous day in Cologne. Heusinger told him that the two cases, those of the Auschwitz criminals and Stashinsky, were legally intertwined. Both trials, he said, demonstrated "how an all-powerful state apparatus could deform and enslave the human character." Judging by Dodd's notes, they did not formally discuss whether the accused in the Auschwitz trial would be treated in the same way as Stashinsky—as accessories to murder rather than perpetrators—but Heusinger's comments suggested that it was a possibility. The verdict in the Stashinsky trial had created a precedent that was now influencing the trials of Nazi criminals in West German courts. After his meeting with Heusinger, Dodd went to see the primary author of the Stashinsky verdict, Heinrich Jagusch. They talked about Stashinsky, his crimes, and his future. Dodd now felt prepared to meet the man he had heard so much about.[4]

The meeting began soon after 2:00 p.m. The senator greeted the former KGB assassin and told him that he had "rendered an important service by telling the truth." Dodd then launched into his questions. The senator wanted to know what Stashinsky could tell him about other assassinations, including ones that appeared to be suicides—a subject that Dodd's committee had been investigating for some time. One such case was that of the Soviet secret agent Walter Krivitsky, who defected to the West in 1937 and wrote the book *I Was Stalin's Agent*, exposing Soviet methods of espionage and assassination abroad. In February 1941, Krivitsky had been found in a Washington hotel, lying in a pool of blood, allegedly a suicide.

Another case was that of Paul Bang-Jensen, a young Danish diplomat who refused to turn over to the United Nations a list of participants in the Hungarian Revolution of 1956, as he believed that it would be leaked to the Soviets. He was found dead in Queens, New York, in November 1959. As had been the case with Krivitsky, Bang-Jensen's body was found with a suicide note explaining his reason for taking his own life.[5]

Stashinsky tried to be as helpful as he could. Dodd remembered later that Stashinsky described to him "in detail how he murdered Bandera . . . and how he followed him day by day, learned his habits, met him on the stairway of the apartment house." Stashinsky had no firsthand knowledge of other assassinations committed by the KGB, but he knew well the culture of the institutions he worked for and could make informed guesses.

Commenting on the matter, he said that "in the Soviet Union it was taken for granted that this is the way one deals with certain types of political enemies in other countries."

Stashinsky also told Dodd that "it was his definite impression that he functioned as part of a worldwide apparatus." He knew that he had been acting on orders coming from the very top of the Soviet hierarchy. He also knew that assassinations would continue after the public outrage over the assassination of Bandera had ebbed. "He said," reads Dodd's travel diary, "that it was his firm impression that he was to be assigned to the same kind of work in one of the major English speaking countries." Senator Dodd was particularly impressed by the replica of the spray pistol that Stashinsky had used to assassinate Bandera. After the meeting, which lasted close to two hours, Dodd went to see Yaroslav Stetsko, the no. 3 man on Stashinsky's hit list.[6]

Dodd left West Germany, as he later recalled, with a much better understanding of how the KGB apparatus worked. In March 1965, the US Senate Internal Security Subcommittee finally conducted its hearings, focusing particularly on the Stashinsky case. The subcommittee's report appeared in print under the title *Murder International, Inc.: Murder and Kidnapping as an Instrument of Soviet Policy*. The main title echoed the name that the American press had given Mafia hit men of the 1930s and 1940s—"Murder, Inc." The introduction, written by Senator Dodd, stated that although the Stashinsky trial had "attracted only episodic attention in the press of the Western world," it deserved to be "ranked with the great trials of history." Dodd explained its importance as follows: "The evidence presented at the trial established for the first time in a court of law that the Soviets employ murder as an instrument of international policy and that, despite the so called 'liberalization' which is supposed to have taken place since Stalin's death, the international murder apparatus of the Soviet Government continues to operate full blast."[7]

48

JUDEX

When Dodd left Karlsruhe on April 10, 1964, Stashinsky was taken back to his prison cell. Rumor had it that he was serving his sentence in Landsberg Prison, some forty miles from Munich. At this point, he had more than five years of imprisonment still ahead of him. His lawyer, Helmut Seidel, had filed a request for clemency, but there was no telling whether it would be granted.

There was also more bad news from outside the prison walls. On June 23, 1964, Inge, apparently traumatized by the ordeal, filed for divorce. We do not know how Stashinsky reacted to the news. But it is easy to imagine Inge's motivations. She was afraid for her life and, according to *Stern* reporter Gerd Heidemann, had begun psychiatric treatment. Heidemann interviewed Inge in early November 1962, soon after the Stashinsky trial. The interview was arranged by Erwin Fischer of the Federal Prosecutor's Office, who assured Inge that she could trust Heidemann and tell him everything. Unfortunately, she was unaware that since 1953 Heidemann had been working for the Stasi—the East German secret police—under the code name "Gerhardt." He went to prison in 1985 for selling forged diaries purported to be Hitler's, while still on the list of active Stasi agents. Heidemann would later claim that he was a double agent—a claim that would have given Inge little solace.[1]

Bogdan Stashinsky was relatively safe in prison, but what would happen after his release? Where could he find safe haven from his former KGB colleagues? During his meeting with Senator Dodd, Heinrich Jagusch told the American visitor that "Stashinsky's testimony had been most helpful, but when he was released, Germany would be very unsafe for him." Jagusch hoped that "arrangements could be made for him in a safer country." Jagusch was an important ally, but he would soon be forced out of office, leaving Stashinsky largely unprotected.[2]

Dr. Jagusch's political troubles began soon after he read the verdict in the Stashinsky trial. A propaganda campaign launched in the East accused him of being a committed Nazi. Then the same *Stern* reporter, Gerd Heidemann, published photographs revealing the face of one of the investigators in the case considered by Jagusch, revealing the fact that the judge was sharing confidential materials with the journalist. Things got much worse a few months after Dodd's visit to Karlsruhe. In September 1964, Jagusch broke the corporate ethics code by publishing in *Der Spiegel*, West Germany's leading political weekly, an article that exposed the release of a suspected East German spy from a federal prison, allegedly in exchange for the release of a number of political prisoners in East Germany. The article, which questioned government policy and the position taken on the issue by Jagusch's superiors, was unsigned. Another of Jagusch's articles appeared in the same magazine in early November 1964. It questioned the actions of the General Prosecutor's Office, which had sanctioned the arrest of a *Der Spiegel* journalist on charges of espionage. This article was signed with the pseudonym "Judex"—taken from a popular French movie about a mysterious avenger. Both pieces were controversial and attracted a great deal of publicity. The hunt for the author began, and soon one of the Munich newspapers pointed a finger at Jagusch.[3]

When approached by Bruno Heusinger, the head of the Federal Criminal Court, Jagusch denied the charge. But he soon changed his mind and admitted to being "Judex." His career at the High Court was all but over. He had offended almost everyone—proponents of improved relations with the East by arguing against the release of a communist spy, and hardliners by questioning the unlawful arrest of a journalist on espionage charges. Most importantly, he had lied to his superiors and to his own colleagues. Since the Stashinsky trial, there had been accusations floated against Jagusch, probably with support and encouragement from the East, that he had taken part in the Nazification of German trade unions under Hitler. Jagusch had denied the charge, and his superiors and colleagues at the High Court had supported him. He lost their support after the publication of his *Spiegel* articles.[4]

In January 1965, Jagusch was suspended on charges of lying about his membership in the Nazi Party. A month later he was allowed to retire for health reasons. Off the bench, he reinvented himself as an authority on German traffic law, but his political legacy remained the verdict that he had handed down in the Stashinsky case. The ruling had a direct impact on dozens of trials of former Nazi officials, including the Auschwitz trial, which ended in the fall of 1965. In a mirror of the Stashinsky trial, the accused were convicted not as primary perpetrators but as accessories to murder. Robert Mulka, the adjutant to the camp commander, received a fourteen-year sentence, a far cry from the death sentence imposed by a Warsaw court in 1947 on the camp commander and Mulka's superior, Rudolf Höss. It would take the German parliament seven years to change the criminal code and remove the loophole that the Stashinsky ruling had created. Because the new code did not come into force until the mid-1970s, quite a few accused Nazi criminals were able to use the "Stashinsky defense" in the German courts. In 1973, Ludwig Hahn, a former commander of the German secret police (SD) in Warsaw who had supervised the liquidation of the Warsaw ghetto and taken part in the suppression of the 1944 Warsaw Uprising, received a twelve-year sentence. The West German press directly linked its leniency to the Stashinsky precedent.[5]

With Jagusch gone, there was one less person at the top of the German judiciary who was concerned about Stashinsky's safety after he served his sentence. It is not known whether Senator Dodd ever acted on Jagusch's prompting to find a safe haven for Stashinsky. But Dodd's days as a powerful senator with influence over world events—and Stashinsky's future—were numbered.[6]

In June 1966, the US Senate Select Committee on Standards and Conduct held hearings on Dodd's trip. His political opponents were alleging that his real purpose had been to help his friend Julius Klein, a retired brigadier general in the US Army who handled public relations for West German companies in the United States. Klein had been criticized for promoting companies that had previously profited from the Nazi regime and its crimes. In response, other West German companies had ceased to employ him as their public relations representative. It was now argued by Dodd's accusers that he had gone to Germany not primarily to see Stashinsky, but to lobby on behalf of General Klein and help him regain some of his lost business. The charges were never proved, but Dodd was censured by the Senate in 1967 on a separate charge of using reelection campaign funds for his own purposes. The investigation came in the wake of Dodd's partially successful attempts to regulate the firearms industry and resulted from the efforts of industry lobbyists.

The man who thanked Stashinsky for telling the truth stayed in office until 1971, but he lost all his power and prestige before that. The Soviet media celebrated the senator's downfall. Many in the Soviet government considered him to be one of the worst enemies the Soviet Union had ever had.[7]

49

VANISHED

tern magazine in Hamburg was the first to break the news. "He was met by agents of the US Intelligence Service, the CIA," wrote the magazine reporter, "and immediately taken to the United States in a military plane." The reference was to Bogdan Stashinsky's release from prison. The *Stern* reporter also touched upon Inge's fate. She had divorced Bogdan in June 1964, but, according to the federal prosecutor Erwin Fischer, who had been helping her through the years, she was well provided for and happy again. Was she married, and if so, to whom? It was anyone's guess.

The *Stern* story appeared in mid-February 1969 and was immediately picked up by the Associated Press and wired to newspapers all over the world. The KGB took special note of the *Stern* publication. In late March, the KGB chief in Ukraine reported on the story to his Communist Party boss. Inside the CIA, officials also noted the *Stern* account, and a copy of it ended up in the agency's files dealing with the assassination of President Kennedy. The only official agency to comment on the news publicly was the West German Ministry of Justice. On February 18, 1969, a spokesman for the ministry declared that Stashinsky, then thirty-eight years of age, had been released and allowed to leave the country for his own protection. The spokesman would not say exactly where Stashinsky had gone. But he did say that the departure had taken place a full two years earlier. The former KGB assassin had been released after serving only two-thirds of his sentence.[1]

This was the first public announcement about Stashinsky since March 1965, when the media had reported that President Heinrich Lübke of West Germany had turned down an appeal for clemency filed by Stashinsky's attorney. Now the *Stern* reporter wrote that upon his release on New Year's Eve 1966, Stashinsky was picked up by the CIA agents. According to the report, the Americans considered him a very valuable agent. The *Stern* article served as a starting point for numerous speculations about the fate of the spy who had disappeared into thin air after his early release from prison. Some suggested that he had probably been transferred to the United States for good. But anyone who wanted to pick up Stashinsky's trail was at least two years behind him.[2]

While the world wondered if the CIA was harboring Stashinsky, CIA experts were in fact still debating whether they could trust the former Soviet agent. Perhaps, after all that had taken place, he was still part of a clever KGB plot to undermine Western security. James Jesus Angleton, who served as head of CIA counterintelligence for many years (1954–1975), was paranoid about the possible KGB penetration of the CIA—he considered every KGB defector a plant. It was only after Angleton's resignation on Christmas Eve 1975 that the agency took another look at the Stashinsky case.

The report, which was ready on April 22, 1976, began with a telling statement: "This memorandum has been written in an attempt to determine whether there is sufficient information to support KGB agent Bogdan Nikolaevich Stashinsky's claim that he assassinated Ukrainian émigré leader Stepan Bandera in Munich in October 1959." The sixteen-page report, which went through every bit of information the CIA had gathered on the Stashinsky case, came to the carefully formulated conclusion that Stashinsky most likely did what he claimed to have done. The only unexplained evidence was the trace of cyanide in Bandera's stomach, an element that Stashinsky's spray pistol was not supposed to leave. Otherwise, claimed the author of the report, it was "difficult to see what the KGB would gain by Stashinsky's confession."

The report gives no indication that Stashinsky was ever in fact brought to the United States, let alone allowed to live there after undergoing plastic surgery, as the rumors suggested in journalistic circles. If the *Stern* magazine reporters who broke the story of Stashinsky's release were correct in their assertion that the Americans had picked up Stashinsky, then they must have taken him somewhere other than the United States. Had he been brought to the United States and placed under the authority of Angleton and his people at the CIA, Stashinsky most likely would have experienced the same kind of treatment that KGB defector Yurii Nosenko had been subjected to. Nosenko had spent three years in solitary confinement and was given drugs to make him tell the "truth"; he was released from CIA captivity only in 1967 and declared a bona fide defector only in 1969.

The author of the 1976 CIA report stated that Stashinsky had been released in 1967 after serving two-thirds of his sentence. "He was given iron works training by German authorities and resettled under another name in another country." The report did not specify the country. Wherever Stashinsky went after being released from the West German prison, he was clearly in hiding.[3]

The only hint that Stashinsky had let slip appeared in advice he gave to the no. 3 man on his Munich death list, Bandera's second-in-command, Yaroslav Stetsko. "I do not think there is any real protection against a murder ordered by the KGB," wrote Stashinsky from his prison cell. "But the carrying out of such crimes could be made far more difficult." Stashinsky advised Stetsko and other possible KGB targets to change their first and last names and their places of residence at least once every three years, and their country of residence as often as possible. In each country they should choose common aliases, avoiding Slavic names. Their names and addresses should not appear in telephone books and directories. A second alias should be chosen for use in their residence, and they should be trained to recognize shadowing. "Complete secrecy must be the first commandment," wrote Stashinsky.[4]

50

KREMLIN GHOST

Bogdan Stashinsky disappeared from the pages of the press after the 1969 surprise announcement about his early release from prison. But his crimes, and even more, his confession, continued to influence Cold War politics as well as the lives of people directly involved in his case for years to come. For a number of such individuals, that influence was anything but benevolent.

In the summer of 1973, his name came up in connection with a US government investigation into an alleged plot to assassinate Leonid Brezhnev on a visit to the United States. In early June, the Soviet embassy in Washington informed the US Secret Service that, according to their sources, a group of Ukrainian nationalists, headed by Bandera's former associate Yaroslav Stetsko, was conspiring to assassinate the Soviet leader. The killers were allegedly fanatical young Ukrainians who had fought in the Vietnam War and were now undergoing special training in the United States. They were planning to dress in police or US Army uniforms and attack Brezhnev, who had succeeded Khrushchev in 1964. One of the alleged plotters was a US Army lieutenant colonel named Nicholas Krawciw.

The Secret Service checked the Soviet inquiry with the CIA, who identified Stetsko from the Stashinsky file. Stetsko, the CIA told its Secret Service contacts, was on the KGB hit list. The FBI immediately got on the case, and soon realized that the plot was a figment of the Soviet imagination. Stetsko, who by that time had become the leader of the Bandera organization, had been planning to visit the United States, but he did not do so. His alleged associates in the plot either stayed out of politics altogether or belonged to a rival faction of the Organization of Ukrainian Nationalists that would not cooperate with him on any project, much less the assassination of Leonid Brezhnev.

One of the alleged plotters, Osyp Zinkewych, was a publisher of dissident literature that was being smuggled out of Ukraine. He believed in the power of the written word, not of a fired bullet. Krawciw had served two tours of duty in Vietnam and had distinguished himself as an intelligence officer at his post in Israel in 1972, prior to the Yom Kippur War. Like many other members of the Ukrainian community in the United States listed by the Soviets, Krawciw knew nothing about a plot to kill Brezhnev. It became apparent that the Soviets were trying to unleash American law enforcement agencies on the Ukrainian organizations that were planning to protest Brezhnev's visit to the United States. FBI sources reported that the leading Ukrainian newspaper in the country, the *Ukrainian Weekly*, was calling on its readers to take an active part in the protests. Brezhnev, wrote the newspaper, would be "smiling with a knife behind his back."[1]

The only guns that Leonid Brezhnev saw during his visit were two pistols presented to him by his favorite Hollywood actor, Chuck Connors, whose westerns the Soviet leader had come to admire. The protests took place in New York and other cities despite the best efforts of the KGB to stop them. The largest was held on Sunday, June 17, 1973, in front of the United Nations headquarters in New York. Close to a thousand Ukrainian protesters chanted, "Brezhnev go home, leave the U.S. alone." One of the alleged participants in the plot, Askold Lozynskyj of the Bandera organization's youth wing, addressed the crowd, calling attention to the irony that the government of the "land of free" was eager to do business with the government of the "land of the oppressed." In the end, it was the Ukrainian nationalists' demonstrations, not their bullets, that constituted the biggest threat to Soviet dignitaries traveling abroad.[2]

Leonid Brezhnev knew that better than anyone else. In May 1975 he completed his rise to the pinnacle of Soviet power by removing his long-time rival, the former KGB chief Aleksandr Shelepin, from the Politburo. The official reason for the removal was Shelepin's tarnished image abroad, as shown by mass demonstrations in London protesting his visit to Great Britain. Ever since the Stashinsky trial, Shelepin had become known in the West as the mastermind of political assassinations.

In the United States, that role was highlighted in the report of Senator Thomas Dodd's committee. "According to the testimony of Stashinsky," wrote Dodd in his introduction, "at the top of the list of Soviet officials directing this [murder] apparatus was Alexander N. Shelepin, Chairman of the State Security of the USSR. Today this former commander-in-chief of the 'Department of Blood-Wet Affairs' is Deputy Premier of the Council of Ministers, Member of the Presidium, and Secretary of the Central Committee, Communist Party, USSR. His presence in these high posts under the 'new' administration strongly suggests that murder will continue as an instrument of Soviet policy, as it has since the days of Lenin himself." Speaking to US politicians on the occasion of the Captive Nations Week's observance in July 1965, Yaroslav Stetsko, no. 3 man on Stashinsky's hit list, accused Shelepin of ordering the killing of President Kennedy.[3]

For years Shelepin had been forced to avoid traveling to the West with official Soviet delegations because a West German judge had issued an order for his arrest in connection with the Stashinsky trial. It was only after the West German government canceled the order under strong Soviet pressure that Shelepin, then chairman of the Soviet Trade Union Association, felt he could travel to the West on official visits. In the spring of 1975, he accepted an invitation from the head of the British trade unions to visit that country. A political scandal exploded in London as soon as news of the visit reached the British parliament. The opposition Tories demanded that the government deny him an entry visa, and the governing Labourites said that it was a mistake to have invited him. One Labour parliamentarian stated that Shelepin was the most unwelcome guest since the prominent Nazi Rudolf Hess had flown to Britain in 1940.

Still, Shelepin decided not to cancel the visit. He wanted to test his new immunity from prosecution. He was met not only by unhappy parliamentarians but also by outraged members of the Ukrainian community. There were 3,000 people protesting Shelepin's visit on the streets of London. The former KGB chief was forced to cut his visit short and go back to Moscow, only to be removed from the Politburo shortly thereafter. His political career was over.[4]

Shelepin lost his position at the top of the Soviet hierarchy not because his colleagues in the Politburo saw anything wrong with the KGB chief overseeing assassinations abroad, but because Leonid Brezhnev took advantage of the protests in the West to finish off his main political opponent. Brezhnev's reference to Western public opinion as the reason for Shelepin's dismissal made a strong impression on the Soviet political elite. The person most affected by it was Yurii Andropov, Brezhnev's appointee to Shelepin's former post at the helm of the KGB in 1967 (following Vladimir Semichastny). Like Shelepin, Andropov was a party apparatchik who harbored strong political ambitions. He learned an important lesson from the Shelepin/Stashinsky affair: if he was caught assassinating people abroad, his prospects of rising to the top in the USSR would vanish.

Under Andropov, the KGB would stop assassinating political opponents of the Soviet regime. Andropov also did his best to avoid antagonizing the West through harsh persecution of leading dissidents. The two most important opposition figures of the 1970s, Aleksandr Solzhenitsyn and Andrei Sakharov, received—by Soviet standards—very mild treatment at the hands of the KGB. The first was exiled to the West, the second to a provincial Soviet city. Both avoided prison sentences. By treading carefully, Andropov became head of the Soviet state after Brezhnev's death in November 1982.[5]

51

ON THE RUN

As the fallout from the public scandal created by Stashinsky's defection to the West influenced the political struggles within the Soviet Politburo, the KGB was on the lookout for its former employee. In November 1962, the month after the Stashinsky trial ended, Vladimir Semichastny, Aleksandr Shelepin's successor and Vladimir Andropov's forerunner as chief of the KGB, approved a plan of "special actions" against "particularly dangerous traitors." Those on the list included Bogdan Stashinsky.

In his memoirs, Semichastny explained the logic behind this and other Soviet attempts to kill former KGB agents as follows:

> I myself, as chairman of the KGB, never had the right to make unilateral decisions on the physical liquidation of people. [Western] propaganda to the contrary was based above all on the principle of carrying out Soviet laws outside the motherland, which applied above all to defectors from our ranks whose names were known. If a Chekist [KGB man], a Soviet citizen, or a soldier who had sworn to serve the motherland and the existing order betrayed his country and fled to the West, then, according to current Soviet law, he could be taken to court and tried despite his absence. And if he was

sentenced to death in those proceedings, after that the question could be raised of carrying out the sentence.[1]

The document, signed by Semichastny in November 1962, specified that "as these traitors, who have given important state secrets to the opponent and caused great political damage to the USSR, have been sentenced to death in absentia, the sentence will be carried out abroad." KGB counterintelligence units were supposed to conduct surveillance of the defector's family members within the Soviet Union, check their correspondence, and search their homes in hopes that the defectors would try to establish contact. Counterintelligence units abroad were to track down traitors in their countries of residence so that specially trained killers from the Thirteenth Department, responsible for active measures, could carry out the sentence. In the case of Anatolii Golitsyn, a KGB officer who defected to the West in December 1961, the plan was to assassinate him if he were ever called to testify before a US Senate or congressional committee.[2]

Stashinsky's whereabouts after his release were known only to a small circle of West German officials. In 1971, General Reinhard Gehlen, who by then had retired as head of the West German Foreign Intelligence Service (BND), published his memoirs, in which he suggested that he knew what had happened to the former KGB assassin. Gehlen confirmed earlier statements by West German officials that Stashinsky had been released after serving only part of his sentence. "Today the KGB's 'torpedo' is living as a free man somewhere in the world he chose on that day in the summer of 1961, a few days before the wall was erected across Berlin," wrote Gehlen. The general never revealed this exact location.[3]

If Stashinsky was not in the United States, then where had he gone? The answer was unexpectedly provided by another retired general, Mike Geldenhuys, in a series of interviews that he gave in early March 1984 to a South African newspaper reporter. Geldenhuys was the sixty-year-old former head of the secret branch of the South African security service, the Bureau for State Security (BOSS), which was known for its rough counterintelligence tactics and human rights violations in dealing with the liberation movement led by the African National Congress. In June 1983, eight months before granting the interviews, Geldenhuys had retired as police commissioner, the highest police office in the country.

On March 5, 1984, the *Cape Times*, the oldest South African daily newspaper, ran the interviews. The piece began with Geldenhuys's biography and a description of Stashinsky's killing of Lev Rebet. The killing of Bandera would be included in the next issue of the newspaper. In the interview, the retired general claimed that Stashinsky had come to South Africa from Germany, and that he, Geldenhuys, then a colonel and second-in-command at BOSS, had been the first South African official to interrogate the new settler. Geldenhuys described some aspects of Stashinsky's life in South Africa but refused to disclose others. "Stashinsky's dossier is one of the world's best kept secrets," he told the reporter, "and in fact is still partly so, since Stashinsky's new identity and whereabouts would never be disclosed." If a KGB assassination team was still hunting for Stashinsky, this was an important clue as to where Stashinsky had started his new life. The problem was that the Soviet Union had no diplomatic relations with South Africa, and carrying out any operation in that country would be a logistical nightmare. Besides, Geldenhuys told the newspaper, no one would now be able to recognize Stashinsky.

Geldenhuys told the reporter that although Stashinsky had escaped the death sentence in West Germany, his life was in danger, and his release from prison had been arranged in the utmost secrecy well before the end of his sentence. "In the meantime we were approached by the West German Security Service and asked to give this man asylum in South Africa because they were convinced it was the only country where he would be comparatively safe from KGB agents," continued the general. "We agreed." There were only three people in the entire country who knew about the secret resettlement: Geldenhuys; his boss, the chief of the South African security service, Hendrik van den Bergh; and the prime minister of South Africa, B. J. Vorster.

According to Geldenhuys, Stashinsky had come to South Africa in 1968, at least one year after his release from prison. The South Africans did not regret accommodating the request of their West German colleagues. According to Geldenhuys, Stashinsky "was able to supply our intelligence service with a vast amount of invaluable information on the structure and operations of the Russian secret service." In South Africa, Stashinsky allegedly not only acquired a new identity but also underwent plastic surgery to change his appearance. He also got a new job and remarried.

"We got him a job in which he did very well for himself," Geldenhuys told the reporter, "and sometime after that he met a girl from Durban and they fell in love. When they got married at the registry office somewhere in the Republic, he asked me to be his best man. We had formed a bond of friendship that still exists today and I was delighted to accept." Geldenhuys said in the interview that in his bank vault he kept a picture of himself posing with Stashinsky and his wife after the wedding. Geldenhuys never mentioned Inge Pohl or anyone else accompanying Stashinsky to South Africa.[4]

The Associated Press and other wire agencies picked up the story on the whereabouts and post-prison life of the former KGB assassin and sent it around the world. Many, including members of the Bandera and Rebet families, questioned whether the report could be true. There are reasons to believe it was. Of the two people besides Geldenhuys who supposedly knew Stashinsky's identity in South Africa, one was still alive. The former prime minister and then president, J. B. Vorster, had died in September 1983, but Hendrik van den Bergh was in excellent health, working on his chicken farm and writing his memoirs after being pushed out of government in 1980. According to General Geldenhuys's biographer, Hanlie van Straaten, as of the summer of 2013 the general had in his archive a photo of President Vorster, van den Bergh, and himself. The photo was the only item in the file labeled "Stashinsky."[5]

Geldenhuys's story was also corroborated by earlier media reports that on June 23, 1964, less than two years after the trial, Inge had divorced Stashinsky, formally ending the relationship that had shaken the KGB world to its foundations. She had then completely disappeared from sight. Was her divorce a ploy to throw off the KGB? Or did she disappear in order to rejoin Stashinsky upon his release? After news of Stashinsky's early release was leaked to the press, a federal prosecutor told *Stern* that Inge was being provided for and was living happily. No one could say whether it was Stashinsky who was providing for her and whether she was living with him. We do know that she almost certainly never returned to East Germany. In 1986 the tombstone was removed from the grave of Stashinsky and Inge's son, Peter. According to German law, a cemetery plot can be cleared for reuse twenty-five years after the burial if no one is looking after the grave.[6]

Stashinsky, by all accounts, remained in South Africa. There were rumors that in the 1970s he served as an adviser to South African–backed units fighting in Congo. Was that the job that General Geldenhuys said BOSS had found for him? It's certainly possible: in 1967, the year Stashinsky was released from prison, the South African police became involved in counterinsurgency operations in Rhodesia. The first special forces personnel for the mission were trained at a secret police base in Durban, the city Stashinsky's new wife had reportedly come from. Gerhi Strauss, the newspaperman who interviewed Geldenhuys and broke the story about Stashinsky's transfer to South Africa, also lived and died in Durban. All this could be coincidence, of course, but it also could be evidence of Stashinsky's life after prison.[7]

The new clandestine police force needed to be trained in fighting insurgents. Stashinsky, who had experience in fighting the liberation movement in Ukraine, could provide helpful advice. If that was indeed the case, Stashinsky's story had an ironic and sad ending. Rescued by Inge, he returned to his old habits with her gone. He would not be the first assassin to leave one totalitarian regime to earn his living from another. In the 1950s, Nikolai Khokhlov, another KGB assassin turned defector, was advising the South Vietnamese dictator Ngo Dinh Diem on how to organize an effective struggle against the partisan movement in his country. To different degrees, both Khokhlov and Stashinsky were experts on counterinsurgency, and while in the West they shared strong anti-Soviet convictions. It would make sense for them to join what was heralded by many as a worldwide struggle against communism.[8]

Of the two conjectures about Stashinsky's country of residence after his release—the United States and the Union of South Africa—the latter seems more plausible. But if the Geldenhuys story is accurate, then it casts many elements of Stashinsky's life and career in a new light. The ironworks training that Stashinsky received in West Germany, it would appear, proved useless to him. It is not clear where or how he spent the year 1967, but by 1968 he was working for the South African secret police, which used tactics similar to those of the KGB in putting down the liberation struggle of another oppressed people. He also lost the woman who had inspired him to shake off the embrace of the KGB and the Soviet system.

In a telephone conversation with the author on April 1, 2013, General Geldenhuys confirmed that Bogdan Stashinsky had indeed been in South Africa in the late 1960s and 1970s. He also confirmed to his biographer, Hanlie van Straaten, the authenticity of the interviews he gave in 1984. But he claimed to remember nothing else. While the general's selective memory may be a result of time and the aging process, it may also indicate that he is not at liberty to speak about a man who is still alive and relies on the protection of his former boss.[9]

52

HOMECOMING

"The slightly stooped man with bald spots and gray hair, who looks considerably less than his age, does not at all resemble the Bogdan Stashinsky I have seen in photographs," wrote the Ukrainian freelance journalist Natalia Prykhodko, beginning her description of the man who introduced himself as Bogdan Stashinsky. She claimed to have met with the former KGB assassin in the summer of 2011 through a friend in the Ukrainian security service. According to the friend, Stashinsky, then approaching his eightieth birthday, wanted to set the record straight. He was ready to give an interview.

In the old man's apartment in downtown Kyiv, the journalist found a bust of Joseph Stalin and a portrait of Winston Churchill on the wall. The old man was friendly but asked her not to use a tape recorder. The interview was conducted in Ukrainian, and the journalist, who primarily spoke Russian, asked readers to take into account that not all the peculiarities of Stashinsky's speech were adequately reflected in her notes. The interview appeared in one of Kyiv's leading newspapers in August 2011, a few weeks before Ukraine celebrated its twentieth anniversary of independence. It had an intriguing title: "Bogdan Stashinsky: I Fulfilled My Duty to Ukraine."

In the interview with Prykhodko, the man who called himself Stashinsky repudiated quite a few elements of his story as it has been known in the West. He told the journalist that he had joined the KGB out of conviction, and it was out of conviction that he had killed Bandera and Rebet. He believed that Soviet rule had brought progress and well-being to his homeland. The most striking revelation, however, had to do not with Stashinsky's political beliefs but with his escape to the West. It was a special operation planned by Aleksandr Shelepin himself, said the old man, and it had proved a success. Shelepin, whose previous career had been associated largely with the Young Communist League, was concerned about his reputation among his older colleagues in the Soviet leadership. By letting the world know that he had ordered the successful killing of Bandera, Shelepin supposedly wanted to show his peers how tough he was. On Shelepin's personal orders, Stashinsky was supposed to turn himself in and tell the whole truth about the assassinations. The plan was that after serving his sentence, which would certainly not be too long, given his voluntary confession, he would be whisked back to the Soviet Union by a KGB team. Stashinsky, a strong believer in Soviet ideology, had agreed to sacrifice himself.

It had all worked exactly according to Shelepin's plan. Things went wrong only after the CIA allegedly transferred Stashinsky to the United States after his release from the West German prison. "I was released before my term was up and taken to Washington," Stashinsky told the young journalist. "There I was suspected of playing a double game, and they decided to send me to Latin America, to Panama, for a time, under surveillance, and supposedly to acquire new habits. I understood that. I was more than careful: I understood that they could liquidate me at any moment." A KGB team came to Panama in 1968 to rescue Stashinsky, taking him first to Africa and then, in 1970, back to the Soviet Union.

What about his personal life? He was indeed married to Inge, who, like him, was a KGB agent out of conviction rather than necessity. They indeed had a son, whom they had left with the KGB in Moscow in August 1961, when they had gone to East Berlin and then to the West. The body of the child buried in Dallgow was supplied by the KGB from an East Berlin hospital. The old man said that he had divorced Inge, who settled in East

Germany after the operation, but her intelligence career had suffered because Stasi officials distrusted KGB agents. After a difficult childhood, their son had settled in Ukraine. He became a professor at Kyiv University and was in touch with his father. Stashinsky had never tried to get in touch with his parents or sisters back in Borshchovychi near Lviv. Their political views differed from his, said the old man. No compromise was possible.[1]

It was an amazing story—one that was picked up and treated seriously by some of the most astute Ukraine-watchers in the West. Taras Kuzio, a senior fellow at the Center for Transatlantic Relations, Johns Hopkins University, was appalled that Stashinsky was allegedly collecting a pension in an independent Ukraine. "One of the KGB's master assassins reared his head in Kyiv this summer," wrote Professor Alexander Motyl of Rutgers University in his blog on the *World Affairs* website. Still, he had doubts about the authenticity of the interview, which were shared by many of his readers. One of them questioned the details of Stashinsky's story as presented by Prykhodko. "She could easily end all speculation by revealing a photo of Stashinsky . . . since there is absolutely NO danger to Stashinsky today, as no one would waste a bullet nor gas on this ancient relic," wrote an agitated reader of the blog. The commenter also suggested that DNA evidence might be used to establish the man's true identity.[2]

The interview indeed raised numerous questions. The very idea that Shelepin was seeking publicity in the West flies in the face of the internal political struggles of the Kremlin in the 1950s and 1960s. The American part of the story appears equally groundless in light of CIA documents known today. The interview was only the latest manifestation of the growing interest in Stashinsky and his story in today's Russia and Ukraine.[3]

The Soviets had lost the clandestine war of assassins and poison guns they had fought in the 1950s and 1960s. They had been defeated in the court of public opinion and had failed to achieve either the short-term or the long-term goals associated with the killing of Bandera. Today, veteran KGB officers are the first to admit that instead of undermining the Ukrainian nationalist movement in the West, the murder reinvigorated it. The crime also did nothing to temper the idea of political independence in Ukraine. In December 1991, thirty-two years after the assassination of Stepan Bandera, Ukraine declared its independence from the Soviet Union, and in so doing helped to bring about the collapse of the Soviet Empire. But Stashinsky and his crimes were never completely forgotten either in Moscow or in Ukraine. Forever linked together in public memory, Bandera and Stashinsky appeared as two antipodes in the political and ideological struggles that preceded the Russian invasion of Ukraine in 2014.

Stashinsky's name first reappeared in Russian newspapers in the fall of 2006 in connection with the poisoning by radioactive plutonium of the former KGB officer and outspoken critic of Vladimir Putin, Aleksandr Litvinenko. Reacting to Western media reports that the assassination had been carried out by Russian intelligence agents, Sergei Ivanov, the spokesman for the Russian foreign intelligence service, issued a statement that read: "Since 1959, when the Ukrainian nationalist Stepan Bandera was eliminated, Soviet intelligence and its successor, the Foreign Intelligence Service, have not practiced the physical liquidation of individuals objectionable to Russia." Few observers in the West took the statement at face value. If anything, it only reminded readers of Moscow's long tradition of using political killings as an instrument of foreign policy.[4]

In Ukraine, Stashinsky's name first made headlines again in the fall of 2008, when the Lviv city administration raised the price of tickets on city trams and buses by a whopping 33 percent for the general public and more than 40 percent for students. To "sell" the price hike to the public, the city issued 50,000 copies of leaflets that stated: "Treason to the homeland begins with an unpaid ride." Stashinsky appeared in the news regularly after that. Those were the heydays of the democratic Orange Revolution in Ukraine, which brought the pro-Western president Viktor Yushchenko to power. When Yushchenko was poisoned with dioxin in 2004, many believed it to be the work of the Russian secret service. National pride was on the rise in Ukraine, and numerous nationalist groups treated Stepan Bandera as their hero. President Yushchenko even awarded him posthumously with the title of Hero of Ukraine.[5]

As the political climate in Ukraine underwent another dramatic transformation with the rise to power of the Russian-backed government of Viktor Yanukovych in early 2010, so did the political values attached to Bandera and Stashinsky. Just as Bandera was being heralded as a Ukrainian national hero by newly revived nationalist forces, the pro-Russian websites got busy undermining the Bandera cult by lionizing his assassin, Bogdan Stashinsky. Natalia Prykhodko's interview with the person calling himself Stashinsky contributed to a larger trend of presenting Stashinsky in a more positive light. "This mysterious interview . . . authentic or just a hoax, make[s] evident that Ukraine under Yanukovych is quickly turning back to honoring KGB 'values,'" wrote a visitor (in broken English) to Alexander Motyl's blog at the World Affairs website. "Also, it . . . show[s the] KGB [as] more mighty than [it was] in reality."[6]

Among some Western veterans of Cold War–era espionage, there was a growing suspicion that the secret services of Russia were behind the "revive Stashinsky" campaign. In April 2011, a few months before the publication of Prykhodko's interview, an English-language blog appeared on the web ostensibly written by Bogdan Stashinsky himself. The author began his first post with the following statement: "I am strongly communistic. I believe in helping my country to create a better Soviet Union. To fulfill this goal I gathered information, took on aliases and killed." In the same month a leader of the National Bolshevik Party of Ukraine, a marginal group in the eastern city of Kharkiv, called on the city authorities to name a city park after Stashinsky.[7]

In 2014, with the Euromaidan protests, the escape to Russia of President Viktor Yanukovych, who was ousted by the Ukrainian parliament, and the Russian government's subsequent invasion and annexation of the Crimea, Stepan Bandera returned to Ukraine yet again as a symbol of his homeland's freedom and independence. Bandera's name figured prominently on the banners of self-defense units that fought on Kyiv's Maidan Square and then marched to Eastern Ukraine to fight the Russian-backed insurgency there.[8] In August 2014, in the midst of the Russian hybrid war in the Donbas region of Eastern Ukraine, unidentified perpetrators desecrated Bandera's burial site in Munich, knocking down the cross on his grave—an act that was met with condemnation in both Germany and Ukraine, bringing back memories of the desecration by KGB thugs of Jewish cemeteries in West Germany. Around the same time, the rebel websites in Donbas revived the old KGB theories that Bandera had been assassinated by West German agents.[9]

While once again raising the banner of Ukrainian independence from Moscow, the vast majority of Ukrainians today reject the radical nationalist ideology of Bandera, along with his strategy and tactics. In the midst of the Ukrainian crisis and mass mobilization of Ukrainian patriotism in May 2014, the leader of the largest nationalist party, *Svoboda* (Freedom), won only slightly more than 1 percent of the popular vote, while in the fall of 2014 his party failed to cross the 5 percent threshold required to obtain seats in parliament. Bandera stands today as the prophet of a minority radical nationalist faith that flourished in the first half of the twentieth century. The majority has opted for the European values and a new pluralistic society. Very few embrace the cause of the assassin or the Soviet strategy of assassinating Ukrainian nationalist leaders in the 1950s.[10]

Newspaper reporters who have gone to Stashinsky's native village in the past few years to interview members of his family found none of them in the village. "His parents could not get over it," said one of the neighbors about their reaction to the news that Stashinsky had assassinated Stepan Bandera. "They said that they had given their whole lives to Ukraine, and their son had brought them such shame. Maria, his sister, said that she had disowned her brother. It would have been better had they been exiled to Siberia: had God allowed them to return, they would not have been afraid to look people in the face. His father soon died; his sister Maria was sick all her life. Iryna, too, did not live long—she developed cancer of the stomach and died. They knew nothing but misfortune. At least after death, they should be remembered with a kind word."[11]

Neighbors believe that Bogdan Stashinsky returned to his native village at least once. According to a local legend, fresh flowers appeared on the graves of Stashinsky's parents soon after his release from prison. Another legend has it that he still comes to the village from time to time to check on his parents' house, which now belongs to a different family. To be sure, say the villagers, no one can recognize him any more—he is a ghost in his own homeland and a tragic figure who is regarded as a traitor by every side he had ever been on.[12]

EPILOGUE:
THE COLD WAR REDUX

James Bond walks into the office of his boss, whose true name remains a secret to us—we know him only by the first letter of his last name, "M." They have a conversation that ends differently from any other that Bond has had with his bosses, male or female, over the years. He reaches into his jacket pocket, extracts an unusual kind of gun, and shoots it at his boss, releasing a poisonous liquid. It is only at the last moment that "M" presses a concealed button on his chair. A bulletproof glass screen descends from the ceiling, separating him from his rogue agent. The stream of pressurized poison hits the glass wall. Bond himself loses consciousness. "Cyanide," says the internal security chief, who rushes into the office after the shooting. He orders everyone to leave the premises. Miss Moneypenny, covering her mouth with her hand, watches in horror as her beloved agent is dragged out of the office.

This is a key moment in Ian Fleming's last Bond novel, *The Man with the Golden Gun*. It was made into one of the most popular James Bond movies, with Agent 007 played by Roger Moore. Written in 1964, at the height of the Cold War, the novel includes elements of true espionage stories then current in the world media. The image of Bond, brainwashed by the Soviets and shooting a gun that spits liquid cyanide, comes directly from newspaper reports on the Bogdan Stashinsky trial. The Munich killings are actually discussed by Bond and "M" in Fleming's novel immediately before Bond tries to kill his boss. "Did they happen to mention the murder of Horcher and Stutz in Munich last month?" asks "M," trying to convince Bond that the KGB is anything but a champion of world peace.[1]

When it comes to the use of the poison gun, Stashinsky succeeded where Bond failed. But the Stashinsky saga, its popular culture incarnations notwithstanding, presents a classic example of the failure of assassination as a tool of international policy. Although the assassin fulfilled his task, the murders themselves failed to achieve their ultimate goal, and on becoming public knowledge, they did major damage to the masterminds behind them.

Conceived as part of the counterinsurgency effort in the final stages of guerrilla warfare in the Ukrainian territories recently conquered by the Soviet Union, the assassination of Stepan Bandera was carried out long after that movement had been effectively suppressed and its ties with foreign centers taken under control and manipulated by the Soviet secret services. Carried out at the insistence and with the enthusiastic approval of the Soviet political leadership, the assassination achieved a result contrary to the one envisioned by its instigators. Instead of creating confusion in the ranks of the anti-regime forces and provoking a power struggle among the leaders of the most militant émigré organization, it removed a leader who was no longer popular or dangerous from the scene, turning him into a martyr and providing his supporters with a tool for mobilization that they had previously lacked.

Stashinsky's escape to the West, and his readiness to reveal what he knew about the Soviet assassination program, severely damaged the credibility of the Soviet leadership and tarnished the image of the Soviet Union abroad. The assassin's testimony and the public relations disaster that followed—risks involved in any government-backed assassination—were ultimately the result of major blunders on the part of the Soviet security apparatus in East Berlin and a breach of the established Soviet practice of forbidding intelligence officers and agents to marry foreign nationals. In both cases, the interference of the political leadership was at fault—a sign of the exuberance and hubris in the Kremlin following a successful strike against a high-profile enemy of the regime.

The newly married couple managed to outwit the KGB. Raised in East Germany but employed in West Berlin, Inge Pohl had never accepted or learned to tolerate communist ideology and the Soviet way of life. Her planned recruitment by the KGB, if it ever took place, brought no tangible results. Facing standard economic hardships in the Soviet capital, she had little difficulty convincing her husband to defect to the more prosperous West. Stashinsky, born and raised in a patriotic Ukrainian family outside Soviet territory, had no strong attachment to the Soviet state or its ideology. He was recruited through blackmail and forced to spy on his own family and countrymen. Brought up as a Christian, he also had moral qualms about the killings he was forced to commit. The threat that the couple's plans to defect might be uncovered by the KGB made them speed up their preparations, and the unexpected death of their son provided the opportunity they were looking for. Stashinsky and his wife acted on the belief that they could find safety from KGB assassins only by confessing and obtaining the protection of Western security services.

Some of the most astute observers of the Stashinsky trial compared the defendant to the main character of Fyodor Dostoyevsky's novel *Crime and Punishment*. "Stashinsky is an ideological Raskolnikov," wrote the correspondent of the *Kölnische Rundschau* (Cologne Review) in his commentary on the trial and its verdict. Like Raskolnikov, Stashinsky struggled with severe moral dilemmas, confessed under the influence of a woman he loved, and finally was sentenced to the same term: eight years. But even more striking parallels can be found between Stashinsky's story and the one told in Joseph Conrad's novel *Under Western Eyes*. The main character of this 1911 masterpiece, a young man called Razumov, betrays to the Russian police a fellow student who seeks his protection after committing a terrorist act. The police recruit Razumov as an agent and send him to Switzerland to penetrate a circle of Russian revolutionaries. There he meets and falls in love with the sister of the man he betrayed. Unable to withstand the moral pressure, Razumov eventually confesses both to the woman he loves and to the revolutionaries on whom he came to spy.[2]

When it comes to the KGB assassination program, the Raskolnikov/Razumov problem appears to be a factor in the defection of two Soviet secret agents, Nikolai Khokhlov and Bogdan Stashinsky, who were both considered loyal and committed to communist ideals. The American and West European intelligence services were only too happy to take advantage of the Dostoyevskian crises haunting their opponents. The problem was that the CIA and its West European partners too often resorted to the same methods as their opponents. "We do disagreeable things so that ordinary people here and elsewhere can sleep safely in their beds at night," says Control, a character in John le Carré's novel *The Spy Who Came in from the Cold*, as he tries to persuade a subordinate in the British intelligence service to assassinate one of its perceived opponents.[3]

David Cornwell, the British intelligence officer who used the pen name John le Carré, knew what he was writing about. But the Western spy agencies running assassination programs never experienced the embarrassment that befell the Soviet agencies during the Stashinsky trial. This was primarily because despite what the James Bond novels and movies suggest, in reality such killings were largely outsourced to "freelancers," quite often common criminals. The Western services supplied only the targeting and planning, finances, and logistical support. If the Soviets generally went after leaders of émigré groups whom they considered citizens of the USSR, the Americans stayed away from their own citizens and targeted foreigners. This was a significant difference between the political cultures of the two Cold War superpowers. In the tradition of the tsars, the Soviets believed that people like Bandera, who may never have been Soviet citizens but were born on territory later acquired by the Soviet Union, were their subjects and thus legitimate targets for assassination.[4]

Despite the obvious differences in choice of targets and methods employed to "eliminate" their opponents, both Soviet and American intelligence services in the 1950s and 1960s resorted to assassination in order to deal with the same phenomenon—insurgency aroused by the weakening or disintegration of empires. In ordering the killings of Bandera and Rebet, the Soviets were seeking to protect their empire from the threat of disintegration, which, despite their best efforts, came to pass in 1991. The Americans did not have a formal empire of their own to protect; but, for all its anticolonial rhetoric, the US government had a stake in keeping other empires afloat in areas that Washington considered vulnerable to communist subversion. Leaders of independent countries, like Fidel Castro of Cuba, Patrice Lumumba of the Democratic Republic of Congo, Achmad Sukarno of Indonesia, and Rafael Trujillo of the Dominican Republic, could be targeted because of their pro-Soviet leanings, independent political actions, or, as in the case of Trujillo, because of policies they maintained that were regarded as conducive to a communist-type revolution.[5]

Over time, international scandals caused by the exposure of KGB and CIA assassinations forced both parties to put a hold on their assassination programs. The Russian authorities claimed that their Soviet predecessors did so immediately after Stashinsky's testimony became public. They could not, however, refuse to help their comrades in arms, so they played a role in the Bulgarian security service's assassination of dissident Georgi Markov in September 1978. Markov was shot by an umbrella-shaped pistol, courtesy of the KGB. In the United States, the investigation into CIA activities conducted by a US Senate committee led by Frank Church influenced President Jimmy Carter's decision to officially end the assassination program in 1978.

The end of the Cold War ushered in a new era of international relations. It brought liberalism to Eastern Europe, ended apartheid in South Africa, and helped achieve a short-lived Israeli-Palestinian reconciliation in the Middle East. But it also produced a wounded and humiliated Russia, created numerous newly independent nations that had to sort out relations with their former masters and neighbors, and revived a number of formerly frozen interethnic and international conflicts. As the new millennium began, former KGB officers reached once again for their Cold War–era assassination manuals in hopes of reshaping the world according to their wishes. The Russians sought to preserve what was left of their empire and surround themselves with friendly (i.e., subservient) states and leaders.

In February 2004, authorities in Qatar arrested three Russian citizens on charges of killing the acting president of the rebellious republic of Chechnya, Zelimkhan Yandarbiyev. One of those arrested had diplomatic immunity, but the other two were put on trial and given life sentences for their role in the assassination, which took place in Qatar's capital of Doha. The following year they were extradited to Russia in order to improve Russo-Qatari relations. The Russian authorities refused to admit that their agents had been sent to Qatar to carry out the assassination. A spokesman for the Russian intelligence service reiterated that Moscow had stopped conducting assassinations abroad after the Stashinsky scandal. Despite their protestations, most considered Yandarbiyev the second Chechen president to be killed by the Russian government. Eight years earlier, his predecessor, Dzhokhar Dudaev, had been killed in Chechnya by a guided missile launched from a Russian military aircraft.[6]

In the fall of 2004, world news agencies reported on the mysterious poisoning of Viktor Yushchenko. Yushchenko was a pro-Western candidate in the Ukrainian presidential election. Traces of dioxin found in his body raised the suspicion that Russia was the source of the poison and might have masterminded the attempt—few countries had poison laboratories attached to their security services, and even fewer had reason to use them against Yushchenko. Yushchenko did not die, and many theories circulated about what might have happened.

In November 2006, another opponent of the Kremlin, the former KGB officer Aleksandr Litvinenko, died in London after being poisoned by radioactive polonium. This was the second time that Moscow was alleged to have used a radioactive substance in an attempt to kill an opponent. The first target, in 1957, was Nikolai Khokhlov, who survived the attempt. In the case of Khokhlov, radioactive poison was allegedly added to his coffee; in Litvinenko's case, to his tea. The British authorities asked the Russian government to extradite a former KGB officer whom they believed was involved in the murder of Litvinenko. Moscow refused the request.[7]

A report released in January 2016 on the poisoning of Aleksandr Litvinenko concluded that he had been killed by two agents of the Russian Federal Security Service (FSB). "The FSB operation to kill Mr. Litvinenko was probably approved by Mr [Nikolai] Patrushev and also by President Putin," read the report, naming the head of the FSB and the sitting Russian president as the people ultimately responsible for the assassination. The hard evidence implicating the Russian leadership was not there, but once again, as in Stashinsky's case, the trail of evidence had pointed to the very top of the Moscow power pyramid.[8]

The Russian intelligence services are not the only ones reviving the Cold War–era practice of political assassination. By all accounts, the CIA is far ahead of its competitors, relying more on its mastery of technology than on its human assets. As in the Cold War, the Russians are going after those whom they consider their own, while the Americans prefer to kill "others." The new opportunities offered by Predators—unmanned aerial vehicles or drones that can attack targets from the sky—give the CIA a clear advantage over its rivals and puts its officers on the cutting edge of the rapidly changing art of assassination.

The program began in 2004 and, over the course of nine years, has resulted in the assassination or targeted killing of more than 3,300 individuals, supposedly Al Qaeda operatives who found themselves on the longest-ever CIA hit list. The program reached its apogee in 2011. According to experts at the Washington-based New America Foundation, that year alone there were more than 120 drone strikes in the tribal areas of northern Pakistan, the main target area of the drone program. Close to 850 individuals were killed. Of those, about 50 were either innocent or never had their identities and affiliations established. This is by far the lowest available estimate of the number of innocent victims. According to one report, only 35 out of 200 individuals killed by drones in northeastern Afghanistan between January 2012 and February 2013 were the intended targets.[9]

The world has changed significantly since the Cold War. What remains largely the same, however, is the logic used to justify assassination as a legitimate tool of government policy. "I would say that since the war, our methods—ours and those of the opposition—have become much the same," declares Control in Le Carré's *The Spy Who Came in from the Cold.* "I mean you can't be less ruthless than the opposition simply because your government's 'policy' is benevolent, can you now?" The benevolent policies of government continue to figure as the main moral argument in favor of continuing programs of targeted killing. The Cold War is maybe over, but the recent rise in East-West tensions and the emergence of new challenges to the established international order make the return to Cold War–era methods of struggle almost irresistible to the former Cold War rivals. In that sense, the Stashinsky story is more than a piece of history. It is also an insight into the present and forewarning for the future.

ACKNOWLEDGMENTS

I became interested in Bogdan Stashinsky's story after reading excerpts from his trial testimony that were first published in Ukraine in 1993, more than thirty years after the trial. The testimony, taken from the earlier and much more comprehensive edition of trial materials published in Munich and unavailable in Ukraine, struck me as a surprisingly candid account of crimes committed by a man who seemed to have every reason not to tell the truth. They offered a unique insight into the modus operandi of the Soviet secret services and an individual's relation to the state that turned him into a traitor.

My reading of Stashinsky's testimony left a number of questions unanswered. His statements often sounded self-serving and sometimes improbable. After all, could a lone KGB agent have carried out not one assassination but two? And what happened to Stashinsky after the trial? Why was he given only eight years for committing two murders and released two years early? Where did he go after his imprisonment? Also, if the testimony he gave was part of a deal he made with the court, how much of it was true?

The idea of checking Stashinsky's story against the existing body of evidence came to me during a visit to Munich. Following the example of Alex Motyl, who prepared for writing a novel that featured Stashinsky as a character by tracing the Soviet agent's movements before and after the two murders he committed there, I, too, retraced Stashinsky's steps. On the basis of Stashinsky's court testimony, I drew a map and walked the routes myself. Stashinsky's assertions were borne out by my experiment. In that regard, at least, he had told the truth.

More comparative data became available when I learned about the existence of declassified CIA files dealing with the political activities and assassination of Stepan Bandera, as well as activities of his followers and rivals from the ranks of the Ukrainian emigration. The information in the CIA files helped me verify and supplement the evidence given by Stashinsky during his trial. So did sources and testimony that emerged from the Soviet side. Once again, it turned out that Stashinsky had told the truth—but not the whole truth. It was up to me to fill in the gaps in his narrative.

Any subject involving the history of intelligence services is difficult, not only because much remains secret but also because there are numerous cover stories and deliberate efforts to mislead that linger for decades, as the Stashinsky case seemed to exemplify. To collect the kind of sources I wanted to see and find my way through the labyrinth of Cold War espionage history, I needed a lot of support, and I am happy to thank those who helped me the most.

My special thanks go to my friends and colleagues Frank Sysyn and Zenon Kohut. Frank invited me to two of the conferences he organized in Munich, and Zenon accompanied me on Stashinsky's trails in Munich from Karlsplatz, where Lev Rebet was killed, to Zeppelinstrasse, where Bandera had worked, and Kreittmayrstrasse, where he died. They also introduced me to Andrii Rebet, the son of Lev Rebet and probably the only surviving participant in the Stashinsky trial of October 1962. I am grateful to Andrii Rebet for the interview he granted me during one of my visits to Munich and for the help that his wife, Ivanna Rebet, offered me with the library collections at the Ukrainian Free University in Munich. The university's chancellor, Dr. Nicolas Szafowal, advised me on the Stasi archives pertaining to the Stashinsky case and shared information on the life trajectories of Bandera's associates after his assassination.

Dr. Roman Procyk of the Ukrainian Studies Fund in the United States agreed to refer my questions about post–World War II Munich to his mother, who well remembered how the Ukrainian community had lived in that city in the late 1940s and early 1950s. He also helped me arrange an interview with Dr. Anatol Kaminski, who was close to Lev and Daria Rebet at the time of the assassination of Lev Rebet.

My special thanks also go to Andriy Portnov, who introduced me to one of his best students at the Free University of Berlin, Maria Przyborowska. I could not have asked for a better assistant than Maria, who traveled repeatedly to Dallgow, the Berlin suburb where Inge Pohl was born and from which Bogdan and Inge made their way to the West in August 1961. Maria did her best to locate Inge's neighbors and relatives. Unfortunately, there were none. But in the parish archive, Maria managed to discover the record of the burial of Peter Pohl and biographical information about his mother.

A colleague of mine at Harvard, Emmanuel K. Akyeampong, helped me acquire copies of rare newspapers from the Republic of South Africa, to which Bogdan Stashinsky emigrated after his release from prison in West Germany. I am grateful to General Mike Geldenhuys, the former police commissioner of South Africa, for granting me a telephone interview, and to his wife, Annatje Geldenhuys, for arranging it. The general's biographer, Hanlie van Straaten, was exceptionally kind in agreeing to pass on to the general the materials I wanted him to read and the questions I had with regard to those materials.

I am also grateful to Tomas Sniegon of the University of Lund for sharing with me the notes of his interviews with the former head of the KGB, Vladimir Semichastny, and to Serhy Yekelchyk of the University of Victoria in Canada for pointing me to the latest literature on Stepan Bandera. In Kyiv, Andriy Kohut and Mariia Panova helped me to find my way in the rich collections of the Archive of the Security Service of Ukraine. In Warsaw, Dr. Marcin Majewski of the Polish Institute of National Memory provided me with files relating to Stashinsky. In the United States, Olha Aleksic assisted me with access to the Mykola Lebed Papers at the Harvard Ukrainian Research Institute, and Lev Chaban and Lubow Wolynets were very helpful in arranging my work on the Yaroslav Padoch Papers at the Ukrainian Museum and Library of Stamford, Connecticut. Professor Leigh McWhite provided access to the James O. Eastland collection at the

University of Mississippi. In Canada, I am grateful to Oleh Romanyshyn of the newspaper *Ukrainian Echo* and to Roman Senkus of the Canadian Institute of Ukrainian Studies for helping me access a collection of newspaper clippings on the assassination of Stepan Bandera.

My friend and longtime editor Myroslav Yurkevich once again helped me with my English prose. Hiroaki Kuromiya and Jim Klingle read the manuscript and gave it their enthusiastic approval. Mary Sarotte posed some important questions about my treatment of Stashinsky as the main character of the book, which helped me rethink his personal story. My wonderful literary agent, Jill Kneerim, became fascinated with the Stashinsky story and gave me numerous excellent suggestions on how to make it even more appealing. And I was very lucky that Lara Heimert of Basic Books agreed to add it to the impressive list of spy stories issued by this distinguished publishing house. It gave me an opportunity to work again with Lara and the outstanding team that produced my two previous books, *The Last Empire* and *The Gates of Europe*. I am especially grateful to Leah Stecher, Collin Tracy, Kathy Streckfus, Jennifer Thompson, and Betsy DeJesu.

Once again, it was my wife, Olena, who was the inspiration and driving force behind this new book project. My daughter, Olesia, helped me edit the manuscript and offered suggestions for improving it. I followed her advice to the letter.

NOTES

PROLOGUE

1. Richard Deacon and Nigel West, *Spy! Six Stories of Modern Espionage* (London, 1980), 127; Karl Anders, *Murder to Order* (New York, 1967), 51–54; *Moskovs'ki vbyvtsi Bandery pered sudom*, ed. Danylo Chaikovs'kyi (Munich, 1965), 194–198.

CHAPTER 1: STALIN'S CALL

1. Nikita Sergeevich Khrushchev, with an introduction, commentary, and notes by Edward Crankshaw, translated and edited by Strobe Talbott, *Khrushchev Remembers* (Boston, 1970), 262; Dmitrii Vedeneev and Sergei Shevchenko, "Priznalsia, zabiraite," *2000*, February 14, 2002; Tarik Cyril Amar, *The Paradox of Ukrainian Lviv: A Borderland City Between Stalinists, Nazis and Nationalists* (Ithaca, NY, 2015), 242–248; Iuliia Kysla, "'Post imeni Iaroslava Halana.' Osinnii atentat u L'vovi," *Ukraïna moderna*, January 6, 2014, http://uamoderna.com/blogy/yuliya-kisla/kysla-galan.

2. William Taubman, *Khrushchev: The Man and His Era* (New York, 2004), 179–207.

3. Khrushchev, *Khrushchev Remembers*, 146–147; "Bandera, Stepan," in *Encyclopedia of Nationalism* (San Diego, 2001), 2: 40–41; Mykola Posivnych, *Stepan Bandera* (Kharkiv, 2015); Grzegorz Rossoliński-Liebe, *Stepan Bandera: The Life and Afterlife of a Ukrainian Nationalist: Fascism, Genocide, and Cult* (Stuttgart, 2014).

4. Khrushchev, *Khrushchev Remembers*, 228; Grzegorz Motyka, *Ukraińska partyzantka, 1942–1960* (Warsaw, 2006); Volodymyr Viatrovych, *Druha pol's'ko-ukraïns'ka viina* (Kyiv, 2012).

5. Paul Robert Magocsi, *A History of Ukraine: The Land and Its Peoples* (Toronto, 2010), 696–700; Jeffrey Burds, "Agentura: Soviet Informants' Networks & the Ukrainian Underground in Galicia, 1944–48," *East European Politics and Societies* 11 (1997): 89–130; Yuri M. Zhukov, "Examining the Authoritarian Model of Counter-Insurgency: The Soviet Campaign Against the Ukrainian Insurgent Army," *Small Wars and Insurgencies* 18, no. 3 (2007): 439–466.

6. Bohdan R. Bociurkiw, *The Ukrainian Greek Catholic Church and the Soviet State (1939–1950)* (Edmonton, 1996); Vedeneev and Shevchenko, "Priznalsia, zabiraite"; Amar, *The Paradox of Ukrainian Lviv*, 240–242; Kysla, "'Post imeni Iaroslava Halana.'"

7. Pavel Sudoplatov and Anatoli Sudoplatov, with Jerrold L. and Leona P. Schecter, *Special Tasks: The Memoirs an Unwanted Witness—A Soviet Spymaster* (New York, 1995), 253 (hereafter Sudoplatov, *Special Tasks*).

8. Amar, *The Paradox of Ukrainian Lviv*, 243; Sudoplatov, *Special Tasks*, 254.

9. Khrushchev, *Khrushchev Remembers*, 262–263.

CHAPTER 2: MASTER KILLER

1. Sudoplatov, *Special Tasks*, 24–38.

2. Myroslav Yurkevich, "Organization of Ukrainian Nationalists," in *Encyclopedia of Ukraine*, vol. 3 (Toronto, 1993); Roman Wysocki, *Organizacja ukraińskich nacjonalistów w Polsce w latach, 1929–1939: Geneza, struktura, program, ideologia* (Lublin, 2003).

3. Sudoplatov, *Special Tasks*, 249–253, 378; Nikita Petrov, "Shtatnyi gosudarstvennyi ubiitsa (reabilitirovannyi): Dva dnia iz zhizni Pavla Sudoplatova," *Novaia gazeta*, August 7, 2013; Nikita Petrov, "Master individual'nogo terrora: Portret Èitongona, kollegi Sudoplatova," *Novaia gazeta*, February 26, 2014.

4. Sudoplatov, *Special Tasks*, 255–256; Dmytro Viedienieiev, "Iak zahynuv Shukhevych i shcho mohlo statysia z ioho tilom," *Istorychna pravda*, August 8, 2011; Olesia Isaiuk, *Roman Shukhevych* (Kharkiv, 2015).

5. Aleksandr Pronin, "Likvidatsiia 'Volka,'" *Stoletie*, March 25, 2014; Andrei Sidorchik, "Palach dlia terrorista: Ubiitsu Bandery nagradili ordenom," *Argumenty i fakty*, March 12, 2014; Posivnych, *Stepan Bandera*, 216; Sudoplatov, *Special Tasks*, 378.

CHAPTER 3: SECRET AGENT

1. Stashinsky's Trial Transcripts, in *Moskovs'ki vbyvtsi*, 127.

2. Ihor Derev'ianyi, "Rozstrily v'iazniv v chervni-lypni 1941 r. Iak tse bulo," *Ukraïns'ka pravda*, June, 24, 2011; Lesia Fediv, "Vin ubyv Banderu," *Shchodennyi L'viv*, May 22, 2008; Ivan Farion, "Iak by mohla, sama ubyla b ubyvtsiu Bandery . . . ," *Vysokyi zamok*, October 14, 2015.

3. Stashinsky's Trial Transcripts, in *Moskovs'ki vbyvtsi*, 125–127; Farion, "Iak by mohla, sama ubyla b ubyvtsiu Bandery. . . ."

4. Amar, *The Paradox of Ukrainian Lviv*, 245–253; Roman Heneha, "Uchast' l'vivs'koho studentstva v rusi oporu v druhii polovyni 1940-kh—na pochatku 1950-kh," *Ukraïns'kyi istorychnyi zhurnal*, no. 3 (2007): 97–112; Irina Lisnichenko, "Shcherbitskii postoianno tverdil Semichastnomu," *Fakty*, January 19, 2001.

5. Volodymyr Ovsiichuk, "Pivstolittia tomu . . . ," in *Osiahnennia istorii: Zbirnyk na poshanu profesora Mykoly Pavlovycha Koval's'koho z nahody 70-richchia* (Ostrih, 1999), 13–17; Vitalii Iaremchuk, "Students'ki roky M. P. Koval's'koho," in ibid., 18–29; Evgenii Chernov, "N. P. Koval'skii: O vremeni i o sebe," in *Dnipropetrovs'kyi istoryko-arkheohrafichnyi zbirnyk*, vol. 1 (Dnipropetrovsk, 1997), 11.

6. Stashinsky's Trial Transcripts, in *Moskovs'ki vbyvtsi*, 130–131.

7. Oleksandra Andreiko, "Narys pro istoriiu sela Pykulovychi," *Forum sela Pykulovychi* http://xn—b1albgfsd8a2b7j.xn—j1amh.

8. Stashinsky's Trial Transcripts, in *Moskovs'ki vbyvtsi*, 135–137; Rossoliński-Liebe, *Stepan Bandera*, 351; Svitlana Voroz, "Ioho vchynkam nemaie vypravdannia," *Holos narodu*, November 23, 2013; Roman Vasyl'ko, "Zlochyn: Khto hostryv sokyru?"

OUN-UPA, http://oun-upa.org.ua/articles/vasylko.html; Vedeneev and Shevchenko, "Priznalsia, zabiraite."

9. Ovsiichuk, "Pivstolittia tomu"; Mikhail Kravchenko, "Trezubets v petle," *Russkoe voskresenie*, www.voskres.ru/army/publicist/kravtshenko.htm.

10. Stashinsky's Trial Transcripts, in *Moskovs'ki vbyvtsi*, 137.

CHAPTER 4: PARACHUTIST

1. Dmytro Viedienieiev and Hennadii Bystrukhin, *Dvobii bez kompromisiv: Protyborstvo spetspidrozdiliv OUN ta radians'kykh syl spetsoperatsii, 1945–1980-ti rr.* (Kyiv, 2007), 288–303, 392–409.

2. John L. Steele, "Assassin Disarmed by Love: The Case of a Soviet Spy Who Defected to the West," *Life*, September 7, 1962, 70–77, reprinted in Allen Dulles, ed., *Great True Spy Stories* (New York, 1968), 419–435; here, 421–422; Stashinsky's Trial Transcripts, in *Moskovs'ki vbyvtsi*, 137.

3. Viedienieiev and Bystrukhin, *Dvobii bez kompromisiv*, 290, 392–395; Stephen Dorril, *MI6: Inside the Covert World of Her Majesty's Secret Intelligence Service* (New York, 2000), 223–248; Peter Gross, *Operation Rollback: America's Secret War Behind the Iron Curtain* (New York, 2000), 171; Kevin C. Ruffner, "Cold War Allies: The Origins of CIA's Relationship with Ukrainian Nationalists," in *Fifty Years of the CIA* (Langley, VA, 1998), 29–30.

4. *Stepan Bandera u dokumentakh radians'kykh orhaniv derzhavnoi bespeky (1939–1959)*, ed. Volodymyr Serhiichuk (Kyiv, 2009), 3: 69–77, 95–96, 105.

5. Sudoplatov, *Special Tasks*, 257–259; Dmytro Viedienieiev and Iurii Shapoval, "Maltiis'kyi sokil: Abo dolia Myrona Matviieika," *Dzerkalo tyzhnia*, August 11, 2001; Viedienieiev and Bystrukhin, *Dvobii bez kompromisiv*, 392–399.

6. Stashinsky's Trial Transcripts, in *Moskovs'ki vbyvtsi*, 137–138; Viedienieiev and Bystrukhin, *Dvobii bez kompromisiv*, 300–309; Georgii Sannikov, *Bol'shaia okhota: Rasgrom vooruzhennogo podpol'ia v Zapadnoi Ukraine* (Moscow, 2002), 16–18.

CHAPTER 5: STREETS OF MUNICH

1. Leonid Shebarshin, *Ruka Moskvy: Zapiski nachal'nika Sovetskoi razvedki* (Moscow, 1996), 150–152.

2. Stashinsky's Trial Transcripts, in *Moskovs'ki vbyvtsi*, 138–141; *Shchit i mech maiora Zoricha*, television documentary, www.youtube.com/watch?v=pm5q_32UluE; Viedienieiev and Bystrukhin, *Dvobii bez kompromisiv*, photo of Colonel Aleksei [Oleksii] Daimon following p. 504; O. Daimon, "V okupovanomu Kyievi," *Z arkhiviv VUCHK-HPU-NKVD-KHB: Naukovyi i dokumental'nyi zhurnal* 12, no. 1 (2000): 245ff.; Sannikov, *Bol'shaia okhota*, 18.

3. David E. Murphy, Sergei A. Kondrashev, and George Bailey, *Battleground Berlin: CIA vs. KGB in the Cold War* (New Haven, CT, 1997), 256–259; George Blake, *No Other Choice: An Autobiography* (New York, 1991), 166–167.

4. Dmytro Lykhovii and Lesia Shovkun, "Demokrat v OUN i persha zhertva KGB," *Ukrainska pravda*, October 12, 2011.

5. Stashinsky's Trial Transcripts, in *Moskovs'ki vbyvtsi*, 141–146; Andrii Rebet, "Lev i Dariia Rebet: Moï bat'ky," paper delivered on June 24, 1998, at the Ukrainian Free University, Munich, manuscript, 13.

6. Ivan Bysaha and Vasyl Halasa, *Za velinniam sovisti* (Kyiv, 1963); Stepan Mudryk-Mechnyk, *OUN v Ukraïni i za kordonom pid provodom S. Bandery (Prychynky do istorii, spohad)* (Lviv, 1997), 128–129; *Moskovs'ki vbyvtsi*, 145, 616–617.

7. Stashinsky's Trial Transcripts, in *Moskovs'ki vbyvtsi*, 154–160; Karl Anders, *Murder to Order* (London, 1965), 25–28.

CHAPTER 6: WONDER WEAPON

1. Stashinsky's Trial Transcripts, in *Moskovs'ki vbyvtsi*, 161–164.

2. Ibid., 164–165.

3. Ibid., 166–167.

4. Ibid., 175–177; Anders, *Murder to Order*, 25–32.

5. Anders, *Murder to Order*, 115; Nikolai Khokhlov, *Pravo na sovest'* (Frankfurt, 1957), 113–138; "Shpion, kotoryi byl otravlen KGB, no vyzhil," *APN Nizhnii Novgorod*, January 12, 2006, www.apn-nn.ru/contex_s/26820.html; Boris Volodarsky, *The KGB's Poison Factory: From Lenin to Litvinenko* (Minneapolis, 2010), 184.

CHAPTER 7: GREETINGS FROM MOSCOW

1. Stashinsky's Trial Transcripts, in *Moskovs'ki vbyvtsi*, 170–172; Anders, *Murder to Order*, 35–36.

2. Author's interview with Andrii Rebet, Munich, July 1, 2012.

3. Stashinsky's Trial Transcripts, in *Moskovs'ki vbyvtsi*, 172–174; Anders, *Murder to Order*, 35–37.

4. Ibid., 174, 248–249, 615; Author's interview with Anatol Kaminsky, a close associate of Daria Rebet, July 27, 2012; Memorandum for the Record, Subject: Meeting with AECASSOWARY 2 [Mykola Lebed] and 29 [Fr. Mykhailo Korzhan], April 3, 1962, 1, Aerodynamic: Contact Reports, vol. 45, NARA, RG 263, E ZZ-19, B 23.

5. Stashinsky's Trial Transcripts, in *Moskovs'ki vbyvtsi*, 174; Anders, *Murder to Order*, 10–11, 38–39, 57; Dmitrii Prokhorov, *Skol'ko stoit prodat' rodinu* (St. Petersburg, 2005), 255.

CHAPTER 8: RED SQUARE

1. Stashinsky's Trial Transcripts, in *Moskovs'ki vbyvtsi*, 184–185; Anders, *Murder to Order*, 44–45; "Sem' sester Stalina: Ili kak stroilis' pervye sovetskie neboskreby," *Fact Magazine*, February 12, 2011, www.magazinefact.com/articles/72-figures-and-faces/751-qseven-sistersq-of-stalin-or-how-the-first-soviet-skyscrapers-were-built.

2. Stashinsky's Trial Transcripts, in *Moskovs'ki vbyvtsi*, 187.

3. "Ishchenko Georgii Avksentievich," in Nikita Petrov, *Kto rukovodil organami gosbezopasnosti, 1941–1954: Spravochnik* (Moscow, 2010), 430–431.

4. Stashinsky's Trial Transcripts, in *Moskovs'ki vbyvtsi*, 182–183; *Romantyk shakhiv ta ioho epokha: Stepan Popel'*, comp. Ivan Iaremko (Lviv, 2009).

5. Interview of Lieutenant General Vasilii Khristoforov, head of the Registration and Archives Directorate of the Federal Security Service of the Russian Federation, in the television documentary *Tainy razvedki: Likvidatsiia Stepana Bandery* (2012).

6. Stepan Bandera, "Nad mohyloiu Ievhena Konoval'tsia," in Stepan Bandera, *Perspektyvy ukraïns'koï revoliutsiï* (Kyiv, 1999), 587–591.

7. Stashinsky's Trial Transcripts, in *Moskovs'ki vbyvtsi*, 149–150, 184.

8. Ibid., 186–187; Anders, *Murder to Order*, 45.

9. Stashinsky's Trial Transcripts, in *Moskovs'ki vbyvtsi*, 185–187; Nikolai Khokhlov, *Pravo na sovest'* (Frankfurt, 1957).

CHAPTER 9: HERR POPEL

1. Stashinsky's Trial Transcripts, in *Moskovs'ki vbyvtsi*, 194–198; Rossoliński-Liebe, *Stepan Bandera*, 354; Anders, *Murder to Order*, 51–54; Richard Deacon and Nigel West, *Spy! Six Stories of Modern Espionage* (London, 1980), 127.

2. Stashinsky's Trial Transcripts, in *Moskovski vbyvtsi*, 198–199; Steele, "Assassin Disarmed by Love," 430.

CHAPTER 10: DEAD ON ARRIVAL

1. "Delving Behind the Scenes of the Death of Stefan Bandera," CIA report, July 14, 1960, Stephen Bandera Name File, vol. 2, National Archives and Records Administration (NARA), RG 263, E ZZ-18, B 6, 15; "Ivan Kashuba's Comments Regarding Bandera's Last Moments of Life," CIA, January 4, 1960, Attachment D, ibid., 1; Wiesław Romanowski, *Bandera: Terrorysta z Galicji* (Warsaw, 2012), 5–8.

2. *Moskovs'ki vbyvtsi*, 23–24, 33, 42; Romanowski, *Bandera*, 8.

3. "Delving Behind the Scenes," 11; *Moskovs'ki vbyvtsi*, 24–25.

4. Edward Page Jr., AmConGen, Munich, to the Department of State, "Mysterious Poisoning of Stepan Bandera, Leader of the Organization of Ukrainian Nationalists (Banderists)," October 26, 1959, Stephen Bandera Name File, vol. 2, NARA, RG 263, E ZZ-18, B 6; "Delving Behind the Scenes," 9–10; *Moskovs'ki vbyvtsi*, 39; *Stepan Bandera u dokumentakh*, 3:85–88; Rossoliński-Liebe, *Stepan Bandera*, 350.

5. *Moskovs'ki vbyvtsi*, 465–466; Romanowski, *Bandera*, 9.

6. Stashinsky's Trial Transcripts, in *Moskovs'ki vbyvtsi*, 249; *Münchener Merkur*, October 20, 1959; cf. *Moskovs'ki vbyvtsi*, 26; Rossoliński-Liebe, *Stepan Bandera*, 349.

7. David Irving, *The Secret Diaries of Hitler's Doctor* (London, 2005), 108, 119, 138, 242–243, 247, 269, 280; Gilbert Shama, "Pilzkrieg: The German Wartime Quest for Penicillin," *Microbiology Today* 30 (August 2003): 120–123; *Moskovs'ki vbyvtsi*, 34–36.

CHAPTER 11: FUNERAL

1. *Moskovs'ki vbyvtsi*, 471–475.

2. Ibid., 27, 471–473, 481, 487–488; Memorandum for the Record, November 18, 1959, Subject: Contact with AECASSOWARY 2 [Mykola Lebed] on October 22 and 23, 1959, 1, Aerodynamic: Contact Reports, vol. 44, f. 2, NARA, RG 263, E ZZ-19, B 23.

3. *Stepan Bandera u dokumentakh*, 3: 85–92; Romanowski, *Bandera*, 27.

4. Stepan Mudryk, *U borot'bi proty moskovs'koi ahentury* (Munich, 1980), chap. 14; Iaroslav Svatko, *Misiia Bandery* (Lviv, 2003), 57–59; *Moskovs'ki vbyvtsi*, 22, 39; Rossoliński-Liebe, *Stepan Bandera*, 350.

5. Mudryk, *U borot'bi*, chap. 14; Ivan Farion, "Shchob vriatuvaty Banderu, udar avta pryiniav na sebe . . . ," *Vysokyi zamok*, December 28, 2008.

6. Munich [base of operations] to Director [CIA], November 24, 1959, IN 11793, Stephen Bandera Name File, vol. 2, NARA, RG 263, E ZZ-18, B 6; Random Notes, The Role of Ivan Kashuba, May 2, 1960, ibid.; "Delving Behind the Scenes," 17; "Ivan Kashuba's Comments," 1.

CHAPTER 12: CIA TELEGRAM

1. Munich to Director, IN 37607, October 15, 1959, Stephen Bandera Name File, vol. 2, NARA, RG 263, E ZZ-18, B 6.

2. Sheridan Sansegundo, "William Hood: Of Moles and Double Agents," *South Hampton Star*, June 9, 2005.

3. Charles Hawley, "The US Soldier Who Liberated Munich Remembers Confronting the Nazi Enemy," *Spiegel International*, April 29, 2005.

4. John Fiehn, "Munich: New Center of Spy Intrigue," *Chicago's American*, January 17, 1960; Marta Dyczok, *The Grand Alliance and Ukrainian Refugees* (New York, 2000), 42–169.

5. Richard Breitman and Norman J. W. Goda, *Hitler's Shadow: Nazi War Criminals, U.S. Intelligence, and the Cold War* (Washington, DC, 2010), 77–80; *Stepan Bandera u dokumentakh*, 3:115–225; Anatol' Kamins'kyi, *Proloh u kholodnii viini proty Moskvy: Prodovzhennia vyzvol'noï borot'by iz-za kordonu* (Hadiach, Ukraine, 2009), 40–58.

6. Breitman and Goda, *Hitler's Shadow*, 80–82, 40–58; Dorril, *MI6*, 231–235.

7. Breitman and Goda, *Hitler's Shadow*, 82–83, 85–88; Kamins'kyi, *Proloh u kholodnii viini proty Moskvy*, 3–39.

8. Munich to Director, IN 37607, October 16, 1959, Stephen Bandera Name File, vol. 2, NARA, RG 263, E ZZ-18, B 6; Munich to Director, IN 38209, October 18, 1959, ibid.; Munich to Director, IN 38504, October 19, 1959, ibid.

CHAPTER 13: UPSWING

1. Director to Munich, Frankfurt, DIR 13898, March 20, 1958, Stephen Bandera Name File, vol. 2, NARA, RG 263, E ZZ-18, B 6; Munich to Director, IN 49176, March 27, 1958, ibid.

2. Munich [General Consulate] to Secretary of State, Department of State, 10490, October 16, 1959, Stephen Bandera Name File, vol. 2, NARA, RG 263, E ZZ-18, B 6; Stepan Bandera to Osyp Bandera, November 1, 1955, in Posivnych, *Stepan Bandera*, 191–194; Stepan Bandera to Jaroslav Padoch, February 7, 1959, Jaroslaw Padoch Collection, no. 208, Ukrainian Museum and Library, Stamford, Connecticut.

3. Timothy Snyder, *The Reconstruction of Nations: Poland, Ukraine, Lithuania, Belarus, 1569–1999* (New Haven, CT, 2004), 154–178; John-Paul Himka, "Ukrainian Collaboration in the Extermination of the Jews During the Second World War: Sorting Out the Long-Term and Conjectural Factors," in *The Fate of the European Jews,*

1939–1945: Continuity or Contingency, ed. Jonathan Frankel (Oxford, 1997), 170–189; Alex J. Motyl, "The Ukrainian Nationalist Movement and the Jews: Theoretical Reflections on Nationalism, Fascism, Rationality, Primordialism and History," in *Polin: Studies in Polish Jewry,* ed. Anthony Polonsky and Yohanan Petrovsky-Shtern, vol. 26 (Oxford, 2014): 275–295.

4. Munich [General Consulate] to Secretary of State, Department of State, 10490, October 16, 1959, Stephen Bandera Name File, vol. 2, NARA, RG 263, E ZZ-18, B 6; Page, "Mysterious Poisoning of Stefan Bandera"; Telegram from the Embassy in the Soviet Union to the Department of State, October 13, 1962, *Foreign Relations of the United States [FRUS],* 1961–1963, vol. 5, no. 245.

5. CIA Memorandum, "Meeting with UPHILL Representatives," May 26, 1961, 1, Stephen Bandera Name File, vol. 2, NARA, RG 263, E ZZ-18, B 6; Chief of Base, Munich, to Chief, S[oviet] R[ussia Division], October 5, 1959, DOI 70–17, ibid.; Munich to Director, IN 38209, October 18, 1959, ibid.; "Delving Behind the Scenes," 4; Chief of Base, Munich, to chief S[oviet] R[ussia], DOI 70–17, October 5, 1958, Stephen Bandera Name File, vol. 2, NARA, RG 263, E ZZ-18, B 6; "Visit of Bandera to the USA," Attachment to EGMA 45003, August 27, 1959, ibid.; Reinhard Heydenreuter, "Pidhotovka ta zdiisnennia zamakhu na Stepana Banderu 1959 r. v dzerkali miunkhens'kykhs' politsiinykh aktiv," in *Ukrains'kyi vyzvol'nyi rukh* 11 (Lviv, 2007): 217.

6. E. H. Cookridge, *Gehlen: Spy of the Century* (New York, 1972); James H. Critchfield, *Partners at the Creation: The Men Behind Postwar Germany's Defense and Intelligence Establishments* (Annapolis, MD, 2003), 200–218.

7. "Herre, Heinz-Danko (1909–1988)," in Jefferson Adams, *Historical Dictionary of German Intelligence* (Lanham, MD, 2009), 183.

8. Critchfield, *Partners at the Creation,* 96.

9. *Moskovs'ki vbyvtsi,* 22, 36; "Delving Behind the Scenes," 4–6; Romanowski, *Bandera,* 24.

10. Romanowski, *Bandera,* 22–23; "Delving Behind the Scenes," 4–6; Munich to Director, IN 38504, October 19, 1959, Stephen Bandera Name File, vol. 2, NARA, RG 263, E ZZ-18, B 6.

CHAPTER 14: PRIME SUSPECT

1. Director to Munich, Frankfurt, DIR 01687, November 5, 1959, Stephen Bandera Name File, vol. 2, NARA, RG 263, E ZZ-18, B 6.

2. "Research Aid: Cryptonyms and Terms in Declassified CIA Files Nazi War Crimes and Japanese Imperial Government Records Disclosure Acts," www.archives .gov/iwg/declassified-records/rg-263-cia-records/second-release-lexicon.pdf.

3. Chief of Base, Munich, to Chief, S[oviet] R[ussia Division], November 12, 1959, EGMA 45907, 2, Stephen Bandera Name File, vol. 2, NARA, RG 263, E ZZ-18, B 6; Romanowski, *Bandera,* 32–33.

4. Viedienieiev and Shapoval, "Maltiis'kyi sokil."

5. Ibid.; Viedienieiev and Bystrukhin, *Dvobii bez kompromisiv,* 392–410; Adam Kaczyński, "Spadochroniarze OUN: Historia desantów z 14 maja 1951 r.," *Inne Oblicza Historii,* https://ioh.pl/artykuly/pokaz/spadochroniarze-oun-historia-desantw-z--maja --r,1071.

6. "Delving Behind the Scenes," 11.

7. Ibid., 11–12.

8. Chief of Base, Munich, to Chief, S[oviet] R[ussia Division], November 12, 1959, EGMA 45907, 1, 2; "Delving Behind the Scenes," 10.

9. Chief of Base, Munich, to Chief, S[oviet] R[ussia Division], November 12, 1959, EGMA 45907, 1, 2; "Delving Behind the Scenes," 10.

CHAPTER 15: ACTIVE MEASURES

1. Stashinsky's Trial Transcripts, in *Moskovs'ki vbyvtsi*, 199; Anders, *Murder to Order*, 57.

2. Murphy, Kondrashev and Bailey, *Battleground Berlin*, 257–58; Anatolii Gus'kov, *Pod grifom pravdy. Ispoved' voennogo kontrrazvedchika. Liudi, fakty, spetsoperatsii* (Moscow, 2004), chap. 10; Eduard Khrutskii, *Teni v pereulke* (Moscow, 2006), 53–55; G. K. Zhukov, *Vospominaniia i razmyshleniia* (Moscow, 2002), 1: 331–33.

3. Murphy et al., *Battleground Berlin*, 264–266; "Soviet Use of Assassination and Kidnapping," CIA report, 1964, Center for the Study of Intelligence, https://www.cia .gov/library/center-for-the-study-of-intelligence/kent-csi/vol19no3/html/v19i3a01p _0001.htm.

4. Christopher Andrew and Oleg Gordievsky, *KGB: The Inside Story of the Foreign Operations* (New York, 1990), 384–385; Marc Fisher, "E. Germany Ran Antisemitic Campaign in West in 60s," *Washington Post*, February 28, 1993.

5. Murphy et al., *Battleground Berlin*, 325–326; *FRUS, 1958–1960*, vol. 8, *Berlin Crisis, 1958–59*, no. 348.

6. *Moskovs'ki vbyvtsi*, 468; Heydenreuter, "Pidhotovka ta zdiisnennia zamakhu na Stepana Banderu 1959 r.," 211–220.

7. *Stepan Bandera u dokumentakh*, 3:593, 601; B. Aleksandrov, "Neshchastnyi sluchai ili ubiistvo?" *Komsomol'skaia pravda*, October 22, 1959; B. Aleksandrov, "Sledy vedut k Oberlenderu," *Komsomol'skaia pravda*, October 25, 1959.

8. *Moskovs'ki vbyvtsi*, 587–589; *Stepan Bandera u dokumentakh*, 3:593, 601; Philipp Ther, "War Versus Peace: Interethnic Relations in Lviv During the First Half of the Twentieth Century," *Harvard Ukrainian Studies* 24 (2000): 251–284; Volodymyr Viatrovych, "Iak tvorylasia legenda pro Nakhtigal," *Dzerkalo tyzhnia*, February 16, 2008; Taras Hunczak, "Shukhevych and the Nachtigall Battalion: Soviet Fabrications About the Ukrainian Resistance Movement," *The Day* (Kyiv, 2009), no. 22; John-Paul Himka, "The Lviv Pogrom of 1941: The Germans, Ukrainian Nationalists, and the Carnival Crowd," *Canadian Slavonic Papers* 53, nos. 2–4 (2011): 209–243; Serhii Riabenko, "Slidamy "Lvivs'koho pohromu" Ivana Dzhona Khymky, *Ukrains'ka pravda*, February 20, 2013.

9. Michael Lemke, "Kampagnen gegen Bonn: Die Systemkrise der DDR und die West-Propaganda der SED 1960–1963," *Vierteljahrshefte für Zeitgeschichte* 41 (1993): 151–174; DEFA Studio for Newsreels and Documentaries, Eyewitness 1959 / W 88 www.defa.de/DesktopDefault.aspx?TabID=412&FilmID=Q6UJ9A0040QW; Rossoliński-Liebe, *Stepan Bandera*, 357–359; Tennent H. Bagley, *Spymaster: Startling Cold War Revelations of a Soviet KGB Chief* (New York, 2013), chap. 12.

10. Stashinsky's Trial Transcripts, in *Moskovs'ki vbyvtsi*, 225.

CHAPTER 16: HIGH HOPES

1. Stashinsky's Trial Transcripts, in *Moskovs'ki vbyvtsi*, 202.

2. Teodor Gladkov, *Lift v razvedku: "Korol' nelegalov" Aleksandr Korotkov* (Moscow, 2002); Sudoplatov, *Special Tasks*, 48, 138–139; 241–244.

3. Khokhlov, *Pravo na sovest'*, 113–138; "Shpion, kotoryi byl otravlen KGB, no vyzhil," *APN Nizhnii Novgorod*, January 12, 2006, www.apn-nn.ru/contex_s/26820.html.

4. Volodarsky, *The KGB's Poison Factory*, 184.

5. Murphy et al., *Battleground Berlin*, 264–266.

6. Stashinsky's Trial Transcripts, in *Moskovs'ki vbyvtsi*, 202–203; Anders, *Murder to Order*, 59–60.

7. Stashinsky's Trial Transcripts, in *Moskovs'ki vbyvtsi*, 202–203; Anders, *Murder to Order*, 59–60.

8. Stashinsky's Trial Transcripts, in *Moskovs'ki vbyvtsi*, 188–189.

CHAPTER 17: MAN AT THE TOP

1. Typescript of Vladimir Semichastny's memoirs with his personal corrections, in the archive of Professor Tomas Sniegon, University of Lund, Sweden, 66. Cf. Vladimir Semichastny, *Bespokoinoe serdtse* (Moscow, 2002), 193; "Ékspertnoe zakliuchenie k zasedaniiu Verkhovnogo suda RF, May 26, 1992," *Memorial*, www.memo.ru/history /exp-kpss/Chapter5.htm; Leonid Mlechin, *Zheleznyi Shurik* (Moscow, 2004), 237.

2. Khrushchev, *Khrushchev Remembers*, 146–147; Posivnych, *Stepan Bandera*, 11–14; Sudoplatov, *Special Tasks*, 357, 378.

3. Sudoplatov, *Special Tasks*, 249, 252–253, 378.

4. Ibid., 355; Georgii Sannikov, *Bol'shaia okhota: Razgrom vooruzhennogo podpol'ia v Zapadnoi Ukraine* (Moscow, 2002), 19, 342–343; Breitman and Goda, *Hitler's Shadow*, 83.

5. Sannikov, *Bol'shaia okhota: Bor'ba s vooruzhennym podpol'em OUN v Zapadnoi Ukraine* (Moscow, 2008), 249; "Diadei v organakh KGB nemalo, a umeniia nashchupat vraga eshche ne vsegda khvataet," *Kommersant Vlast'* 994, no. 40 (October 8, 2012).

6. Filipp Bobkov, "A. N. Shelepin," *Federal'naia sluzhba bezopasnosti Rossiiskoi Federatsii* www.fsb.ru/fsb/history/author/single.htm!id%3D10317982%2540fsbPublication .html.

7. Leonid Mlechin, *Shelepin* (Moscow, 2009); Christopher Andrew and Oleg Gordievsky, *KGB: Intelligence Operations from Lenin to Gorbachev* (New York, 1990), 463; Herbert Romerstein, "Disinformation as a KGB Weapon in the Cold War," *Journal of Intelligence History* 1 (Summer 2001): 54–67.

CHAPTER 18: PRIVATE MATTER

1. Anders, *Murder to Order*, 60; Stashinsky's Trial Transcripts, in *Moskovs'ki vbyvtsi*, 204.

2. Aleksandr Sever, *Smert' shpionam! Voennaia kontrrazvedka Smersh v gody Velikoi Otechestvennoi voiny* (Moscow, 2009), 410; A. A. Sokolov, *Anatomiia predatel'stva: "Superkrot" TsRU v KGB. 35 let shpionazha generala Olega Kalugina* (Moscow, 2005), 33; Vitalii Pavlov, *Operatsiia Sneg: Polveka vo vneshnei razvedke KGB* (Moscow, 1996), 116.

3. Stashinsky's Trial Transcripts, in *Moskovs'ki vbyvtsi*, 204; Anders, *Murder to Order*, 61.

4. *Moskovs'ki vbyvtsi*, 620; Anders, *Murder to Order*, 38–39, 60, 114; Steele, "Assassin Disarmed by Love"; Peter-Ferdinand Koch, *Der Fund: Die Skandale des Stern Gerd Heidemann und die Hitler-Tagebuch* (Hamburg, 1990), 107–121; Annemarie Lange, *Führer durch Berlin* (Berlin, 1963), 121; Excerpts from a report on meeting with the agent "Lipski," Archives of the Polish Ministry of Internal Affairs, Instytut Pamięci Narodowej, Warsaw, IPN BU 01355/196/J (1074/4/48), 1–2.

5. *Moskovs'ki vbyvtsi*, 620; Anders, *Murder to Order*, 60.

6. Anders, *Murder to Order*, 61.

7. Stashinsky's Trial Transcripts, in *Moskovs'ki vbyvtsi*, 208.

CHAPTER 19: AWARD

1. "Simvoly zovushchie k miru i progressu," *Pravda*, December 7, 1959, 4; "Vsenarodnyi prazdnik," *Pravda*, December 6, 1959, 1.

2. Stashinsky's Trial Transcripts, in *Moskovs'ki vbyvtsi*, 204–205; Anders, *Murder to Order*, 62.

3. Stashinsky's Trial Transcripts, in *Moskovs'ki vbyvtsi*, 206; Anders, *Murder to Order*, 62–63.

4. William Hood, *Mole: The True Story of the First Russian Spy to Become an American Counterspy* (Washington, DC, 1993), 68.

5. Stashinsky's Trial Transcripts, in *Moskovs'ki vbyvtsi*, 208–211, 226; Anders, *Murder to Order*, 63–64.

CHAPTER 20: PROPOSAL

1. Anders, *Murder to Order*, 64; Murphy et al., *Battleground Berlin*, 488; Tennent H. Bagley, *Spy Wars: Moles, Mysteries, and Deadly Games* (New Haven, CT, 2008), 123–131; "Fabrichnikov, Arkadii Andreevich," *Mezhdunarodnyi ob'edinennyi biograficheskii tsentr*, http://wwii-soldat.narod.ru/200/ARTICLES/BIO/fabrichnikov _aa.htm; Sannikov, *Bol'shaia okhota* (2002), 343–344; "Kravchenko Nikolai Nikolaevich," in Petrov, *Kto rukovodil organami gosbezopasnosti*, 505–506.

2. Stashinsky's Trial Transcripts, in *Moskovs'ki vbyvtsi*, 209–211; Anders, *Murder to Order*, 64.

3. Anders, *Murder to Order*, 64–65; Stashinsky's Trial Transcripts, in *Moskovs'ki vbyvtsi*, 212.

4. Hood, *Mole*, 23.

5. Stashinsky's Trial Transcripts, in *Moskovs'ki vbyvtsi*, 212–213; Anders, *Murder to Order*, 64–65; Rossoliński-Liebe, *Stepan Bandera*, 355.

6. *Moskovs'ki vbyvtsi*, 620; Anders, *Murder to Order*, 38–39, 60, 114; Steele, "Assassin Disarmed by Love"; Peter-Ferdinand Koch, *Der Fund. Die Skandale des Stern Gerd Heidemann und die Hitler-Tagebuch* (Hamburg, 1990), 110–111.

7. Stashinsky's Trial Transcripts, in *Moskovs'ki vbyvtsi*, 210–215; Anders, *Murder to Order*, 65.

CHAPTER 21: INTRODUCING THE BRIDE

1. Stashinsky's Trial Transcripts, in *Moskovs'ki vbyvtsi*, 215–216; Anders, *Murder to Order*, 67–68.

2. Koch, *Der Fund*, 114–116.

3. "Razoruzhenie—put' k uprocheniiu mira, ukrepleniiu druzhby mezhdu narodami: Doklad tovarishcha N. S. Khrushcheva na sessii Verkhovnoho Soveta SSR," *Pravda*, January 15, 1960, 1–2; The Kitchen Debate (Nixon and Khrushchev, 1959), 2 parts, www.youtube.com/watch?v=z6RLCw1OZFw&feature=relmfu.

4. Stashinsky's Trial Transcripts, in *Moskovs'ki vbyvtsi*, 215–216; Anders, *Murder to Order*, 67–68. For transcripts of conversations wiretapped by the KGB in the Moscow hotels in the late 1950s, see Osobyiarkhiv Litvy (KGB Litovskoi SSR), opis 3, delo 8411–3.

5. Stashinsky's Trial Transcripts, in *Moskovs'ki vbyvtsi*, 218–219, 226; Koch, *Der Fund*, 116–117.

6. Anders, *Murder to Order*, 68; Deacon and West, *Spy!*, 126; Koch, *Der Fund*, 116.

CHAPTER 22: MONTH OF THE SPY

1. Koch, *Der Fund*, 117–118.

2. Stashinsky's Trial Transcripts, in *Moskovs'ki vbyvtsi*, 217–218; *Imena Moskovskikh ulits: Putevoditel'*, ed. K. G. Efremov, 5th ed. (Moscow, 1988), 141.

3. Stashinsky's Trial Transcripts, in *Moskovs'ki vbyvtsi*, 217, 227; Koch, *Der Fund*, 117–118; Hood, *Mole*, 176–177.

4. "The Summit Conference of 1960: The Intelligence Officer's View," *Central Intelligence Agency*, https://www.cia.gov/library/center-for-the-study-of-intelligence/csi-publications/books-and-monographs/sherman-kent-and-the-board-of-national-estimates-collected-essays/8summit.html.

5. "The Paris Summit Falls Apart," UPI, www.upi.com/Audio/Year_in_Review/Events-of-1960/The-Paris-Summit-Falls-Apart/12295509435928-2; David Lawrence, "Infiltration of Communists Still Serious Problem Here," *Evening Independent*, June 16, 1960; Bem Price, "Poor Spies Pose War Threat," *Victoria Advocate*, July 30, 1991, 3A.

6. *Krovavye deianiia Oberlandera: Otchet o press-konferentsii dlia sovetskikh i inostrannykh zhurnalistov, sostoiavsheisia v Moskve 5 aprelia 1960 goda* (Moscow, 1960); Hermann Raschhofer, *Political Assassination: The Legal Background of the Oberländer and Stashinsky Cases* (Tübingen, Germany, 1964); Viatrovych, "Iak tvorylasia legenda pro Nakhtigal'"; "Völkerrechtliche Praxis der Bundesrepublik Deutschland im Jahre 1960," in *Max-Planck-Institut für ausländisches öffentliches Recht und Völkerrecht* (1963): 345–346; *Moskovs'ki vbyvtsi*, 44–46, 592–595.

CHAPTER 23: GOING IN CIRCLES

1. *Moskovs'ki vbyvtsi*, 34–35, 592; "Delving Behind the Scenes of the Death of Stefan Bandera," CIA report, July 14, 1960, Stephen Bandera Name File, vol. 2, National Archives and Records Administration (NARA), RG 263, E ZZ-18, B 6, "The Visit of the

Oberkomissar of the German Criminal Police, Adrian Fuchs," CIA, May 2, 1960, Attachment C, ibid.

2. "Matviieiko Miron, shef sluzhby bezpeki OUN, 'Usmikh', agent angliiskoi razvedki 'Moddi': protokoly doprosov," *Novosti Ukrainy*, http://noviny.su/smi-00000 745.html; Author's interview with Anatol Kaminsky, July 27, 2012.

3. "Research Aid: Cryptonyms and Terms in Declassified CIA Files."

4. Chief of Base, Munich, to Chief, S[oviet R[ussia Division], May 2, 1960, EGMA 48874, 1; Stephen Bandera Name File, vol. 2, National Archives and Records Administration (NARA), RG 263, E ZZ-18.

5. "Delving Behind the Scenes," 1–2.

6. Ibid., 3–4.

7. Ibid., 7–18; "The Visit of the Oberkommissar," 3.

8. Viedienieiev and Bystrukhin, *Dvobii bez kompromisiv*, 408; Random Notes, "Role of Ivan Kashuba," May 2, 1960, Stephen Bandera Name File, vol. 2, NARA, RG 263, E ZZ-18, B 6; Chief of Base, Munich, to Director, [Central Intelligence Agency], November 29, 1961, IN 29726, 1–3, Subject Files: AEDOGMA/AEBATH, NARA, RG 263, B 5.

CHAPTER 24: MOSCOW BUGS

1. Anders, *Murder to Order*, 69; Stashinsky's Trial Transcripts, in *Moskovs'ki vbyvtsi*, 227.

2. "Narodnoe khoziaistvo SSSR/1960/Sel'skoe khoziaistvo," www.mysteriouscountry .ru/wiki/index; Robert W. Gibson, "Reporter Returns. Soviet Life: Big Changes Since 1960," *Los Angeles Times*, April 17, 1986.

3. "Rasstreliannyi gorod," *Trud*, July 2, 2007 www.trud.ru/article/02-06-2007 /116699_rasstreljannyj_gorod.html.

4. Steele, "Assassin Disarmed by Love," 432; Stashinsky's Trial Transcripts, in *Moskovs'ki vbyvtsi*, 227; Anders, *Murder to Order*, 70.

5. Peter Grier, "Cleaning the Bug House," *Air Force Magazine*, September 2012, www.airforce-magazine.com/MagazineArchive/Pages/2012/September%202012 /0912embassy.aspx.

6. Stashinsky's Trial Transcripts, in *Moskovs'ki vbyvtsi*, 217, 229–230; Anders, *Murder to Order*, 70–71; Koch, *Der Fund*, 119.

CHAPTER 25: FAMILY

1. Stashinsky's Trial Transcripts, in *Moskovs'ki vbyvtsi*, 230–231; Anders, *Murder to Order*, 71.

2. Lesia Fediv, "Vin ubyv Banderu," *Shchodennyi L'viv*, May 22, 2008.

3. "Toi samyi Bohdan," *Ekspres*, October 14, 2010; Iurii Lukanov, "Try liubovi Stepana Bandery: Stsenarii dokumental'noho televiziinoho fil'mu," 1998, www.oocities.org/yuriylukanov/start_files/dorobok/dorobok01.htm; Stashinsky's Trial Transcripts, in *Moskovs'ki vbyvtsi*, 143; Ivan Farion, "Iak by mohla, sama ubyla b ubyvtsiu Bandery . . . ," *Vysokyi zamok*, October 14, 2015.

4. Iuliia Kohut, "L'viv u stratehichnykh planakh rosiis'koho tsaria," Travel Lviv: Tury po L'vovu, http://travellviv.com/uk_statti_petro1.html.

5. Stashinsky's Trial Transcripts, in *Moskovs'ki vbyvtsi*, 231–232; Anders, *Murder to Order*, 71–72; Koch, *Der Fund*, 119.

CHAPTER 26: CHANGE OF PLANS

1. "Baryshnikov Vladimir Iakovlevich," in Petrov, *Kto rukovodil organami gosbezopasnosti*, 182–183; Dmitrii Tarasov, *Bol'shaia igra SMERSha* (Moscow, 2010), 11–13.

2. Stashinsky's Trial Transcripts, in *Moskovs'ki vbyvtsi*, 232–233; Anders, *Murder to Order*, 72; Steele, "Assassin Disarmed by Love," 433.

3. Stashinsky's Trial Transcripts, in *Moskovs'ki vbyvtsi*, 233; Anders, *Murder to Order*, 73.

CHAPTER 27: NEW YEAR

1. Stashinsky's Trial Transcripts, in *Moskovs'ki vbyvtsi*, 210, 226; Anders, *Murder to Order*, 72–73.

2. Stashinsky's Trial Transcripts, in *Moskovs'ki vbyvtsi*, 233.; Koch, *Der Fund*, 119.

3. Stashinsky's Trial Transcripts, in *Moskovs'ki vbyvtsi*, 218; see photo of Stashinsky sisters following p. 695.

4. Stashinsky's Trial Transcripts, in *Moskovs'ki vbyvtsi*, 232.

5. Ibid., 234; Steele, "Assassin Disarmed by Love," 433; Anders, *Murder to Order*, 73.

6. Anders, *Murder to Order*, 73–74.

CHAPTER 28: BACK TO SCHOOL

1. Stashinsky's Trial Transcripts, in *Moskovs'ki vbyvtsi*, 234–235; see photocopies of Stashinsky's official evaluation, passport, and student identification card following p. 695.

2. Sannikov, *Bol'shaia okhota* (2008), 17.

3. Stashinsky's Trial Transcripts, in *Moskovs'ki vbyvtsi*, 235; Anders, *Murder to Order*, 75–76.

4. Inge's letter as shown in *Tainy razvedki: Likvidatsiia Stefana Bandery*, television documentary, 2012, http://my.mail.ru/community/russkiemaloross/tag/%D1%F2%E0%F8%E8%ED%F1%EA%E8%E9.

5. Steele, "Assassin Disarmed by Love," 434; Inge Pohl's police testimony, in *Moskovs'ki vbyvtsi*, 620–621; Anders, *Murder to Order*, 76; Koch, *Der Fund*, 119; Rossoliński-Liebe, *Stepan Bandera*, 355.

CHAPTER 29: TELEPHONE CALL

1. Stashinsky's Trial Transcripts, in *Moskovs'ki vbyvtsi*, 235, Inge Pohl's police testimony, in ibid., 621.

2. Stashinsky's Trial Transcripts, in *Moskovs'ki vbyvtsi*, 235–236; Anders, *Murder to Order*, 89.

3. Stashinsky's Trial Transcripts, in *Moskovs'ki vbyvtsi*, 236; Anders, *Murder to Order*, 90–91; Aleksandr Bogomolov and Georgii Sannikov, *Bez protokola: Nevydumannye istorii* (Moscow, 2010), 210; Mlechin, *Zheleznyi Shurik*, 240.

CHAPTER 30: BERLIN

1. "Zadanie Rodiny vypolneno! Raport geroia-kosmonavta Germana Titova tovarishchu N. S. Khrushchevu na Vnukovskom aėrodrome, 9 avgusta 1961 g.," *Pravda*, August 10, 1961, 1; "Genii i trud naroda tvoriat chudesa: Rech N. S. Khrushcheva," *Pravda*, August 10, 1961, 2.

2. "Vystuplenie N. S. Khrushcheva po radio i televideniiu 7 avgusta 1961 g.," *Pravda*, August 8, 1961, 1–2; John F. Kennedy, "The Berlin Crisis," July 25, 1961, www .presidentialrhetoric.com/historicspeeches/kennedy/berlincrisis.html; Frederick Kempe, *Berlin, 1961: Kennedy, Khrushchev and the Most Dangerous Place on Earth* (New York, 2011), 269–322.

3. Stashinsky's Trial Transcripts, in *Moskovs'ki vbyvtsi*, 236; Anders, *Murder to Order*, 90–91; Koch, *Der Fund*, 119.

CHAPTER 31: DOWN TO THE WIRE

1. *Moskovs'ki vbyvtsi*, 238, 621; Anders, *Murder to Order*, 92–97.

2. Kempe, *Berlin 1961*, 337.

3. *Moskovs'ki vbyvtsi*, 238, 621; Anders, *Murder to Order*, 94, 97; Kempe, *Berlin 1961*, 336; Steele, "Assassin Disarmed by Love," 434–435.

4. Kempe, *Berlin 1961*, 339–340, 345–346.

5. Stashinsky's Trial Transcripts, in *Moskovs'ki vbyvtsi*, 245; Anders, *Murder to Order*, 94–95; Kempe, *Berlin 1961*, 343–345; Steele, "Assassin Disarmed by Love," 434–435; Koch, *Der Fund*, 119–120.

CHAPTER 32: SHOCK WAVE

1. Records of the Rohrbeck Evangelische Kirchengemeinde Archive, Dallgow.

2. Sannikov, *Bol'shaia okhota* (2008), 18; Anders, *Murder to Order*, 98.

3. Bogomolov and Sannikov, *Bez protokola*, 248; Sannikov, *Bol'shaia okhota* (2002), 16–18; Aleksandr Sripnik, "17 mgnovenii iz zhizni veterana razvedki Konstantina Bogomazova," *Ezhenedelnik 2000*, November 13, 2009.

4. *Stepan Bandera u dokumentakh*, 3: 590–593; "Umer neposredstvennyi rukovoditel' operatsii po ubiistvam Stepana Bandery i L'va Rebeta," *Novosti Ukrainy*, June 25, 2008, http://rus.newsru.ua/ukraine/24jun2008/sviatohorov.html; Anatolii Tereshchenko, *Komandir razvedgruppy: Za liniei fronta* (Moscow, 2013); Sannikov, *Bol'shaia okhota* (2002), 15–17; Georgii Sannikov, "General Zubatenko," *Lubianka*, no. 8 (2008): 228–235.

5. Sannikov, *Bol'shaia okhota* (2008), 17–18; Aleksandr Skripnik, "Shchit i mech Aleksandra Sviatogorova," *2000*, no. 50 (December 13–19, 2013), www.szru.gov.ua /index_ua/index.html%3Fp=3317.html.

6. Gladkov, *Lift v razvedku*, 571–574; Murphy et al., *Battleground Berlin*, 301–304; Bogomolov and Sannikov, *Bez protokola*, 174.

7. Skripnik, "Shchit i mech Aleksandra Sviatogorova."

8. Sannikov, *Bol'shaia okhota* (2002), 16–17; Memorandum for the Record, April 22, 1976, Subject: Assassination of Stefan Bandera, 6, Stephen Bandera Name File, vol. 2, NARA, RG 263, E ZZ-18, 6; Andrew and Gordievsky, *KGB: The Inside Story*, 386; Evgenii Chernykh, "Slukhach Sovetskogo Soiuza," *Komsomol'skaia pravda*, December 20, 2012.

9. Anders, *Murder to Order*, p. 68; Viedienieiev and Bystrukhin, *Dvobii bez kompromisiv*, 271–274, photo of Oleksii Daimon following p. 504; "Personal File no. 301: Major Daimon, Aleksei Filimonovich," Archive of the Security Service of Ukraine (Kyiv), Fond 12, no. 17587; Zhan Kots'kyi [Ivan Kotovenko], "Buzynovyi dyskurs. Intermetstso." Maidan. Arkhivy forumiv Maidanu, http://maidanua.org/arch/arch2004 /1083958049.html.

10. Interview of Lieutenant General Vasilii Khristoforov, head of the Registration and Archives Directorate of the Federal Security Service of the Russian Federation, in television documentary *Tainy razvedki: Likvidatsiia Stepana Bandery* (2012); Memorandum for the Record, April 22, 1976, Subject: Assassination of Stefan Bandera, 6; Aleksandr Fursenko and Timothy Naftali, *"One Hell of a Gamble": Khrushchev, Castro, Kennedy and the Cuban Missile Crisis, 1958–1964* (London, 1998), 334.

CHAPTER 33: DEFECTOR

1. Joseph J. Trento, *The Secret History of the CIA* (New York, 2005), 185–188; John le Carré, "Introduction," *The Spy Who Came in from the Cold* (New York, 2012); Kempe, *Berlin, 1961*, 354–358; Murphy et al., *Battleground Berlin*, 378–381.

2. Memorandum for the Record, April 22, 1976, Subject: Assassination of Stefan Bandera, 2; Hood, *Mole*, 118.

3. Memorandum for the Record, April 22, 1976, Subject: Assassination of Stefan Bandera, 2; Rossoliński-Liebe, *Stepan Bandera*, 351.

4. Murphy et al., *Battleground Berlin*, 343–346; Michał Goleniewski personal file, Archives of the Polish Ministry of Internal Affairs, Instytut Pamięci Narodowej (Warsaw), IPN BU 01911/97/1; Tennent H. Bagley, *Spy Wars: Moles, Mysteries and Deadly Games* (New Haven, CT, 2007), 48–49; Leszek Pawlikowicz, *Tajny front zimnej wojny: Uciekinierzy z polskich służb specjalnych, 1956–1964* (Warszaw, 2004), 217ff.

5. Memorandum for Chief, S[oviet] R[ussia Division], August 24, 1961, 1–2, Stephen Bandera Name File, vol. 2, NARA, RG 263, E ZZ-18, B 6.

6. Chief of Station, Germany, to Chief of S[oviet] R[ussia Division], EGOA 15811, October 10, 1961, Aerodynamic: Operations, vol. 22, f. 1, 1–2, NARA, RG 263, E ZZ-19, B 14; Memorandum for the Record, April 22, 1976, Subject: Assassination of Stefan Bandera, 5; Iurii Lukanov, "Vin nazyvav sebe 'Mykola Sereda, ukraïnets' z Sumshchyny,'" *Hazeta po-ukraïns'ky*, December 18, 2012; Stashinsky's Trial Transcripts, in *Moskovs'ki vbyvtsi*, 256.

7. Memorandum for the Record, April 22, 1976, Subject: Assassination of Stefan Bandera, 9.

8. Ibid., 2; Rossoliński-Liebe, *Stepan Bandera*, 354–355.

CHAPTER 34: INVESTIGATION

1. Kempe, *Berlin 1961*, 405–407; John F. Kennedy, "Remarks on Signing Peace Corps Bill," September 22, 1961, John F. Kennedy Presidential Library and Museum, www.jfklibrary.org/Asset-Viewer/Archives/JFKPOF-035-045.aspx.

2. Stashinsky's Trial Transcripts, in *Moskovs'ki vbyvtsi*, 252–254, photos following p. 695; Karl Anders, *Mord auf Befehl* (Tübingen, Germany, 1963), photos following p. 32.

3. Stashinsky's Trial Transcripts, in *Moskovs'ki vbyvtsi*, 178, 255; Memorandum for the Record, April 22, 1976, Subject: Assassination of Stefan Bandera, 2.

4. Julia Lalande, *"Building a Home Abroad": A Comparative Study of Ukrainian Migration, Immigration Policy and Diaspora Formation in Canada and Germany After the Second World War*, PhD diss., University of Hamburg (Düsseldorf, 2006), 347–352; Stashinsky's Trial Transcripts, in *Moskovs'ki vbyvtsi*, 255–256.

5. Memorandum for the Record, Subject: Meeting with AECASSOWARY 2 [Mykola Lebed], April 19, 1962, 1, Aerodynamic: Contact Reports, vol. 44, f. 2, NARA, RG 263, E ZZ-19, B 23; "Geheimdienste: Bart ab," *Der Spiegel*, November 29, 1961.

6. Anders, *Murder to Order*, 115–116.

CHAPTER 35: PRESS CONFERENCE

1. *Who Actually Killed Ukrainian Nationalist Stepan Bandera: The Dirty Affairs of the Gehlen Secret Service* (Toronto: Canadian Slav Committee, 1961), 2–3.

2. Chief of S[oviet] B[loc] Division, Memorandum: Aerodynamic—KGB Operations Against Ukrainian Emigres, April 12, 1967. Aerodynamic: Operations, vol. 36, NARA, RG 263, E ZZ-19, B 20.

3. *Who Actually Killed Ukrainian Nationalist Stepan Bandera*, 3–13; *Pravda pro te, khto spravdi vbyv Stepana Banderu: Chorni dila helenivs'koï rozvidky* (Toronto: Canadian Slavonic Committee, 1961), 5–22; Rossoliński-Liebe, *Stepan Bandera*, 356.

4. "Spione," *Der Spiegel*, June 27, 1962; Stashinsky's Trial Transcripts, in *Moskovs'ki vbyvtsi*, 265–266; Norman J. W. Goda, "CIA Files Related to Heinz Felfe, SS Officer and KGB Spy," Government Secrecy e-prints, www.fas.org/sgp/eprint/goda.pdf; Murphy et al., *Battleground Berlin*, 435–439; Evgenii Primakov et al., *Ocherki istorii rossiiskoi vneshnei razvedki*, 6 vols. (Moscow, 2002), 5:127; Chief of Base, Bonn, to Chief, E[astern] E[urope Division], EGMA27257, March 23, 1964, Subject: Protocol of Felfe Trial, 36–37, Heinz Felfe Name File, vol. 3, f. 2, NARA, RG 263, E ZZ-18, B 16; CIA Report, "KGB Exploitation of Heinz Felfe: Successful KGB Penetration of a Western Intelligence Service," 120–122, NARA, RG 263, CIA Subject Files, Second Release, Box 1.

5. *Moskovs'ki vbyvtsi*, 50–55.

6. Memorandum for the Record, April 22, 1976, Subject: Assassination of Stefan Bandera, 9; *Moskovs'ki vbyvtsi*, 50–55; *Osyp Verhun rozpovidaie* (Kyiv, 1962); M. Maksymenko, M. Davydiak, and O. Verhun, *Provokatory na Zakhodi prodovzhuiut' diiaty* (Kyiv, 1963); "Memo from Colleagues in the USSR," Archives of the Polish Ministry of Internal Affairs, Instytut Pamięci Narodowej (Warsaw), IPN BU 01355/196/J (1074/4/48), 39.

7. V. Nikitchenko, "Vsem nachal'nikam upravlenii KGB pri SM USSSR," November 27, 1961, Archives of the Security Service of Ukraine, Kyiv, fond 16, opys 1, no. 930,

fol. 210; V. Nikitchenko "Vsem nachal'nikam upravlenii KGB pri SM USSSR," February 14, 1962, Archives of the Security Service of Ukraine, Kyiv, fond 16, opys 1, no. 932, fols. 37–39.

CHAPTER 36: HIGH POLITICS

1. *Abendpost*, no. 268 (November 18–19, 1961). Cf. a Polish translation of the *Abendpost* article in the Archives of the Polish Ministry of Internal Affairs, Instytut Pamięci Narodowej (Warsaw), IPN BU 01355/196/J (1074/4/48), 13–19.

2. "Geheimdienste: Bart ab"; "Germans Hold Russian: Ex-Soviet Agent Reported to Admit Bandera Killing," *New York Times*, November 18, 1961; "Ex-Red Agent Admits Killing 2 Exile Chiefs," *Chicago Daily Tribune*, November 18, 1961.

3. *Moskovs'ki vbyvtsi*, 55–57, 62–63; Mlechin, *Zheleznyi Shurik*, chap. 5.

4. "President Kennedy Delivers Major Policy Speech at UW on November 16, 1961," HistoryLink, www.historylink.org/index.cfm?DisplayPage=output.cfm&File_Id=968.

5. "Geheimdienste: Bart ab"; John L. Steele, "Assassin Disarmed by Love."

6. *Moskovs'ki vbyvtsi*, 67–68; Charles H. Pullen, *The Life and Times of Arthur Maloney: The Last of the Tribunes* (La Vergne, TN, 1994).

7. *Moskovs'ki vbyvtsi*, 82–83, 89; Denis Smith, *Rogue Tory: The Life and Legend of John G. Diefenbaker* (Toronto, 1997).

8. "Stevenson Lashes at Russian Colonialism," *Ukrainian Weekly*, December 2, 1961; *Moskovs'ki vbyvtsi*, 84; Joe Holley, "Lev E. Dobriansky: Professor and Foe of Communism, 89," *Washington Post*, February 6, 2008; Lev E. Dobriansky papers, 8 boxes, Hoover Institution Archives.

9. *Moskovs'ki vbyvtsi*, 68–72; "Soviet Agent Confesses Killing Bandera and Rebet as 'Enemies of Soviet Regime,'" *Ukrainian Weekly*, November 28, 1961; "Yaroslav S. Stetsko Was Next on the KGB List," *Ukrainian Weekly*, December 2, 1961; "Ukrainians Picket Soviet U.N. Mission in Protest over Murder of Bandera," *Ukrainian Weekly*, December 9, 1961.

CHAPTER 37: CONGRESSMAN

1. Stashinsky's Trial Transcripts, in *Moskovs'ki vbyvtsi*, 267.

2. *Memorial Addresses for Thomas Joseph Dodd*, 92nd Cong., 2nd sess., 1972 (Washington, DC, 1972); *Report of the Select Committee to Investigate Communist Aggression and the Forced Incorporation of the Baltic States into the U.S.S.R.: Third Interim Report of the Select Committee on Communist Aggression, House of Representatives, Eighty-Third Congress, Second Session, Under Authority of H. Res. 346 and H. Res. 438* (Washington, DC, 1972).

3. Christopher Matthews, *Kennedy & Nixon: The Rivalry That Shaped Postwar America* (New York, 1997), 52–54.

4. Lisa Phillips, *A Renegade Union: International Organizing and Labor Radicalism* (Champaign, IL, 2013), 105–106; 410–411; Matthews, *Kennedy & Nixon*, 46–50; James Srodes, *Allen Dulles: Master of Spies* (New York, 2000), 410–411; Garry Wills, *Nixon Agonistes: The Crisis of the Self-Made Man* (New York, 2002), 24–28.

5. *Investigation of Senator Thomas J. Dodd: Hearings of the Committee on Standards and Conduct. United States Senate. Eighty-Ninth Congress, Second Session, June 22, 23,*

24 and 27, and July 19, 1966, Part 1: *Relationship with Julius Klein* (Washington, DC, 1966), 329–330; Jonathan H. L'Hommedieu, "Baltic Exiles and the U.S. Congress: Investigations and Legacies of the House Select Committee, 1953–1955," *Journal of American Ethnic History* 31, no. 2 (Winter 2012): 41ff.; "Congressman Kersten, Friend of Ukrainians, Dies," *Ukrainian Weekly,* November 11, 1972.

6. Memo for W. C. Sullivan, in Russ Holmes Work File, Release of Certain FBI Documents to the Senate Select Committee, Mary Ferrrell Foundation.

7. *Memorial Addresses for Thomas Joseph Dodd; Report of the Select Committee to Investigate Communist Aggression and the Forced Incorporation of the Baltic States into the U.S.S.R.*

8. *Investigation of Senator Thomas J. Dodd,* 20–21.

9. "The Attack on the Romanian Legation in Berne—February 1955," *Stancodrescu,* November 7, 2008, http://stancodrescu.over-blog.com/article-25803233.html; *Investigation of Senator Thomas J. Dodd,* 318.

10. John L. Steele, "Assassin Disarmed by Love," *Life,* September 7, 1962, 70–72; Memo for W. C. Sullivan, in Russ Holmes Work File, Release of Certain FBI Documents to the Senate Select Committee, Mary Ferrrell Foundation; W. A. Branigan to W. C. Sullivan, January 14, 1964, in FBI Warren Commission Liaison File 62–109090, Mary Ferrell Foundation; *Investigation of Senator Thomas J. Dodd,* 321.

11. *Investigation of Senator Thomas J. Dodd,* 21; *Moskovs'ki vbyvtsi,* 345, 603.

CHAPTER 38: KARLSRUHE

1. "Russians Ignore Protest by Allies—Guards at Wall Exchange Fire," *New York Times,* October 9, 1962.

2. "Police Guard 'Spy' on Poison Deaths Charge," *Evening News* (London), October 8, 1962; *Moskovs'ki vbyvtsi,* 106.

3. *Moskovs'ki vbyvtsi,* 106–107.

4. *Inside Dr. No Documentary* (DVD) in *Dr. No* (Ultimate Edition, 2006); David Schoenbaum, *Die Spiegel-Affäre: Ein Abgrund von Landesverrat* (Berlin, 2002); David Manker Abshire, *Triumphs and Tragedies of the Modern Presidency: Seventy-Six Case Studies in Presidential Leadership* (Westport, CT, 2001), 185.

5. Arkadii Vaksberg, *Toxic Politics: The Secret History of the Kremlin's Poison Laboratory—from the Special Cabinet to the Death of Litvinenko* (Santa Barbara, CA, 2011), 203; *Moskovs'ki vbyvtsi,* 107.

6. Volodymyr Stakhiv, "Protses proty B. Stashyns'koho," in *Pro ukraïns'ku zovnishniu polityku, OUN ta politychni vbyvstva Kremlia* (Hadiach, Ukraine, 2005), 298–299; *Moskovs'ki vbyvtsi,* 107–109.

7. Borys Vitoshyns'kyi, "Vbyvnyk pro svoï zlochyny," *Shliakh peremohy,* October 12, 1962.

8. Stakhiv, "Protses proty B," 299–300.

9. *Moskovs'ki vbyvtsi,* diagram of the courtroom with seating arrangements following p. 695; Stakhiv, "Protses proty," 299–300; Author's interviews with Andrii Rebet, Munich, July 1, 2012, and Anatol Kaminsky, July 27, 2012.

10. Borys Vitoshyns'kyi, "Pershyi den' protsesu," *Shliakh peremohy,* October 10, 1962; *Moskovs'ki vbyvtsi,* 115, 120.

11. Deacon and West, *Spy!*, 152; Liubov' Khazan, "Pisatel' i diplomat Sergei German: 'Stepan Bandera pogib ot tsianistogo kaliia, . . . '" *Bul'var' Gordona*, February 19, 2013; Koch, *Der Fund*, 107.

CHAPTER 39: LOYALTY AND BETRAYAL

1. "Heinrich Jagusch, deutscher Jurist; Bundesrichter (1951–1965); Dr. Jur.," *Munzinger Biographie*, http://195.226.116.135/search/portrait/heinrich+jagusch/0/10106 .html; Arthur J. Olson, "German Receives Five Years as a Spy," *New York Times*, January 31, 1960; Allen W. Dulles, *The Craft of Intelligence: America's Legendary Spy Master on the Fundamentals of Intelligence Gathering for a Free World* (Guilford, CT, 2006), 108.

2. Stashinsky's Trial Transcripts, in *Moskovs'ki vbyvtsi*, 121–123, Anders, *Murder to Order*, 99–101.

3. Stashinsky's Trial Transcripts, in *Moskovs'ki vbyvtsi*, 124.

4. Ibid., 124–134; Georgii Sannikov's interview in the television documentary *Tainy razvedki: Likvidatsiia Stepana Bandery* (2012).

5. *Moskovs'ki vbyvtsi*, 115–116.

6. Adriana Ohorchak and Kateryna Shevchenko, *Ukraïns'kyi rodovid* (Lviv, 2001), 221; *Moskovs'ki vbyvtsi*, 472.

7. Stashinsky's Trial Transcripts, in *Moskovs'ki vbyvtsi*, 134; Dominique Auclères, *Anastasia, qui êtes-vous?* (Paris, 1962).

8. Stepan Lenkavsky to Jaroslaw Padoch, July 16, 1962, Jaroslaw Padoch Archive, Correspondence, no. 238; Vedeneev and Shevchenko, "Priznalsia, zabiraite."

9. Vitoshyns'kyi, "Pershyi den' protsesu."

10. Stepan Lenkavsky to Jaroslaw Padoch, May 17, 1962, Jaroslaw Padoch Archive, Correspondence, no. 238; Stashinsky's Trial Transcripts, in *Moskovs'ki vbyvtsi*, 140.

11. Stashinsky's Trial Transcripts, in *Moskovs'ki vbyvtsi*, 144; Oleksandra Andreiko, "Narys pro istoriiu sela Pekulovychi," http://xn—b1albgfsd8a2b7j.xn—j1amh; Iurii Lukanov, "Try liubovi Stepana Bandery: Stsenarii dokumental'noho televiziinoho fil'mu," 1998, www.oocities.org/yuriylukanov/start_files/dorobok/dorobok01.htm.

12. Vitoshyns'kyi, "Vbyvnyk pro svoï zlochyny"; Stashinsky's Trial Transcripts, in *Moskovs'ki vbyvtsi*, 139–140.

13. Stashinsky's Trial Transcripts, in *Moskovs'ki vbyvtsi*, 140, 146.

CHAPTER 40: FIRST MURDER

1. Borys Vitoshyns'kyi, "Na slidakh svoiei zhertvy: Druhyi den' protsesu proty Stashyns'koho," *Shliakh peremohy*, October 12, 1962.

2. Author's interview with Andrii Rebet; Memorandum for the Record, Subject: Meeting with AECASSOWARY 2 [Mykola Lebed] and 29 [Fr. Mykhailo Korzhan], April 3, 1962, 1, Aerodynamic: Contact Reports, vol. 45, NARA, RG 263, E ZZ-19, B 23.

3. Andrii Rebet, "Lev i Dariia Rebet: Moï bat'ky," paper delivered on June 24, 1998, at the Ukrainian Free University, Munich, manuscript in author's possession, 12–14.

4. "Tsikavyi dokument," *Ukraïns'kyi samostiinyk: Spetsiial'nyi vypusk* (Munich, 1962), 50–56; Author's interview with Andrii Rebet.

5. Stashinsky's Trial Transcripts, in *Moskovs'ki vbyvtsi*, 154.

6. *Moskovs'ki vbyvtsi*, 140, 146.

7. Borys Vitoshyns'kyi, "Cholovik z Moskvy," *Shliakh peremohy*, October 12, 1962; Stashinsky's Trial Transcripts, in *Moskovs'ki vbyvtsi*, 163.

8. "Tsikavyi document," 50–56; P. Hai-Nyzhnyk, "Het'manych Danylo Skoropads'kyi (1904–1957): Do istoriï vstanovlennia starshynstva v Het'mans'komu Rodi ta spadkoiemstva v ukraïns'komu monarkhichnomu rukhovi," *Kyïvs'ka starovyna*, no. 4 (2002): 110–125.

9. Stakhiv, "Protses proty," 311–312; Stashinsky's Trial Transcripts, in *Moskovs'ki vbyvtsi*, 173.

CHAPTER 41: BIG DAY

1. Borys Vitoshyns'kyi, "Z nakazu TsK partiï Stashyns'kyi zamorduvav providnyka," *Shliakh peremohy*, October 14, 1962; *Moskovs'ki vbyvtsi*, 181–182.

2. Borys Vitoshyns'kyi, "Ia pidnis zbroiu i vystrilyv," *Shliakh peremohy*, October 16, 1962; Borys Vitoshyns'kyi, "Shliakhy kryvavoï kar'iery," *Shliakh peremohy*, October 21, 1962; Borys Vitoshyns'kyi, "Potvorne oblychchia Moskvy: Pidsumky pershykh dniv sudu proty Stashyns'koho," *Shliakh peremohy*, October 21, 1962; Stashinsky's Trial Transcripts, in *Moskovs'ki vbyvtsi*, 184–199.

CHAPTER 42: DOUBT

1. *Moskovs'ki vbyvtsi*, 95.
2. Stakhiv, "Protses proty B," 314–315.
3. *Moskovs'ki vbyvtsi*, 174–180.
4. Stashinsky's Trial Transcripts, in *Moskovs'ki vbyvtsi*, 200–201, 251–260.
5. *Shliakh peremohy*, October 10, 1962; *Moskovs'ki vbyvtsi*, 115–116.
6. Vitoshyns'kyi, "Potvorne oblychchia Moskvy."
7. Stepan Lenkavsky to Jaroslaw Padoch, July 16, 1962, Jaroslaw Padoch Archive, Correspondence, no. 238.
8. Stashinsky's Trial Transcripts, in *Moskovs'ki vbyvtsi*, 240–244.
9. Ibid., 239–240.
10. Ibid., 267–270.
11. Ibid., 228.
12. Ibid., 199–200.

CHAPTER 43: PROSECUTION

1. Stashinsky's Trial Transcripts, in *Moskovs'ki vbyvtsi*, 271; "Bohosluzhennia v Karlsruhe," *Shliakh peremohy*, October 16, 1962.

2. "Legal Arguments by Chief Public Prosecutor Dr. Kuhn," in *The Shelepin File: Planned and Executed Murders of Ukrainian Political Leaders* (London, 1975), 33–42; Stashinsky's Trial Transcripts, in *Moskovs'ki vbyvtsi*, 281–291; *Investigation of Senator Thomas J. Dodd*, 21.

3. *Moskovs'ki vbyvtsi*, 240.

4. Petro Kizko, "Stashyns'kyi—uosoblennia shpyhuns'koï systemy," *Shliakh peremohy*, October 21, 1962; Vitoshyns'kyi, "Potvorne oblychchia Mosky"; *Moskovs'ki vbyvtsi*, 403–404; "Chomu Stashyns'kyi utik na Zakhid i pryznavsia do zlochyniv?" in *Moskovs'ki vbyvtsi*, 617–620.

5. Memorandum for the Record, April 22, 1976, Subject: Assassination of Stefan Bandera, 6.

6. Stashinsky's Trial Transcripts, in *Moskovs'ki vbyvtsi*, 291–297.

7. Stepan Bandera, "Lesia Bandera (1947–2011): 'Tatu, Ty ie symvolom dlia tsiloï kraïny . . . ,'" *Ukraïns'ka pravda*, August 29, 2011.

8. "Speech by Miss Natalia Bandera," in *The Shelepin File*, 53–56; Stashinsky's Trial Transcripts, in *Moskovs'ki vbyvtsi*, 305–307, 382–383.

CHAPTER 44: DEVIL'S ADVOCATES

1. Stashinsky's Trial Transcripts, in *Moskovs'ki vbyvtsi*, 297–303.

2. Ibid., 297–303; "Slovo pani mgr. Dariï Rebet," *Ukraïns'kyi samostiinyk* (special issue, 1962): 28–29; Author's interview with Andrii Rebet.

3. "Mr. Kersten's Plea at Stashynsky's Trial," in *The Shelepin File*, 15–20; Stashinsky's Trial Transcripts, in *Moskovs'ki vbyvtsi*, 308–316; *Investigation of Senator Thomas J. Dodd*, 324; Legal Arguments by Attorney Dr. J. Padoch," in *The Shelepin File*, 50–53.

4. Stashinsky's Trial Transcripts, in *Moskovs'ki vbyvtsi*, 316; Stakhiv, "Protses proty B," 342.

5. Stashinsky's Trial Transcripts, in *Moskovs'ki vbyvtsi*, 316–326; Stakhiv, "Protses proty B," 342; Dariia Rebet, "Vyna, diisnist' i dotsil'nist'," in *Ukraïns'kyi samostiinyk* (special issue, 1962): 29–32; Dariia Rebet, *Na perekhrestiakh vyzvol'nykh zmahan'* (Hadiach, Ukraine, 2003), 57–60.

CHAPTER 45: VERDICT

1. *Daily Telegraph*, October 16, 1962; *Berliner Zeitung*, October 18, 1962; *Moskovs'ki vbyvtsi*, 359, 434–436.

2. "Sentence and Oral Opinion of the Court," *The Shelepin File*, 21–33.

3. Ibid.

4. *Moskovs'ki vbyvtsi*, 343–344; Jaroslaw Padoch to Stepan Lenkavsky, October 19, 1962, Jaroslaw Padoch Archive, Correspondence, no. 238; "The Soviet Killer's Orders Were: Liquidate Them!," *Detroit News*, December 3, 1962.

5. "Legal Arguments by Chief Public Prosecutor Dr. Kuhn," 37; "Sentence and Oral Opinion of the Court," 32.

6. *Moskovs'ki vbyvtsi*, 343.

7. Ibid., 393–394.

8. Ibid., 361, 367–369; *Investigation of Senator Thomas J. Dodd*, 334.

9. *Moskovs'ki vbyvtsi*, 346–352, 622.

CHAPTER 46: UNANSWERED LETTER

1. *Investigation of Senator Thomas J. Dodd*, 23–24, 314–315.

2. Jaroslaw Padoch to Stepan Lenkavsky, October 19, 1962, Jaroslaw Padoch Archive, Correspondence, no. 238; Stashinsky's Trial Transcripts, in *Moskovs'ki vbyvtsi*, 297, 341–342, 368; "2 Yanks Will Charge Nikita with Murder," *Daily News*, October 17, 1962; *Investigation of Senator Thomas J. Dodd*, 325; Philip Agee, *Inside the Company: CIA Diary* (New York, 1975), 611.

3. *Investigation of Senator Thomas J. Dodd*, 314–318, 325.

4. Ibid., 336–337, 350.

5. Melvyn P. Leffler, *For the Soul of Mankind: The United States, the Soviet Union and the Cold War* (New York, 2007), 182–192; Jonathan Haslam, *Russia's Cold War: From the October Revolution to the Fall of the Wall* (New Haven, CT, 2011), 210–213.

6. Memo for W. C. Sullivan, in Russ Holmes Work File, Release of Certain FBI Documents to the Senate Select Committee, Mary Ferrrell Foundation; *Investigation of Senator Thomas J. Dodd*, 338–341.

7. "William J. Hood Dies; CIA Man Who Signed Off on 'Unusual' Oswald Cable," February 15, 2013, JFKFacts, http://jfkfacts.org/tag/william-j-hood.

CHAPTER 47: GUEST FROM WASHINGTON

1. *Investigation of Senator Thomas J. Dodd*, 365.

2. "Soviet Use of Assassination and Kidnapping," CIA report.

3. *Investigation of Senator Thomas J. Dodd*, 25–26; "Memorandum of Conversation, Federal Republic of Germany Chancellor Konrad Adenauer and Dean Acheson, Special Envoy of US President Kennedy, Bonn, West Germany, 23 October 1962," in *The Global Cuban Missile Crisis at 50: New Evidence from Behind the Iron, Bamboo, and Sugarcane Curtains, and Beyond*, eds. James J. Hershberg and Christian F. Ostermann, vol. 2, Cold War International History Project Bulletin 17/18 (Washington, DC, 2012), 624–625.

4. *Investigation of Senator Thomas J. Dodd*, 25–26, 353–365.

5. Ibid., 365–367; *The Bang-Jensen Case: Report to the Subcommittee to Investigate the Administration of the Internal Security Act and Other Internal Security Laws of the Committee on the Judiciary*, United States Senate, 87th Cong., 1st sess. (Washington, DC,1961); Memorandum, Senator Dodd to Jay Sourwine, Re: Stashynsky Hearings, September 23, 1963, folder 12-53b. File Series 4: Legislative Subseries 10: Internal Security Subcommittee, James O. Eastland Collection, Archives and Special Collections, J. D. Williams Library, University of Mississippi.

6. *Investigation of Senator Thomas J. Dodd*, 365–367, 387, 479.

7. *Murder International, Inc.: Murder and Kidnapping as an Instrument of Soviet Policy*, United States Congress, Senate Committee on the Judiciary, Subcommittee to Investigate the Administration of the Internal Security Act and Other Internal Security Laws (Washington, DC, 1965); *Investigation of Senator Thomas J. Dodd*, 480; "Stashynsky, Bogdan N.," Folders 12-53a and 12-53b.

CHAPTER 48: JUDEX

1. Deacon and West, *Spy!*, 152; Koch, *Der Fund*, 109, 120; "Hitler Diaries: Agent Was 'Communist Spy,'" BBC News, July 29, 2002, http://news.bbc.co.uk/2/hi/europe/2159037.stm.

2. Author's interview with Andrii Rebet; *Investigation of Senator Thomas J. Dodd*, 365.

3. John Gimbel, "The 'Spiegel Affair' in Perspective," *Midwest Journal of Political Science* 9, no. 3 (August 1965): 282–297, esp. 292; [Heinrich Jagusch], "Handeln mit Verrätern?" *Der Spiegel*, September 9, 1964; Koch, *Der Fund*, 120; Judex, "Droht ein neuer Ossietzky-Fall?" *Der Spiegel*, November 4, 1964; Gerhard Ziegle, "Rätsel um Heinrich Jagusch: Warum log der Senatspräsident seinem Vorgesetzten ins Gesicht?" *Die Zeit*, November 20, 1964.

4. Hans Joachim Faller, "Heinrich Jagusch," in *Juristen im Portrait: Verlag und Autoren in 4 Jahrzehnten* (Munich, 1988), 431–437.

5. Ziegle, "Rätsel um Heinrich Jagusch"; J. C., "Ex-Nazi Judges," *AJR Information* 20, no. 2 (April 1965): 2; Hermann Raschhofer, *Political Assasination: The Legal Background of the Oberländer and Stashinsky Cases* (Tübingen, Germany, 1964); "Urtail: Ludwig Hahn," *Der Spiegel*, no. 24 (1973); "Closing Argument [of] Professor Dr. Cornelius Nestler in the Criminal Proceeding Against John Demjanjuk (Presented before the Munich District Court on April 13, 2011)," www.nebenklage-sobibor.de/wp-content/uploads/2011/04/SKMBT_C203110509153301.pdf; Martin Rath, "Lehrbuchfall Staschynskij: Als extralegale Hinrichtungen einmal vor Gericht kamen," Legal Tribune Online, May 8, 2011, www.lto.de/recht/feuilleton/f/lehrbuchfall-staschynskij-als-extralegale-hinrichtungen-einmal-vor-gericht-kamen.

6. *Investigation of Senator Thomas J. Dodd*, 362, 365, 292–293, 479; Erich Schmidt-Eenboom, "Empfänglich für Geheimes: Die (west)deutschen Nachrichtendienste im Äther," in Klaus Beyrer, *Verschlüsselte Kommunikation. Geheime Dienste-Geheime Nachrichten*, *Umschau* (Heidelberg, 1999), www.desert-info.ch/download/pdf/PDF-Forum/Kreipe.pdf; E. W. Kenworthy, "Helms Says Dodd Conferred with CIA Before Europe Trip," *New York Times*, July 27, 1966, 19.

7. Jonathan S. Wiesen, *Germany's PR Man: Julius Klein and the Making of Transatlantic Memory* (New York, 2007); *Investigation of Senator Thomas J. Dodd*, 577–578; "Dodd, Thomas," in *American National Biography* (New York, 2000); "Antikommunism ego vera," "Zachem Dodd zanimaetsia politikoi?" and "Porok ne nakazan," *Literaturnaia gazeta*, April 9, 1968, 15.

CHAPTER 49: VANISHED

1. Khazan, "Pisatel' i diplomat Sergei German; "CIA II, Assassin 280," Harold Weisberg Archive, Digital Collection, http://jfk.hood.edu/Collection/White%20Materials/White%20Assassination%20Clippings%20Folders/Security%20Folders/Security-CIA-II/CIA%20II%20140.pdf.

2. "Deep Mystery Shrouds Whereabouts of Stashinsky," *Ukrainian Weekly*, March 15, 1969; *The Ukrainian Bulletin*, Ukrainian Congress Committee of America, vols. 17–19, 28.

3. Memorandum for the Record. April 22, 1976, Subject: Assassination of Stefan Bandera, 6; Tom Mangold, *Cold Warrior—James Jesus Angleton: The CIA's Master Spy Hunter* (New York, 1992); "Nosenko, Yurii Ivanovich," in Richard C. S. Trahair and Robert L. Miller, *Encyclopedia of Cold War Espionage, Spies, and Secret Operations* (New

York, 2012), 261–263; Hendrik van Bergh, "Mord in München," *Das Ostpreußenblatt*, October 27, 1979.

4. "The Preparation of the Murder of Yaroslav Stetsko," in *The Shelepin File*, 60–61.

CHAPTER 50: KREMLIN GHOST

1. Stetsko CIA File, nos. 100–107; Susan Rich, "Nicholas Krawciw," *International TNDM Newsletter* (Dupuy Institute), 28, www.dupuyinstitute.org/pdf/v2n4.pdf.

2. Bruce Lambert, "Chuck Connors, Actor, 71, Dies; Starred as Television's 'Rifleman,'" *New York Times*, November 11, 1992; "The Rifleman Meets Leonid Ilyich Brezhnev," www.riflemanconnors.com/leonid_brezhnev.htm; Ihor Dlaboha, "N.Y. Ukrainians Demonstrate Against Brezhnev's Visit to U.S.," *Ukrainian Weekly*, June 23, 1973.

3. *Investigation of Senator Thomas J. Dodd*, 480; Willard Edwards, "Shelepin's Role in Murder Told," *Chicago Tribune*, January 7, 1966.

4. Robert Merry, "The KGB's Ex-chief Had Britons Seething," *Chicago Tribune*, March 15, 1975; "Stunde der Rache: Generalsekretär Breschnew ist einen Mann los, der sich an seine Stelle setzen wollte. Politbüro-Mitglied Alexander Schelepin," *Der Spiegel*, April 21, 1975.

5. Leonid Mlechin, *KGB: Predsedateli organov gosbezopasnosti. Rassekrechennye sluzhby* (Moscow, 2006), chaps. 12 and 14.

CHAPTER 51: ON THE RUN

1. Typescript of Vladimir Semichastny's memoirs, in Tomas Sniegon's archive, 66. Cf. the abridged and censored Russian version in Semichastny, *Bespokoinoe serdtse*, 193.

2. Christopher Andrew and Vasili Mitrokhin, *The Sword and the Shield: The Mitrokhin Archive and the Secret History of the KGB* (New York, 1999), 367.

3. Reinhard Gehlen, *Der Dienst. Erinnerungen, 1942–1971* (Mainz, Germany, 1971); Reinhard Gehlen, *The Service* (Cleveland, OH, 1972), 241.

4. Gerhi Strauss, "Ex-KGB Assassin Now Lives in SA," "Stashinsky's First Perfect Murder as a KGB Agent"; "The Farm Boy Who Became Police Chief," all in *Cape Times*, March 5, 1984, 11.

5. Associated Press, "Ex-KGB Agent Living in S. Africa," March 5, 1984; "KGB Man Given Asylum," *Times of India*, March 6, 1984; "Assassin of Rebet, Bandera Living in South Africa," *Ukrainian Weekly*, March 18, 1984; "Kolyshnii ahent KGB B. Stashyns'kyi znaishov prytulok u PAR," *Svoboda*, March 14, 1984; Hanlie van Straaten's e-mail messages of July 12 and 16, 2013, to the author about her conversations with Geldenhuys.

6. Deacon and West, *Spy!*, 152; Khazan, "Pisatel' i diplomat Sergei German"; Records of the Rohrbeck Evangelische Kirchengemeinde Archive, Dallgow.

7. "South African Police: Special Task Force. History," www.sapstf.org/History.aspx; Legal notice no. 30811, *Green Gazette*, February 29, 2008.

8. Anatolii Lemysh, "My mnogo utrachivaem ot togo, chto boimsia vser'ez kopnut' nashu istoriiu," *Den'*, October 24, 1998; Vladislav Krasnov, *Soviet Defectors: The KGB*

Wanted List (Stanford, CA, 1986), 30; report and notes on the Soviet use of parapsychology, in Nikolai Khokhlov papers, boxes 1, 3, Hoover Institution Archives.

9. Record of author's conversation with General Geldenhuys on April 1, 2013, in author's archive; Hanlie van Straaten's e-mail messages of July 12 and 16, 2013, to the author about her conversations with Geldenhuys.

CHAPTER 52: HOMECOMING

1. Natalia Prykhod'ko, "Bohdan Stashyns'kyi: Ia vykonav svii obov'iazok pered Ukraïnoiu," *Livyi bereh*, August 8, 2011.

2. Taras Kuzio, "Émigré Strategies Face Soviet and Ukrainian Realities," *Kyiv Post*, November 17, 2011, www.kyivpost.com/opinion/op-ed/emigre-strategies-face-soviet -and-ukrainian-realit-117131.html; Alexander J. Motyl, "A KGB Assassin Speaks," Ukraine's Orange Blues, *World Affairs*, November 18, 2011, www.worldaffairsjournal .org/blog/alexander-j-motyl/kgb-assassin-speaks.

3. Iurii Andrukhovych, "Chuvyrla u chudovys'ko," *Khreshchatyk*, March 12, 2008; Serhii Herman, *Inge: Roman* (Kyiv, 2012); Roman Babenko, "Z koho Serhii Herman napysav vbyvtsiu Bandery Stashyns'koho," *Bukvoïd*, December 5, 2012; "Love Is Stronger Than KGB," *Fresh Production*, July 26, 2012, http://freshproduction.com/en /lyubov-silnee-kgb; "Gruzinskii rezhisser snimet film ob ubiitse Bandery s kinozvezdami Gollivuda," *Zerkalo nedeli*, December 7, 2012.

4. "SVR otritsaet prichastnost' k otravleniiu Litvinenko," News RU, November 21, 2008, www.newsru.com/russia/20nov2006/svr.html.

5. "U L'vovi bezbiletnykh pasazhyriv porivniuiut' z ubyvtseiu Bandery," *Komentari*, November 28, 2008; "Yushchenko and the Poison Theory," BBC News, December 11, 2004, http://news.bbc.co.uk/2/hi/health/4041321.stm; David Marples, "Stepan Bandera: The Resurrection of a Ukrainian National Hero," *Europe-Asia Studies* 58, no. 4 (June 2006): 555–566; Alex J. Motyl, *Ukraine, Europe and Bandera*, Cicero Foundation, Great Debate Paper no. 10/05 (March 2010); Andre Liebich and Oksana Myshlovska, "Bandera Memorialization and Commemoration," *Nationalities Papers* 42 (2014): 750–770.

6. Motyl, "KGB Assassin Speaks."

7. Nikolai Kuznetsov, "Natsional-bol'sheviki Khar'kova prizvali pereimenovat' Molodezhnyi park," *Gorodskoi dozor*, April 26, 2011; Bogdan Stashinsky blog, http://assassinstashynsky.blogspot.com/2011/04/log-5-public-confession.html; Author's interview with Anatol Kaminsky.

8. Anthony Faiola, "A Ghost of World War II History Haunts Ukraine's Standoff with Russia," *Washington Post*, March 25, 2013; Andreas Umland, "Stepan Bandera, das Faschismuskonzept, das "Weimarer Russland" und die antiukrainische Propaganda- kampagne des Kremls," Voices of Ukraine, May 12, 2014, http://maidantranslations .com/2014/05/12/stepan-bandera-das-faschismuskonzept-das-weimarer-russland-und -die-antiukrainische-propagandakampagne-des-kremls.

9. Andrew Wilson, *Ukraine Crisis: What It Means for the West* (New Haven, CT, 2014); "Nazi-Kollaborateur und ukrainischer Held," *Die Welt*, August 18, 2014; Stepan Petrenko, "V chuzhom piru pohmel'e, ili kto i zachem ubil Banderu?" *Zaria Novorossii*, October 14, 2014, http://novorossy.ru/articles/news_post/v-chuzhom-piru-pohmele -ili-kto-i-zachem-ubil-banderu.

10. Cnaan Liphshiz, "For Ukrainian Jews, Far-Right's Electoral Defeat Is the Proof That Putin Lied," Jewish Telegraphic Agency, June 2, 2014, www.jta.org/2014/06/02 /news-opinion/world/for-ukrainian-jews-far-rights-electoral-defeat-is-proof-that -putin-lied; "Chomu Svoboda ne proishla v parlament?" OSP-UA, October 29, 2014, http://osp-ua.info/politicas/42990-chomu-partija-svoboda-ne-proyshla-v-parlament .html.

11. Lesia Fediv, "Vin ubyv Banderu," *Shchodennyi L'viv*, May 22, 2008.

12. Ibid.; Mariia Hoiduchyk, "Toi samyi Bohdan: Maty Stashyns'koho, diznavshys', shcho syn vbyv Banderu, zbozhevolila," *Ekspres*, October 14, 2010, http://e2.expres.ua /article/1245.

EPILOGUE: THE COLD WAR REDUX

1. Ian Fleming, *The Man with the Golden Gun* (New York, 1965), 15–18.

2. *Moskovs'ki vbyvtsi*, 389–392; Fyodor Dostoyevsky, *Crime and Punishment* (New York, 2011 [1866]); Joseph Conrad, *Under Western Eyes* (Mineola, NY, 2003 [1911]).

3. John le Carré, *The Spy Who Came in from the Cold: A George Smiley Novel* (New York, 2012), 15.

4. Andrew and Mitrokhin, *The Sword and the Shield*, 355–358; Archie Brown, *The Rise and Fall of Communism* (New York, 2009), 206–207, 644–645.

5. Athan G. Theoharis, ed., with Richard Immerman, Loch Johnson, Kathryn Olmsted, and John Prados, *The Central Intelligence Agency: Security Under Scrutiny* (Westport, CT, 2006), 169–172; Tim Weiner, "CIA Plotted Killing of 58 in Guatemala," *New York Times*, May 28, 1997.

6. "Russia Behind Chechen Murder," BBC News, June 30, 2004, http://news.bbc .co.uk/2/hi/middle_east/3852697.stm; "Russian Foreign Intelligence Service Denies Its Participation in the Death of Yandarbiyev," NewsInfo, February 13, 2004, www .newsinfo.ru/?a=radio&sa=view_new&id=49407.

7. Boris Volodarsky, *The KGB's Poison Factory: From Lenin to Litvinenko* (Minneapolis, 2010), 62–116, 137–181, 189–253.

8. "Full Report on the Litvinenko Inquiry," *New York Times*, January 21, 2016.

9. "Drone Wars Pakistan: Analysis," New America, http://securitydata.newamerica .net/drones/pakistan-analysis.html; Daniel Byman, "Why Drones Work: A Case for Washington's Weapon of Choice," *Foreign Affairs* (July-August 2013): 32–43; Audrey Kurth Cronin, "Why Drones Fail: When Tactics Drive Strategy," *Foreign Affairs* (July-August 2013): 44–54; Marina Fang, "Nearly 90 Percent of People Killed in Recent Drone Strikes Were Not the Target," *Huffington Post*, October 15, 2016, www.huffingtonpost.com /entry/civilian-deaths-drone-strikes_us_561fafe2e4b028dd7ea6c4ff.

INDEX

Serhii Plokhy is the Mykhailo Hrushevsky Professor of Ukrainian History at Harvard and the director of the university's Ukrainian Research Institute. The prize-winning author of nine books, including *The Last Empire* and *The Gates of Europe*, Plokhy lives in Arlington, Massachusetts.